T0377171

AFRICAN ETHNOGRAPHIC STUDIES OF THE 20TH CENTURY

Volume 32

CHANGING SOCIAL STRUCTURE IN GHANA

CHANGING SOCIAL STRUCTURE IN GHANA

Essays in the Comparative Sociology of a new State and an old Tradition

JACK GOODY

LONDON AND NEW YORK

First published in 1975 by the International African Institute.

This edition first published in 2018
by Routledge
2 Park Square, Milton Park, Abingdon, Oxon OX14 4RN

and by Routledge
711 Third Avenue, New York, NY 10017

Routledge is an imprint of the Taylor & Francis Group, an informa business

© 1975 International African Institute

All rights reserved. No part of this book may be reprinted or reproduced or utilised
in any form or by any electronic, mechanical, or other means, now known or
hereafter invented, including photocopying and recording, or in any information
storage or retrieval system, without permission in writing from the publishers.

Trademark notice: Product or corporate names may be trademarks or registered
trademarks, and are used only for identification and explanation without intent to
infringe.

British Library Cataloguing in Publication Data
A catalogue record for this book is available from the British Library

ISBN: 978-0-8153-8713-8 (Set)
ISBN: 978-0-429-48813-9 (Set) (ebk)
ISBN: 978-1-138-59322-0 (Volume 32) (hbk)
ISBN: 978-0-429-48906-8 (Volume 32) (ebk)

Publisher's Note
The publisher has gone to great lengths to ensure the quality of this reprint but
points out that some imperfections in the original copies may be apparent.

Disclaimer
The publisher has made every effort to trace copyright holders and would welcome
correspondence from those they have been unable to trace.

CHANGING SOCIAL STRUCTURE IN GHANA:

Essays in the Comparative Sociology
of a New State and an Old Tradition

Edited with an Introduction by

JACK GOODY

INTERNATIONAL AFRICAN INSTITUTE
London

1975

To

Meyer Fortes,

scholar of Ghanaian life

ISBN 0 85302 041 8

© International African Institute 1975
210 High Holborn, London WC1V 7BW

Printed in Great Britain by Clarke, Doble & Brendon Ltd, Plymouth

CONTENTS

List of Figures   *v*

List of Tables   *vi*

Introduction

JACK GOODY, *University of Cambridge*   *vii*

Economics

KEITH HART, *University of Manchester*
Swindler or Public Benefactor? - The Entrepreneur
in his Community   1

JEREMY EADES, *Ahmadu Bello University, Nigeria*
The Growth of a Migrant Community: The Yoruba
in Northern Ghana   37

G.K. NUKUNYA, *University of Ghana, Legon*
The Effects of Cash Crops on an Ewe Community   59

MARGARET PEIL, *University of Birmingham*
Female Roles in West African Towns   73

Religion

JACK GOODY, *University of Cambridge*
Religion, Social Change and the Sociology
of Conversion   91

MALCOLM MCLEOD, *University of Cambridge*
On the Spread of Anti-witchcraft Cults in
Modern Asante   107

Kinship

POLLY HILL, *University of Cambridge*
The West African Farming Household   119

ESTHER N. GOODY, *University of Cambridge*
Delegation of Parental Roles in West Africa
and the West Indies   137

ENID SCHILDKROUT, *University of Illinois, Urbana*
Economics and Kinship in Multi-ethnic Dwellings   167

CHRISTINE OPPONG, *University of Ghana, Legon*
A Study of Domestic Continuity and Change: Akan
Senior Service Families in Accra   181

iv

D. PAUL LUMSDEN, *York University, Toronto*
Resettlement and Rehousing: Unintended Consequences
among the Nchumuru   201

Politics

A.F. ROBERTSON, *University of Cambridge*
Composition and Procedure in Ahafo Councils   229

Education

PENELOPE ROBERTS, *University of Ife*
The Village School Teacher in Ghana   245

REFERENCES   261

BIBLIOGRAPHY   272

INDEX   283

LIST OF FIGURES

Figure 1	Map of Ghana showing places and peoples discussed	*facing page*	*vii*
Figure 2	Genealogy of Ile Olowo	*page*	44
Figure 3	Anlo district	*page*	60
Figure 4	Chores and child care	*page*	192
Figure 5	Financial provision	*page*	192
Figure 6	Financial management	*page*	192
Figure 7	Krachi District today, showing Nchumuru villages	*facing page*	202
Figure 8	A block of D-type V.R.A. houses (New Grube)	*facing page*	203
Figure 9	Ahafo	*facing page*	229
Figure 10	Speaking time of Local Council Members	*facing page*	240

vi

LIST OF TABLES

Table 1   Relationship of people responsible for taking male migrants to northern Ghana   *page* 49

Table 2   The economically active labour force in selected cities, employed only (percentages)   79

Table 3   Gonja (northern Ghana): Generation of foster parent for four samples   143

Table 4   Relationship between child and foster parent in three southern Ghana societies: Boys   146

Table 5   Relationship between child and foster parent in three southern Ghana societies: Girls   146

Table 6   Generation of foster parent: comparision of northern and southern Ghana: (combined samples)   147

Table 7   Children in three Jamaican communities living with neither parent; Percent living with kin and with non-kin; Percent of all children living with foster parents. (Clarke 1966: Appendix 5)   150

Table 8   West Indian fostering relationships: Generation   155

Table 9   Comparison of northern Ghana, southern Ghana and West Indian fostering relationships, by generation of foster parent. (From totals of Tables 6 and 8)   161

Table 10   Couples jointly participating in financial responsibilities, by ethnic origin   194

Table 11   Male students' attitudes to the husband's financial responsibilities by ethnic origin   195

Table 12   Husbands performing household tasks, by ethnic origin   196

Table 13   Men students' attitudes to housework, by ethnic origin   197

Table 14   Size of 244 Nchumuru households as of Sept. 1969   219

Table 15   Number of houses involved in each household by Sept. 1969   220

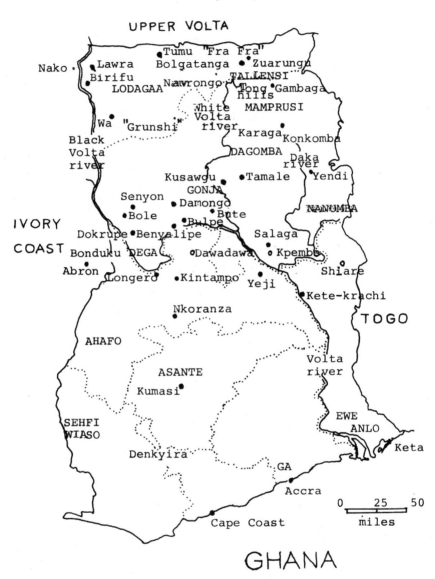

Figure 1
Map of Ghana showing places and peoples discussed
(ethnic units in capitals)

INTRODUCTION

Some three years ago, I revisited Northern Ghana with a Ghanaian friend who worked as a statistician with a large firm. We visited his village and recorded the myth associated with the performances of a secret society, to which he belonged, a myth that I had recorded by hand some twenty years before. After attending the rites of that society, some of the company went along to the meeting of the local Young Men's Association, whose main object was to improve and modernise the village. It would be simple to draw contrasts between the 'traditional' and 'modern' elements in this situation and to characterise the people participating in these spheres as 'men of two worlds'. Politicians too, have frequently to switch from concerns of party to concerns of chiefship. Such a shift occurs not only in the normal process of securing one's local base, but also when a man is out of power in terms of the 'national' scene, he may seek an alternative route to positions of influence.

It is easier from the outside to see these situations in terms of two worlds, one of which is disappearing before the advances of the other. To the extent that this is true (and it is the assumption of most 'modernisation' studies) the progression is certainly a slow one, a process in which many elements of the traditional situation undergo change rather than get rejected outright. Indeed some have queried the relevance of new institutional forms to these new nations, seeing the 'traditional' sector as controlling most of the important allocations (Zolberg 1968). The weight to be given to 'traditional' or 'modern' factors will clearly vary in different institutional contexts. But the study of the contemporary situation must take account of both sorts fo factor and therefore be concerned with problems of change as well as of continuity.

This book presents the results of some recent research into social change in Ghana. Each of the essays deals with some aspects of the changing situation, not necessarily today's change but at least change that is relevant to what is happening today. It thus continues the interest of social scientists in the situation that lies before their eyes rather than in a reconstruction of a society that may have existed in pre-colonial times.

There is (of course) nothing wrong with such reconstructions. But whereas anthropologists at the turn of the century (and perhaps for two or three decades afterwards) could observe societies little affected by the advent of Europeans, at least as political rulers, clearly this is no longer true today. The Yoruba and the Frafra communities which Eades and Hart describe in Tamale and Accra did not exist at that time. Moreover the process of establishing these communities at a considerable distance from their homeland has *viii*

influenced conditions in the home territory, as well as constituting evidence of yet more extensive changes.

To reconstruct the earlier situation, enquiry on the spot is clearly of paramount importance. Reasonable guesses about those situations can still be made by means of careful enquiry and the exercise of sound judgement. But the focus of such an investigation is inevitably on the past and on continuities from the past; the present, the changing situation, is residual to one's other work. One is not interested in the functioning social system, in the social system that operates before one's eyes, but in reconstructing the 'original' Baganda or Ashanti social organisation as it existed in pre-colonial times.

Clearly as the years slip by, fieldwork becomes less and less use for discovering the truth about pre-colonial society - or what many prefer to call savage or primitive. This is the crisis of empirical anthropology (the pure 'theoretician' does not have to get that close to contemporary reality). The techniques it prefers (i.e. fieldwork) are no longer suited to the societies it favours (i.e. the traditional). Today even studies of rural areas have to take account of networks that stretch to and from the towns, whether these be social, political, economic or religious. Indeed this limitation of the purely village study has long been true of many African societies, where trade, government, religious cult or literary activity has required a wider canvas for adequate analysis.

What is the anthropologist to do? Does he return to the armchair and let the historian reconstruct what has virtually disappeared and the sociologist study what has taken its place? Certainly he can play a useful role as the mediator between the dead and the living, the specialist in past cultures, the provider of comparative material, the inventor of intuitive insights. But his tool would be a vast Human Relations Area File combined with the written record of colonial penetration, not the testimony of the fieldworker able to make his own observations and formulate his own questions. It would be the anthropology of past societies, a kind of historical sociology of other cultures.

In this book we adopt (like others) a different approach and suggest another possibility for anthropology today in the context of studies of a particular new nation. It is one that continues a recent tradition of social anthropology, especially in Britain, which emphasised the value of observational studies combined with theoretical concerns. These studies try to show that the fieldworker with a wide comparative background (that is, in the range of pre-industrial societies) has a positive role to play in contemporary social science. The documentary techniques of the historian cannot be ignored (though we have not used them much in the present studies). The questionnaires and surveys of the sociologists of literate societies are useful tools (and have been used by Hart, Oppong, Roberts, Lumsden and others). But the basic data for the work we present is a set of detailed observations, the outcome of a prolonged period of residence among the people themselves and a knowledge of the local language. Apart from the emphasis on fieldwork and on an understanding of the traditional social structure, the kind of study undertaken has much affinity with the sort of sociological study carried out by Luckham on the Nigerian military where, in the chapter on peer groups, for example, he attempts to combine:

(a) historical data on the role of peer groups in two military coups,
(b) statistical data from the Gazettes etc., on common training and criss-crossing of careers of the coup participants,
(c) observations on the manner in which officers associate with their peers, go out drinking with them, chat about their friendships among their course mates and show deference towards their senior officers (Luckham 1971:13).

Just as Luckham is inevitably involved in the sociology of the military of new nations, so too Hart becomes involved in the comparative sociology of micro-economic behaviour, Oppong in the comparative sociology of resettlement, Robertson in the comparative sociology of committee behaviour and myself (peripherally at least) in the comparative sociology of conversion.

The study of new nations thus provides a testing ground for theory and at the same time helps to break down the barriers between disciplines that have arisen in particular social contexts and that so pre-occupy the minds of the many students and staff in the social sciences. We think such a perspective is important for research and that such work can be carried out without loss of the academic quality that has been gained by studies of such well-known topics as kinship terms, descent systems and ritual behaviour. But it is also important for the purposes of teaching both anthropology and sociology, separately or together, that students be introduced to the analysis of data from the contemporary situation in societies that are neither wholly 'traditional' nor wholly 'modern'. It is for this reason that we include a selected bibliography of social research on Ghanaian society. Work on the 'traditional' systems has been mainly excluded, as the references are readily available elsewhere. The present list of works shows the extent and quality of social research carried out in Ghana, making that country a particularly useful focus for the study of 'other cultures' in the world of today, in the closing decades of the twentieth century.

JACK GOODY
Cambridge

SWINDLER OR PUBLIC BENEFACTOR? - THE ENTREPRENEUR IN HIS COMMUNITY

KEITH HART

In all relatively open economic systems it is possible for a few individuals to enrich themselves largely through their own efforts. The relationship betwen individual enrichment and social welfare is, however, a matter of dispute.

One set of ideologies is associated with the new rich themselves and those who proprogate their virtues. Success is attributed to hard work, abstinence, ambition, perseverance, skill and initiative, a quick eye for opportunities, luck and perhaps 'a good woman behind me'. According to this view, success is due to the positive personal qualities of the individual concerned; no-one else really suffers when success comes this way. If the envious point out that some people are liable to get hurt by the individual's single-minded pursuit of profit, it is usually claimed in mitigation that the public good is enhanced by his success in the long run: his enterprise generates additional social welfare either through a net increase of the total social product (provision of more goods, services and jobs) or through eventual redistribution of wealth gained at no-one else's expense (the charitable benefits of industry). In this way individual enrichment may be idealised as a public benefaction, the mainspring of social progress.

Another set of ideologies is associated with those who oppose the new rich: individual enrichment is here attributed to lack of moral principle, isolationism, selfish greed, exploitation of others, theft (both direct and indirect) and numerous other anti-social vices. In every sense the community suffers from having such a person in its midst and public welfare is inevitably harmed. Individual wealth is seen largely as a product of transfers of value grabbed by force or sneaked by deception; wealth, created by others, is unjustly concentrated into the hands of a few persons selected by their lack of an ordinary social conscience. According to this view any long-term economic growth resulting from such a process is small compensation to those unfortunate enough to have been expropriated by the new rich on their way to the top. The essential feature of accumulation is thus the transfer of part of the social product to the benefit of one section of the community at the expense of the rest. In this way the successful individual is epitomised as a swindler and a public nuisance, the negation of social harmony.

These two contrasting images of the new rich may be encountered in real life situations, where social conflict arising from individual enrichment often take the form of ideological disputes about the morality of both particular persons and the process in general. The very existence of wide discrepancies in personal wealth poses a problem of justification and explanation which each of us depending on his own experience, tends to resolve by consistent adherence to one ideological pole or the other, whether positive or negative.

CHANGING SOCIAL STRUCTURE IN GHANA

But must we leave it at that, simply as an example of the relativity of social constructions of reality? Is it not possible to settle the dispute at some other level, by having recourse to theory or 'the facts'? When we turn to western economic theory for an assessment of the social consequences of individual enrichment, we only find two broad political camps corresponding roughly to the opposed ideologies set out above: each has prejudged the issue according to its commitment to a social world view. 'Functional' theory (the Weberian tradition) sees in the 'entrepreneur' a symbol of rationality and progress; 'conflict' theory (the Marxist tradition) identifies the 'capitalist' as a socially divisive expropriator of wealth produced by others.[1] It is unlikely then that the argument would be capable of resolution at the level of abstract generalisation, since all social theories, as ideologies, legitimate their findings by selective reference to some of the facts, while ignoring other, perhaps equally or more important dimensions to the problem. The tendency towards polarised judgements in real life is accentuated when the validity of entire social systems is called into question.

The position adopted in this paper is that social life, unlike the simplified reductions found in ideology and theory, is a *dialectical* process, in which individuals and groups seek to resolve fundamental contradictions operating as opposed pressures on their behaviour and thought. The process of personal enrichment highlights the contradiction between self and other, individual and society, private and public interests. At the bottom lies the contradiction, at least in the short-term, between accumulation and consumption. Conflict, both within the individual himself and in his exchanges with those around him, is the inevitable product of this clash of interests: but this may be offset by compensating measures which allow the individual to maintain viable, solidary relationships with his fellows and which reduce the antipathies and social conflict generated by his personal success. Given that social behaviour is never as consistent as ideology and sociological typification make it out to be, the basis of any theoretical account of the relationship between individual enrichment and social welfare must lie in the variety of possible resolutions to the dialectic as encountered in real life.

It is this paper's aim to examine the social correlates of individual accumulation in a particular time and place, to see whether variations in the degree of ideological and practical opposition to the new rich may be grounded in (a) an unprejudiced analysis of the mechanisms of accumulation adopted by particular categories of individual and (b) an empirical account of their strategies for conducting exchanges with their social environment. The problem is a general one in history: as a recent commentator has remarked when discussing the issue in relation to African development, '.... emphasis on accumulating money as against meeting social obligations worried many people in the United States and Europe in the early years of industrialisation. John D. Rockefeller was highly unpopular most of his life; English literature is filled with hostile references to the 'new men', such as in Dickens' 'Hard Times' ' (Kamarck 1967:51). The interesting question is not to wonder whether accumulation of money and social obligations are in conflict - they clearly are; it is to ask why certain kinds of accumulation give rise to serious conflict in practice, while others do not. The wider issues of political choice and sociological prediction also depend on the question being framed in this way: in short, which strategies of accumulation are compatible with an enduring, co-operative social fabric and which lead to its potentially violent

SWINDLER OR PUBLIC BENEFACTOR? 3

disruption? A major aim of the paper is thus to generate analytical categories which can be applied to the empirical problems in a wide-ranging number of social contexts. The particular case study chosen is appended to this discussion as a concrete illustration of what is thought to be a general dialectical process.

II

Very few analytical propositions are arrived at in a vacuum; and, before proceeding to elaborate the theoretical framework used in this study, it would probably be helpful if I were to outline the history of ideas and experience which lies behind the present analysis.

There are many cases for which my approach may be relevant (and I am aware of several), but the central case which this generalising model has been designed to fit was the product of an anthropological field study conducted in Ghana during 1965-68.[2] The study focussed on a number of self-made men and women who originated in one district of N.E. Ghana and, at least potentially, shared an ethnic label referring to that district, 'Frafra'. Some of them lived in their home village at the time of the study, others had moved to an urban centre within the Frafra district and others were migrants resident in Southern Ghana's major cities. These accumulators (let us call them, without prejudice, 'entrepreneurs') were selected for study on one of two grounds - either (i) they were the commercial stars of this ethnic group, so widely known to most Frafras in Ghana that I could hardly miss them or (ii) they were small entrepreneurs at various stages of the accumulation process, less widely known but identified by me as prominent in a more restricted milieu, such as a village or a slum quarter.

All of these individuals presented accounts of their lives and social relations which I interpreted as providing (through their selection and emphasis of apparently verifiable events) ideological justification for their chosen path of material accumulation. All of them were described to me by others around them, and the two sets of accounts were often in conflict. In addition to these verbal statements, I was able to observe certain events and interactions over a prolonged period and sought, by means of various checks, to establish 'objectively true' pictures of each individual's career built up from fragments of information gained in many ways. These personal histories, combining material transactions, social relations and ideological statements, were of highly varied quality, depending on the time devoted to each.

An underlying theme to emerge from these researches was that tensions between the claims of individual enrichment and those of social obligation were resolved in a number of practical ways and these various resolutions were often reflected in the somewhat idealised statements put out by actors of different kinds. The questions that I addressed to this problem were all concerned with the developing relationship between the entrepreneur and members of his community, whether it be home village or urban ethnic group. Could the demands of individual accumulation and membership in a 'traditional' community be reconciled? If they could not, what strategies were appropriate for emancipation from these ties? Conversely, why did village and ethnic solidarities apparently carry so much weight, when they inhibited the possibility of realising a successful strategy for personal enrichment?

4 *CHANGING SOCIAL STRUCTURE IN GHANA*

In taking this line, I was strongly influenced by the views of individual entrepreneurs, several of whom were by far my most intimate informants. A frequent topic in their conversation was the drag on their ambitions of continued ties with members of their natal community:

'When they see this man is better, they want him to be worse, and they will always keep on coming, coming and you are giving, giving, giving. And then you will stand in the same shoes as they are - you will have nothing to give and they cannot give you anything. So you are poor and that is the level they really want to bring you to.' (Politician and businessman in Accra).

In like vein, the converse opinion of many members of their networks was that these entrepreneurs were prone to neglect solidary relations of a morally binding nature. My initial analysis was based on an assimilation of this cognitive perspective and a reading of comparative entrepreneurial history and sociology.[3] The overriding concern of this literature was to demonstrate the 'economic rationality' of the entrepreneur as he fought to secure extra profits (and social progress) in the face of obstacles put up by the forces of reaction. Unsurprisingly, I adopted a 'modernisation' approach to the problem of entrepreneurial development. The epitome of 'modern men', these accumulators of privately owned assets escaped, with a few exceptions, from the pressing obligations of kinship, neighbourhood and ethnicity through conversion to Islam or Christianity and by moving into new social milieus, where individualism was more positively sanctioned. They were ascetic, hardworking savers and investors whose economic rationality was in conflict with the norms of traditional values emphasising generosity and equality. As innovative types *par excellence* their unconventional choices set important precedents for their fellows. Although the mass of Frafras remained in stagnant poverty and were hidebound by tribal morality, the success of these few entrepreneurs was a source of great emulation for many and this small group constituted as such a major force for change, principal actors in the historical process leading to the erosion of existing social solidarities.[4] Imbued with the spirit of this analysis I wrote a paper in 1969 which stressed the positive contribution made by small entrepreneurs of this type to Ghana's development in the fields of long-distance trade, transport, housing, contracting and urban services. (Hart 1970)

The overall picture was consistent and therefore credible, were it not for the omission or glossing over of a number of impressions, facts and partial analyses which did not quite square with the general argument. Later I tackled the problem from an entirely different source and with another literature in mind. I became interested in the vast range of non-wage activities through which large numbers of ordinary poor Ghanaians made a sometimes precarious living in the towns. Preoccupation with this mass of petty transactions in what I chose to call the 'informal economy' brought to light the 'rationality' of various mechanisms of income sharing and social security provision which extended kinship and urban ethnicity made possible. Private accumulators looked rather different from this point of view and I came to realise that not all the self-employed, turning over a steady income, were would-be entrepreneurs who had failed to accumulate.[5]

A growing acquaintance with the literature of political economy and development economics led me to investigate the macro-structural relations between urban capitalism, rural production and the great amorphous rural-urban labour market of the self-employed. At this stage my attention

SWINDLER OR PUBLIC BENEFACTOR?

was drawn to previously neglected features of Frafra entrepreneurship which together conform closely to the negative stereotype of the 'petty capitalist'.[6] Many accumulators were crooks, spivs, money lenders, extortionists, slum landlords, food hoarders and speculators who even sold water for profit, whose initial capital had been acquired shadily more often than not and whose unbridled individualism threatened the emergent adaptations with which the majority of Frafras sought to protect themselves against poverty, insecurity and exploitation. Moreover, the efforts of these small-time accumulators were of negligible social value in the face of massive income drain from Ghana facilitated by continuing relations of neo-colonial domination in sectors completely outside their control.

But this picture too, equally convincing because internally consistent, disturbed me because it precluded the possibility that small entrepreneurs, taken as a group, might be making a substantial contribution to real income growth in Ghana. Swindler or public benefactor? The polarised contrasts of popular sentiment and economic sociology succeed only in establishing that opposed points of view are possible, even likely, both in social life itself and in its academic analysis. This paper was conceived first as an attempt to set up an analytical framework capable of transcending the banal level of circular reasoning and self-fulfilling ideology, and second as a brief and partial application of the framework to a particular set of empirical circumstances, even though the details of the case were not collected with the testing of this framework in mind.

To relate the problem: what are the various ways in which individual entrepreneurs accumulate wealth? How do they manage their relationships (material, social and ideological) with other members of their community while raising their own income level? What are the consequences of individual enrichment for social welfare, conceived of either in terms of the total social product or of its distribution? These questions present a number of analytical difficulties which it would be advisable to confront before becoming involved in the case study itself. The following sections III and IV may be glossed over by readers who have little interest in theoretical problems.

III

The most obvious analytical problems are the following: (1) to identify the 'entrepreneur' as an actor (emic) or observer (etic) category, or as both; (2) to put a boundary around the term 'community' without object-ifying either it or the individual's orientation to it; and (3) to specify the terms under which social relationships will be analysed. It may then be possible to produce an abstract account of the accumulation process and its social consequences, by means of which particular cases may be investigated.

First, the term 'entrepreneur' is used ubiquitously in social science and history to denote a bewildering variety of persons. In the third world, anyone who is not either a peasant farmer or a wage earner is liable to be classified as an entrepreneur; in anthropology, anyone who does something novel or manipulative, maximises profit or even acts persistently to further his own interest is likely to be called an entrepreneur; even in economics, 'some writers have identified entrepreneurship with the

CHANGING SOCIAL STRUCTURE IN GHANA

function of uncertainty-bearing, others with the co-ordination of productive resources, others with the introduction of innovations and still others with the provision of capital', (Hoselitz 1952: 98). It is clear that the word is normally used by analysts to mean whatever they like.

The classical definition of the entrepreneur, however, was designed to identify that human agency which combined the factors of production (land, labour, capital, technology) in working enterprises. Later Joseph Schumpeter (1961) concentrated on this factor as the main source of innovation, in order to explain how economies changed over time. The entrepreneur as a distinctive personality type is a convenient mechanism for turning static individualistic models of the utilitarian type into dynamic theories of social and economic change. And so it is in this form, as a generalised 'innovator', that the entrepreneur has been incorporated into anthropological analysis, largely through the work of Barth, Geertz and Long.[7] Marxist analysis of the laws of motion of industrial societies dispenses with the need to employ personality types in seeking an understanding of the dynamics of economic transformation. Here, the entrepreneur as a separate category is submerged in the division **between** the two great classes of workers (the owners of labour-power) and **capitalists** (the owners of capital and those who work on their side), **whose struggle** contains the dynamic of the social system.

The basic problem with a term like 'entrepreneur' is that it is an **'emic'category** of western culture, with implicit connotations of large-**scale business** leadership of a kind which is historically very specific **indeed.** The entrepreneurial firm of nineteenth century western Europe **and America** was a peculiar kind of socio-economic formation which is **perhaps** not so commonly encountered in the world today as is the label associated with the period of its efflorescence. I use the term, for want of a better, to denote not even a status, (never mind a class), but rather an economic role which may be only an aspect of the behaviour of individuals whose primary position in society is not necessarily defined by the term. Entrepreneurship refers here to a category of instrumental activity - the individual accumulation and investment of surpluses, realised in the form of capital assets which are productive of further wealth and managed by the owner himself.[8] Those who engage in this activity are conforming to entrepreneurial role behaviour, a role which may be played by anyone to a greater or lesser degree and which implies no functional specialisation to the exclusion of other roles. Note that entrepreneurship and self-employment are by no means synonymous, since the latter does not necessarily imply an expanding capital stock - the independent artisan or trader may be engaged simply in the static reproduction of his own subsistence rather than in accumulating surpluses. Entrepreneurs in this paper are thus self-employed accumulators of material surpluses.

It could be argued that my definition would be better served by the label 'capitalist'.[9] Both terms suffer from having specific associations with western economic history and political theory, which reduce their value as general etic categories. Marx's analysis of the capitalist mode of production is, however, far too precise to allow any extension of the term without causing considerable confusion. 'Entrepreneur' has been employed more vaguely in a wider variety of contexts than has the term

SWINDLER OR PUBLIC BENEFACTOR? 7

'capitalist', and for this, perhaps frivolous reason I choose it as my
label instead of seeking a neologism. A further point to be borne in
mind is that, if entrepreneurial accumulation is to be a pure analytical
category, care must always be taken to distinguish between its use in
the analysis of particular social contexts and the emic categories used
by actors to identify individuals labelled by the observer as 'entrepreneurs'.

The second main problem involves the use of the term 'community' in
this context. Conventional macro-economic analysis usually proceeds by
placing an artificial boundary round a social entity (be it a town, region,
country or international zone), in order to analyse internal relations
of production and distribution as well as flows of goods and services
across the boundary (the import/export trade). The volume of external
transactions determines how open the economy is; if it is very low, the
system may be legitimately regarded as closed for most analytical
purposes. It is with a similar end in view that I use the term 'community'
- as a matrix of social relations capable of being given an objective
boundary by the observer and (but not necessarily) recognised by the
actors as providing in certain contexts a possible basis for collective
identification against the outside world.[10] The matrix usually, but not
necessarily has a fixed territorial dimension. Most individuals may be
located in a multiple, hierarchical series of overlapping and discrete
social matrices of this kind. Membership in any one community must
always be putative and relative for any individual: some will be more
committed to internal relations than others. Nevertheless, it is always
analytically possible to trace for each person only those relations
which lie within a given social matrix of which he is a member, while
treating all those relations with persons lying outside the boundary
as an undifferentiated 'import/export trade'.

The central problem is to establish which order of 'community' is
most valid for the question at hand. Economists tend to talk of national
systems because of prevailing accounting techniques and policy-making
bodies; Marxist economists and sociologists are likely to take an even
wider universe than a single nation state as their analytical starting
point; and regional economics has begun the systematic study of parts
of national systems. Anthropologists are generally forced by the nature
of their enquiries to limit analysis to a village, a rural district, a
factory, an urban neighbourhood or even a dispersed social network such
as a migrant ethnic group. In these cases, selection of a boundary is
often an ex post facto rationalisation for a fieldwork decision taken
long ago.

The point is that, once a boundary has been chosen as a starting
point, internal relations must be analysed as a systematic whole and
relations crossing the boundary are of paramount significance (even
though they are often neglected by analysts who focus for convenience on
intra-community relations), since it is these external relations which
determine whether the social entity so bounded may be legitimately
regarded as a closed system or rather as an open system whose internal
relations are in some important ways shaped by relations originating
in a more inclusive social entity, such as the nation or perhaps the
world itself.

The question of whether a given level of analysis is appopriate must,
of course, always depend on the kind of problem being tackled: if most

of the answers are to be found outside the boundary chosen for analysis, then the choice was a poor one. The danger is that, once the analysis is committed to a given kind of community, the observer will objectify the boundary as real and finite (rather than as a heuristic device), treating the multiple affiliations of actors contained within it as *dominated* by that cluster of social ties which he has chosen to emphasise. The relative significance of community ties for each individual will vary considerably and cannot be prejudged; indeed we should be wary of analyses which treat all members of the community as homogeneous in their degree of commitment to it.

We have now arrived, rather laboriously, at an operational meaning for the phrase 'the entrepreneur in his community': having selected a bounded social matrix of some kind, we will analyse the activities of individuals located within it whose economic activities may be said to consist in part of the accumulation of material surpluses.

One further distinction is necessary, however. Individuals are rarely self-contained: most accord a qualitatively different priority to their relations with co-resident close kin (the domestic group). Indeed the level of mutuality of decision-making within the immediate range of conjugal family relations is usually such that the basic unit of analysis is in some contexts more appropriately the domestic group than the individuals who make up its numbers. Entrepreneurs are perhaps notably egoistic, but between the individual and his community there always exists the mediating range of close kinship relations within the domestic group. It is advisable, therefore, to differentiate between family and community relations. The four elements of our analysis may thus be conceived as **three** concentric circles radiating out from a single point - ego (the **entrepreneur**): close kin (his domestic group): community (however **operationally** defined): rest of the world (differentiated, whenever **appropriate**, in order to account for significant external relations). It is the community boundary, and not any one egocentric domestic group within it, which provides the starting point for analysis.

The third cluster of analytical problems concerns the framework adopted for studying the social relations linking entrepreneurs with other actors. The relationship between the entrepreneur and his community has often been seen as lying in a conflict between individual motivation and social values. But concentration on the subjective dimension usually produces excessively monistic and unverifiable theories of social behaviour. Analysis in these terms often reduces the complexity and contradictions of human behaviour and ideas in action to simple psychological types and universal group norms, each of which are portrayed as stable, consistent and rational subjective states. Moreover, selection of this analytical focus implies that the observer must locate the origins of behaviour in inferences made about deep psychological stimuli, when all he usually has to go on are observed or reported events and verbal reflections of various kinds.

I have already suggested that shifts in behaviour and thought over time and between places are too complex to be capable of reduction to internally consistent models of a highly subjective nature. In this paper I choose to analyse the relationships between persons as an impermanent set of material and immaterial transactions giving rise to a consciousness which may sometimes be articulated by the actors as open statements about the nature of these exchanges to the extent that these expressions of

SWINDLER OR PUBLIC BENEFACTOR?   9

attain any internal consistency they may be said to constitute an
'ideology', which, grounded as it is in common experience, is likely to
be shared in some degree by a social category, such as a status group
or class. Material transactions (the 'economic' component) involve the
exchange of goods or their equivalent; immaterial transactions (the
'social'component) are conceived of here as an exchange of services without
formal payment; expression of consciousness are the 'ideological'
dimension to these relationships.

All of these elements of human behaviour may be observed and analysed
without having recourse to speculation about the inner subjective states
which may have 'caused' the actors to behave the way they did. If this
paper seeks to establish analytical generalisations, they should be capable
of being located in the dialectic between actual exchanges and the
ideological expressions which relate to them. The social behaviour and
thought of actors are in turn conceived of as the product of dialectical
contradictions encountered in social life.

Again, perhaps an overlarge theoretical hammer has been used to
crack what some might think a smallish nut; it must be said, however, that
these definitional problems are both highly contentious and most relevant
to the ensuing discussion. We have reached the position where relations
between individual entrepreneurs and others, both within and outside the
boundaries of domestic group and community, can be seen as exchanges
having an economic, social and ideological dimension. It is now possible
to construct out of these elements a theoretical model for the analysis
of the accumulation process and its social consequences.

IV

The individual entrepreneur, if he is to retain effective links with
his community, has to maintain a balance in his career between private
accumulation and community consumption. It is the working premiss of
this paper that, instead of treating all forms of accumulation as having
broadly similar social effects, we should analyse with some exactness
the economic, social and ideological exchanges connecting the entrepreneur
and his domestic group with the wider community and beyond; that a finer
analysis of this kind will generate predictions about the level of social
conflict likely to be encountered by various kinds of entrepreneurial
activity; and that the relationship between individual accumulation
and social development, both in general and in specific historical cases,
will be clarified. A number of distinctions, particularly relating to
economic exchanges, must be made for this analysis to proceed without
unnecessary confusion.

Let us assume that, at the beginning of his career, the entrepreneur's
total income is equal to his total domestic expenditure and that this
level of consumption is not markedly different from the norm for most
members of his community. The first requirement is to gain a surplus of
income over consumption needs. Surpluses can be generated in two ways,
either by saving out of domestic income and increasing the productivity
of family labour, or by securing a net addition to domestic resources through
income transfer. The first method, or the face of it, *produces* surplus
value without making anyone else worse off; the second involves the
circulation of surplus value, as a result of which one man's gain is another's

10 *CHANGING SOCIAL STRUCTURE IN GHANA*

loss. This distinction is crucial to any understanding of the social effects of individual accumulation.[11]

Personal and domestic savings may be generated by: (1) reducing domestic consumption levels (abstention) (2) working harder oneself and producing more (3) expansion of productive family labour inputs (4) increasing the efficiency of production through e.g. economies of scale, greater co-ordination of labour,improved skills, technological innovation and better means of storing surpluses (5) a natural stroke of good fortune, such as a minerals find. As a consequence of all of those measures the social surplus as a whole is increased and the total amount of value produced in the world is in most cases greater than before.

But individual surpluses may also be generated by transfer of assets and income; (6) inheritance and marriage payments (7) gift, a public handout or some similar windfall (8) credit or loan (9) rent and interest payments (10) exaction of tribute (11) manipulative skill in markets and monopoly pricing (12) theft (13) an increase over time in the relative price of goods and services sold by the domestic group. All of these transfers involve only the distribution of the social product, having the effect of concentrating surpluses in one man's hands through circulation of value rather than its production.

Finally, surpluses may be generated by (14) the acquisition of labour producing surplus value (more than it receives for its own consumption), e.g. help from the community, wage labour, pawns and slaves. This form of surplus accumulation is more complicated than the others since , although production may be increased by making the producers work harder or more effectively than before, the issue may be seen as a question of distribution in that the workers' share of their product is less than it could be. This problem lies at the heart of the dispute between Marxists and non-Marxists over the amount of income transfer between the two classes engaged in capitalist production. The case is put in a rather extreme manner by Mandel:

> '... nowhere in the world has ... the production of a growing mass of surplus value been the result of voluntary abstinence on the part of producers who thus make savings and become rich. Everywhere... it has been the outcome of an appropriation, a grabbing by one part of human society of the social surplus product which has been produced by the rest of this same society. This appropriation may indeed be the result of an 'abstinence', namely, that of the producers ... Unfortunately it has been the grabbers and not the unwilling heroes of this abstinence who have emerged enriched from the ordeal.

(Mandel 1968:89 his italics)

Perhaps - but assertions of this kind are an inadequate substitute for reasoned empirical analysis, however valuable they may be as support for a critical ideology.

The transfer of income to the entrepreneur may not always be counted as a cost to his community: in many cases the transfer may be achieved at the expense of persons outside, so that the total amount of value circulating within the community is increased. (The classic case would be Robin Hood, but the profits from external trade would be a less exotic example.) Moreover, some gains by income transfer within the community may be perceived as entirely legitimate and encounter little public opprobrium.

SWINDLER OR PUBLIC BENEFACTOR? 11

We may summarise this section of the argument as follows. Entrepreneurial accumulation of material surpluses can occur by any of three means: (a) an increase in the net social surplus achieved without any transfer of value taking place (b) a transfer of value from outside the community (c) a transfer of value from inside the community. Only (c) is objectively injurious to the community by concentrating in private hands surpluses which would otherwise have been available for public consumption; and even some of these intra-community transfers may be culturally defined as legitimate. Both (a) and (b) especially, but also (c), constitute a potential source of benefit to the community as a whole, depending on the destination of the surplus.

Surpluses generated by any combination of the means listed above may be channelled in varying proportion to the following uses - (1) capital investment in productive assets or hire of labour (2) a savings fund (3) interest-bearing speculation and usury (4) rent and interest payments, replacement of fixed capital, taxation and similar costs (5) increased personal and domestic consumption (6) redistribution of material welfare by direct donation to members of the community and outsiders. Only capital investment generates additional social surpluses in the long run; a savings fund may be used eventually for productive investment or consumption; money loans may be made to producers or consumers. These three uses of the surplus, when added to fixed outgoings, determine the amount left for immediate consumption; the balance between personal consumption and redistribution affects the short-term income distribution conequences of entrepreneurial accumulation.

As far as relationships between the entrepreneur and his community are concerned, the destination of these surpluses is critical. But two further dimensions to the question enter here - the time horizon employed for assessing the net results of income flows, and the extent to which the community economy is an open one. Capital investment and savings may reduce community consumption in the short-term, but they hold out the prospects of increased income yields in the future, by adding to the total amount of value produced and made available for distribution later. Alternatively, an individual's emphasis on private accumulation now may be offset by great personal generosity later. The time dimension, and in particular how long people are prepared to wait for jam tomorrow, is thus an important aspect of the entrepreneur's exchanges.

Secondly, it is a matter of crucial significance whether the entrepreneur's expenditures on investment and consumption remain within the community or flow out of it. The entrepreneur could be a source of income drain in a number of ways: by using imported factor inputs, by investing his money abroad, by paying out large sums to agencies located beyond the community boundary, by consuming overpriced imported luxuries, and by making large donations to bodies outside the community. On the other hand, he could be a substantial source of community prosperity: by using internal factor inputs, circulating his money within the community, creating demand for local goods and services (the multiplier effect) and ensuring that any redistribution is to the other members of his community, not outsiders. The more open the community economy, the more likely it is that the entrepreneur will be a source of income drain; in a closed economy, his activities are likely to increase the total amount of value in circulation in the long run. Those who, like Frank (1969), argue that indigenous entrepreneurs in the third world are a major source of income drain from rural to urban areas and from underdeveloped to

12 *CHANGING SOCIAL STRUCTURE IN GHANA*

metropolitan countries, must show empirically that the internal benefits of entrepreneurial activities are outweighed by income loss.

It is clear that, for any individual entrepreneur, a number of choices present themselves at different stages of his career. The balance between accumulation, consumption and redistribution at any one point in time is likely to be correlated with the size of surplus in hand. In the initial stage, when he is struggling to break out of the subsistence nexus, he is likely to control his personal and domestic consumption, while fiercely resisting transfers from himself to the community: in other words he will be stingy. During the middle stage of consolidation and expansion, he may continue to maximise the rate of surplus accumulation through capital formation and investment: this course brings him into head-on conflict with those around him; or he can afford to relax somewhat to pay out a bit more on personal and family consumption as well as on redistribution and profit sharing. At the same time he may be able to point to the indirect fruits of his labours in the form of increased community prosperity. In the final stage of his declining years, the rate of accumulation may be reversed and he may even allow accumulated surpluses to be converted into rentier investments, the pursuit of political office and social prestige, conspicuous consumption, the advancement of his children and large-scale redistribution. At any time, of course, the entrepreneur may suffer a reversal (perhaps through a miscalculation of the appropriate balance of expenditures) which reduces him to the subsistence level or to a substantially lower rate of surplus accumulation and consumption.

The extent to which individual enrichment brings collective material benefits must, therefore, vary substantially; and it is predicted that the degree of social conflict generated by entrepreneurial activities will be a direct function of this economic variable. But not all exchanges are economic in nature and the ideological (subjective) factor has some independent influence on the social consequences of individual enrichment. Even if the material flows from the entrepreneur to his community are exiguous, he may (a) compensate by rendering social services and behaving acceptably within the community (b) ignore or move out of the community. In the first case the effect of material transactions is counter-balanced in some degree by the entrepreneur's social behaviour and openly expressed ideology of commitment to the community: and in the second, he closes off non-utilitarian exchanges with members of the community by means of isolationism or escape.

Perception of the social justice of income inequalities is a difficult, and often unpredictable variable. The community at large may fail to differentiate between the ways wealth is accumulated, treating all rich people either as positive reference points for status emulation or as targets for revolutionary attack. Again, in some cultures ostentatious private consumption is socially meritorious and in others abstention from display is a public virtue. Absolute income levels may be less significant for the perception of inequality than changes in the relative incomes of individuals and groups over time. All of this may be so, and I would certainly not suggest that actors invariably share the rationality of this analysis; nevertheless I maintain that social conflict may in large measure be predicted from an analysis, along the lines suggested in this paper, of the objective exchange relationships and income flows linking entrepreneurs and their community.

SWINDLER OR PUBLIC BENEFACTOR?

We may predict, therefore, that conflict (both actual and ideological) between the entrepreneur and his community will be greatest when the following conditions are met: when accumulation is achieved by a culturally unacceptable transfer of value from the community to the entrepreneur, when conversion of surplus income into capital formation and private consumption leaves little for immediate redistribution to the community and has negligible indirect effects on community prosperity in the longer term (especially if the entrepreneur is a major channel for income drain out of the community) and when he rejects community standards of social behaviour. Conversely, conflict will be minimised when the effect of entrepreneurial accumulation is only to increase the amount of value in circulation at no cost to the community itself, when surpluses generate internal economic growth and the redistribution rate is high, and when community norms of approved behaviour and ideology are closely observed by the entrepreneur. To adopt a game analogy, the one extreme is a zero sum game with the entrepreneur as winner and everyone else the losers, while the other is an in an increasing sum game in which everyone wins. Between these poles lie a number of compromises in which the balance of advantage shifts over time from the community to the entrepreneur and back again.

Finally, social conflict and its ideological expression will be substantially increased if individual accumulation becomes crystallised in a new social division of labour, whereby entrepreneurs emerge as a distinct, self-conscious and enduringly powerful status group. As long as the rate of upward and downward mobility associated with entrepreneurial activities in a particular social context is high, the emergence of a capitalist division of labour will be inhibited. Moreover, the rate of capital formation in the community as a whole is inversely related to the degree of community co-operation needed for accumulation by individuals. The long run social consequences of accumulation therefore depend intimately, though not exclusively, on the success with which entrepreneurs are able to resist domestic and community pressures towards immediate consumption.

The contradiction between individual enrichment and social welfare is thus a real one, which produces in the short term a dialectical dilemma between private and public interests. This dilemma may be resolved in a number of ways: (1) by enriching oneself and one's family at the expense of no-one else in the community, through a combination of hard work, skill and asceticism (2) by causing economic growth in the community as a whole and devoting a sufficient part of one's income to internal redistribution for others to judge one's retained wealth to be fair (3) by adopting conventional social attitudes, the overt symbols of community membership, and being of service to others in the community (4) by moving into another community which positively sanctions individualism, provides more effective material support or sees itself as benefitting from any transfers of value taking place (5) by the single-minded pursuit of profit in isolation from wider social ties and through any means, however morally disreputable, including theft, extortion and exploitation.

The last expedient, of course, is not a resolution of the dilemma at all. Nevertheless it is this image (which forms the basis of the negative view of the entrepreneur as 'swindler') which lies behind most stereotypes of the entrepreneur in popular ideology and Marxist political economy. The first two interpretations of the entrepreneur's private and public roles combine to provide the positive stereotype of the entrepreneur as

14 *CHANGING SOCIAL STRUCTURE IN GHANA*

genius and public benefactor: they form the one-sided ideology of an accumulating class and its apologists, as well as allowing the rich to sleep at night. The third and fourth strategies have been identified by social anthropologists, [12] conscious of the moral and social pressures which may be brought to bear on small entrepreneurs in face-to-face communities.

In principle, this analysis of the accumulation process may be applied to a large number of historical situations over a range of levels, from the micro to the macro. To this writer it seems to be immaterial whether the unit of analysis is a single individual and his immediate social network or a class of entrepreneurs and the national society of which they are part - the basic components of the approach are equally applicable at any level. The case to be analysed may be the problems faced by independent artisans and traders in village India, the role played by financial speculators, merchants and industrialists in the development of class antagonisms in Britian, or the economic activities of racial and religious minorities throughout history. The analytical framework was not developed with these situations explicitly in mind - the immediate problematic concerns some small operators from one part of Ghana - but it is hoped that, with some modification, a full exposition of the kind outlined above serves the purpose of drawing attention to the almost infinite variety of ways through which the individual accumulation of surpluses may be conducted. All too often important dimensions to the problem are neglected by social scientists operating with cultural and ideological blinkers on: as the following case study will show, these blinkers are extremely difficult to shed.

V

In this section, the subjects of the study are introduced, the entrepreneurs and their community identified and some individual cases briefly outlined.

The study focused on a group of people selected by their common district of origin, which in modern Ghana is recognised by the ethnic label 'Frafra'. These people live in a densely populated part of N.E. Ghana which is predominantly rural savannah. Their homeland is a unified administrative entity - the Frafra local council area - and it consists mainly of agricultural settlements linked by a network of paths and roads. In the middle of these villages lies a new cosmopolitan urban complex, Bolgatanga, which has become in recent years a major entrepot and regional service centre, with its large market, lorry park and government buildings.

Frafras number about a quarter million or 3 per cent of Ghana's population, but their identification as a 'tribe' is problematic. In the 1930's Fortes studied the Tallensi who, together with two other socio-linguistic groups (the Nabdams and Gurensi), make up the Frafra 'supertribe'. [13] Although at home local identities usually take precedence over the Frafra label, the term is widely used, and usually recognised as valid by members of all three groups, in the national context.

For many years Frafras have migrated from an increasingly over-crowded homeland (where population densities are often 450 per sq. mile or more), first to the surrounding rural areas of the North, then to the cocoa farms and mines of Ashanti, and latterly to the rapidly growing towns and cities of Southern Ghana. This migration has been one of labour circulation and mostly involves males in the 15 - 45 years age group, although some men take their families with them away from home. Rights in patrilineal land and property are not forfeited my migrants, nor is succession to political and ritual office impeded by long term absence: for these and other reasons, almost all migrants eventually return home to reap the benefits which are customary as one grows older. Today at least a quarter of all Frafras live away from home, and for adult males the absentee rate in most villages is 50 per cent or more. Moreover, although most migrants make frequent visits back home, Ghana's labour market situation is now such that extended stays abroad are more common than short periods of temporary employment in the South.[14]

The label 'Frafra' acquires meaning for migrants from their continued links with home. But all major urban centres and most minor ones have a substantial community of Frafras, a partially floating population which is in general marked by a high degree of internal interaction and mutual dependence. These migrants are linked to each other and to their homeland by a continuous flow of personnel in all directions - Frafras are very mobile, thanks to the much improved system of transport and communications. They constitute in this way of network of individuals and quasi-groups spread throughout Ghana, sharing an identity based on a common place of origin and on a degree of linguistic and cultural unity which is greater, the more localised the focus of ethnic categorisation.

Any ethnic group is cross-cut by other axes of stratification, but in Ghana the distribution of occupational, educational and similar advantages is tied to the historical penetration of British colonialism inland from the coast. As very recent beneficiaries of this process, Frafras are remarkably homogeneous in most respects: avenues of upward social mobility through education, for example, have been open to them in any numbers only during the last decade, at a time when the higher end of the labour market was already becoming saturated. When we speak then of Frafras who had reached 20 years and beyond in the 1960's, the vast majority are to be located in the massive underclass of Ghanaian society, without white-collar employment (1 in 200) and without any education (1 in 100). They are mostly cultivators, small traders and labourers: they are poor and, as a group, have a national reputation for great criminality. They are culturally conservative, laying great emphasis on marriages and funerals; their religion is still ancestor worship - Christians and Moslems each accounted for only 3 per cent of the Frafra population in 1960.

The Frafra elite - those who have managed to rise noticeably above the rest - is both very small and not of particularly high status in Ghana as a whole; but each individual in it is far more exposed and widely known than men of equal status who come from more advantaged regions. The elite is composed of various sub-elites, which tend to overlap in the case of particular individuals - the politicians (national, local and 'traditional'), the white collar workers, including a handful of professionals (most of the former living within the Frafra district and the latter outside it), a miscellaneous group of men and women who have achieved a degree of eminence in their chosen occupation (some soldiers and policemen, for example), and most important of all, the self-made rich or entrepreneurial elite (who are to be found mainly in Bolgatanga and the cities of Southern Ghana).

16 *CHANGING SOCIAL STRUCTURE IN GHANA*

These eminent individuals, with some variation, usually retain strong links with members of their own natal community and ethnic group, and never escape entirely from the 'Frafra' label. The Frafra elite is recruited in a very open fashion - most of its members belong to the first generation - and the possibility of upward mobility, usually through the medium of entrepreneurial accumulation, is a common source of aspiration for most Frafras. The spirit of capitalism is thus widespread among members of this ethnic group and independent economic activity, outside agriculture and wage employment, is a very noticeable feature of their lives. But in the long run, despite the individual success stories of the few 'stars' who made it out of the ruck, the mass of ordinary Frafras are condemned to lives of poverty and routine work, whether they leave home or not. In the pecking order of Ghanaian society they come very close to the bottom and the riches of a small number of accumulators stood in stark contrast to the unsuccessful striving for self-improvement and routinised failure which were the lot of most Frafras.

Consequently, it is hardly surprising that Frafras have developed, under conditions of shared poverty and individual insecurity, an articulated morality based on recognition of the mutual depedence of kinsmen and ethnic 'brothers'; nor is it unpredictable that those who manage to enrich themselves should be a widespread target for the aspirations, hopes, fears and antipathies of their less fortunate fellows. It is the nexus of relationships and contradictions inherent therein which provide the operational meaning of the phrase 'the entrepreneur and his community' in this case.

There are simpler examples of a community boundary than the recognition of a shared cultural identity based on natal origin by a geographically dispersed ethnic network of the kind depicted here. Nevertheless, it is within a boundary of this sort that I seek to locate the Frafra 'new rich'. Most Frafras maintain relationships with members of their family, lineage, village and ethnic group which take on different meanings according to the situation the individual finds himself in. Generally, therefore, the community boundary of ethnic insiders - a solidary group of individuals linked by a shared natal origin - is defined situationally; indeed the location of the community boundary may well be a matter of dispute between individuals and, as such, it is more equivocal and negotiable than many other associational ties.

Despite the potentially shifting nature of the boundary, this study draws it round that social matrix of people who, by reason of their birthplace and continued links with their home of origin, may be said to be Frafras. Within the Frafra homeland, the boundary of natal community is likely to be placed no higher than the clan settlement. Identification of common membership within such a boundary carries with it the expectation of social solidarity, to be expressed with a negotiable degree of intensity. Inside that boundary are a number of individuals who by virtue of material accumulation, have been called 'entrepreneurs'. These entrepreneurs engage in exchange relationships with members of their natal community, whether this be, at various times, a clan settlement or an urban ethnic brotherhood. It is these relationships, together with the ideological statements to which they give rise

SWINDLER OR PUBLIC BENEFACTOR? 17

on both sides, that are the subject of this study. Frafra entrepreneurs maintain a highly variable commitment to their relations with home kin and other Frafras; some of them find only a small part of their social identity in the label 'Frafra'; but all of them can be studied in relation to their natal community and that is the purpose of this particular exercise.

Next, we should ask whether the 'entrepreneurs' identified in this analysis correspond to any homogeneous categories of the actors themselves. The traditional stereotype of the rich man *(nera gu'la)* implies the acquisition of material wealth (in the form of crops, livestock, personal possessions, wives and offspring) through stewardship of inherited lineage property and perhaps through his own achievements as a farmer, trader or community leader. It is universally a term of approbation. Other categories which are still in use include the 'man of property' *(bondaana)* and the 'big man' *(bom kate,*implying physical strength or social power): whereas the former carries the connotation of private wealth, the latter belongs unequivocally to the public arena of political competition. Both terms may occasionally be used in a pejorative way. The modern term which comes closest to my category 'entrepreneur' is 'money man' *(ligeredaana)*. If the *nera gu'la* contains the positive stereotype of traditionally acquired riches and prestige, the 'money man' has succeeded through domination of the market and thus typifies the changed nature of economic power today. Money in the bank is now a more reliable measure of enrichment than the traditional assets of the *nera gu'la*. The term 'money man' is on the whole used in a morally neutral fashion.

Most people whom I identified as 'entrepreneurs' would be labelled 'money man' or 'man of property' by Frafras. A few accumulators, at an early stage of the self-enrichment process, would escape emic categorisation as 'rich', but were included in my sample as 'entrepreneurs'. Few of the entrepreneurs qualified as the 'traditional rich man' and only a few more could be called men of power, 'big men'. But the most successful entrepreneurs qualified for all these emic labels and stand at the apex of the entrepreneurial ladder to social prestige within the Frafra community.

Finally, as a relief from this abstracted discussion, I present six brief cases which together provide a concrete illustration of the sort of people who were selected for study as 'Frafra entrepreneurs'.

To restate the etic definition reached above (p.6) entrepreneurship refers in this paper to 'the individual accumulation and investment of surpluses, realised in the form of capital assets which are productive of further wealth and managed by the owner himself'. The following cases, with the exception of A and D (who are rich by any standards in Ghana), show that these 'entrepreneurs' are individually very small fry indeed from the point of view of the national economy.

A was born in 1928, the second son of a poor Tallensi farmer. At the age of 40 he was a senior non-commissioned officer in the army at Accra. He owned five houses and nine commercial vehicles which, together with numerous part-time trading and investment activities, brought in an annual income of around £20,000. His consumption expenditure, allowing for a steady rate of capital accumulation and saving, accounted for a large part of this income: he had 11 wives, 17 children, a floating household of 80 persons, scores of dependents and clients throughout Ghana, and in 1968 he provided the financial

18   *CHANGING SOCIAL STRUCTURE IN GHANA*

support necessary for his brother to become the chief of their home village. Soon afterwards he retired from the army and moved lock, stock and barrel back home.

B was some four year older and also an N.C.O. in Accra. His home was a section of Bolgatanga and his father had been a serviceman. In his youth he had known great hardship, but the 1950's and 1960's saw him accumulate two houses, a mini-bus, a corn mill and several other income-yielding assets. A monogamous Christian, he lived in Accra with his wife (a trader), while his five children attended missionary schools. He was rather isolated in the migrant community and was ambivalent about returning home one day.

C was born around 1925 in a Gurensi village. He left home at the age of 12. After a lifetime of working as a cook/steward, while plying a number of ancillary trades (most of them shady), he lived in his own house in Accra with two wives, four children and a number of younger male relatives. Although at one stage he had £2,000 in the bank and at another owned two commercial vehicles, in 1968 C's fortunes were recovering only slowly after a short gaol sentence had all but smashed his entrepreneurial career. He had no plans to return home permanently, although his links with people from his village were strong.

D was born about 50 years ago into a Gurensi family which was notoriously poor. Again, after a fluctuating migrant career, by the mid-1960's he had built up in Bolgatanga an impressive collection of enterprises. He owned eight houses and two private cars, ran a fleet of heavy lorries, was boss of the transporters' union and a political activist, traded in thousands of head of cattle at a time, as well as in bulk purchases of maize and rice, supplied food to local institutions, ran a petrol station for a time and, as a building contractor, had been responsible for several of the new apartment and office blocks springing up in the town. A pillar of the Bolgatanga Moslem community (which included many non-Frafra business associates), he had six wives but was thought to be sterile. Illiterate and speaking no English, D relied on an army of employees, helpers and hangers-on to run his affairs.

E is a 50 year old childless female divorcee, who lives with a distant relative in Bolgatanga. She started trading in the South with her ex-husband, but now stays mainly in the North where she keeps up close relations with her natal kin in a nearby village. Her main trade is in guinea corn (sorghum) for beer brewing, but she also buys beans and maize wholesale and sends groundnuts, rice and fowls to trading partners in the South. She employs youths to pull hand-carts in the market and to hire out bicycles, has a house in Bolgatanga which yields rents and formerly ran a five-ton truck. She is popular among her neighbours and no longer spends most of her profits on lovers.

F is 70 years old and has never left his Tallensi village birth-place where he is now the head of a large co-resident lineage, based on 10 closely related male agnates with their many wives and children. A benevolent patriarch, he has built up from an inherited advantage of fertile land and herds a highly co-operative

SWINDLER OR PUBLIC BENEFACTOR?

enterprise based on food farming, livestock raising and trading
a gin distillery, a corn mill and labour migrant remittances.
One of his sons also farms tobacco and hires out bicycles. F
is next in line for the office of earth priest in his village.

The sample of 71 entrepreneurs was as heterogeneous as these six
cases, perhaps more so.[15] Nevertheless, some patterns of Frafra entrepreneurship emerged clearly enough to permit tentative generalisation.
The next two sections attempt to draw out from the complicated case
material a few points of relevance to this paper's central topic: the
evidence for these summary statements is necessarily curtailed.

VI

The working hypothesis of this paper is that the degree of
ideological and practical opposition encountered by entrepreneurs in
their community is likely to be a function of (a) the actual methods
adopted for the accumulation of surpluses by different categories of
individual and the objective consequences of this process for the
distribution of social welfare within the community, and (b) the
strategies adopted by entrepreneurs for resolving the contradictions
between private and public interests which inevitably arise in their
exchanges with other members of their community. The aim of this
section is thus to ask of Frafra entrepreneurs; how do they do it? -
before proceeding in Section VII to examine how they manage their
relationships with other Frafras.

A brief account of the accumulation process must differentiate
three spheres - the home village, Bolgatanga and the cities of the South
(Accra and Kumasi). [16] Many individuals move freely between these spheres
at different points of their career (see case A above) and the more
successful entrepreneurs, such as case D above, usually have interests
in all three. But the opportunities for accumulation in these spheres
are sufficiently different to warrant separate treatment.

In the past, individual accumulation at home was constrained by
the exercise of rights over labour and property by family elders, acting
as stewards of joint lineage land and herds. Nevertheless, provided
that he made himself available for collective family work when required,
a young man was free to acquire property in his own right through his
own efforts. Even so, it is said that a father retained an over-right
over personal property acquired by his son's individual enterprise.[17]
And in general it was only when a man became 'fatherless' that he
succeeded to the management of lineage assets and was able to own
private property. Despite these constraints, personal accumulation
was not only possible, but, in Fortes' words, 'individual initiative,
ambition and independence of action, within the limits imposed by their
social and material order, are common' (Fortes 1945: 9).

The traditional means of accumulation are still evident in Frafra
villages today: they consist essentially of food production on personal
plots, raising of small and large livestock, trading surpluses in local
markets and even long-distance import-export trade, usury or pawning
and craft specialisation. A man would usually have to rely on his own
labour and that of his conjugal family: a wife was thus an essential aid
to accumulation and, with the brideprice being normally four cattle to

be paid over a negotiable period, most young men were dependent on the older managers of lineage herds for the privilege of getting married. Livestock were the key to the traditional accumulation process: every young man was made a gift of a fowl or a goat, usually by his mother's brother and, if he were astute and lucky, by the gradual process of natural increase, trade and conversion of good surpluses into livestock, he could build up a substantial number of fowls, goats and sheep, leading eventually to the direct purchase of cattle on the market. Livestock rustling and robbery of all kinds seem to have been a frequent short-cut in this process. It all meant that the gerontocratic system of inheritance could be by-passed by energetic individuals but only with considerable difficulty.

Today, despite numerous technological innovations in agriculture and the introduction of new crops, agriculture and livestock raising in Frafra villages follow broadly the same pattern. Wage labour is more common in some parts of the district, but an overall land scarcity and the absence of a market in land makes it difficult for individuals to accumulate solely on the basis of agrarian pursuits. Case F above is a rare example of agricultural enterprise based on a pooling of lineage labour and funds: co-operative units today usually contain no more than two or three adult males. All the activities listed as 'traditional' can now be pursued more gainfully thanks to the development of regional and national markets: trading and transportation of foodstuffs, the manufacture for export of straw and leather artifacts, moneylending and the purchase of crop futures, secondary occupations (diviner, roofing expert, blacksmith) - all of these have benefitted from the extension of markets into rural areas.

In addition, a number of novel economic activities have entered Frafra village life in the post-war period and each constitutes a further opportunity for some people to accumulate without leaving home. The village store trader is a newcomer whose position is due to the entry of the small impedimenta of western civilisation into the budgets of most villagers - cigarettes, aspirin, kerosene, matches and the like. He is often able to use cash surpluses generated by monopoly pricing for usury and speculation, as well as for capitalising production on his own behalf. Another rapidly growing industry in the villages (subject to government regulations) is the commercial manufacture and sale of millet beer and gin. Profits are also to be made on an increasing scale from the investment of surpluses in capital equipment (bullock ploughs, flour mills, bicycles) which can be hired in many villages. Finally, the pursuit of 'traditional' chiefly office has now been elevated to the status of a substantial political racket, entailing large expenditures and bringing considerable financial rewards to the successful operator. Chiefs are often the wealthiest inhabitants of Frafra villages and they are usually surrounded by the financial corpses of their less successful competitors for office.

The rural economy of the Frafra district is thus much more diversified and commercialised than in Fortes' time. But opportunities for accumulation are still restricted by the availability of land (which limits agrarian production for export) and by the size of local markets (which means that each village has room only for one store, flour mill and gin distillery). Moreover, although individuals are better placed to accumulate surpluses, they must still face severe normative pressure from elder kinsmen if they neglect collective work for the pursuit of private profit. Collective demands on an individual's labour can be oppressive and, in general, genealogical succession to stewardship of joint lineage assets remains the only uncomplicated road to relative affluence in the Frafra villages.

But the rural economy is now extremely open and, in addition to long-distance migration and commerce, the existence of Bolgatanga in the heart of the Frafra homeland has revolutionised village life. A major market and employment centre is now only walking distance or a short bicycle ride from most villages; and trucks bring villagers into town from the outlying areas, (the farthest of which are only 15 - 20 miles away). In Bolgatanga there are more opportunities for accumulation by Frafras than anywhere else in Ghana, since here they have the advantage of being local residents without the restrictions of village economy and society.

The key to accumulation in Bolgatanga lies in the twin complex of market and lorry park, each of which, apart from serving the local region, is a focal point in the long-distance trading and transport networks that link Southern Ghana with neighbouring countries to the North. Frafras operating out of Bolgatanga are important traders and brokers in foodstuffs, livestock, fowls, cola and various indigenous manufactures, such as cloth, iron tools and tourist goods (see case E above). They also play a prominent part as commercial transport owners in the lorry park, which is dominated by Moslems, Frafra and non-Frafra alike. Although risky the profits from lorry ownership are potentially very great and made more secure by membership in the nationwide cartel of Moslems which operates Ghana's main transport centres (see case D above).[18]

Most of the really wealthy Frafra entrepreneurs have accumulated riches from   trade and transport operations in Bolgatanga. But the town offers several other opportunities for capital investment: in housing, built or bought by the entrepreneur as rented accommodation; in service industries like catering, vehicle maintenance, bicycle hire, corn and rice milling etc.; in construction and food contracting for local government; and, when kin networks make the land and labour available, in absentee farming and livestock rearing on a large scale in the surrounding villages. As well as those who already live in Bolgatanga villagers and southern migrants can participate in the town's economy through partners and investment media requiring minimal local supervision, such as rented accommodation.

Bolgatanga therefore provides an open invitation for any ambitious Frafra youth with an eye for the main chance; he no longer needs to travel South for his fortune - ample opportunity is at hand on his doorstep. He may acquire starting capital by working as a market porter *(kayakaya)*, odd-job man in the market, lorry park messenger, trader in cola left-overs, bicycle repairer, apprentice craftsman, breadseller or as one of any number of similar roles. With adequate patronage, cheap board and lodging from relatives and ordinary good fortune, it has been possible for many Frafra entrepreneurs to accumulate substantial assets in Bolgatanga from a beginning as small as this. Although a lucky break in the market place is not exactly the same as a gift of a fowl from one's mother's brother, the same principle of self-betterment by manipulative skill and hard work from an insubstantial beginning, is still held out as the model of Frafra accumulation. The Bolgatanga entrepreneur is in a unique position to make money, since he is relatively free of village ties, but can draw on the assistance of home kin whenever necessary; and he is a native in a booming entrepot where the opportunities for successful enterprise are continually expanding.

22   *CHANGING SOCIAL STRUCTURE IN GHANA*

A number of the more successful entrepreneurs are to be found in the South, where opportunities for advancement are far more widespread, but competition is keener. Cases A, B, and C above provide examples of migrant entrepreneurship without substantial investment in the Frafra homeland, although the two are sometimes successfully combined.

Most Frafra migrants in Ghana's southern cities are unskilled, illiterate wage workers. As such, they are trapped in a nexus of low income and high living costs. They can reduce the latter by abstaining from all but essential personal expenditures and living free with relatives for a time. But an enduring solution to the problem of surplus accumulation can only be found by supplementing wage income. Some income supplements are associated with the job itself: employment as a domestic servant or policeman often carries with it additional perquisities in the form of food, lodging and clothing allowances. But, more substantially, these and many other occupations are a potential source of 'nick off'[19] and sometimes bribes. Steady peculation of materials (food, bricks, even gold) is the single most common source of an initial capital surplus for Frafra workers; and those whose employment allows them to perform a 'gatekeeper' role are the perennial recipients of bribes.

As well as these on-job supplements, migrant workers are much given to moonlighting and job-duplication, both inside and out of the wage labour market.[20] In addition to wage employment, there are a host of small-scale self-employed activities, ranging from gardening through petty trade to hairdressing and photography, which offer the assiduous migrant the opportunity of accumulation through a combination of several sources of income, each of them claiming only part of his time. Frafras believe that the poor only become rich through 'trickery'and it is certainly true that criminal activities are both a ready source of surplus income and scarcely disapproved within the migrant community. Thieves, hustlers, receivers, gamblers and con-men flourish in the slums of Accra and Kumasi: and some of them manage to convert surpluses into legitimate enterprises.

Entry into the 'informal economy' of Ghana's cities is extremely open, for capital and skill requirements are usually low. Frafras participate freely, on a part-time and full-time basis in the different non-wage sectors (with the exception of the artisan industries, such as tailoring, carpentry and shoe-making, which they have been slow to enter as apprentices), where they may amass small surpluses for immediate re-investment in a variety of deals and petty enterprises - trading dealing, speculation and money lending are the most common ways in which Frafra migrants put small capital sums to work for them.

As well as direct earnings from wages, illegitimate activities and self-employment, some Frafras manage to get hold of lump sums in the form of gratuities and loans received from an employer or kinsman. Patronage of this kind is the only alternative to self-acquired funds (with the possible exception of assistance from the financially independent wife): for Frafra migrants are never able to borrow money from the banks, and interest rates in the informal loans market are on the whole too prohibitive to make acquisition of working capital by this means profitable.

Most migrants never transcend the level of petty enterprise enlisted so far - their earnings fluctuate, often dramatically, but capital

SWINDLER OR PUBLIC BENEFACTOR?

surpluses of any size are beyond the reach of the majority. For the successful few, substantial capital investments, as in Bolgatanga, are generally restricted to housing for rent (more profitable in Accra) and commercial transport (more risky than in Bolgatanga). The failure rate in transport is very high indeed, but the potential profits continue to attract unwary novices. Other enterprises requiring considerable inputs of capital are trading stores, catering establishments, large scale market trade, construction and maintenance contracting, and utilities, such as water supplies and flour mills. With some variation the overall picture is not dissimilar to Bolgatanga: in Kumasi, some Frafras even manage fairly large cocoa and food farms as a side line.[21]

Out of this fragmented account of migrant entrepreneurship, a number of general points emerge. Most entrepreneurs remain wage earners as long as it is feasible to do so, since they often build their enterprises around their work-place and are reluctant to sacrifice the stable income which a job ensures. Second, they tend to diversify their investments rather than specialise: this allows them to develop a mixed portfolio combining high and low risk enterprises. Third, the initial stages of accumulation especially have a 'make or break' quality which means that the budding entrepreneur, with all his resources committed, does not have the reserves to withstand adverse market trends or a series of inefficient decisions. Fourth, sudden reverses of fortune are a common occurrence, often because the entrepreneur lacks necessary skills, contacts and experience: ease of entry usually implies easy failure in the heat of open competition. Fifth, illiterate migrants are fully exposed to the vagaries of a corrupt and capricious bureaucracy which they often understand imperfectly or not at all: those who move with ease inside local government and state licensing circles have a decided advantage over their competitors. Sixth, many trading and similar activities are dominated by ethnic or religious rings which make life difficult for the outsider trying to break in. Seventh, although patronage and 'soft' loans are a great help to some entrepreneurs at an early stage of their careers, most have to make it entirely by their own efforts. Eighth, it cannot be overemphasised that illegitimate income sources play a significant part at some stage of almost every migrant entrepreneurial career. Ninth, the major constraint on accumulation beyond a certain point lies in the entrepreneur's time: most Frafras find it extremely difficult to delegate responsibility to reliable assistants or to engage workers who do not consume all the surplus which their additional labour generates. Last, in these circumstances, the migrant's immediate circle of close kin and particularly his wives are in a position to enhance or ruin his enterprises. Wives often take on a crucial economic role as business partners and, when they are themselves independently employed, may even be a source of money reserves and risk capital if needed.

Finally this review of methods of surplus accumulation must make explicit reference to women who, except as the wives of male entrepreneurs, are excluded from this paper for reasons of simplicity. Frafra women whether single or married, seem to be limited to trade, catering, prostitution and moneylending for independent income. In the villages, these opportunities are more or less restricted to local market trade and occasional beer-brewing; Bolgatanga and the southern towns allow for a range of retail, wholesale and processing activities especially in the food and drink trades. Commercial sex on a freelance basis is a potentially lucrative source of additional

24   *CHANGING SOCIAL STRUCTURE IN GHANA*

income in urban areas, where wage employment is, with the exception of a few well-educated women, almost entirely a male province. It is beyond the scope of this paper to enquire why these female entrepreneurs should be so limited in the range of their economic activities. Most Frafra women play a subordinate role in the households of their husbands or male kinsmen.22

In summary, Frafra entrepreneurs are only rarely 'businessmen' of the kind one is likely to encounter in a local chamber of commerce. They are simply the more successful operators in an open system of individualised accumulation which attracts the interest of almost all Frafras, most of whom eventually resign themselves to lives of routinised poverty. Only a few of the 71 Frafras whom I identified as 'entrepreneurs' would be thought rich by the mass of Ghanaians, when compared with the bureaucratic elite and Southern Ghana's chiefs, cocoa-farmers and businessmen. In the scale of their enterprises and life-style, they would appear to most outsiders as scarcely differentiated at all from the ordinary run of poor Ghanaians. But in the Frafra context, they have risen well above the income level of most Frafras and, as such, are the commercial stars of this disadvantaged ethnic group.

Income flows are notoriously difficult to pin down, but I was able to calculate the money value of fixed assets and working capital for the sample of 71:27% owned assets worth less than £1,000; 38% were valued at between £1,000 and £5,000; 17% between £5,000 and £10,000; and 18% over £ 10,000 (of whom cases A and D above owned capital assets in excess of £25,000). These sums may not appear to be very much, but in the context of Ghana's wage and price structure - where the government minimum wage in the mid 1960's was less than 9 per month - they are fairly substantial. In many cases, income turnover was simply not reflected in the value of capital stock, and this in itself is one of the aspects of Frafra entre-preneurship which it is the purpose of the next section to explain.

VII

This bald account of the mechanisms of Frafra accumulation must serve as the background to an analytical discussion of the typical exchange relationships (material, social and ideological) which link Frafra entre-preneurs and their community of origin. All the information presented so far relates to the *sources* of entrepreneurial surpluses - how capital may be accumulated. The argument developed in Section IV above predicts that, if surpluses are derived from transfers within the community, and especially if some ethical illegitimacy may be attached to these transfers, the entrepreneur is liable to encounter considerable opposition from those around him. The evidence of the case study is rather equivocal on this point, and this in turn may be a function of the indeterminacy of the community boundary postulated by the analysis. The situation of the village entrepreneur is easier to establish, because of the limited range of his social relationships, than that of the Frafra entrepreneur in Bolgatanga or Accra, where the ethnic community is crosscut by so many other social ties. Nevertheless some degree of generalisation is possible.

In the village, the accumulator is faced with two distinct sets of social relationships: on the one hand, his close kin with whom he is usually co-resident (his father, brothers and a few very near agnates, plus his own conjugal family of wives and children) and on the other,

SWINDLER OR PUBLIC BENEFACTOR?

the remainder of the village community with whom he conducts the majority of his face-to-face relationships outside the home. It is virtually impossible to accumulate riches in a Frafra village without creating antagonisms within one's circle of immediate kinsmen. Younger men are likely to offend their elders by spending too much time working exclusively for themselves, mature men are almost always in competition with their brothers and near agnates for control of scarce lineage resources in the form of land, labour and livestock; as fathers and lineage elders themselves, they are prone to being accused (often with justice) of exploiting the labour of their womenfolk and adult children without sharing the rewards, or of diverting joint property to their own private ends. These conflicts make the management of domestic social relations an extremely difficult art for the agricultural entrepreneur, but, for those few (like case F, above) who can turn these internecine quarrels to advantage or build up a fund of mutual trust in their families, the circle of close kin constitutes an invaluable cluster of resources on which he may draw. On the whole, however, the blackest accounts of an individual's path to riches are to be heard from his nearest relatives, most of whom can usually point to some way in which the accumulator overrode their interests for the sake of concentrating resources in his own hands.

Outside the range of close kin, Frafra village entrepreneurs are less likely to encounter conflict with their community neighbours. Even within the domestic sphere, conflict can be allayed by working as hard towards collective production as for private ends. And income generated in the individual's spare time (of which there is plenty in the dry season) without use of family resources constitutes an unequivocal net addition to the social surplus: the busy craftsmen or fowl trader is likely to be commended as a hard worker, whose success owes much to perseverance and skill. The majority of trading incomes are derived from the export of surpluses and as such are a source of conflict neither in theory nor in fact.

Village storekeepers, gin distillers and flour mill operators are usually able to secure unreasonable profits from their monopolies: but because these market transactions are in a way impersonal, the transfers of internal real income which take place meet with little odium. Usury and futures- buying on the other hand are socially risky because they are obviously personalised forms of exploitation. Chiefs frequently exploit their fellow villages in a number of ways, usually creaming off surplus village income and labour in order to recoup the massive expenditures they paid out to a higher echelon chief to win their office in the first place. Perhaps predictably, men who enrich themselves in ways such as these at the expense of the village community as a whole, are likely to be more popular in their immediate kinship networks than the agricultural/export trade entrepreneur whose activities tend to swallow up scarce lineage resources.

To summarise, village entrepreneurs encounter some opprobrium at various levels, depending on whether their activities may be perceived as direct exploitation by those who come into contact with them. In general, however, they acquire surpluses through inheritance, hard work and production for export to urban areas, relying heavily on an expanding conjugal family for significant accumulation in the long run. As such they may legitimately present themselves in a positive light as the 'traditional rich man' *(nera gu'la)*, objects of emulation by the wider

26   *CHANGING SOCIAL STRUCTURE IN GHANA*

public and antagonism from their closer agnates. It is mainly in the
fields of agriculture, livestock rearing and rural manufacture of goods
for export that Frafra entrepreneurship adds substantially to the *production*
of social surpluses.

But by far the greatest number of Frafra entrepreneurs are to be
found outside their home village, in Bolgatanga and the urban South. It
is with their situation that the remainder of this paper is primarily
concerned. The two spheres may be treated together for most purposes,
as cosmopolitan commercial economies in which the typical forms of
accumulation are common to both. The main differences are that wage
employment is more significant in the South and the strong Islamic
content of Bolgatanga trading and transport networks imports a special
flavour to entrepreneurial relationships there. In both, the community
of people sharing a common origin is rather indeterminate and the definition
of a close network of kinsman more elastic than in the village. It would
be tedious to work exhaustively through the categories of surplus listed
above, when assessing the sources of material surplus accumulated by urban
entrepreneurs. It will be sufficient to indicate the main ways in which
this classification may be applied to the Frafra case, at the same time
showing that actors' ideologies make play with contrasting objective
features of the accumulation process.

If we take an overview of Frafra accumulation outside the villages,
it can be fairly said that surpluses are generated more often by transfer
of value than by its production. Thrift, hard work, use of family labour
and innovation are obvious enough in the cases of many entrepreneurs; and
capitalist surpluses find their way into the production process in numerous
fields, such as construction, transport and utility provision. But the
vast part of entrepreneurial income is derived within the sphere of
circulation, whereby an existing stock of value is transferred from one
section of the society to another. Having said this, it must also be
pointed out that most urban surpluses come from outside the reference
group of the ethnic community: crooks, traders, moneylenders and transporters do their business with the general population, of whom only a
minority are Frafras. It is true that some enterprises are actually built
up around a clientele of co-villagers and fellow Frafras: and in these
cases, considerable conflict is normally generated by disputes over the
form and rate of payment for goods and services purchased. Reliance on
demand generated by ethnic loyalties has some advantages and many drawbacks.
In general, therefore, the urban entrepreneur's surpluses are not recog-
nisably accumulated at the expense of other members of his community.
Frafras are quick to point out if a certain entrepreneur's money is 'clean'
or 'dirty'(i.e. honest or crooked) and they may use this as a moral weapon
in the event of conflict emanating from another source, but, as long as
his victims lie outside the reference group, his standing in the community
is not seriously threatened.

Out of the possible forms of transfer listed before, it is my contention
that inheritance, gifts and loans play a negligible role in the generation
of entrepreneurial surpluses. British tax collectors are often amazed by
the frequency with which the income of the self-employed is attributed to
transfers of this kind, transfers which are both legitimate and subject
to little or no tax. It is the same with studies of African entrepreneurs,
which frequently list 'help' from kinsmen or the patronage of an anonymous
donor as the source of their starting capital.[23] These sources provide

SWINDLER OR PUBLIC BENEFACTOR? 27

a convenient mythological cover for processes of accumulation which rarely stand up to intensive scrutiny. I came across a few concrete cases of the helping hand of benevolent patronage, and many more claims that gifts and similar payments had played a prominent role in the entrepreneur's career; but the abiding impression, as far as Frafras are concerned, was that the most common sources of surplus income were manipulation of markets, theft, usury, speculative deals and a host of more or less dishonest operations, which enabled the sharp manipulator to acquire capital without contributing directly to the production of social welfare. The poor do not have so much that they can afford to donate large capital surpluses to each other, nor do the relatively rich often transfer part of their wealth voluntarily to a young man in need of a lucky break: the only way the poor can acquire surpluses, without having to work excessively hard, is by fiddling a slice of the social cake to which they would not ordinarily be entitled.

Here we have the basis of an ideological conflict - Frafra entrepreneurs and those who feel kindly towards them tend to stress their own legitimate efforts, their strivings and deprivations, their lucky breaks and their genuinely productive activities; on the other hand, the pervasiveness of crooked dealings in entrepreneurial careers and the importance of income transfers in general undermine this image of the boy who made it to the top through legitimate self-help and socially valuable enterprise. I have already mentioned in Section II above how my own analysis has shifted over time in the features of Frafra accumulation which are chosen for emphasis. But, even if many Frafra entrepreneurs are or have been crooked, this does not often bring them into direct conflict with members of their own community. The way they managed to become rich was not usually in itself a bone of contention: and as a result, the methods used by entrepreneurs to accumulate surpluses could be widely emulated by other Frafras and their most successful exponents legitimately celebrated as heroes. Where the conflicts really started was over the *destination* of the entrepreneurial surpluses and the mechanisms developed by entrepreneurs for dealing with their close kin and other members of the ethnic community.

The contradictions of individual enrichment were felt most keenly in the linked spheres of family labour and consumption. As was pointed out in the previous section, a major barrier to accumulation beyond a certain level lies in the entrepreneur's need for reliable unsupervised labour capable of handing over most of the profits to him. All entrepreneurs face this difficulty at some stage: those who hire strangers are inevitably disappointed and those who look to their own kinsmen (including their wives) often discover that the distinction between entrepreneurial and family income is not appreciated. Conversely kinsmen might feel cheated of the legitimate rewards for their co-operation and labour. It is a cleft stick from which only a handful of social genuises emerge unscathed. Consequently Frafra enterprise is characterised by grievances of this kind expressed on both sides of the accumulator's family, many of them understandable from either point of view. In this sense the urban entrepreneur is little better placed to avoid family conflict than his rural counterpart.

But the critical problem which divided Frafra entrepreneurs from their ethnic community was the *consumption* dilemma. The destination of surpluses was, to Frafras at least, invariably more important than their origin. As if it were not hard enough to transcend all the structural

CHANGING SOCIAL STRUCTURE IN GHANA

constraints on entrepreneurial accumulation, the main difficulties which Frafras claimed to encounter lay in trying to prevent the premature destruction of surpluses in expenditures benefitting their families, co-villagers and anyone else who could lay claim to a shared ethnic identity. They were particularly hard-pressed when it came to determining the appropriate allocation of their earnings between the threefold demands of net accumulation (the funds available for capital investment, savings and interest-bearing loans, after the fixed costs of enterprise have been deducted), personal or domestic consumption, and redistribution for consumption by others within and outside the entrepreneur's community. Whatever the reality of transactions involving fellow Frafras, it was invariably the case that entrepreneurs identified their most serious problem as restricting intra-ethnic exchanges involving material losses to themselves.

On the other side, there may have been some individual grievances about personal exploitation by a particular entrepreneur (and he, more often than not, would be a close kinsman); but there was no widespread feeling among Frafras of general exploitation by entrepreneurs as a status group. Extremely widespread, however, was the feeling - directed at individuals and the status group - that in refusing to share immediately what they had, these accumulators undermined the morality of the group, by seeking to better themselves rather than pool whatever transient gains might come into their hands.

The dominant ethic of exchange among Frafras is one of open-ended reciprocation which, in the long run, would ensure that benefits were equalised among members of the same group. For a population of generally poor people, who are exposed to great insecurity and who do not expect to be any better off when they die than when they were born, this moral injunction to share available resources is a rational form of social insurances. It is, of course, no less rational to seek to better one's own material position by placing oneself and one's family on a permanent higher income level. These two rationalities lie at the basis of the entrepreneur's dilemma - how to divide his resources between a public social security fund of reciprocal exchanges between familiars and private accumulation towards a personalised form of security provided by capital investments. The balance between the two is never finally resolved and each individual has to seek his own answer to the dilemma: it is an answer, moreover, that is likely to be constantly shifting in response to changed circumstances and prospects.

The notion that private accumulation necessitates a restriction of reciprocal exchanges within the ethnic community is made explicit in the remark quoted above, when a Frafra entrepreneur spoke of those around him seeking to reduce him to their level of poverty. We must ask how these community claims are manifested, why they carry any weight and what solutions, however temporary, are commonly found by successful accumulators.

There are an almost infinite number of ways in which surpluses may be drawn off into the entrepreneur's community - into financing the expansion of joint lineage assets, notably cattle; helping out one's lineage agnates with bridewealth payments, making loans and gifts to people who have little intention of ever paying back, as long as their circumstances remain more reduced than those of the donor; meeting temporary or regular

SWINDLER OR PUBLIC BENEFACTOR?

claims to support relatives; keeping an extra-large extended household of people who eat free; allowing customers to avoid payment for goods and services purchased from the enterprise; throwing big parties (such as funeral wakes); spending a lot on communal drinking; putting money into ethnic social security funds from which others will draw dispro - portionately owing to their great need; keeping up an extensive political clientele; pursuit of office (traditional or modern); conspicuous consumption on behalf of the 'family name' (e.g. payments to praise-singers and musicians, purchase of expensive clothing for parading at ceremonials, etc). The list could be extended. Some forms of expenditure obviously involve a greater degree of moral constraint than others - the above categories may be perceived as a rough ranking of priorities to Frafra ideal normative standards, with items towards the end of the list constituting more voluntaristic commitments for personal ends.

The pressures towards increased personal and domestic consumption may be no less great and indeed they often conflict with the claims of the wider community, adding a further dimension to the accumulation/ consumption dilemma. Private consumption is related to the developmental cycle of the domestic group: it can become an especially serious problem when the entrepreneur is confronted with the demands of an increasing conjugal family - for better and more food, clothing, housing and the like, for the expenses of children's education (potentially a major source of income drain) and the finances involved in being a polygamist, particularly when additional wives are not expected to play any productive role in their husband's enterprises. Apart from family considerations, young single men and older married men alike are always exposed to the allurements of 'city lights' and the snares of vanity: opportunities to spend on consumer durables, personal display and fast living (women, drink and gambling) are much greater in cities such as Accra than in the villages of the Frafra homeland.

The propensity of would-be accumulators to spend beyond their means and to go bust as a result is a well-recognised cause of entrepreneurial failure. A Tallensi proverb captures this crippling tendency to spend too much, too soon - 'a bird cannot scratch for food', they say, 'before its feet have touched the ground *(niing n pu luu, ka pu peera)*. We might say that many Frafras seek to fly before they have grown wings. Premature consumption and redistribution of income was also spoken of as a 'leaking anus', uncontrollably draining away the individual's investment resources, as surely as diarrhoea will clean out the contents of his intestines. The self-projected image of Frafra accumulation is thus one of an entrepreneur conducting a running battle with his personal proclivites and the demands of those around him.

On the face of it, these difficulties could be resolved by a little self-control and the will to put aside claims backed only by moral sentiment. But the social obligations of kinship and ethnicity are not so easily dismissed. The entrepreneur is tied to his close kin and ethnic community by a number of relationships which have varying significance at different stages of his life career. He needs his lineage kin at first for the means of getting married (cattle); he needs the social security of an urban ethnic brotherhood and access to homeland, in case his entrepreneurial strategies fail totally; he needs co-operation and trust-worthy labour supply, which he will find nowhere else if not in his immediate domestic circle and community of origin; he needs to pursue any ambitions for political power and status elevation within the ethnic

30 *CHANGING SOCIAL STRUCTURE IN GHANA*

community, because outside it an illiterate Frafra with a few slum dwellings and trucks carries virtually no weight in Ghanaian society; and finally, unless he is a convert, he will be bound by a shared religious morality and a community of worshippers, based on the ancestor cult.[24]

Complete escape from the obligations of extended kinship and urban ethnicity therefore carries with it a terrible personal risk which few are prepared to take - self-reliance and the rejection of ties associated with one's origin offer the prospect of destitution in the event of financial failure. Most Frafra entrepreneurs prefer to make an uneasy compromise between private interests and public morality. But what is confused compromise in fact, often emerges as black and white contrast in the ideological utterances of the actors themselves.

I once interviewed a Frafra entrepreneur in Accra (Case B above), who,without any prompting from me, produced an account which was classically Weberian in its polarised simplicity. He portrayed himself as a poor boy who, bereft of any help from lineage kin and cast adrift by misfortune in Accra, had managed to pull himself up by his own boot- straps only through systematic self-denial, reliance on his wife and the rejection of all other social relationships. A soldier and a Christian, he claimed not to have been home for twenty years, wanted nothing to do with other Frafras and sought only to provide for his conjugal family's security through his entrepreneurial endeavours. He rejected traditional religion ('you cannot vote for two parties at the same time'), economic co-operation between brothers, kinship norms in general and even those elements of Frafra migrant life like drinking together, joining mutual aid societies and holding funeral parties, which sought to perpetuate home solidarities in the city. Instead he was a model exponent of rational economic behaviour (commitment to his job, keen budgeting and cumulative investment), a Christian ethic compatible with personal asceticism and an individualised notion of social responsibility centring on the monogamous nuclear family.

This man had not been reading Parsons at night classes. His self- portrait contained enough of the observable truth to be credible, and it was reinforced by the comments of other migrants who also stressed his isolationism - 'Ask him how many visitors he has! Another man will eat penny himself and spend a shilling (on others), but not B. And that is why he has money and we do not.' But the portrait was a caricature which, in the initial telling, distorted reality by excluding any information that failed to conform to his idealised resolution of the conflicting pressures operating in his life. I later discovered that B was quite heavily involved in exchanges with his kin and other Frafras and relied for much of his entrepreneurial activity on relationships within the ethnic community; that he did visit home regularly and supported lineage kin there; that he was anxious for his children to retain their ethnic identity despite a mission education; and, as a lineage elder back home, had a far more equivocal attitude to traditional religion in practice.

The point is that idealised self-portraits (and the casual remarks of outsiders), just like Weberian ideal types in western sociology, should never be mistaken for the reality they purport to depict. B identified a strong underlying tendency in his behaviour and he sought to reduce his actions to a pattern consistent with that tendency; but in fact he was

SWINDLER OR PUBLIC BENEFACTOR?

engaged in a far more complex dialectical process of seeking to reconcile the two poles of a contradiction in his life without ever managing to eliminate either. Nor should we prejudge the future of his internal struggle: the perfectly emancipated 'modern man' may or may not revert in the future to a state of closer integration with his moral and social community of origin. It would be unwarrantably deterministic to suppose otherwise.

At a more general level, I observed a marked correlation in my sample of entrepreneurs between success as an accumulator and religious affiliation; Christians and Moslems were significantly richer than non-converts and there were more of them in the sample than in the comparable Frafra population as a whole.[25] This observation is clearly conducive to an explanation along the following lines: faced with severe pressures against accumulation from members of their natal community, many Frafra entrepreneurs sought to escape by joining a religious congregation which did not place the same degree of moral restriction on self-enrichment. Such a conclusion may be sociologically convincing and, as such, it could join the growing ranks of comparative evidence linking entrepreneurship and religious non-conformity in the third world.[26] But to focus on this aspect, to the neglect of many others, simply because it fits in nicely with an O.K. sociological theory - Max Weber's link between capitalism and protestantism in the West - is to bowdlerize social life. The reality of Frafra entrepreneurship is, as I have shown, a good deal messier than the homogenised picture of sanctimonious accumulators with God on their side. Sociological theories of this kind are analogous to B's selective self-portrait: they are ideal types which do not simplify reality - they distort it by omitting large chunks of the picture. Moreover the bias of the distortion is in the same direction: towards a whitewash of the true character of entrepreneurship in the real world.

There is more than one kind of resolution to the entrepreneurial dilemma (as indicated in Section IV), and Frafras have found several. Some tried to hide their wealth, by making highly covert investments and resisting all forms of personal display: those who tried this ploy included a number of traders who could plead poverty owing to a run of bad luck, and no one was any the wiser. Most entrepreneurs have to isolate themselves at the initial stages of accumulation or after a reversal, but the majority attempt to buy their way back into general favour later on. Redistribution of surpluses within the community is, in any case, the most common form of conflict resolution. In this way Frafra entrepreneurs accumulate resources and then redistribute a large part to others, without significantly increasing in the long run either their own standard of living or the rate of fixed capital formation. Dissipation of assets and income, almost as soon as they have been acquired, is most frequently a means of pursuing political power and social prestige within the entrepreneur's community of origin. This rationale is more acceptable than self-enrichment and capital accumulation for its own sake. Thus over time, material resources, concentrated by a private individual in exchange for some public odium are later redistributed in exchange for social status and ideological deference. An enduring class of capitalistic accumulators is in this way prevented from developing and the Frafra social product is increased only to the extent that their entrepreneurs succeed either in transferring income from outside sources in the first place or in generating economic growth.

CHANGING SOCIAL STRUCTURE IN GHANA

The fluctuating nature of entrepreneurial careers is well-illustrated by A's exchanges with his kin and community over a period of 25 years (see Case A above). As a young man he stood by, while his father and elder brother ransacked his room in vain, looking for trading profits which he had stored elsewhere. Later he ran a large extended household, bought a lorry and went broke. Forced to change his ideas, he isolated himself completely from all but his wives and business contacts. At this time he would beat up his wives in order to extract the last penny of their takings from petty trade. Then, as his fortunes picked up, he was able to relax somewhat and leave them to their own devices. When his income became huge, he could afford to be expansive.

An example of his latterday largesse occurs every year when he visits home for a month to attend the traditional harvest festival. From a box full of notes and coins, he distributes £1000 to women, children, male clients, musicians and anyone else who takes his fancy. He rationalises this generosity as follows: 'By giving them money they are all happy with me and pray to their ancestors that, when I go back South, I'll get the same amount to bring back next year and spend. I have seen that a man who has and does not give, God takes it away from him.' This spree is conceived of as annual shareout of dividends, as insurance against social antagonism and even mystical attack. The ancestors are looked after too: one year I saw him sacrifice 27 guinea fowls, 19 chickens, 2 goats, a sheep and a dog to his father and the other spirits of his lineage. 'If I miss any of them out, they will bring sickness, it is a year's pay for them or something like a loan.'

A also spent several thousands of pounds buying the chiefship of their village for his brother. At the moment he can afford to be open-handed and he, unlike most other Frafra entrepreneurs, seems to have found a successful formula for making money and keeping a vast army of followers reasonably happy. He is already the most powerful man in the Tallensi area (even when he is in the South) and his riches are merely a vehicle for the expression of his ambitions in this respect. If he were to suffer a series of reverses, the pattern of his social relationships and his ideology of collective commitment would necessarily change for the moment and he would have to restrict his outgoings once more. But, as he stands now, A is the polar opposite of B. - the traditional big man, as against the modern privatised individual. As such these two men come close to representing the extremes between which the majority of Frafra entrepreneurs are to be located, making some kind of compromise between dialectically opposed interests.

The overall picture of Frafra entrepreneurship is thus much more complicated than is implied by making a simple link between thrift and social or ideological emancipation from the ties of kinship and ethnicity. Shifts in the balance of material and social exchanges between individuals and their community are reflected in contrasting ideological statements which tend to reduce the confused and dialectical conflicts of real experience to over-simplified extremes. In general, however, we may observe that Frafra entrepreneurs, far from draining off income from their natal and ethnic communities, are, in the long run, a source of substantial increase in the total amount of social welfare circulating within the community of Frafras. They achieve this in the main by redistribution of benefits derived from elsewhere, more than by stimulating economic growth. In consequence there are very few objective grounds for Frafras, at any rate,

SWINDLER OR PUBLIC BENEFACTOR?

to regard this kind of accumulation as exploitation and the home-bred entrepreneurial type is widely admired and emulated by them. But the short-term problem, of accumulation versus consumption by self and others, is a source of unavoidable interpersonal conflict and embarrassment, embracing an elastic range of relationships and serving as a major deterrent to individual enterprise in a large number of cases. It is, of course, convenient for those who have failed to enrich themselves to portray their state as a product of self-sacrifice to the common good; and the new rich themselves may represent their detractors as merely 'envious'. But the grievances of the poor are usually justified, for it is undoubtedly true that the spirit of individual accumulation, if widely disseminated through their ranks, undermines a universalistic community ethic of poverty-sharing. The fact that most Frafra experience this conflict of aspiration as a personal dilemma at some stage in their lives, or even throughout their careers, only points to the deep-lying nature of the contradiction between individualised and collective adaptations to the problems of poverty, hardship and insecurity.

If one were to stress one feature of Frafra accumulation at the expense of others, it would be to suggest that the Frafra entrepreneur is ultimately constrained by his limited organisation resources. Unable to expand his labour force by the recruitment of reliable wage employees and business partners, he must try to secure the co-operation of kinsmen and others from his natal community whom he feels he can trust. But that trust, if it is to work successfully, must be based on his recognition of an ethnic of open-ended reciprocity and mutual obligation, which in itself has the effect of diverting accumulated surpluses towards the maintenance of these solidary relationships rather than into increased capital formation and unlimited economic expansion. The central paradox of Frafra entrepreneurship is contained in the struggle of each individual to resolve the conflicting demands of personal accumulation and social equity. Entrepreneurs of this kind are thus not a stable psychological or sociological type, but individuals enmeshed in a variety of exchanges with their social environment throughout the course of their fluctuating careers.

VIII

In conclusion, perhaps I should recapitulate by stating what this paper has not been. It has not attempted a complete account of the why and how of entrepreneurial development in the Frafra case. Such an account would require, for one thing, a much more systematic reference to relationships and situations in which the closed circles of kinsmen and ethnic groups play no part. Rather, we began with a question about stereotypes. Hardworking saver and public benefactor or swindler and public nuisance? Which of these two consistent sets of images comes closer to the truth of individual accumulation? We saw that these images were part of wider ideologies, generated to a large extent by objective economic and social circumstances. And when ideological perceptions are in part a function of one's relationship to the accumulation process, these images of support and opposition are bound to be relative. This is particularly the case when accumulation takes the form of a transfer of value from one section of society to another.

It was felt, as a result of this reasoning that the question of the social consequences of individual enrichment could never be resolved unless a particular group of accumulators could be placed in the context of an

34 *CHANGING SOCIAL STRUCTURE IN GHANA*

analytically bounded community. An ethnic group was almost certainly a poor test case for this theory because of the rather inconclusive nature of relations contained within its boundaries. Nevertheless, by examination of the relationships between Frafra entrepreneurs and their community of origin, it has been tentatively demonstrated that the ideological perception of entrepreneurial activity is related concretely to the form of economic and social exchanges linking entrepreneurs with those around them and that the two, in dialectical combination, provide significant indicators of the degree and form of support or conflict generated by individual accumulation. More generally it is claimed that an exchange approach, stressing the shifting nature of individual careers and the variety of responses to real life contradictions, throws more light on entrepreneurial development than a simple-minded opposition of stable personality types and inflexible group values.

NOTES

1. The opposing versions of the nature of the social division of labour in the nineteenth century social theory and political economy (see, e.g. Marx 1970 and Durkheim 1964) are well described in Giddens (1971: 224-242).

2. Fieldwork in urban and rural areas of both North and South Ghana led to a University of Cambridge Ph.D. thesis, which is unpublished (see Hart 1969). Whenever the ethnographic present is used in this paper it refers to the period 1965-68.

3. In particular: Weber (1958), Schumpeter (1961) and Rostow (1960), all of whom adopt favourable attitudes towards the entrepreneur as agency of social and economic change.

4. This was the main message of my Ph.D. thesis (Hart 1969).

5. The 'informal economy' of Ghana's cities is discussed in Hart (1973).

6. Major sources of neo-Marxist influence in this respect have been Mandel (1968) and Baran (1973).

7. Barth ed. (1963) - see especially Paine (1963) and the editor's introduction - Geert (1963) and Long (1968).

8. This definition owes something to Barth (1963); it differs somewhat from that offered by Katzin (1964: 182) for small African entrepreneurs.

9. The label preferred by, for example, Hill (1970bĵ.

10. Cf. Barth ed. (1969).

11. The distinction is essentially that drawn by Marxists between 'primitive accumulation' (transfers of surplus value) and 'capitalist accumulation' proper (the entry of capital into the production of surplus value) - see Marx (1970:part VIII) and Mandel (1968:c.4.)

12. By, for example, Parkin (1972) and Long (1968) respectively.

13. See Fortes (1945, 1949) and - a paper specifically on social change - (1936). The meaning of Frafra as a tribal label is discussed in Hart (1971).

14. See Hart (1974) for an account of Frafra migration.

15. This sample formed the empirical basis for my Ph.D. thesis (Hart 1969).

16. These were the places in which I did intensive fieldwork.

17. See Fortes (1949:139).

18. Ghana's Islamic transport system owes its origin to a Syrian trading company operating between the wars in N. Ghana and beyond (see Hart 1970:109).

19. English 'nick-off' - U.S. 'rip-off'.

20. See Hart (1973) for an extended treatment of urban income opportunities.

21. The propensity of Ghana's small entrepreneurs to diversify their interests, at the cost of specialisation, is discussed in Hart (1970) and Garlick (1971)

22. I have a paper in preparation which deals with this topic explicity: 'Changes in the social division of labour and patterns of female employment in Ghana', paper for the 1974 B.S.A. conference at Aberdeen on 'Sexual divisions in society'.

23. See, for example, Garlick (1971:36) where the results of a survey of African traders show that starting capital was supposed to be generated by either personal savings or gifts and loans from relatives.

24. These suggestions are elaborated in Hart (1971).

25. See Hart (1969:378-387) for an early discussion of this issue. Only 60% of the sample, as compared with 79% of the total Frafra population in 1960, were adherents of traditional (pagan) religion. Moreover, entrepreneurs who were converts to Christianity and Islam or were agnostics, accounted for a very high proportion of the more successful Frafra accumulators.

26. The classic exposition is, of course, Weber (1958); anthropological studies which have made comparable findings include Geertz (1963), Long (1968) and Parkin (1972). There are many more examples in the literature.

THE GROWTH OF A MIGRANT COMMUNITY: THE YORUBA
IN NORTHERN GHANA

J.S. EADES

The coming of independence to the majority of African states and the breakup of the colonial empires has brought with it a recurrent problem which seems to be increasing rather than diminishing in intensity. This is the position of alien immigrants who were welcomed during the colonial period by the Europeans who saw them as bringing with them essential services and entrepreneurial skills. Since independence, the large colonial possessions have been broken down into mostly small autonomous nation states, and within these new frontiers, aliens are regarded with increasing suspicion and resentment by governments wishing to create employment opportunities for their own people and to gain a measure of control over their economies. The result has been a series of expulsions of aliens in several countries. In 1969, seven weeks after assuming office, the Busia administration in Ghana announced that aliens in the country without valid residence permits had fourteen days to obtain them or leave. This resulted in the mass exodus of nationals of other countries, and especially of Nigerian origin, in the first two weeks of December. But the Ghanaian 'compliance' order was not an isolated example, though the number of people involved was greater than elsewhere. Nigerian nationals have also been expelled from the Ivory Coast, Gabon, and, more recently, Zaïre: there were considerable repatriations of personnel after the breakup of French West Africa; and most recently of all, large numbers of Asians have been ordered out of Uganda.[2]

Thus this is a serious and recurring problem which has many facets. It raises legal questions concerning the definition of citizenship in the countries concerned, and economic questions about the likely impact of the expulsions on the economic life of the indigenous population. But from a sociological viewpoint, a pre-requisite for understanding the expulsions and the reasons behind them is to examine the migration process and the factors underlying it which led to the formation of the migrant communities in the first place. This paper will provide some of the background to the expulsions from Ghana in which the group most affected were Yorubas from Western Nigeria. Though comparative newcomers to trading in Ghana, compared with, say, the Hausa or the Mossi, by 1957 the Yoruba had established themselves in a position of virtual monopoly in the major markets of Ghana in the sale of some commodities, notably provisions, cloth and small manufactured goods. But in addition to the large towns, almost any village of any size in the rural areas as well had its resident Yoruba trader who, together with his wives, was usually the only local source of these items.

In addition to their success in trading, however, perhaps the most noticeable fact about the Ghana Yoruba was their comparative failure to assimilate with the Ghanaians, and the tenacity with which they maintained their ethnic identity (J.R. Goody 1970:135ff)·

This paper therefore will attempt to provide insights into the linked

38 *CHANGING SOCIAL STRUCTURE IN GHANA*

phenomena of Yoruba entrepreneurial success and Yoruba social isolation. In order to do so it will adopt a slightly different approach from much of the literature on migration and urbanisation in Africa. Recent writing has tended to adopt four main foci. The first of these is structural, and has attempted to create for the urban environment the same sort of analytical framework that kinship theory provided for functionalist anthropology: the result has been considerable discussion of networks and network theory and the extent to which it can provide this framework (Epstein 1961: Mitchell 1969). The second focus is institutional; voluntary associations, religious, cultural, ethnic and recreational, have received much attention, together with their role in socialising the migrant in the urban situation (Banton 1957); Little 1957 and 1965). The third is cultural; the breakdown of traditional value systems in the melting pot of city life. Here terms such as 'detribalisation' and 'retribalisation' have been defined and redefined (Cohen 1969:1-2; Watson 1970; Mayor 1961). The fourth is political: the power and authority relations of migrants with their host groups (Skinner 1963; Cohen 1969; Schildkrout 1970a and b). In adopting these foci, however, social scientists have had little cause to pay much attention to the links between migrants and their home communities, and the exact relationship between the social structure of the home community and the migration process. Migration instead involves disruption of the migrants' links with home and their 'traditional' values. They become 'detribalised', or, where there is obviously little assimilation, 'retribalised', but in either case the migrant community is seen as autonomous, and its members have little contact with their place of origin. An extreme example of this is to be found in Cohen's work on the Hausa community in Ibadan, where he writes:

Sabo is a highly autonomous, multipurposive community ......
(and) is very far from being a social or cultural extension
of Hausaland. Sabo culture and system of social relations
differ radically from their counterparts in Hausaland in such
important respects as stratification, pattern of marriage,
occupational structure, nature of the chieftaincy, and the
composition and organisation of domestic units and so on.
Sabo culture is thus distinct from northern Hausa culture.
(Cohen 1966:33)

Elsewhere he writes:
'Hausa cultural tradition is not the crucial factor in the formation
of these (i.e. Hausa) communities in Yoruba towns'. (Cohen 1969:15).

This paper on the other hand will argue that in the case of the Yoruba in Northern Ghana, at least, consideration of the social structure and cultural norms of the home community can provide insights into both the nature of the migration process and the maintenance of Yoruba ethnic identity. Indeed it is only with reference to such consideration that it is possible to explain the position of the Yoruba in Ghana at all.[3] It will start therefore by briefly outlining the position of the Yoruba in Ghana as a whole, and will then focus on the north of Ghana where my own work was carried out. It will go on to consider in detail the migration of Yoruba to Tamale, and the relationship of these migration patterns to Yoruba social structure in Nigeria, and finally it will consider the nature of the migrant community that arose as a result.

THE GROWTH OF A MIGRANT COMMUNITY   39

Distribution and migration of the Yoruba

In 1948, the census recorded 48,000 Nigerians in Ghana, and by 1958, Stapleton estimated that the figure had increased to 56,000 (Stapleton 1959). In fact, the increase in the number of Nigerians, and especially the number of Yoruba, had been far more rapid than he thought and the 1960 census showed that there were more than 114,000 Yoruba alone in the country. By 1969, the number had probably risen to over 200,000.[5] This rapidly increasing population had several marked characteristics. Firstly most of the adults were engaged in a single occupation - petty trading. Secondly the Yoruba, as noted above, were very evenly distributed throughout the country and had penetrated into the most remote rural areas in their search for trading opportunities. Thirdly, the great majority of the Yoruba in Ghana came from just four areas of Yorubaland. These were: Oyo North Division, and especially the towns of Shaki, Igboho, Igbetti, Kishi and Shepeteri; Oshun North-West Division and especially Ogbomosho; Offa and the nearby smaller towns of Oyan and Inisha; and Ilorin. Fourthly in any given area of Ghana would be found large clusters of migrants from the same towns in Nigeria. The massive Ogbomosho group predominated in Kumasi, while the Ilorin formed the majority in Accra.[6] People from the Offa area were widely distributed over the whole of the south of the country, the Offa being found in large numbers in Koforidua, and the Oyan in the diamond towns of Oda and Akwatia (Stapleton 1959; Peil 1971:211). The Shaki were as widely distributed in the north as the Offa and Inisha in the south. They were especially strong in the border towns of Yendi and Bawku where many of them were engaged in smuggling goods back and forth into Togo and Upper Volta. The Igboho were concentrated in Tamale, Walewale, Bolga and Bawku, while the Igbetti were located almost solely in Tamale, apart from small groups in Yendi and Damongo. The Ogbomosho formed the largest Tamale group and many of these were traders who had been initially unsuccessful in Kumasi and had tried their luck further north. Apart from two other small groups in Wa and Gambaga, however, there were few other Ogbomosho north of the Volta.

The Yoruba in Tamale at the time of the exodus therefore consisted mainly of people from the four towns of Ogbomosho, Igboho, Igbetti and Shaki. There were in addition small numbers of migrants from other towns including Otu, Ilorin, Oshogbo, Shepeteri and Offa. As in the rest of Ghana there were very few migrants from the cocoa-producing areas of Yorubaland such as Ibadan, Ondo, Ife, Ekiti, Ijebu and Egba.[7] The total strength of the Tamale community in 1969 I would estimate at about 3100.[8]

Of the Yoruba men, about two-thirds were traders. The rest were either traders who had failed and turned to other work like driving or government labour, or the younger educated men in clerical and teaching positions. An even larger percentage of the women were involved in trading, though mostly on a very small scale. Most of them had started trading with between £5 (¢10) and £40 (¢80) capital, given them by their husbands on marriage, though many of them had had experience in trading from an early age through helping their mothers. Only a handful of women, though, really corresponded to the stereotype of the rich and independent Yoruba woman trader, and nearly all the richer women came from Ogbomosho.[9]

40 *CHANGING SOCIAL STRUCTURE IN GHANA*

There was for instance only one Igbetti woman trading on a large scale[10] and it is no coincidence that she lived with Ogbomosho women in an Ogbomosho-owned house, and her closest friends were from Ogbomosho. Most of the older Igbetti women had been employed weaving when they first arrived in Ghana, and one of them said that she had only taken up trading because Ghanaian women heard that she was a 'Lagosian', and, assuming that she must be a trader had come to buy from her. She started to stock a few goods as a result and later gave up weaving.

Tamale itself is situated in the southwestern corner of the Dagomba kingdom and is by far the largest town in the north of Ghana. Unlike Yendi or Salaga, it was not a large town before the arrival of the British, though there was a market there (Levtzion 1968:120). In 1905 they moved the headquarters of the Northern Territories there from Gambaga, and the town started to grow rapidly. It soon became a large military and administrative centre, as well as the hub of the communications network for the area. The population grew from over 2000 in 1911 to 12,000 in 1931[11] and 42,000 in 1960. Roads radiated from it to Yendi in the East, Kumasi in the South, Wa and Damongo in the West and Bolgatanga, Bawku and Ougadougou in the north. By 1969, Tamale was becoming a major urban centre. It already had five secondary schools, two large military establishments and an agricultural station in addition to the government offices. An industrial estate and an international airport had also been proposed. There were branches in the town of the G.N.T.C. as well as the other expatriate and Indian wholesale firms, and as a final mark of urban status, the expatriate club and the polo ground had been joined by a Kingway store and two Lebanese-owned cinemas. With a relatively large proportion of the population earning regular wages as soldiers, government workers, labourers and so on, a demand was created comparatively early for the cloth, provisions and other items which became the Yoruba's stock-in-trade after about 1945.

By 1969, Tamale had two main markets. There were few Yoruba in the New Market which was patronised mainly by Dagomba selling bulk food-stuffs.[12] The Old Market, built by the British, was right in the centre of the town, and it was here that the Yoruba predominated. 234 of the 700 council-allocated stalls were rented by Yorubas, but these included most of the best-stocked stalls in the market. Only 42 of these were rented by women and most Yoruba women sold from headloads or from a kiosk or table placed in front of their husbands' stalls, or by the streets near their houses. In addition, nearly 200 stalls had been built independently on market land, most of them by Yoruba, and these traders paid 5p. a day to the council in lieu of a regular monthly rental.

The main lines dealt in by the Yoruba were well-defined. Nearly all the women sold provisions - sardines, tinned milk, sugar, soap and detergents together with matches, cigarettes and some native medicines. Only a few of the richer women travelled outside Tamale to buy goods, usually to Kumasi. Most bought from Yoruba men selling provisions by the carton in Tamale market, though some husbands would buy goods for their wives on their own

THE GROWTH OF A MIGRANT COMMUNITY

41

trips to the south. The men dealt in provisions which they sold to other traders (usually Ghanaian or Yoruba women) by the carton or dozen; in cloth - which they sold in six- and twelve-yard pieces to mainly Ghanaian tailors, seamstresses and retailers; and finally in a bewildering range of small manufactured items collectively known as *worobo* or *nyamin-nyamin*, (Rouch:1956:117) [13], including singlets, wallets, rubber shoes, cutlery, flashlights, batteries, ball-point pens, contraceptives, locks, and almost anything else that could be bought in bulk from Lebanese and Indians in the south and sold at a profit in the north. The more successful traders had usually been dealing in the same lines for many years, while the less successful ones were constantly changing in attempts to find commodities that would bring in a steady profit. Most of the buying was done in Kumasi and Accra, and a trader would travel down between one and five times a month depending on his capital and turnover. Many delegated the buying or the care of the stall while they were away to junior relatives working under them. The amount of goods bought on each trip varied considerably: most traders would take between £100 (¢200) and £300 (¢600) but richer ones would at times take considerably more. Visits to the south with less than ¢100 (¢200) were uneconomical, and in such cases the buying could be handled by a friend (who would in return receive part of his lorry fare). Alternatively close friends might provide short-term loans.

Most of the large trading firms (G.B.T.C., U.A.C., U.T.C. etc) had branches at Tamale, where goods could be bought wholesale. In practice, the supplies of many goods, especially cloth and provisions, were very limited, and obtaining them depended on the ownership of a passbook or on familiarity with the storekeepers and often a willingness to bribe them. The occupational structure of Tamale created a much heavier demand for these goods than could be met by the firms, and one of the main roles of the Yoruba men was to help meet the demand by transporting the goods up independently. Only a few Yoruba men resident in Tamale did the bulk of their buying in Tamale itself: these included the poorest traders and a handful of successful ones who were well-known to the storekeepers of the large firms.

As elsewhere in Ghana, Tamale market is one of the cycle of six in the area held on successive days. The other markets [14] are all within easy reach of Tamale by either cycle, or in more recent years, by the ubiquitous mammy lorry. Many of the Tamale Yoruba would travel to these markets or send junior relatives, thus considerably increasing their turnover. Most Yoruba men I interviewed had spent some years travelling on this market circuit, but after becoming better established, they could afford to stay in Tamale all the time while their regular customers would come to them from the villages on Tamale market day. Another way for the younger trader to get established in Tamale was with a locally made barrow *tereko*. About two dozen Yoruba men in Tamale had these, stationing them at strategic points like Kingsway, the Post Office, the petrol stations and the lorry parks, and their barrow would be heavily laden with a wide variety of small manufactured goods. Many of the barrow boys later graduated to market stalls of their own, passing on the barrows to their junior relatives.

One of the main reasons the Ghana Government gave for the expulsions of the aliens was their involvement in smuggling and illegal currency dealing. Many of the richest Yoruba in Tamale (mainly Shaki) had apparently

42 *CHANGING SOCIAL STRUCTURE IN GHANA*

empty stalls and little visible stock, but carried out most of their trade in the house at night. Many Shaki had also settled in Yendi, Bawku and the border towns in Togo, and there was a flourishing trade in CFA francs and in Nigerian pounds which had grown up since the imposition of currency restrictions by the Ghana Governments in 1961. Many Yoruba needed foreign exchange to build houses or support relatives in the home town and their main sources included Hausa kola traders, and other Yoruba smuggling goods into Togo.[15] Many goods smuggled into Ghana were also being manufactured there, but many Ghanaians were prepared to pay more for (what they considered to be) a higher quality imported item. The Yoruba with their international connections were ready, willing and able to help meet this demand. Cigarette sellers for instance would keep a few of the 'better' (i.e. smuggled) ones for regular customers, without which they would have been unable to attract business, and the cigarette would be subjected to a series of esoteric tests to determine its origin before money changed hands. Similarly, imported wax prints were considered to be better than the Akosombo product;[16] imported skin-lightening creams and antiseptic soaps were also preferred; and even imported A.P.C. tablets were considered superior. In addition to these regular lines, periodic shortages of sugar, tomato paste, sardines and matches would also send the energetic Yoruba looking elsewhere for supplies.[17] Most Yoruba in Tamale probably dealt in smuggled goods from time to time as they could be disposed of very quickly, the demand always exceeding the supply. But most of these goods were initially handled by a small ring of Shaki men acting as distributors and brokers. They were the first people that smugglers from Yendi and Bawku approached, after which news would be sent to buyers that the goods had arrived and were on display. Despite the profits, however, smuggling was risky and many traders had been in difficulties after being arrested or having their goods confiscated by the border guards. The leading brokers stayed in business by utilizing a network of contacts among police and customs officials, and would be the first down to the police station to plead on behalf of one of their number who had been waylaid by the authorities.

It was only in the smuggling trade however that Yoruba trading organisation was relatively complex. Otherwise the most obvious feature of Yoruba trading in Tamale was the large number of small-scale traders selling similar ranges of goods. Apart from the younger men working for their senior relatives, each Yoruba was working for himself, and even the younger men would eventually be set up as independent traders after a period of service, often upon their marriage. But the Yoruba acted at a single level of trade, transporting goods from the large firms and Lebanese in the south, and selling them to the retailer or straight to the customer in the north. This contrasts with the situation described for instance by Cohen in his work on the cattle and kola trades, which are characterised by elaborate role differentiation, the emergence of powerful broker figures with their followings, and by a trade organisation controlled at every level between production and consumption by a single ethnic group (Cohen 1965;1966; and especially 1969:71-97). The Yoruba trading in Tamale consisted of non-hierarchical independent small-scale trading units, and the next section will consider features of the migration process which might account for this.

THE GROWTH OF A MIGRANT COMMUNITY 43

Processes of migration

The bulk of the Yoruba in Tamale were made up of the four groups from Ogbomosho, Igboho, Igbetti and Shaki, and the core of each of these groups consisted of large clusters of kin.[18] To illustrate the connection between kinship organisation and migration, I will examine in some detail the history of migration to Ghana from a single compound in Igbetti. While there are obvious difficulties in asserting that the history of any one family in trading is in any way 'typical', nevertheless we may be able to pinpoint features which are common to a large number of migration histories both in Igbetti and the other main towns represented in Tamale.

Igbetti is one of the most northerly towns in the Western State of Nigeria, lying 50 miles north of Ogbomosho and 35 miles north-west of Ilorin. It is the nearest town to the deserted site of Old Oyo from which many Igbetti lineages trace their origin. As a rough estimate I would put the population in 1971 at around 15,000.[19] The vast majority of the adult males are farmers, the main crops being yams, maize and millet. Land is plentiful in the district and many men from the Ilorin area have come across to farm there. This factor together with the enormous market which is held in the town every four days and which ensures good prices and easy transport for the produce,perhaps makes farming a more attractive, prospect than it is in the neighbouring towns.[20]

The kinship system of the northern Yoruba is based on the agnatic lineage and has been much discussed in recent years (Lloyd 1962;Bender 1970; Bascom 1969). In Igbetti most of the lineages trace descent from an ancestor two or three generations before the present elders, who is often said to have come to the town from Old Oyo or one of the other evacuated settlements in the area. This rather shallow generation depth is probably due to the fairly recent foundation of the town during the long succession of nineteenth century wars, rather than to foreshortening of the genealogy (Lloyd 1955:243; Bascom 1969:42). During these years, the impressive granite outcrop which looms over the town provided a natural fortress for people from the surrounding villages against a succession of attacks.

Traditionally all members of the agnatic lineages lived together in large rectangular compounds *(Ile)* but in Igbetti in recent years these have been progressively demolished and up to five or six smaller and more compact structures built on the site of each. Ile Olowo is a medium-sized compound. It now consists of nine smaller structures, four of which are on the site of the old large compound demolished in 1959. These structures are still adjacent to each other, but new land will have to be found for any further building. The genealogy of the lineage associated with the *Ile* is shown in Figure 2.

Figure 2

Skeleton Genealogy of Ile Olowo, Igbetti, showing the relationship of those involved in the migration to Ghana from the compound

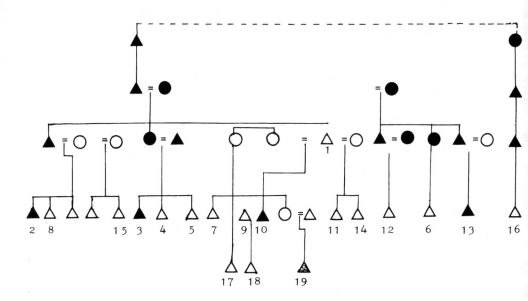

1. Alhaji Sadiku
2. Sanusi
3.-5. Sule and brothers
6. David
7. Lasisi
8. Amuda
9. Sumanu
10. Salami
11. Tijani
12. Jimoh
13. Amadu
14. Ganiyu
15. Fasasi
16. Braimah
17. James
18. Mumuni
19. Karimu

THE GROWTH OF A MIGRANT COMMUNITY 45

The Yoruba predominance in the markets of northern Ghana developed out of the trade in Yoruba woven cloth [21] and other commodities in the early years of the present century. This trade probably dates back to the early 19th century or even before [22], but it was the early colonial period which saw the greatest increase in Yoruba trading activity in northern Ghana. The reasons for this are perhaps threefold. First the more settled colonial conditions, especially in Borgu which lay across the trade route, allowed groups of Yoruba traders to pass freely. Secondly, the development of the cocoa industry in Ghana and the rise of urban centres in the south led to the import of food-stuffs from the Northern Territories on an increased scale, and thus an increase in the amount of money in circulation there. Thirdly, the same period saw a decline in the Mossi cloth industry to the north of Ghana (Skinner 1962:386-7). If the first factor allowed Yoruba traders to penetrate to northern Ghana at all, the two others caused a rapid growth in the number of traders in the area in the first three decades of the century. As early as 1908, the Assistant Commissioner at Navrongo noted that there were Yoruba trading there along with Hausa and Mossi [23], and about the same time some of my own informants or their fathers started to appear in various parts of the north.

It seems likely that the first Yoruba to arrive there were Shaki, trading in beads, natron, and antimony from northern Nigeria. The first Igbetti to go to Ghana was Alhadji Sadiku [24], the present head of Ile Olowo, who went with a group of Shaki traders in about 1910. He took with him capital gained from farming with his senior brother and he stayed first at Yendi and Gambaga before going to Tamale when the town began to grow and attract migrants. He returned home to marry seven years later and after his marriage and an attempt to learn Arabic, he returned to Ghana in 1924, taking with him several friends and junior relatives and porters. The relatives included Sanusi, the son of a senior brother, Sule and his two brothers, the sons of a sister, and David, the son of another sister. This time he was trading in Yoruba cloth. Until the 1930's the means of transporting cloth was by headloads, and the route to Ghana lay through Djougou and Lamakara to Yendi and Tamale, though other more northerly routes were used on occasions. A strong porter could carry up to 40 men's cover cloths, the journey took between three and seven weeks depending on the route and the weather conditions, and the cloth was carried on foot round the towns and villages of northern Ghana. In the 1930's however, the pattern began to change. Tamale was by now a considerable size and there was an increasing demand for European goods which the Yoruba started to cater for. Indicative of this demand is the decision of the U.T.C. to open a branch in the town in 1929 [25]. The Yoruba who had sufficient capital, however, preferred to buy in the south rather than in Tamale itself. The road to Kumasi was now open for most of the year and the middle 1920's saw an enormous increase in the lorry traffic passing between the two towns [26]. In the rural markets the cycle was becoming a familiar sight and some of the Yoruba also started to deal in cycle parts [27]. Now the traders in Nigerian cloth gradually began to transport it by road, rail and steamer instead of with headloads. Tamale market grew enormously and the 1931 Census records 305 Yoruba in the Tamale area [28]. Many of these would have been groups of traders related to each other, working under the direction of a senior trader, and performing a variety of roles in the trade in cloth and other goods. By 1939, the heads of most of the clusters of kin that formed the core of the Yoruba community in the north up to the time of the exodus

46   *CHANGING SOCIAL STRUCTURE IN GHANA*

were already established in Tamale.

The Ile Olowo group was no exception. In 1933 Sadiku returned home again leaving Sule and his relatives in Ghana. They were starting to sell pans brought up from the south by one or other of them in addition to Nigerian cloth. Lasisi, Sadiku's eldest son, came over with a group of porters in 1936 to join them. Sule was in charge of purchasing and transporting the Nigerian cloth. The situation at this time was rather like that described by Amselle for the Kooroko, with a senior relative at home directing trading operations among his junior relatives established elsewhere (Amselle 1971). Lasisi was however dissatisfied with the way the others were trading and he could see that their capital was fast diminishing. He wrote to his father to tell him to come back to Ghana which Sadiku did in 1943. He brought with him Samanu, his second son, who also had ambitions to learn Arabic and become a Mallam. On his arrival, Sadiku paid off the debts the group had incurred, divided the remaining capital among his junior relatives, and left them to trade independently of each other. He himself went off to Damongo together with Amuda who had replaced Sanusi who returned home to marry and farm. Sadiku stayed there until 1949 when his senior brother died and he returned to Igbetti where he was now the oldest male member of Ile Olowo. One by one the other junior relatives had also returned home. Sule died in 1945, and Samanu took the news home to Nigeria where he stayed to learn Arabic. David and one of Sule's brothers went broke, and they used the remaining capital of the third brother to transport the three of them home. Amuda remained in Ghana but gave up trading: in 1950 he got a job with the Public Works Department as a bulldozer driver and later moved to Tema to work on the site of the new town.

Lasisi was thus the only one of the group still trading in Ghana at this point and unencumbered by his less efficient relatives he began to make progess. He had started trading on his own with the division of the capital between the various members of the group in 1944, and his assets at that time consisted of £16 worth of European cloth, £7.10s. which he had managed to save, and a cycle worth £3.10s. which he hired out from time to time. He remained trading in Tamale, selling mostly European cloth, until 1949 by which time he had managed to save up enough capital to return to Nigeria to buy Yoruba cloth. In the period after the war this was much in demand owing to the scarcity of European cloth. On his first trip home he took with him £300; on the second he took £300; and for the third he was able to increase it to £500 by selling off four cows he had acquired. Thereafter for several years he returned to Nigeria at four-monthly intervals to buy, and Nigerian cloth remained his sole interest until a sharp increase in the duty on it forced him to return to the sale of European cloth about 1955. By the early 1950's, therefore, he was well established in Tamale. He had acquired two wives and was building himself a house in Tamale, and as his business expanded, he began to take a whole series of junior relatives to Tamale to help him. In 1951, he took his half-sibling, Tijani. In 1956 he loaned Tijani £60, but Tijani had little success trading in Tamale. He moved to Damongo where his father had been trading previously, and had more success there as a cycle repairer, farmer, and exporter of dried meat to Techiman. In 1958, he was joined by Ganiyu, his junior brother, who worked for two years as an apprentice cycle-repairer after which he returned to Igbetti

THE GROWTH OF A MIGRANT COMMUNITY

to learn Arabic from Samanu. Tijani was then joined by Fasasi, a half-sibling of Amuda, who had been a cycle repairer in Igbetti and who continued with the work in Ghana. By 1969, Tijani had acquired houses in Igbetti and Damongo, and three wives, one of them Ghanaian. Also with him in Damongo was Amadu, a more distant agnate whom Lasisi had invited to come to Ghana in 1960. He did not work for Lasisi, however, but was given capital of 100 on his arrival, and he joined Tijani in Damongo where he stayed until his death in a road accident in 1967.

In 1952, Lasisi took on his junior full brother, Salami, to whom he gave the remnants of the European cloth he had in stock, while he himself concentrated on Nigerian cloth. Salami proved to be an excellent trader, and when in 1960 Lasisi built himself a larger stall in the market, Salami was given the old one together with £60. His success continued until his sudden death in 1968 by which time he had acquired three wives and a house in Tamale on a site near his brother's.

Jimoh was less of a success. He also joined Lasisi in Ghana in the early 1950's after leaving Ilorin where he had been training as a motor mechanic. Lasisi decided to set him up as a trader, and gave him money to buy cloth in the south. Jimoh spent all the money and in order to buy the cloth he broke into Lasisi's room and removed some more. Unfortunately he was seen and on his return from Kumasi he was met by a delegation of irate relatives at the lorry park. After a confrontation he disappeared and has since lost all contact with the others, though he is believed to be working as a tractor driver in the Volta Region. A second relative who joined Lasisi in Tamale, this time in 1966, was Braimah. He became a washerman with equipment purchased by Lasisi. He returned to Nigeria to marry in 1968 and with capital derived from washing started to trade on his return to Ghana. Lasisi also brought James, his mother's sister's son, from Igbetti to drive a car which he had bought in the early 1960's and to manage a rice farm which he planted in 1967.

The last two people that Lasisi took to Ghana were the eldest son of Sumanu, Mumuni, and Karimu, a young boy who was the son of his junior sister. At the time of the exodus these two were helping him in his shop together with his own two senior sons. His third and fourth sons were both in secondary school and unlikely to trade. Throughout, Lasisi had maintained links with Igbetti. His eldest daughter had been educated there while, in 1959, Lasisi helped to rebuild Sadiku's compound. In 1967 he provided the money for himself, Sadiku and Ganiyu to go to Mecca together.

From the complexity of this single example a paradigm of lineage-based migration can be constructed of general application in both Igbetti and the two other towns under discussion. The initial migrant is usually a junior member of his own sibling group. If he is successful in Ghana he will take with him junior relatives. In time he retires to Nigeria to assume a position of leadership in his own compound. Throughout, the members of the groups have varied success with trading and exhibit a wide range of aptitudes for it. Most of them undergo a period of training, working under a senior relative who will usually be responsible for the expenses of their marriage and for an initial

48   *CHANGING SOCIAL STRUCTURE IN GHANA*

gift (or less often a loan) of capital to set them up as independent traders in turn. If their success continues they may in turn bring further junior relatives to help them. The trader who is unsuccessful, however, will usually return home to farm, or move to another part of Ghana (usually a smaller town or village) to try his luck again. This is an important feature of the migration and explains the wide distribution of the Yoruba traders in the rural areas. Many of these had been unsuccessful in the towns and for them, a move to the rural areas meant higher profit margins, less competition and cheap accommodation. Another option for the unsuccessful is to look for other work such as driving or government labour, or to make use of skills acquired in the home town or Ghana, like tailoring, gold-smithing, or cycle-repairing.

But if it is to his relatives that the successful trader looks for assistant, it is the nature of Yoruba kinship organisation which determines which relatives he will be most likely to call on. Table 1 shows the relationship of the people responsible for the migration of the 195 Yoruba men to Northern Ghana on which I was able to get information in 1970-71. The most obvious inference from this table is that the bulk of migrants to Ghana from Igbetti and the other two towns were taken by close relatives and especially agnatic relatives. Within the lineage there is a tremendous emphasis on seniority, defined by order of birth. All collateral relatives, regardless of either sex or generation are referred to as 'elder sibling' *(egbon)* if they were born before the speaker and as 'younger siblings' *(aburo)* if born after him (Bascom 1969:49). To his *egbon* ego owes service, deference and respect, and he expects the same from his *aburo*. This is reinforced by modes of address - the use of the second person plural and the avoidance of personal names in addressing certain categories of senior relatives (for a full account, see Bascom 1942;1969:49-54).

Thus in his lineage, ego has a pool of junior relatives related to him in a variety of ways which he can call to his aid for trade in Ghana as in other spheres of life, and if his own children are not old enough to be taken along, there are other junior relatives available who are. But recruitment from within the agnatic lineage is not a purely random affair. It will be seen from Tab.1 that it is more common to recruit close relatives than more distant ones, as might be expected. As well as seniority within the lineage, Yoruba also lay emphasis on the unity of the sibling group. Yoruba inheritance rules do not divide the property of a polygynous man equally between the sons; instead it is divided into equal parts according to the number of wives of the dead man who have produced sons, irrespective of the number of sons of each, according to what Gluckman calls the house-property complex. Kinship ideology reflects this economic fact; it is expected that a child's closest relationships will be those with his siblings by the same mother *(omoiya)*, and all the time the group of full siblings will differentiate itself from the children of the same father but different mothers *(obakan)* (Lloyd 1962:279-286; Aronson 1971:31ff). We might expect therefore that the number of migrants recruited by their full siblings will be larger than that recruited by half-siblings or more distant relatives, and among the Igbetti migrants this appears to have been so . A corollary of this unity of the sibling group is that the migrant in search of helpers will first look for them either among his junior full siblings or among the sons of his senior full siblings. It is this latter relationship that formed the nucleus for most of the 10 or so clusters of kin that were the core of the Igbetti community in northern Ghana. Only when these are

TABLE 1: RELATIONSHIP OF PEOPLE RESPONSIBLE FOR
TAKING MALE MIGRANTS TO
NORTHERN GHANA

	Ogbomosho		Igbetti		Igboho		Total	
	No.	%	No.	%	No.	%	No.	%
Parent	4	11.4	4	6.6	10	10.1	18	9.2
Full sibling	7	20.0	6	9.8	13	13.1	26	13.3
Half sibling	1	2.9	3	4.9	6	6.0	10	5.4
Father's full sibling	3	8.6	12	19.7	10	10.1	25	12.8
Father's half sibling	1	2.9	2	3.3	3	3.0	6	3.1
Father's sibling's son	1	2.9	0	0.0	0	0.0	1	0.5
Other agnatic relatives	1	2.9	4	6.6	1	1.0	6	3.1
Matrilateral relative	3	8.6	6	9.8	12	12.1	21	10.8
Affinal relative	0	0.0	0	0.0	3	3.0	3	1.5
Non-relative	1	2.9	4	6.6	6	6.1	11	5.6
Went independently	3	8.6	17	27.9	34	34.3	54	27.7
Born in Ghana	10	28.6	3	4.9	1	1.0	14	7.2
TOTAL	35	100.0	61	100.0	99	100.0	195	100.0

A note on the sample. In the circumstances in which the fieldwork
was carried out, it was impossible to obtain a random sample, and
these migrants were those that happened to be available for interview in 1971. All the Igbetti and the Ogbomosho were resident in
the Tamale district, while the Igboho sample contains a number of
people from Bawku, Bolgatanga and other towns in the north, many
of whom had started their trading careers in Tamale.

50   *CHANGING SOCIAL STRUCTURE IN GHANA*

unsuitable or unavailable will a man then consider his half-siblings and their sons or more distant relatives.

Although the basic structure of Yoruba kinship is the agnatic lineage, yet the terminology is cognatic as are the patterns of exogamy, and women by no means lose their rights in their natal lineages on marriage. Indeed they might well move home temporarily either on divorce or the death of their husbands, and after the menopause, they are likely to do so permanently. Women who are senior in age are important parties to lineage discussion, household activities and the organisation of *rites de passage*. In some cases, they may be joined in their natal compounds by one or more of their children, whose descendants in time may become incorporated into the lineage. This cognatic element in Yoruba kinship has led to some controversy in recent years as to whether the Yoruba in certain parts of the Western State should in fact be called cognatic or agnatic in terms of their social organisation (Lloyd 1962; 1966b; Bender 1970,1971). What concerns us however is the close ties that exist between groups in full-siblings, whether male or female, and it is not surprising that many migrants to Ghana were recruited by matrilateral relatives and especially their mother's full siblings.

But while Yoruba patterns of social organisation emphasise the solidarity of agnates, and especially full siblings, Yoruba socialisation patterns also encourage individualism and self-reliance. As well as helping his father on the farm, a Yoruba boy is traditionally given a piece of land to farm for himself in the afternoons and evenings, and many migrants to Ghana accumulated their initial capital by working for themselves in just this way. Yoruba traders in Ghana also emphasised self-reliance and economic independence, and the result was a proliferation of small-scale trading units. On the basis of the factors outlined above we might predict that trading relationships based on full siblings would be more durable than those based on the half-sibling or more distant relationships. There is some evidence that this is so but a full analysis of this material is beyond the scope of the present paper. But even in the relatively durable trading partnership between two full siblings, tensions can arise. There is often the fear that the younger partner is quietly embezzling funds for his own use. That this happened in many cases in Ghana is certain, and it would have been very easy to do in the absence of fixed prices and where much of the buying and selling outside Tamale was entrusted to the junior brother. But in considering fission in the Yoruba trading enterprise we must take into account the nature of the items dealt in and the organisation of trade. With the gradual switch from the trade in Nigerian cloth to that in manufactured goods from Kumasi and Accra which took place immediately after the Second World War, more complex patterns of co-operation were no longer necessary and this could have only accentuated the fissive tendencies within the Yoruba trading group.

It will be seen from Table 1 that 28% of the migrants to Ghana went independently (i.e. they took their own capital and did not serve under a master before trading independently). Accretion of the migrant community proceeded not only vertically with recruitment of junior agnatic relatives, but horizontally with the recruitment of members of other lineages: here the crucial role is that of the *egbe*. This word has a very wide range of meanings - from traditional age sets (Lloyd 1954:371ff.) to modern cultural and religious associations (Bascom 1969:47; Fadipe 1970:257ff) and informal

THE GROWTH OF A MIGRANT COMMUNITY 51

groups of close friends who meet frequently for relaxation or to discuss matters of common concern. In the 1920's and 1930's a Yoruba needing porters would often persuade members of his *ẹgbẹ* to join him in trips to Ghana. For this the porter would receive a cash payment as well as an introduction to long-distance trading. Many were influenced by their experience as porters to accumulate or borrow their own capital and then to try their luck trading independently. After 1945 porters were replaced by other forms of transport, but in the great expansion of trade in the post-war period, a large number of Igbetti migrated with their own capital at the suggestion of friends already in Ghana. At first people recruited in this way were given accommodation, advice on conditions in the market, and if necessary, loans by the friends who had persuaded them to go. But unlike migrants recruited by relatives, they were working independently from the very start. Many of the friends recruited in this way would also be fellow *ẹgbẹ* members and the *ẹgbẹ* pattern was reproduced in Ghana. Members adopted the same dress on important occasions and played a prominent role in *rites de passage* of one another. A trader would look to his closest *ẹgbẹ* friends for short-term loans to enable him to buy in the south, or in times of crisis, as in 1955 when a market fire burnt down the stalls and destroyed the stocks of several Igbetti men. In the case of one migrant, one of his closest friends was still living with him at the time of the exodus, 20 years after his arrival in Ghana, and another more successful friend had built his own house on the nearest available site. In the drawing rooms of the seven members of this particular *ẹgbẹ*, prominently displayed, were group photographs taken at Christmas some years previously which showed all the members dressed in the same rich type of Nigerian cloth. The members also had stalls in the same line in the market and were selling much the same type of *wọrọbo* that the member who had persuaded the others to go to Ghana had been selling in 1948.

The Yoruba community in Tamale

Having discussed in some detail the processes of migration we now have to consider the nature of the community in Tamale to which these gave rise. The tenacity with which Yoruba in Ghana maintained links with their home towns has been commented on before. Seeing that the migration process was so strongly rooted in agnatic lineages and friendship networks in the home town, this is hardly surprising. The Yoruba migrant was not disrupting or losing touch with his place of origin - indeed he depended on it for assistance in trading which made maintenance of such contacts a matter of importance. These ongoing ties of kinship, friendship and economic obligation found expression in various ways. Most migrants in Ghana intended to return home in later life when it became necessary for them to assume positions of responsibility in the home compound, though this often meant leaving considerable investments in Ghana for junior relatives. Most Yoruba migrants had been married in their towns of origin, even when they had been born in Ghana or had been taken there as small boys. This pattern started to change in the 1960's when it became difficult to send home the large sums of money needed for weddings, and marriages started to be arranged between groups of kin resident in Ghana, but even up to the time of the exodus, most weedings were performed in the home towns. There were constant visits home by members of the various large kinship groups, and one of the first priorities for any successful migrant was to go home to put up a building there. Even if an individual himself did not go home very often, scarcely a year would go by without one or other of his relatives going home and maintaining contact by conveying letters, presents and news. Many of the migrants had sent one or more of their children home to live with their grandparents, and many children attended primary and middle school in their home towns and then joined a relative in Ghana for secondary education. Finally there were the annual meetings of the town improvement unions to which six or more people from each group of migrants in Ghana would be sent as delegates. The four big groups in Tamale all sent representatives to their respective annual meetings and as the choice of delegates varied from year to year, a large percentage of the migrants would return home for this purpose in the course of time. Through these associations the migrants were kept in touch with home affairs and would contribute to a variety of projects in their home towns: from the erection of churches, mosques, markets, dispensaries and postal agencies to bribes to government officials to influence the location of other amenities in the area.

To the outsider the Lagosian community appeared largely undifferentiated, but in fact there were deep divisions between the various large town groups making it up, and a Yoruba migrant's primary loyalty was to his home town. Yoruba failure to inter-marry with Ghanaians has been commented upon, (J.R. Goody: 1970) but it was just as uncommon for a Yoruba to marry a Yoruba from a different town. There existed institutions which brought together Yoruba from different towns, such as the churches, the Yoruba Parapọ Committee, and the Nigerian Community Committee, but a closer look at the function of these bodies shows that they succeeded in reinforcing town loyalties rather than in breaking them down. In the case of the Yoruba Christians, for instance, there were three exclusively Yoruba congregations in the town, two Baptist and one United Missionary Society. Almost all the Igbetti, but none of the other Yoruba attended the U.M.S. church. The larger of the two Baptist congregations, the First Baptist Church,was principally made up of Ogbomosho and Igboho (all the Shaki men in Tamale were Muslim with one exception), but the church was haunted by the resentment of the other groups of Ogbomosho domination and this was one of the factors at the root of a split which took place in 1959, resulting in the formation of the smaller Second Baptist Church. Few Ogbomosho were members of this and many of the congregation came from the minority towns of Otu, Shepeteri and Ilesha.

The Yoruba Parapọ meetings were held at the house of the Yoruba chief in Tamale. These meetings were a useful means of settling disputes between the members of different Yoruba groups and discussing matters of common interest, principally to do with trade and the markets. Membership of the Yoruba Parapọ consisted of representatives from each Yoruba town which had migrants in Tamale, and the number of representatives depended on the number of migrants. Any dispute,therefore, tended to split the meeting along lines of town of origin. The Nigerian Community Committee originated later and was organised after Nigerian independence in 1960 to act as a link between the Nigerian High Commission in Accra and its nationals in Tamale. This body was less than a success. In addition to the tensions between the three main ethnic groups involved (the Ibos withdrew from the meetings after the events of 1966 and the Hausa habitually arrived late for the meetings or not at all), there was the tension between the President who was the Ogbomosho and the Secretary who was not. Apart from welcoming

THE GROWTH OF A MIGRANT COMMUNITY

53

the High Commissioner once and issuing forms for passports which resulted in the embezzlement of £300 (¢600) by the secretary and no passports, the body achieved little in its brief and clouded history.

This touches on the question of the political involvement of the Yoruba with their hosts. As mentioned above, there was a Yoruba chief who had been first appointed by the British in the 1930's in their extension of the policy of indirect rule. Yet zongo politics and tensions between the indigenous and the stranger sections of the community were never the feature of political life in Tamale that they were in Kumasi and the other large towns in the south (cf. Skinner 1963; Schildkrout 1970 a and b; Cohen 1969). There were several factors behind this difference. Firstly Tamale itself was a colonial creation: as a result it was ethnically very diverse and there was no large indigenous population with vested interests which it saw being usurped by stranger interlopers. Much of the resentment at the Yoruba domination in the markets in the south came from the fact that the Akan had the money from cocoa to enter trading, but were denied the opportunity because other groups had previously established a monopoly. In Tamale this was not the case. For many years the Dagomba had been in control of much of the trade in food-stuffs to the south and, as a result, were in control of much of the transport as well. Many of the goods dealt in by the Yoruba were primarily of interest to clerical and other workers, chiefly of southern origin, and many of the Dagomba women who were trading were retailing cloth by the yard, while the Yoruba were only interested in selling larger pieces. By 1969 the Yoruba position in trade vis à vis the Dagomba was one of the symbiosis. It had not yet got to the point of serious competition for scarce resources, though perhaps the beginning of an overlap in interests could be seen with an increasing number of Dagomba women interested in selling provisions.

Also as a result of its origin, the layout of Tamale was such that there were no rigidly segregated ethnic enclaves within it. Admittedly parts of the town were known as 'Accra Town', 'Mossi Zongo', and 'Hausa Zongo', but these were labels of origin and hardly reflected ethnic composition in 1969. Even the Sabon Gida, the traditional Yoruba area of concentration, contained many houses owned by Dagomba and other Ghananians, and in recent years, many Yoruba had built themselves houses in newer parts of the town and moved out.

In this situation of symbiosis rather than conflict, there was little stimulus for the emergence of a Yoruba identity which transcended more parochial loyalties. Naturally the Yoruba recognised their broad cultural similarities, but in conversation with a group of Igboho or Igbetti, one would very soon hear criticism of the Ogbomosho and vice versa. The main foci of social interaction were the regular meetings of the individual town groups and here the main issues were the quarrel over the site of a new mosque and market in Igboho, the chiefship dispute in Igbetti, and the murder of the Bale of Ogbomosho, rather than events in Ghana. The Yoruba naturally showed considerable interest in the Ghanaian election campaign of 1969 but at the level of individual rather than group behaviour. Indded the only action at the group level was to reject all advances from the leading political parties contesting the election, to call a halt to all regular Yoruba meetings in case they should be interpreted as politically motivated, and to stand rigidly aloof from the whole affair.

CHANGING SOCIAL STRUCTURE IN GHANA

But in this pragmatic and individually oriented approach to Ghanaian politics, we can perhaps see another basic difference between the Tamale Yoruba and some other migrant communities. In the case of the Ibadan Hausa, for instance, Cohen vividly describes the role of the 'landlords'. These were the 'big men' of the community who derived their status and influence from their pivotal economic role in the cattle and kola trades. An important part of their influence was their ability to exercise some sort of coercion over their clients who were bound to them by ties of economic interest owing to the complex and differentiated nature of the trade in which they were engaged (Cohen 1969:92-7). Among the Tamale Yoruba, trading activities were less complex and ties of clientship far less important if they existed at all. The emphasis was on individualism. Though there were 'big men' who took a leading part in the deliberations of the various town groups, their authority did not depend on their power to exercise economic coercion or withdraw patronage, but rather on an amalgam of age, proven integrity and a reputation of giving sound advice. Wealth was much less important - indeed the richer men were often so busy that their attendance at these meetings was extremely infrequent and assumption of leadership in their town groups was subordinated to their pursuit of success in their own trading enterprises.

CONCLUSION

It has been suggested in this paper that Yoruba migration to Ghana can only be fully understood by looking at the origins in the social structure of the home towns. Migration developed vertically through the recruitment of junior lineage members and horizontally within networks of friends of similar age, interest and religion. The result was a very tightly knit community in which both patterns of interaction among kin and friendship networks were in many cases derived from the home town. Loyalty to the town of origin, symbolised by the regular meetings of the improvement union branches, formed the basis of community formation and to the individual this loyalty meant an intention to ultimately return to Nigeria to take up the responsibilities either of an elder or title holder in the home compound. Perhaps the different types of migration can be seen as being arranged along a continuum with 'seasonal migration' at one end and 'permanent settlement' with loss of contact with the town of origin at the other. On this continuum, the Yoruba would occupy a position somewhere in the centre. To regard them as permanently settled migrants makes it difficult to explain their failure to assimilate, whereas by adopting a dynamic perspective on the relations between the migrants and their home towns, this failure becomes quite understandable.

In addition through utilisation of these links with their home towns, the Yoruba managed to successfully solve some of the perennial problems of small-scale petty traders. Their system of recruitment ensured that the young trader starting to trade on his own had at once received a sound education in trading methods, knowledge of the best places to purchase a given commodity at the best price, and the capital to exploit this knowledge. His membership of a tightly-knit town community ensured encouragement from friends and relatives who also placed a high value on success in trading, and allowed him privileged access to information on the state of the market in the south from other Yoruba who had just returned. But his acceptance and exploitation of these mechanisms for trading success would

THE GROWTH OF A MIGRANT COMMUNITY

in turn only reinforce his links with his lineage and town of origin. In explaining therefore the success of the Yoruba in commercial activity throughout Ghana, it is essential to keep in mind the dynamic nature of these links with the town of origin: these enabled the Yoruba to exploit vigorously trading opportunities which arose as a result of the rapid economic development of the colonial period, and resulted in a lively increase in their numbers. It is even more important to keep it in mind in the context of post-colonial Africa, where national frontiers are hardening, xenophobia is increasing and the position of the migrant who fails to assimilate becomes more unenviable than ever.

NOTES

1. The fieldwork on which this paper is based was carried out in the Northern Region of Ghana, 1969-70, and in the Western State of Nigeria, 1970-71. I am grateful to the Managers of the Smuts Memorial Fund, University of Cambridge, for the award of a Smuts Studentship as well as an additional grant from the Fund, and to the Department of Education and Science, London, for the award of a Hayter Studentship with which the fieldwork was financed. I am also grateful to Ronald Cohen, Jack Goody and James O'Connell for their suggestions and criticisms.

2. For a comprehensive account of the expulsions of aliens from Ghana and elsewhere, see Peil (1971).

3. More recently some studies have taken into account the interaction between the migrant's places of origin and their urban situation. See Aronson (1971), Plotnicov (1970), and Hart (1969).

4. I am grateful to Mr. Olaopa of the Rehabilitation Division , Western State Ministry of Economic Planning and Reconstruction, Ibadan, for making available figures of returnees from Ghana registered by the Division during 1969-71 on which parts of this section are based.

5. This is necessarily a crude estimate. My estimate of the size of the Tamale community in 1969 is well over double the figure of the 1960 Census (see below n.8.). See also Peil (1971:225-6) for estimates from various sources of the number of Yoruba repatriated ranging from 140-170,000.

6. Stapleton (1959) gives the impression that the Ilorin formed the majority of the Yoruba in Ghana. This is only true of the Accra area.

7. 71.3% of registered returnees to the Western State were from Oyo North, Oshun North West and Oshun North-East (which includes Inisha and Oyan). Offa and Ilorin are of course in Kwara State and I have not been able to obtain figures for the number of repatriates there.

8. This estimate is based on lists of adult men resident in Tamale kept by the secretaries of the Tamale branches of the various town unions, together with my own quantitative data on the number of their dependents.

56 *CHANGING SOCIAL STRUCTURE IN GHANA*

This figure consists of:

Ogbomosho	900
Igbetti	700
Igboho	600
Shaki	450
Other Towns	450

9. This difference between women from the two towns can be shown by the difference in the median estimated monthly value of the trading turnover of the women we interviewed. The figure for the Ogbomosho women in Tamale was over ₡200, and that for the Igbetti women under ₡100.

10. That is to say with a monthly turnover of ₡1000 or more.

11. Census Report, Tamale District, 1931, Ghana National Archives, Tamale, (GNAT) C.456.

12. Few Yoruba were involved in the trade in food-stuffs in Tamale though the situation was different in some other areas of the north, e.g. the Bimbilla area where many Shaki were involved in the yam trade.

13. Yoruba who were literate in English translated these words as 'petty-petty things'.

14. Namely Savelugu, Katinga (nr. Tolon), Kumbungu, Sankpala and Nyankpala. The distance of these markets from Tamale varied from 9 miles (Sankpala) to 23 miles (Katinga). The first three of these markets were much larger than the other two and many Yoruba just attended these and stayed in Tamale on the other days.

15. The Togo border was officially closed for most of the period 1960-66. One of the factors in Yoruba success in the Nkrumah era was the skill with which they evaded many of these restrictions. For the effect of the closure on Ghanaian trade, see Garlick (1968:25).

16. With import duty, the imported cloth sold by the G.N.T.C. in 1969 was near double the price of the Akosombo cloth, often identical in design. Smuggled imported cloth was relatively far cheaper, hence its popularity.

17. Such shortages were frequent in the worsening economic climate of 1961-66. See Rimmer (1966:27).

18. For example over 50 of the 160 or so adult men from Ogbomosho in Tamale came from four compounds in the home town while the great majority of the 135 Igbetti men in Tamale came from only 10.

19. The 1963 census estimate of 25,000 is far too high, but is perhaps less outrageous than the figures given for Igboho (nearly 50,000), Shaki (over 75,000) and Ogbomosho (well over 300,000 making it larger than Kano and the third largest town in Nigeria!). More realistic figures would be about 12,000 for Igboho , 25,000 for Shaki and 100,000 for Ogbomosho. Milone and Olaore have attempted to correct the figures for the Western State as a whole (1971) while Aluko (1966) has outlined the political factors behind the 1963 census.

THE GROWTH OF A MIGRANT COMMUNITY

20. Igbetti informants stressed to me that 'our people are too fond of farming', and indeed it seems that the rate of migration from Igbetti was probably lower than for the two towns, Kishi and Igboho, which with Igbetti make up the Irepo District. All three towns were of a very similar size, yet the Igbetti had only migrated to Tamale in Ghana in any numbers. As well as being well represented in Ghana as Igbetti, Igboho and Kishi also had large contingents in Upper Volta and Niger.

21. The real name of Ile Olowo as well as the names of its members have been changed.

22. The main type was the familiar cloth woven in narrow strips by men on the horizontal loom, especially in the towns of Ilorin and Iseyin (See Bray (1968) on the Iseyin weavers). Other types of cloth included the broader woven cloth produced on the vertical loom by women in Igbetti and the other towns in the area, as well as indigo tie-dyed cloth, mainly from Abeokuta.

23. Clapperton (1829:14-15) and Lander (1838 Vol. I:152) mention the quality of Yoruba cloth and the existence of a trade route from the Kishi area to Salaga.

24. Annual Report on the North Eastern Province by E.O. Warden, 1908. Ms. in GNAT C.489.

25. Annual General Report on the Northern Territories, 1929-30, GNAT C.489

26. This can be clearly seen from the figures of the number of vehicles crossing the ferry at Yeji on the road between Tamale and Kumasi. In 1924, 1377 vehicles crossed the ferry northbound. In 1928 the figures had increased to 5567. Annual General Report for the Northern Territories 1928-29. GNAT C.178.

27. Dagomba District Report 1936. GNAT C.291.

28. Census Report on Tamale District 1931. GNAT C.456.

29. Ogbomosho sent eight, Igboho and Igbetti six each, Shaki four, and the minority towns two or one each, depending on their numbers in Tamale. *Parapọ* is simply the Yoruba word for 'union'.

30. Before the compliance order there were no Yoruba commercial transport owners in Tamale. Yoruba traders therefore had to rely on Dagomba and others for transport to the south. In other parts of Ghana the Yoruba were involved in transport, for instance in the Koforidua area where they had been involved early on in the cocoa industry, and in Accra and Kumasi where many of the richer traders had invested in taxis

31. Cf. the intense struggle of the Hausa in Ibadan to maintain the spatial and cultural integrity of Sabo. Cohen (1969:113-9) and passim.

THE EFFECTS OF CASH CROPS ON AN EWE COMMUNITY

G.K. NUKUNYA

The people of South Anlo[1] have managed over the last forty years to evolve a system of farming around their traditional capital of Anloga which changed the harsh environment into an oasis of progress and prosperity. Faced with problems of land shortage, unbelievably poor sandy soil, sea erosion and drought, as well as with the constant threat of flooding from the unreliable rains and the periodic rising waters of the Volta, they introduced a system of cultivation involving irrigation, heavy manuring, rotation of crops and intensive cultivation. The main crop grown under this system is shallot, *cillium ascolornicum*, locally known as *sabala*, introduced into the area towards the end of the last century, but corn, pepper, okra and other vegetables are also grown.

Anloga, situated only fifteen miles east of the Volta estuary, lies halfway across the dry coastal plain that stretches from Accra right down to Dahomey and therefore enjoys - or rather suffers from - all its essential features. But it also has to reckon with the large Keta Lagoon to the north which with the Volta and the Atlantic surf on the south almost encircles the sandbar on which it stands. Indeed it is this encirclement which provides the area with an insular touch that gives Anloga and its environs their distinctive character, for it is only from the east through Denu that one can reach it by land. Thus it is water which dominates the landscape and presents the place with most of its problems. Periodically, especially around September, the surf becomes wild and not only threatens but actually erodes substantial portions of the coast, only (fortunately) to re-desposit the silt later. But the erosive effects seem to get the upper hand year after year with the result that every year the sandbar becomes narrower. September is also the month in which the waters of the Volta rise and spill over into the lagoon raising its surface above the surrounding lands. It is therefore the most inhospitable month throughout the area.

This coastal belt, which is about forty miles long, is strikingly narrow, (see map) barely two miles at its widest portion at Woe, but in Keta and settlements to the east it is only a few hundred feet wide. Even the wide portions are traversed by long narrow depressions, running almost parallel to the coast line, which get flooded after the major rains of May and June. But water is not the sole problem of the area. On the contrary, the difficulties posed by drought are much more devastating, for the rains are not only scanty, about 30 inches per year, they are also both irregular and extremely unreliable. The soil too is very poor. The southern half of the coastal belt is pure sand which presents a very good spectacle to the sightseer but is of little productive value. Towards the lagoon however it is darker and apparently richer due to admixture with decomposed vegetable matter, but the salt content makes it fatal for most plants the nearer one gets to the lagoon itself. Yet this narrow, forty-mile, coastal stretch has to support nearly 100,000 inhabitants,making land shortage another chronic problem of the place.

Thus for most practical purposes cultivation has not been an important

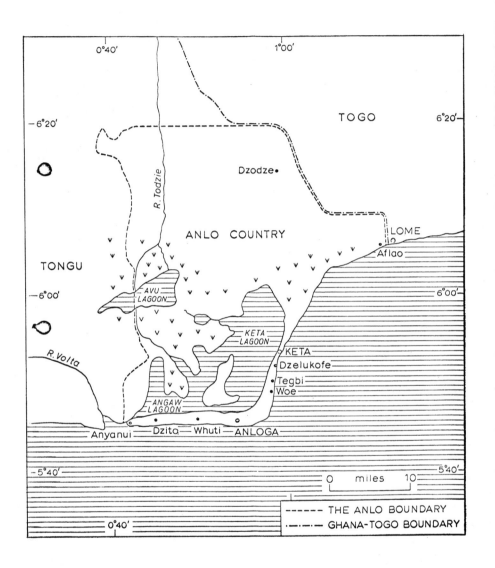

EFFECTS OF CASH CROPS ON AN EWE COMMUNITY 61

proposition in south Anlo in the eastern half because of the unavailability of land, and in the west where more space exists, due to the hazards of flooding and drought. As a result, until the coconut was introduced on a large scale during the last century, only cassava, corn and vegetables were grown on the few sheltered places. Important economic activities included sea and lagoon fishing as well as poultry farming which all past accounts of the area emphasised. [2] In extremely dry years, too, the coastal fringes of the Keta Lagoon, with its brackish water, dry up to leave large incrustations of salt which bring in a considerable income to the locals.[3]

Up to about the 1920s everything seemed to have worked smoothly with the economy. But round about that time, however, the population pressure began to tell on the land (and the sea) resulting in large scale migratory movements from the area. Scores of families of Anlo fishermen started to migrate in search of fresh and richer waters. Some settled permanently in Abidjan in the Ivory Coast and Badagri in Nigeria, but others were content to spend periods of up to three years before returning home. Other important locations are Senya Beraku, Chorkor (in Accra) and Grand Popo in Dahomey. Today colonies of Anlo fishermen can be found on the West African coast from as far north as the Gambia right down to the Congo. Little wonder, therefore, that they have been called 'the pan-African fishermen'. (Hill 1963:64).

One area not greatly affected by this massive exodus is Anloga, the traditional capital of Anlo, and its immediate environs. Just as the population pressure was beginning to tell on the area, shallots, which had hitherto been considered only as a backyard crop, started to receive greater attention. Instead of running away in search of jobs in foreign countries, Anloga farmers decided to make something out of their homeland. Through heavy manuring the land on the edge of the lagoon has been brought under cultivation. Through sanding, the long depressions which used to get flooded during the rains have been made less vulnerable. This was the beginning of an industry which by the 1940s made 'Anloga shallots' household words in Ghana. It was the beginning of an industry on which now depend all the towns west of the district administrative centre of Keta, which embraces a population of about 40,000 inhabitants.

It is not known exactly when or by whom shallots were introduced into the Anloga area. The names of the pioneers now given all happen to be either grandparents of the respective informants or others closely related to them. Both Quansah (1956-57:45-49) and Tettey (1960:1-5) gave accounts of the introduction of shallots in the area in about 1800 but said very little as to how they arrived at this date. What is certain is that by 1877 shallot cultivation had been established in the area. In that year a book published by Johnson Whiteford (1877:73) mentioned how his ship anchored off Quitta (Keta) and was met by natives in canoes loaded with poultry and 'eschalots in baskets'. As there is no suitable ground near Keta on which these could be grown apart from the land now used it is reasonable to assume that the crop was then in cultivation and some surplus was being produced, though it would be far-fetched to presume that the intensive techniques now in use were already present at the time. But by 1930 shallot cultivation had attracted the attention of government agricultural officers. Stein, the agricultural officer operating in the

62 *CHANGING SOCIAL STRUCTURE IN GHANA*

area was unable to describe the industry and to mention four different kinds of the crop under cultivation, namely large and small, red and white (1929:152). The mention of the white shallots for this period is very interesting, for although they have now disappeared almost altogether, the present writer himself recalls their prevalence during the 1940s before the importation of new seeds from Agu [4] led to their eventual extinction.

For quite a long time after the introduction of the crop Anloga and Woe remained the only important growing centres, a position which continued until around 1933 when the industry spread to Tegbi, Dzelukefe and later to Whuti and Dzita. Today shallots are grown in all settlements between Keta and Anyanui, but those two settlements still produce the major part.

Land tenure and system of inheritance

Under the Anlo system of land tenure the ultimate title in the land is vested in clans or lineages, and it is as members of these descent groups that individuals acquire their shallot plots. But although the social structure is based on a patrilineal ideology, diverging transmission of property is practised with the share of a woman passing to her children [5]. Two inheritance procedures operate side by side. In one the property is shared individually among the children and in the other it is shared equally among wives [6] who had issue by the deceased, each widow taking her share for her children. A widow who had no issue by the deceased gets nothing. Whatever the method applied the share of daughters is much smaller than that of sons. Recent trends as demonstrated by court cases [7] seem to suggest that the system of diverging transmission is now being challenged in favour of a more straightforward patrilineal inheritance, but so far no significant changes have been made in this direction.

Shallot plots can also be acquired through gifts from father to children, from husband to wife, or from relative to relative. Fiaboe, as it is known in Anloga, becomes the property of the recipient and is not added to the property of the donor after his death for the purpose of sharing among his children.

Pledging of plots is also common. Under this practice, locally known as Woba, the beds are cultivated by the pledgee until such time that the pledgor is able to settle the debt [8]. Outright purchase of land and plots, said to be rare in the past, now occurs quite frequently under recognised procedures. There is a custom involving the offer of drinks by the vendee, its acceptance by the vendor and the participation of both as well as witnesses in drinking. Other requirements include a formal demarcation of boundaries in the presence of neighbours and the planting of boundary trees at the corners. Boundary pillars, with the name or initials of the new owner inscribed on them, are now preferred. In all these trans-actions the approval of the vendor's lineage head and other elders is considered necessary.

Tenancy is another important arrangement in shallot farming. There are two main systems known locally as *dame* and *fame*. In the first the owner of an unprepared plot grants it to another person to cultivate and the harvest is shared between the two in the ratio of two to one in favour of the tenant. In the second a farmer who has already prepared his plot but finds that he has insufficient seeds for all, hands them to another

EFFECTS OF CASH CROPS ON AN EWE COMMUNITY   63

who provides the seeds, sows them and maintains the crop. The harvest is
then divided into half. The agreement can be terminated by either side after
each harvest. In the case of *fame*, the general understanding is that the
transaction is for that season only, although there is sometimes the need
for renewal. This procedure regarding termination differs, of course, from
tenancy as known in the forest areas of Ghana, and even in the coconut
plantations of the Anlo area and the northern fringes of the Keta Lagoon
where fish fences and traps are used. For one of the principal conditions
of tenancy in customary law is that what is given can never be taken back
again from the person to whom it has been given so long as the tenant
recognises the ultimate title of the owner (Ollennu 1958:103). In the case
of shallot plots, however, the transaction is made only on the understanding
that it is for a specified time and nothing more. This is understandable
in view of local conditions and the nature of the shallot farms. In the
forest areas those who give out land usually have enough to spare and
can afford to do without the plots so long as their share of the harvest
is assured. In the area of the present study, where individual holdings
are not only small but where natural disasters like floods abound, it is
necessary to have an arrangement like the present system of tenancy by
which a farmer afflicted by any of these misfortunes could seek assistance
without necessarily alienating his plots. Moreover unlike many cash crops
of the forest, the shallot is not a tree crop and takes only two months
to mature, so that labour costs and other activities associated with it
are quite different and present a different set of problems altogether.

Thus today, unlike in the past when direct inheritance and gifts were
the only means of getting land, Anloga farmers have developed many new
ways of acquiring plots. The basic traditional system of tenure remains,
but alterations have taken place to meet the conditions necessitated by the
emergence of the crop as a commercial commodity. These tenurial arrangements
ensure that anyone with the capital to buy seeds for cultivation will
normally be able to obtain land during a farming season. Despite the
shortage of land, the physical hazards and the uncertainties they generate
mean that a large number of plots change hands every season. While transfer
is not permanent, the *woba* system can, however, deprive the landowner of the
use of his land (or at least part of it) for a long period.

Intensive cultivation

The land available for shallot farming is very restricted. Only the
low lying areas surrounding the Keta Lagoon and the elongated depressions
already described may be used because the beds upon which the crop is
grown are made on very low ground barely a few feet above sea level. Even
then no area neatly fits the required level without much attention and
detailed manipulation. In short, where the land is found to be too high,
the surface layers have to be removed, and where too low, sand has to be
added to bring it to the required level.

The specialised nature of the plots shows that only those whose lineage
and other relatives have land in the correct locations have access to it
through direct inheritance. In this respect the system of diverging
transmission has the effect of making land available to people who would
not get it through their lineages. But as we have just seen, within the
context of general land shortage in the area, it has the additional effect

64   *CHANGING SOCIAL STRUCTURE IN GHANA*

of further fragmentation leading to smaller portions. Individual holdings are therefore very small, averaging something like half an acre. But almost every year nearly half the total area under cultivation is flooded for several months. No techniques have been developed to check or control the floods and shallot beds covered by the flood waters are left uncultivated. Given the size of the plots, the aim of the system is to obtain the best possible result from the smallholdings.

Details of early techniques of shallot cultivation and the type of organisation that went with it are not known for certain, but since the 1930s a rather intensive system has been in use which requires labour outside the family. Although wives, children and other dependents do help with the farm work, hired labour, made readily available by the dense population, is used for the more exacting tasks of transportation, watering and sanding.

As a rule the plots are divided by narrow gutters into small rectangular beds to allow easy access to the crop for weeding and watering. As the crop is very tender, reaching only one foot above the ground and planted only a few inches apart, walking on the bed can be harmful to the crop and is never allowed. It is in the gutters that the farmer stands in order to reach the crop. The gutters, which are about one foot wide and one foot deep, also serve as irrigation channels during the dry season and as drainage canals after the rains have flooded the beds. As a further check against the flood waters, the sides of each bed are strengthened by a framework made of corn stalks and grass.

The size of the beds differs from place to place and from farm to farm. Even in the same farm no uniform size of beds is maintained. Consequently different and conflicting dimensions have been given by earlier writers. Stein (1929:152-160) mentioned 10 feet x 86 feet as the standard size of beds, Tettey (1960:5) 6 feet x 40 feet, Grove (1966:394) 6 feet x 15 feet and the present writer arrived at an average of 4 feet x 16 feet in 1957 (1957:12-13). It appears also that not only does the bed size differ from place to place but the dimensions are also changing from time to time. For instance the farm in which the 1957 dimensions were taken was found in 1971 to contain beds with an average size of 5 feet x 18 feet.

As already indicated, the shallot crop takes two months to mature and it is possible to raise three main crops a year. But in actual fact this is not possible every year due to the interruption of floods. In between the seasons corn, ground nuts and vegetables are planted. The first sowing season which coincides with the start of the traditional calendar [9] lasts from January to March and is known as *Fedomi* (Nukunya 1957:12-13). The second known as *Fenu* lasts from April to July and the last, *Kele*, covers September to November. The beginning of the sowing, which lasts a month, is decided by the leader of the farmers of an area and is announced by the town crier. It is an offence for any farmer to sow his seeds before or after this period. This is done to ensure that the crops of a particular area mature at about the same time to prevent *yoe*, an insect pest, spreading from the matured crop to the younger ones to which it is very harmful. The pest which provides a perennial hazard usually attacks the maturing crops especially during the dry season.

EFFECTS OF CASH CROPS ON AN EWE COMMUNITY

During the *Fedomi* season which is generally dry, the beds are watered daily for several days before the seeds are planted. At this time and sometimes in the other season the farmer depends not only on the irrigation channels which may get dry but also on wells built all over the farm. These wells, built with cement blocks, are deep enough to maintain constant supply of water even during the dry season.

Since the farmer irrigates his land whenever necessary, the fluctuations and distribution of rainfall do not exert much influence on the farming calendar. He is also able to cultivate the same piece of land for a long time because he does not depend on innate fertility of the soil but regularly enriches the basically poor, sandy soil with multifarious combinations of manures and fertilisers. Indeed it is in the system of manuring that the intensive nature of shallot cultivation is most clearly seen. As has already been mentioned, the soil is basically poor and therefore regular manuring is necessary to maintain fertility. In the event a large number of manures has been introduced, some of which are not even found in the immediate vicinity of Anloga. Principal among these, according to a rough order of importance are *nyimi* (cow dung), *lavi* (fish manure), *druimi* (bat droppings), and *yevudu* (chemical fertilisers, also known as *amedahe-du* or poor man's manure). Chemical fertilisers which the Government is now encouraging farmers to use instead of the traditional ones, are sold at heavily subsidised prices by the Ministry of Agriculture Extension Office at Anloga and also by local commercial firms. *Lavi*, derived from various species of fish, is obtained from the coastal towns and villages east of Anloga. Common species are 'abobi', *anchovie*, 'deyi', *sardinella sp.*, 'agbatsahe' mainly 'ngogbavi', *vomer gibbiceps*, and 'togo', *tilapia melanopleura*. All except the last named are obtained from the sea. Tilapia is the only lagoon fish used. For cow dung and bat droppings, however, the farmer has to travel to Tongu country and villages across the Keta Lagoon.

All the manures have specific functions to perform and are applied at different times of the season. The cow dung, always applied before the seeds are planted, has the dual function of accelerating germination of the seeds as well as enlarging the bulbs. *Lavi*, which may be scattered on the beds before sowing or applied soon after germination, is mainly to help sustain steady growth while the *druimi* and chemical fertilisers mainly develop the stalk and are usually applied a few weeks after germination. It is not necessary to apply all in one season and therefore a series of permutations are used to prevent unnecessary expenditure and excessive manuring. Thus, whereas cow dung is used by all every season, *druimi* and fertilisers may not be applied together because they are known to perform largely the same function. The seasons also affect the type of combinations used. Chemical fertilisers for instance are not applied during the *Kele* season because they lead to excessive heat which is harmful to the crop, but are instead recommended for *Fenu*, the season of heavy rainfall.

The shallot beds require attention throughout the life of the crop, and the addition of manures before sowing and after germination of the seeds has already been mentioned. Even before the seeds are planted, three different types of hoeing take place. Other important activities are weeding, watering and *bomelele*, which means 'breaking the surface'.

66 *CHANGING SOCIAL STRUCTURE IN GHANA*

Two weeks after sowing *lavi* is scattered on the beds and a stick is used
to push it into the soil. Soon afterwards the weeds which have germinated
with the seeds are cleared from the beds to prevent them both from choking
the young crop and competing with it for the manure. This is repeated
if more weeds have grown before the crop begins to mature. And as we have
already seen, during the dry season of *Fedomi* and also in the other seasons
when the rains fall, watering of the beds becomes necessary. *Bomelele* is
done during the rainy season when there is sign of water-logging. The top
soil between the plants is loosened by hand. This loosening is also
necessary if the surface of the beds becomes hardened up during the dry
season due to the alternating effects of watering on the one hand and
heating and evaporation by the sun on the other.

The harvest also brings a new set of activities in its wake. The
harvested crop is left to dry on the farm for two or three days, but many
farmers now prefer to remove it home the same day for fear of thieves whose
activities have increased in recent years. Failing that a night watch is
arranged with friends and neighbours around the farm. The shallots are
then taken home by members of the family assisted by women hired from the
vicinity of the farm. At home they are left under the sun for about a week
for the leaves to be throughly dried. The bigger bulbs are carefully
selected and tied into bundles for sale at Anloga and Keta markets from
where they are exported to Accra and other parts of the country. The
smaller ones, on the other hand, are kept on ceilings of living rooms and
kitchens made with woven palm branches and reeds known as *agbake* to be
used in future as seeds.

A bundle of shallots weighs about thirty pounds and may cost between
2 and 8 depending on the size of the bulbs and nature of the harvest
as a whole in the season. No weights are used, but the farmer by experience
knows the number of bulbs to tie together to get the correct weight. A
government move to introduce a system of weighing in being strongly resisted
because this will disregard the size of the bulbs and their appearance in
fixing the price. But it is hoped that a system of grading which takes
note of these qualities will pave the way for weighing to be introduced.

It has not been easy to arrive at reliable tonnage of shallot products
and exports. Ministry of Agriculture figures quoted by Grove (1966:403)
show that it rose from around 322 tons per annum in 1941 to 1268 tons in
1955. These were based on returns of ferry depots and customs posts. While
all the shallots leaving Anloga have to pass through these posts, no
facilities exist for collecting information on tonnage and it is difficult
to understand how the figures were arrived at. Also since a large proportion
of the harvest is not sold but reserved as future seed any figures based
solely on the finished product are bound to be misleading. Independent
investigation and calculation reveal that the 1970 crop amounted to around
22,000 tons. On this basis, the estimated 1500 acres of land under cultivation
will each yield about 15 tons a year which corresponds to the annual tonnage
per acre the Ministry now gives.

The wealth of farmers differs a good deal. Although the size of farms
is no index to wealth, on the whole richer farmers tend to have larger plots
than poorer ones. Figures given by the farmers themselves suggest that
rich farmers can make as much as £2000 gross in a vintage year while the
average in an ordinary year for the entire farming community may be put at

EFFECTS OF CASH CROPS ON AN EWE COMMUNITY 67

about £500 gross. But in an industry like shallot farming with heavy overhead expenses, the net income is quite low compared with the gross, sometimes falling below a third of the latter. In extremely bad years even heavy losses are incurred. Taken together, however, the industry is substantially profitable as can be seen from the life styles of the farmers.

Shallots and contemporary Anlo society

The cash the industry brings to Anloga farmers has no doubt introduced significant changes both in the landscape and their standard of living. Within the last three decades, storey buildings and bungalows, the goal of every ambitious Anlo youth, have replaced the old traditional mud huts. Secondary school education has suddenly erupted with a gigantic force to a level unknown anywhere in the Volta region. When this last point is considered alongside the slow progress education and Christianity made in their initial stages of development, the effect of shallots in this regard can be seen in its true perspective. Of all the main towns in Anlo, Anloga was the very last to embrace Christianity. From the very beginning the town rejected it because it was seen as a threat to the religious and cultural institutions of the town, which is not only the capital but also the cultural centre of Anlo. Thus it was not until 1906 that the Bremen Mission was able to open the first church in the town, over fifty years after Christianity and schools were brought to Keta. It is therefore a fantastic achievement on the part of Anloga that just within thirty years of the establishment of the first primary school there it should become the first town in what is now the Volta Region to open a secondary school. The Zion College, opened in 1937, owed nothing to the shallot industry for its establishment, but by drawing a large proportion of its students from the area, its development and consolidation as an institution of learning was indirectly affected by the new-found wealth of the local farmers. It also shows the seriousness with which the inhabitants took education once the initial obstacles were removed.

Today school education for boys is considered a matter of course, while nearly half the girls of primary school-going age are at school. And with ten primary and middle schools catering for over three thousand children the town has clearly become a major centre for primary education in the region. The number of secondary schools has now increased to two, both Government assisted, with the local teacher training college making three the number of institutions of higher learning in the town. There are now three institutions which all owe their establishment to local rather than governmental or missionary initiative as is the case in many parts of the country.

Another positive effect of the industry was to arrest the migratory tendency which was gathering momentum around the 1930's. As a result, contrary to the general trend in the area, the population of Anloga increased steadily from about 3000 in 1931 to 5000 in 1948 and 11000 in 1960. The advanced report of the 1970 census has put the new figure at 13000. While emigration is not altogether unknown to the town, there is very little evidence of it apart from the perennial exodus of school leavers for Accra and other large Ghanaian cities and towns. The reason is that despite the land shortage only those who loathe farming and hard work can complain of unemployment in the town. Although the majority

CHANGING SOCIAL STRUCTURE IN GHANA

of inhabitants are farmers and therefore need a reasonable portion of land for their livelihood, the prosperity generated by the industry's success has led to many subsidiary economic activities which are not dependent on land as such. There are, for instance, the farm hands whom almost every farmer needs during each major stage of the farming cycle. There are also the growing numbers of artisans, masons and carpenters, needed for the continuous building works going on in the town. Tailors and dressmakers are also very well placed for good patronage. Even private day nurseries have been opened to care for children of working mothers. Indeed with money around, any able-bodied person in town within certain limits will find something to do. Moreover, although the wages and general income levels of workers in Anloga compare favourably with those in Accra and other big cities, the cost of living is on the whole much cheaper. It is true that imported goods like sardines, corned beef, milk, sugar and beverages cost more here than in the cities, but this is more than offset by the ridiculously low cost of accommodation, locally grown foodstuffs and fish. In the slums of Accra, a single room may cost around 1 for those who have to rent one (and the majority live in family houses which are rent-free) while ten pence should be sufficient to provide a wholesome meal, perhaps with a lot more to spare. It is therefore no exaggeration to say that shallots have helped to stabilise Anloga society. The inhabitants of many Anlo towns and villages indeed point enviously at the lucky position of Anloga and what shallots have done to the town. If only their own home towns or villages could have a comparable industry that would afford them the opportunity to stay at home!

The town's contact with the outside world has also increased greatly. It is connected with both Accra and Ho, the regional capital, by daily mail service. The six-odd self-contained rooms built for the oil prospecting project, now temporarily abandoned, are presently used to augment the catering services of the existing Government rest houses. Nutritious qualities of local foodstuffs, already good in the past due to the abundance of vegetables and fish, have greatly improved with the addition of imported goods like tea, coffee, and milk. There is now a Government clinic in the town but serious cases have to be taken to the Government hospital at Keta twelve miles away. It is a significant mark of the people's wealth, though, that in the case of serious sickness they prefer to travel to private hospitals at Lome, Adidome or Dzodze, many miles away, where they pay large sums of money for services they could well obtain gratis in Keta. In fairness to the farmers, however, it must be mentioned that the Keta hospital, which serves the entire Anlo district, is always overcrowded and therefore service is not always efficient.

As far as the social structure itself is concerned, the changes follow the general pattern described elsewhere for the area (Nukunya 1969:162-208). The major difference here seems to be the presence of over one thousand post-elementary school pupils which certainly adds a new dimension to local social life. Although the teacher training college and one of the secondary schools are fully residential and the second secondary school partly so, their extra-curricular and outward activities cannot be totally divorced from the town's life. Regular visits to the town by the pupils as well as calls by parents, relatives and friends from outside Anloga all add up to make a less homogeneous population. This effect is increased by the presence of teachers and their families, over 90% of whom hail from outside

EFFECTS OF CASH CROPS ON AN EWE COMMUNITY

the Anloga area. Another change stems from the stability of Anloga population already, which makes households built around the nucleur family a more common feature of domestic organisation.

Against these developments may be mentioned the major drawback of the area, namely the ravages of the sea and the lagoons which disturb Anloga, and indeed all the settlements on the sea coast. Although Anloga town itself is quite safe, the damage done elsewhere, especially around Keta, affects every settlement. As we have already seen, the only access to the town by land is from the east through Denu and Keta. But every year in September when the surf becomes wildest and the lagoon overflows its banks, the only road linking these places becomes nearly impassable and sometimes has to be closed to motor traffic. Twice during the last decade, first in 1963 and again in 1969, it was necessary to close the road between Denu and Keta for more than a year. To offset this, a road is now under construction which will link Anloga with Dabala and Sogakofe. When completed, it should reduce the dependence on the eastern route and make Anloga and the entire coastal area less affected by climatic factors.

CONCLUSION

Shallot farming is an indigenous industry in the real sense of the term. The farmers are predominantly illiterate, but the high productivity and the skilled techniques evolved for the intensive cultivation of the crop have been acquired by their own efforts. In this way the system as a whole contradicts the argument often made by experts of agricultural development in the tropics that the main obstacle is the inability of the illiterate peasant farmer to respond positively to innovations due to his resistance to change. In Anloga, no doubt, the difficult environment and shortage of land have contributed to this development. Nonetheless, his achievement has shown that neither environmental limitations nor traditional attitudes should necessarily retard agricultural development.

It is also interesting to note that these developments have not necessarily resulted in any drastic tenurial changes. Whereas certain attitudes to land, such as alienation, have been altered, the position of descent groups and their leaders in the system have largely remained intact. The only real changes will occur if the threat to diverging transmission is sustained.

NOTES

1. Anlo is an Ewe-speaking chiefdom with a population of just over a quarter of a million and an area of 900 square miles. Their social structure is organised on a system of patrilineal descent which involves fifteen dispersed clans and numerous localised lineages. The author, an Anlo himself, did field work there in 1962-3, and has made many visits to the area since 1964. In this paper, emphasis has been placed on Anloga as a convenient way of looking at the problem because it is the centre of the industry and many of the points refer specifically to it. For instance it is the only town,strictly speaking,which has not yet experienced any massive emigration. However, shallot growing has long been an essential occupation of the inhabitants of Woe, though there, unlike Anloga, fishing is equally important. Other principal shallot growing centres now are Tegbi, Whuti and Dzita all of which have in a general way been affected by the changes described.

2. The earliest references to the poulty industry were by Johnson Whiteford (1877:73), and Governor Winiet in his Journal 1850.

3. The most accurage description of the salt industry in is Grove 1966: 386-90.

4. Agu is a town in the mountains in south central Togo from where the best seeds for the Anloga area are obtained.

5. For details of the inheritance system see Nukunya (1971:12-16), where it is claimed that diverging transmission applies to both self-acquired property and to clan or lineage property. Children take over their father's property after his death. Women remain managers and real owners of their share until their death when it passes to the children though the latter could be working this property while their mother lived. A woman's land is inherited by both sons and daughters. See also Bender (1971:76-81).

6. The property is shared among the wives whether they were living with their husbands at the time of his death or were divorced. The important consideration is that they must have children by the husband.

7. See for instance Ollennu (1958:256) for the case of 'Nunepeku and others versus Ametepe', where the agnates tried unsuccessfully to dispossess the maternal relative of the lineage property.

8. What Ollennu (1958:98) says of a pledge applies to the *woba* system: 'Its purpose essentially is not so much to hold the pledged property as security, as to have its use as interest on the amount borrowed or as profit upon the articles or goods lent or given on credit. Therefore when land or other property is pledged, the legal implication is that the pledgee may use it, and that he is not answerable to any deterioration which is the natural consequence of such use'.

9. The traditional Anlo calendar starts with the first full moon in January and ends with the last in December.

EFFECTS OF CASH CROPS ON AN EWE COMMUNITY

10. In spite of the cheap prices at which the fertilisers are sold many farmers complain that the bulbs for which they have been used rot very easily and could therefore not be preserved for a long time. As the seed shallots have to be kept for three to six months before planting, such bulbs do not make good seeds.

11. First of all weed and grass are cleared together with any remaining intercrops like corn and vegetables, all of which are then left to dry on the surface. Clearing of the beds in this way, known in Ewe as *nugaga*, which we prefer to call 'hoe-weeding' is done with a small hoe because it does not involve any deep movement of the soil. Actual hoeing, *nunonlo*, which follows one week later, is done with longer and stronger blades. The soil is moved about one foot upside down while the weeds are cleared and all live roots meticulously removed, but the dry weeds as well as any rubbish left on the bed are well dug in. *Nutotobo* and sowing then follow. *Nutotobo*, which is a mild form of deep hoeing, is an artistic exercise requiring plenty of care and diligence and undertaken only by the farmer himself or any-one well versed in the art. The bed is hoed in such a way as to make the surface very smooth and levelled, but in a dry season it also has the effect of shuffling the watered surface with the soil below. In this respect it may be said that shallot farming is in many ways an art. The neatly cut gutters, the smooth surface of the beds and the round-walled wells, all give a picturesque scenery to anyone observing the farms from a vantage point.

12. The size and appearance of the bulbs are the two qualities used in pricing shallots. The bulbs must not only be large and round, but they must also take a rosy-brown rather than light-grey appearance. One of the reasons why chemical fertilisers are not greatly favoured is their inability to produce this colour in the bulbs.

13. The Norddeutsche Mission, which was the first missionary group to operate in Anlo, was generally referred to as the Bremen Mission before other related churches joined them to form the Evangelical Presbyterian Church.

14. Throughout Eweland and Ghana, the schooling of girls was not considered important because of the belief that the kitchen, which was seen as their rightful place, did not require classroom education. It was only during the last few decades that the schooling of girls started to increase, but still their number falls far short of those of the boys at school.

15. Oil is known to exist off the Anloga sea coast, but its quantity has not yet been fully assessed. Exploratory work started in 1964 when dozens of living quarters for the workers were built, but work has been suspended since the overthrow of the Nkrumah regime. The buildings are now used as extensions of the Government Rest Houses.

FEMALE ROLES IN WEST AFRICAN TOWNS[1]

MARGARET PEIL

Introduction

While female participation in the urban labour force is lower in most parts of tropical Africa than in most developed countries, women in the coastal and forest belt towns from southern Ghana to southern Cameroon have a higher rate of economic activity than do women in most cities of Western Europe or America (Fogarty 1971:514-19). Female employment in West Africa increases rather than decreases with age and is also high for married women even though the fertility rate is among the highest in the world. Rather than being employed in clerical work or manufacturing, the high rate of activity in West African towns is due to the large number of women who are independent traders. Most of these traders are illiterate, since educated women can take up any of the white collar occupations open to men at the same rate of pay, but some educated women still prefer trading as providing opportunities for economic and social independence unmatched in other careers.

This paper is concerned with the interaction between economic and other roles in the lives of urban women in West Africa. The hypotheses are as follows:

1. Marital autonomy is related to economic independence and relative contribution to household expenses. Women who are able to support themselves have more autonomous marriages than housewives. The ordinary woman also has a more autonomous marriage than her elite sister, even though most of the latter are employed, because the former makes a comparatively greater contribution to the household.

2. Labour force participation is related to marital career and age in that older women have more autonomous marriages than young, newly married women. Husbands are concerned to establish control over their wives in the early stages of marriage and older women more often find greater freedom in polygynous marriage, divorce, or widowhood.

3. Women's social life (a) expands with participation in the labour force and (b) is based more on interaction with family and kinsmen and less on formal recreation than men's.

Data used include the wide literature on West African urban life, various national censuses, and sample censuses and interviews collected by the author in two Ghanaian and four Nigerian cities. Studies in Tema and Ashaiman (a planned port/industrial city and its 'free enterprise' suburb twenty miles from the Ghanaian capital) were carried out in 1968 and 1970. Almost identical schedules were used in 1972 in suburbs of Lagos and Kaduna (the federal capital of Nigeria and the former capital of the Northern Region) and in Abeokuta and Aba, large regional centres in the west and east respectively. In all cases, houses were selected by systematic sampling from a series of random starts and census data were collected on everyone living in the sample houses. (Most houses contain

74 *CHANGING SOCIAL STRUCTURE IN GHANA*

several households). Individuals to be interviewed were selected on a quota basis from the census sheets to ensure that various age, occupational, educational, religious, migratory and ethnic categories were represented. Although the numbers in each sample are relatively small (394 to 657 women in the censuses and 25 to 348 women interviewed), the possibility of confirming findings in several cities provides greater support than would a larger number of interviews in one location.

Economic Opportunities

It has been argued that the African woman is less well off in town than she was in the countryside. Schwarz (1972) points to the low income from trade, the high proportion who must depend on concubinage, the increased domination of the husband when the wife contributes nothing to the family's subsistence, the lack of security when she is deserted far from home. This may be an accurate picture of conditions in Kinshasa, where he did his study, but it is dangerous to generalise on the basis of one city or even one country. In some parts of Africa urban women may be limited to beer brewing and prostitution, but in most West African cities they have considerably wider occupational opportunities, more amenities and often less male dominance than in rural areas.

Women are usually self-employed and many do have a low income, but this may not be notably different from their husband's situation. (In the Nigerian towns studied, 43% of employed women interviewed earned less than 100 per year, but so did 23% of the employed men). Unlike East Africans, people in West Africa (especially the Yoruba and Hausa of Nigeria and the Akan and Ga of Ghana) are used to living in towns. Life in these towns may not be notably different from village life except that fewer people are farmers. Women have not been slow to take advantage of opportunities open to them, though the nature of their participation in the labour force depends on various background factors.

Table 2 shows the nature and extent of female participation in the labour force in various West African cities. Comparable data for major francophone cities have not been published, but available data suggest that participation there is lower, at least partly because men have traditionally dominated trading in these areas, aided by Islam. Meillassoux reports (1968:84) that women in Bamako have very few opportunities for earning money. Diop (1965:106) found that only 6% of the women he studied in Dakar were economically active.[2] However, Togo and Dahomey appear to be exceptions. Boserup reports (1970:188) that 66% of the women in Dahomean towns are in labour force. This and the data in Table 2 indicate that female employment is notably higher in the southern parts of states from Ghana to Cameroun than elsewhere in the area.

There is some evidence that rates are higher in the smaller marketing towns than in the capitals of these countries. In Ghana, women in Koforidua were more involved, especially as artisans, than women in Accra and the same was true in my 1968 Tema sample (68% in the labour force), though here more were in white-collar occupations. Participation in Abeokuta is higher than in Lagos and, in my 1972 samples, the same was true of Aba (62%), compared to 42% and 32% respectively of the women in the suburbs of Lagos and Kaduna. This higher participation in provincial centres partly reflects the norms of the rural areas, where most physically able

FEMALE ROLES IN WEST AFRICAN TOWNS

women are employed in subsistence farming and/or trade and also there are opportunities in the less congested and less regulated towns. Markets in Accra and Lagos are extremely crowded and only a small proportion of the women who want market stalls can get them. (When the aliens were expelled from Ghana, there were over 24,000 applicants for about 4000 vacated stalls in various towns). The extra women hawk their goods in the streets or set up a table near their house or anywhere that seems good for business. They sometimes have intermittent battles with policemen trying to enforce laws based on European ideas of urban order and cleanliness and ignoring local business norms. In the end, it is usually the women who win rather than the law, an indication of the former's power in the society. However, the large number of women traders and shortage of space does inhibit some women in the capitsl from trading.

In some areas, Islam also reduces urban women's opportunities are compared to rural women and to Christians. Muslims prefer to keep their wives within the compound, out of contact with other men. This is usually not possible in rural areas, where women are needed to help with the farming. But in towns and villages of predominantly Muslim areas, seclusion of women increases male status. While this rules out wage employment, it does not, at least among the Hausa, prevent the women from trading. Hill (1969) describes a system of house trade whereby grain is brought to the house by the husband and sold through a network of child messengers. Cohen (1969:65) reports the same use of children by Hausa women in Ibadan. Migrant women in towns such as Kaduna may not be able to engage in house trade because they have no access to child labour or because enough women are free to move about to make such a trade unnecessary (except to provide income for the secluded women). The participation rate for the suburb of Kaduna studied was four times as high as the more Islamized city proper. However, Islamic restrictions on participation appear to be much stronger in francophone than in anglophone West Africa. Muslim women in the four Nigerian towns I studied were more often in the labour force than Christian women; there was no difference in the two Ghanaian towns.

Participation in trade is not necessarily a woman's first choice; it depends on alternative opportunities and is thus related to the woman's education, age, marital status and length of residence in the town. Education provides alternatives to trading because many jobs require it, but some women with secondary education become successful market traders or shopkeepers and many women teachers and nurses do some trading on the side. In all four of the Nigerian towns studied, participation in trade increased and wage employment decreased with age, up to fifty when some women retire. Data from Dakar (cited by Boserup 1970:95) indicate the same pattern, though this study of market women showed a higher average age than occurs among the total population of traders because older women are more likely than the young to be stall holders, a mark of success in this field.

Most women marry early and, though they may have several husbands in turn, remain married during most of their reproductive years. Hence, age and marital status are closely related. Marital status affects labour force participation because of the husband's attitudes and because economic activity is seen as more important and more necessary at certain times in the life cycle. Women think of their occupation role as complementary to and not necessarily distinguishable from their roles as wife and mother,

76   *CHANGING SOCIAL STRUCTURE IN GHANA*

but sometimes these roles must take turns. Young women may be required by their husbands to leave wage employment on marriage because they resent the control of other men over their wives. Marris (1961:53) indicates that Yoruba husbands may not provide trading capital until they are sure the marriage will last, and other husbands prefer that their new wives do not work in order to establish dominance over them. Wives may see the first year of marriage as a 'year off', when they get used to being a wife and can devote themselves to their husbands. The next year or two are spent in being a full-time mother. Then they begin to think of returning to business in a small way, combining roles. The husband's enthusiasm for supporting them may dull in time, or a growing family require more income than the husband can provide. At any rate, women in their thirties increasingly turn to trade to improve their position. Some women barely stay solvent, but the successful ones gradually become wealthy and powerful. (Five per cent of the traders in the Nigerian samples were clearing 300 or more per year). These probably leave the running of the household to younger co-wives, relatives, or housemaids. Some divorce their husbands; others are already widows or divorcees who choose not to remarry because, 'What is man? I have my own money' (Ottenberg, quoted by LeVine 1966:191). Whether inside or outside of marriage, they live an independent life.

Clignet (1972:314) shows that labour force participation rates for single, divorced and separated women in Douala and Yaounde are twice as high as those for married women. The rate for single women is fairly low in the Nigerian samples (33%) because many were still in school, but the rates of 83%, 63% and 44% for the widowed or divorced and the polygynously and mongamously married respectively indicate that women who have no husband to support them are necessarily the most active and that polygynous marriage frees women from household duties, allowing them time for trading. In a sense, then, polygyny can be used to get the same benefits as a 'free' woman while following the societal norm of marriage and profiting from the protection and support of a husband. Polygynous husbands tend to be wealthier than those with only one wife and thus more able to provide trading capital for their wives. At the same time, services to them can be shared. It is easier in a polygynous than in a monogamous household to ensure that domestic duties and child care are attended to, so women traders in such households are under less pressure to defer to their roles as wife and mother.

Polygyny in Dakar seems to have a sometwhat different effect than in Nigeria, but the basic principles remain. Grandmaison (1973:100) shows that polygynous women in her Lebou sample were less likely to be in the labour force than the monogamously married. The difference was entirely in the wage-earning sector, and she goes on to show (1973:104-5) that women with enough education for salaried employment were unwilling to put up with a polygynous marriage. Since the Lebou women in polygynous marriages were slightly more likely to be trading than the monogamously married, the difference between Dakar and Nigerian cities may be due to the relatively small proportion of women in the former who trade rather than to a lack of opportunities for polygynous women.

However, trading provides a unique opportunity for all married women to adjust their involvement in the labour force to the needs of the home. American women often feel that they must stay at home because there would be no one to look after the children if they went out to work. In Eastern

FEMALE ROLES IN WEST AFRICAN TOWNS   77

Europe, the state provides supportive services to enable large-scale
participation by women in the labour force. In West Africa, there is no
state provision, but many families of very modest means have a housegirl
to help out (see below). Other women can trade from the house when the
children are young and gradually build up capital. When one child is old
enough to look after the others, the mother can move further from home for
supplies or sales. Working hours are completely adjustable; she can stop
for days or weeks if necessary and return to business as soon as conditions
permit so long as her capital is still intact. Thus, the conflict of roles
is minimised.

Local women are more active in trading than strangers, because the
former have learned the intricacies of the local situation from their
mothers and have networks of contacts to improve their chances of success.
Strangers more often go into prostitution, since this is not something
one does at home or, if they are educated, get wage employment as clerks,
teachers, or nurses.

There are usually relatively more women in professional and clerical
occupations in cities with lower female participation in the labour force
than in cities where more women are economically active (i.e. Monrovia and
Kaduna rather than Abeokuta and Accra). Widespread participation tends to
be of iliterate women engaged in trade; when there are fewer of these,
the women clerks and teachers provide a higher proportion of the labour
force. The chief constraint on this type of employment is the lack of
education for girls. At each stage of educational development, girls are
some years behind boys, so it is only when education becomes almost
universal that they catch up. Lagos and Accra are the only parts of their
countries where there are equal numbers of boys and girls in primary school,
and the proportions continuing beyond primary are still severely imbalanced.
The girl who is educated faces the same problem in finding wage employment
as her male counterpart, except that sexual favours may be expected in
lieu of a money bribe by the future employer.

Women are only occasionally employed as labourers, but increasingly
jobs are available in factories doing light assembly, hand finishing,
or as seamstresses. (Boserup's assertion to the contrary, 1970:112, is
out of date.) Some factories still hire no women at all; in others they
contribute over half the labour force. Such work is attractive because
it usually provides a better, and certainly a more secure, income than
trading, but women often leave when they marry because self employment in
trading or services allows more flexible hours for child care. Factories
do not provide nurseries and very few allow mothers to work different hours
to other workers. Although many seamstresses are illiterate, training in
sewing is often regarded as a fitting 'finish' to a primary education,
making the girl especially attractive as a wife. Established seamstresses
make additional income by training others, either informally on a small
scale or by setting up a 'School of Domestic Science' for ten to twenty
'apprentices' at a time. There were twenty four of these in Aba, a town
of about 300,000 inhabitants. Other women's skills of pot making, cloth
dyeing and weaving are more often practised in villages than in cities.

Services, on the other hand, are mostly limited to the towns. This
includes prostitution, hair plaiting, baby nurses and housemaids as well

78   *CHANGING SOCIAL STRUCTURE IN GHANA*

as a few women in the army and police forces. Prostitution is most important in towns with a severely imbalanced sex ratio, which is not as
characteristic of West as of East Africa. Of the cities in Table 2, only
those in Cameroun have a high rate of prostitution. This country had a
different colonial experience from that of the other four countries,
which may have encouraged this trade. The possibility of polygyny or
'befriending' (living together without any ceremony) and the ease of
divorce if a marriage is based on customary rites rather than a church
or civil ceremony (as are the great majority of West African marriages)
mean that prostitution is significant mainly to short-term urban residents
who do not wish to establish even a temporary alliance - mainly young men
who are saving up for eventual marriage and migrants from a long distance
who prefer to avoid expensive entanglements while in town. Women who
have divorced their husbands in spite of family disapproval may move to
town and practise prostitution while looking for another husband, since
rural norms make it difficult for them to live alone in a village.
Although some prostitutes have 'pilot boys' or madams who organize them,
most prostitution in West Africa is on a more casual basis. Since some
prostitutes trade and some traders provide occasional or regular
sexual services, it may be difficult in some cases to distinguish between
the two. School girls and clerks may also practise occasional prostitution
to increase their income. There is also a shading off from prostitution
to the more permanent status of a 'friend' or 'mutual consent' wife
(usually to a young man) or of 'outside wife' of someone whose position
or first wife's attitude condemns him to official monogamy. But such
relationships are not so common in Ghana or Nigeria as in Kinshasa;
only 2% of the women in the Nigerian samples and 1% of those in the
Ghanaian samples reported 'mutual consent' marriages.

At the bottom of the female economic hierarchy are the housemaids,
young girls living with urban families in the capacity of nurse girl for
the children,cleaner, runner of errands, and general dogsbody. They
make employment possible for the low income as well as the high income
housewife. Many of these girls are relatives who have been sent to town
in the hope that they will attend school, or at least be trained in
trading or some other skill. Where they are not relatives, they are
usually from the same village as the family they are staying with, but
there appears to be an increasing commercialisation of this field in
recent years. Whereas in the past girls were 'fostered' (E. Goody 1971)
and became part of the family, payment is now often made to the girl or
her family and she becomes an employee. There were several cases in the
Nigerian samples of housemaids from a different town and even a different
ethnic group than their employers. These girls are on call night and
day, and may spend long hours hawking goods for their mistress or
looking after the children while the mistress trades in the market.
Their pay (if any) is very low, but the system provides an outlet for
poor rural families who cannot afford to support all of their children
and for young girls who lack education, skills, or capital for trading.
A majority of the housemaids are under fifteen, and ·some are under
eight years of age. If a girl is lucky, she may be better fed than
at home, learn useful skills and make a good urban marriage. If she
is unlucky, she may be mistreated, ill-fed and miserable until she is
old enough to escape. In the past, family ties helped to ensure fair
treatment, since the whole family would be aware of what was going on.

Table 2: The Economically Active Female Labour Force in Selected Cities, Employed Only (Percentages)

Occupation	Ghana[a]			Nigeria[b]			Cameroun[c]		Sierra Leone[d]		Liberia[e]
	Accra	Kumasi	Koforidua	Lagos	Kaduna	Abeokuta	Yaounde	Douala	Freetown	Bo	Monrovia
Professional, technical	4.4	3.6	2.7	5.6	12.3	3.3	7.8	2.8	10.7	16.0	19.6
Managerial, admiristrative	0.4	0.1	0.0	0.3	0.8	0.1			0.8	0.0	4.2
Clerical	3.7	1.0	1.3	6.9	11.4	0.3	5.7	2.2	8.6	2.7	14.8
Sales	72.0	61.3	63.4	71.2	56.4	85.0	19.9	40.8	62.7	50.7	37.5
Farming, fishing, quarrying	0.9	11.9	9.9	0.4	1.6	0.5	26.5	12.9	1.6	19.4	4.0
Transport, communications	0.9	0.5	0.6	0.9	1.2	0.1	0.0	0.0	2.0	0.0	2.1
Craftsmen, labourers	12.1	14.8	18.2	6.9	8.9	9.5	11.2	15.7	9.1	9.7	8.3
Service, sport	5.5	6.8	4.5	7.8	7.4	1.2	28.8	25.6	3.8	1.5	9.5
Total	100.0	100.0	100.0	100.0	100.0	100.0	100.0	100.0	100.0	100.0	100.0
N	49,970	30,476	5819	69,072	2642	46,561	2718	14,477	9615	1028	2931
Economically active	52.0	51.4	64.3	44.0	7.8	62.3	63.4	65.4	23.8	7.8	13.4

Sources:
[a] 1960 Population Census of Ghana, Special Report A, Table 7. Age 15+

[b] 1963 Population Census of Nigeria, Tables 9G and 13; Lagos and Western State, Vol. 2, Tables 8B.2 and 2B.4. Abeokuta figures refer to Abeokuta Division, Urban. Age 15+

[c] 1962 sample census of Yaounde and 1964 census of Douala, unpublished. Data obtained from R. Clignet. Percent economically active from Clignet 1972:314. Age 15+

[d] 1963 Population Census of Sierra Leone, Vol. 3, Table H. Age 10+

[e] 1962 Census of Liberia, Tables 13B and 17B of PC-A4. Age 15+

80 *CHANGING SOCIAL STRUCTURE IN GHANA*

When the housemaid is not a relative, this sanction ceases, but there is evidence that girls can now leave one family for another.

Ethnographic background

How is it possible that such a large proportion of women should be free to engage in independent economic activity, in societies which are still overwhelmingly dominated by men and where the average married woman (and almost everyone is married) has six children? An examination of the position of women in these societies provides some clues to the factors favouring independent female economic activity. The Yoruba women of southwestern Nigeria have been called (LeVine 1966:191) Africa's most independent women. Although about half of the Yorubas are Muslims, seclusion of women has never been popular. Rather, their role as traders is so institutionalised that men expect their wives to be economically independent, providing for themselves and, if possible, contributing to the children's subsistence as well. Southall's comment (1963:55) that 'the traditional obligation to clothe and feed a wife has broken down....in Lagos' is based on a misunderstanding; Lagos women have a traditional obligation to clothe and feed themselves. A study by Galletti (1956:77) found that only 5% of Yoruba women in cocoa-farming families depended completely on their husbands for support. It is significant that the highest rate of female employment in the Nigerian samples was in Abeokuta, a traditional Yoruba town maintaining 'old ways' rather than a rapidly growing modern city. On the scale of female status devised by Sanday (1973), Yoruba women stand at the top, having material control, demand for their produce, political participation, solidarity groups and female deities holding general powers over both men and women. These factors are shown to be closely related to high public status of women in a society. In the Yoruba case, leaders of women's craft and trade guilds could be chiefs in their own right and had direct access to the *obas* (rulers) and thus considerable overt political power in the community as well as status distinct from their husbands and descent groups   (Lloyd 1968:68).

Ibo women of southeastern Nigeria have had a less privileged position. Their mobility as traders was limited in precolonial times, and their income was largely under male control. Their political influence was of the latent, 'behind the scenes' variety. Colonial rule brought peace and wider opportunities, which radically increased their economic standing and power within the household   (LeVine 1966:190; Ifeka-Moller 1973:318). The Aba women's riots of 1929 were largely organised by women traders who saw their income and new freedom threatened by taxes and who used widespread market contacts as efficient means of communication   (Gailey 1971). Ibo women are more ambivalent about trade than the Yoruba. It is suggested that women traders are unfaithful to their husbands and unsuccessful in child-rearing. (This happens elsewhere, but the Ibo seem to take it more seriously.) 'The role of trader is an emergent one for Onitsha women, not sharply separated from the role of wife, but its normative incompatibility with major features of both wife and mother roles...is fairly clearly conceptualized' (Henderson 1972:232). As a result of this ambivalence, women feel guilty about giving time to trade instead of domestic duties and take much less advantage of their financial independence than they might. Much of their wealth is contributed to their marital households, and they show a considerably greater dependence on their

FEMALE ROLES IN WEST AFRICAN TOWNS   81

husbands for decision making than do the Yoruba women.

Independence among Akan women is supported by a matrilineal inheritance system whereby children are the heirs of their mother's brothers
rather than of their fathers. The Queen Mother is an important figure
behind every *ohene* (ruler); she has considerable political influence
during his rule and holds a key role in the choice of a successor.
Women often continue to live in their lineage houses rather than joining
their husband's household. Ga women tend to live in separate sex households and pass material goods in the female line. Thus, both these
southern Ghanaian groups have a traditional independence of location
and action which facilitates trading and the maintenance of capital in
female hands. Like the Yoruba women, they are not under pressure to
pass on their profits to their husbands and thus are able to build up
substantial sums to further their business interests. Although many
women only make enough to provide for themselves, others can afford to
send children abroad for education. For both, a private income allows
autonomy which is often denied to married women in other countries.

As a result of their economic activity, these women play an important
role in modern politics, as they did in the past. The first female head
of the U.N. Security Council was a Liberian. Women were active in
independence movements, and there were several women Members of Parliament
in Ghana and Nigeria. Women chiefs in Sierra Leone have shown very
considerable political acumen, both in getting elected and in mobilising
economic and political resources to further their ends. Unlike the Western
model, Mende and Sherbo culture defines women as 'active and able for
leadership roles'. (Hoffer 1972:162). Ghanaian women are seldom chiefs,
but they have also demonstrated their political power. During the Nkrumah
regime the National Council of Ghana Women, mouthpiece of women traders,
was made an integral wing of the ruling party and was regularly consulted
on government decisions. Women traders in Kumasi were able to get leading
alien male traders deported and the rest moved out of the central market.
(Very few Ghanaian men trade in markets, as opposed to stores, so opposition
can be phrased in terms of locals versus aliens rather than women versus
men). In Nigeria, a government official complained, 'It is astonishing
to note that a good proportion of the economy of Ibadan City Area is being
owned and controlled by women and the so-called petty traders who own
most of the taxi-cabs and mini-buses plying the routes and erect most of
the decent buildings, and yet pay nothing to the local authority on these
property!' (Anon.1971)

Marriage

The most important roles from the standpoint of the women concerned
are those of wife and mother. The two roles are seen as practically
synonymous, since the childless wife has a hard time keeping a husband.
Women in towns marry somewhat later than those in rural areas, but almost
all women want to marry and have families which are large by present
European standards. How does living in towns and participating in the
labour force affect women's marriages?

The move to town is seldom taken by the women alone. She moves with,
or to join, her parents or husband and thus as someone in need of protection

CHANGING SOCIAL STRUCTURE IN GHANA

rather than as an independent person. Towns are seen as potentially dangerous places for 'respectable' young women, though an older woman who is already a successful trader or a divorcee or widow who does not want to return to her paternal home is allowed to make her own decisions. Since most women, therefore, are in town under the authority of a male, the norms of respect and obedience apply. However, urban women are under less constant pressure to conform to these norms. Husbands usually work away from home rather than with their wives on the farm. There is often no male present to take a decision, so the woman must do it. The urban woman is also released from the constant supervision of her husband's relatives, especially her mother-in-law. This means she has considerably greater freedom of action, which is further increased if she is able to support herself. Lucas (1973) reports that the married Midwestern Ibo women he interviewed in Lagos reported that their husbands made major decisions by themselves in 18% of the households where the wife was working and 41% of those where the wife was not working. A sample in the rural area from which they came, where all the women were farming, showed that 25% of the husbands took major decisions by themselves. Though these samples are small, the data suggest that women who stop working when they move to town lose status in the household, while women who continue to work may gain it.

However, the relationship between a woman's income and her marital independence is not a straightforward one. The level of her income relative to her husband's and the use to which it is put appear to be more important than the mere fact of her employment. Because of differential opportunities for earning money, illiterate women traders may have autonomous marriages, whereas educated women married to husbands with high incomes are more likely to have either syncratic or authoritarian marriages. Oppong (1970) has shown from her study of elite marriages in Accra that a woman's power position relative to her husband's is directly related to her contribution to household expenses. Where the wife makes a substantial contribution relative to her husband's there is a greater chance that decisions are reached democratically; where the wife makes little or no contribution (because she has no income or is unwilling to use it for household expenses), the husband usually makes decisions autocratically. The same is true wherever the husband is considerably older than his wife or has considerably more educational or occupational status than she does, but economic contributions seem to be most important. Equality in these factors fosters syncratic decision making. However, the lower the educational level of the spouses, the greater the substitution of automatic for syncratic decision making - each spouse goes his/her own way, making decisions in their own sphere. It is this pattern which characterises average, as opposed to elite, urban marriages where the wife is employed.

Barnard suggests (1968:157) that teachers' wives in Kinshasa must be more submissive than rural wives because their status depends on their husbands. In West Africa, as in Europe, the elite wife must often put up with her husband's authoritarianism because she is dependent on him for maintaining her standard of living. Teachers and nurses earn far

FEMALE ROLES IN WEST AFRICAN TOWNS

less than their doctor or lawyer husbands. Even if she were allowed to keep the children after a divorce (likely only for the matrilineal Akan), she could not afford special schooling for them, a car, entertainment and other perquisites of elite life. Ordinary women have much less to lose; they may be making a substantial contribution relative to their husband's and thus can demand more autonomy of decision making in the household. Those who have read about companionate marriage in the women's magazines and would like to try this European style may get some cooperation if the husband is at the same educational and economic level as themselves, but generally husbands do not like the loss of authority implied in syncratic marrage. Marris (1961:55) indicates that companionate marriage depends on the attachment of spouses to each other to the exclusion of kinsmen, and Oppong's evidence (1973) from Accra confirms that this is still a long way from the norm.

The amount and nature of autonomy can be traced in answers to a number of questions in the Nigerian urban surveys. Respondents were asked whom they would go to for help if they needed money or work or were in trouble with a kinsman or the police. They were also asked when they expected to go home and what they would do with an unexpected gift of 100. Answers to these questions provide data on attitudes toward husbands and willingness to take autonomous action. Generally, a large measure of dependence is evident, but autonomy does increase with age. Participation in the labour force does not necessarily increase autonomy; age and the level of income relative to the husband's are probably more important. Ibo women appear to be more dependent on their husbands than Yoruba women.

Women tend to be much more independent in their use of money than in other aspects of decision making. Even in an obviously autocratic marriage, when the husband would be consulted and his wishes obeyed for even relatively minor decisions, any money which a woman comes by is usually seen as hers to dispose of. Only a third of employed women reported that they contribute regularly to household expenses, though others do so indirectly by filling their own needs. Yoruba women expect to keep their profits for themselves, but help their husbands over financial difficulties (Marris 1961:53). Since either may need help suddenly, their mutual dependence helps to stabilise the marriage. However, lack of ability to reciprocate, to pay back what is seen as a debt, contributes to tension, especially if the debtor is the husband. A few women did say that they would consult their husbands about a sum as large as 100, but most would either use it for trade (45%); send at least part of it to relatives at home (17%); or spend it on clothing (for themselves and the children), food, or consumer goods (16%). These proportions varied little between the towns, and indicate that the norm of female employment has made women fairly autonomous in the domestic economic sphere, even though they are not themselves employed.

Only two women traders said they would give any of the money to their husbands and women teachers were more likely to say they would let their husbands decide on its use than were less educated housewives. Since 100 is a relatively smaller sum for the former than the latter, this finding indicates that the teachers were probably involved in more

CHANGING SOCIAL STRUCTURE IN GHANA

authoritarian marriages (several comments favour this hypothesis) and that economic autonomy is prevalent at lower economic levels of the society even where the wife has no income. Clignet (1970:142) reports that half of the women surveyed in Abidjan who were in the labour force had autonomous budgets, but so did a quarter of the housewives. Fraenkel (1964:131) reports that the head wife in a Kru household in Monrovia controls most of the household income in a manner similar to British working class housewives. Money received by the husband from various household members is turned over to her for subsistence expenses and distribution as trading capital. If the husband is away at sea, the money comes directly to her. Thus, even if the woman does not trade, she is still a major economic decision maker in the household.

Only three quarters of the Nigerian women who were living with their husbands would ask him for money if they needed it; others preferred to ask relatives or friends. Somewhat more would expect their husbands to get them out of trouble with the police. In this case, husbands were seen as responsible for them, in charge, etc. Although some wives would consult their husbands before seeking work, about half considered someone else more useful in helping them find work or in overcoming difficulties which arose while at work. (In the latter case, the husband would seldom be present at the work-place, but about half would consult him about it and some of these expect him to take an active part in settling the problem. This is most feasible where both work in the market or at home.)

Economic independence is not necessarily accompanied by socio-psychologic independence. Women who make their own economic decisions expect to be able to call on their husbands for help and advice in other spheres seen as belonging more properly to men. For example, in contrast to money decisions, women are considerably less autonomous in migration decisions. About half of the migrants reported that they had come specifically at someone's request, usually their husband's, and half of those currently married said that the decision to return home was their husband's, not theirs to make. A few had come to town after their husband's death to live with a son, indicating a felt need to come under male protection. They would return home only on the son's decision. However, there are also some older women who are determined to remain in town regardless of their husband's decision; in some cases, the husband had already gone home. This is partly because the wife would be expected to go to the husband's hometown rather than her own, and older women may not want to make the necessary adjustment. But there are some cases where a successful trader sees no reason to leave her business just because her husband is leaving town. By the time they reach menopause, many women have already lost out to a second, younger wife and others fear that this may happen. If they have children in town, these may be considered more reliable than the husbands. The result may be a divorce, or just a permanent separation.

It is impossible to get accurate figures on divorce, since some marriages (in some countries, the majority) break up without court proceedings which leave a record. But there is general agreement that many West African societies have high rates. Young women may leave the man their parents select in favour of their own choice. Older women may decide to 'retire' from marriage and live with a son

FEMALE ROLES IN WEST AFRICAN TOWNS 85

or return to their lineage home. Lloyd (1968:72) found rates of 2-5% per year in the Yoruba towns he studied. He points out that, among other things, divorce is increased by the lack of sex role identity (both men and women trade) and the women's ability to pay back the brideprice, which leaves their relatives with little reason to defend the marriage. Women's economic and political power gives rise to considerable jealousy within the marriage, frequent accusations of witchcraft (only women are witches) and fears of impotence on the part of males. Successful traders are considered witches by the Nupe and Ibo as well (Nadel, cited by LeVine 1966:190; Henderson 1972:214). Men expect considerable overt subservience from their wives in all these societies, and this may only increase the tension in households where the wife is economically more successful than her husband, or at least economically independent of him. The wife marries chiefly for children, and is quick to move to another if her husband cannot provide them. Yet, the husband's manhood is continually challenged by his wife's independence.

Akan women have a similarly high level of marital instability. The 1960 Ghana census listed 10.7% of urban Akan women as divorcees. If a woman does not choose to remarry, she is usually able to support herself, and obtains security from the support of her matrikin. Akan couples very seldom share finances. Rather than seeing her money supporting the household while the husband's money is sent to his mother and sisters, the wife keeps her income for her own use and to help her children, who cannot expect to inherit from their father (Oppong 1970). Ga women, who are more active traders than the Akan, had an urban divorce rate of 8%, lower than the Akan but nearly twice as high as the Ewe rate (4.3%). Ga married women live with their mothers and sisters and carry on household affairs as well as trade independently of their husbands. The husband's dominance is severely mediated in such a situation, and polygyny needn't provoke divorce, since the wives will not share accommodation. At the same time, the conjugal bond is relatively weak and easily broken.

Ewe women are engaged in the labour force to the same extent as Akan women, but have a higher proportion in the craftsmen and sales categories. Their divorce rates are lower because a strong patrilineal system transfers their ties to their husband's family and provides support for them within the marriage. They have more to lose through divorce, because the husband would send the children home to his patrilineage. In the Ga and Yoruba cases, the husband's family tends to be nearby, so the children can be seen regularly after a divorce. Thus, it appears that the divorce rate has more to do with lineage ties than with labour force participation, though the latter is a contributing factor.

Divorce may be initiated by the husband because of his wife's independence, since men have fewer alternative sanctions than in the past. Wife beating is still possible at all levels of society, but it is probably less common in urban than in rural areas because urban women can use various resources to escape. Religious sanctions, formerly an important male resource, have been lost to widespread Christianity. Finally, and most important to marital stability, sanctions are weakened because the two spouses are now contributing the same thing,

86 *CHANGING SOCIAL STRUCTURE IN GHANA*

money rather than making complementary contributions to household subsistence. The woman who wants to 'play the field' without repaying the bride price leaves her husband little choice but to ignore it or divorce her (Falade 1963.)

Divorces tend to be more likely in polygynous than in monogamous marriages, though Lloyd (1968:76) contends that this is largely because there are more spouses in such marriages who may sue for divorce. A woman may divorce her husband for taking a second wife but if she aspires to be a big trader she may be grateful for a co-wife's assistance. Cooking of West African meals is a very time-consuming process (which is why so many Yoruba families buy meals from traders), and someone is needed to look after the children. However, the relegation of domestic tasks to a junior co-wife may cause trouble, as Henderson (1972:232) indicates for the Ibo: 'Onitsha society provides no clear normative standards.... for allocating tasks of child-rearing between wives, and this informal differentiation of roles therefore tends to create irreconcilable jealousies'. The situation seems to be resolved in Yoruba marriages by all the wives sharing both domestic duties and trading. Still, Grandmaison's evidence (1973:105) indicates that polygyny is most successful when all of the wives are at roughly the same economic level or where the oldest wife is the most successful economically, thus reinforcing her status in the household. The presence of a young, educated wife whose salaried employment gives her a higher economic standing within the household than her place in the age hierarchy would warrant is likely to lead to quarrels, accusations of witchcraft etc.

Clignet and Sween (1969:141) indicate that polygyny continues to have an important place in West African urban life among peoples who have traditionally been highly polygynous. In Abidjan, women as well as men find advantages in such marriages. While Ivorian men are using modern means (salaried employment) to attain a traditional end (polygyny), their wives are using traditional means (polygynous marriage) to attain modern ends (equality, independence of action). Even educated women may favour the role of senior wife because of the increased power it gives them, especially if the husband is wealthy. Thus, institutions can be modified rather than being discarded as the society modernises.

In other areas, such as southern Ghana, where the institution of polygyny has been less important, women use other means for improving their status and their educated and economically successful leaders have worked actively against polygyny. However, ordinary women may still find that it suits their needs. Men with only one wife may object to her economic activitiy because of the opportunities it gives to be sexually unfaithful. The large amount of time which must be spent obtaining supplies, travelling to markets and selling are taken as evidence of lack of concern for their husbands and children. Polygynous women find it easier to be away and to take a lover, since a man who has several wives watches them less closely than the man with only one. Thus, an active trader may find a polygynous marriage produces less role conflict than a monogamous one.

FEMALE ROLES IN WEST AFRICAN TOWNS   87

Social Life

The remaining role to be examined is the social one - women as
kinsmen, co-tenants, neighbours and friends. Data from surveys in
Ghana and Nigeria indicate that women have less contact with their relatives,
inside or outside the town, and participate less in formal associations
and organised recreation than men. Marital status has more effect on
social life than labour force participation.

Young and Willmott (1957) and similar studies in European and American
towns have given the impression that women are much more closely tied to
their kinsmen than men. This was clearly not the case in the Nigerian
cities I studied. Women have less time and money for moving about the
town to visit relatives and also visit home less often, though they may
stay longer once they get home. Housewives visit nearby relatives more
often than employed women, which indicates that an important difference
between Bethnal Green and Lagos is the proportion of wives who work.
Husbands often object to their wives visiting home, since such a visit
may be prolonged for several months and may lead to a divorce. Among
elite couples with official holiday time, it is not unusual for husband
and wife to take their holidays at different times and visit their own
villages separately. People further down the economic ladder are more
likely to come from the same village, and hence they might go home as
a family for Christmas. However, this is more possible for short than
for long-distance migrants, and visits home promote contacts with one's
family of origin which may be divisive for the marriage.

Women tend to leave family, clan and hometown associations to the
men. These associations are always men dominated, and women are valued
chiefly for their monetary contributions. When women join associations,
they tend to favour church and/or savings societies. While many church
societies have a mixed membership, others are run by and for the women.
Women have a more active role in running some religious organisations,
notably the independent sects, than is permitted them in Western-
oriented mission churches, which have the same male-dominant structure
as in Europe. Locally founded sects, on the other hand, may have
women prophetesses and a largely female management. Islam has little
place for women, so very few Muslim women can use religion as a social
outlet. Women's savings societies are an outgrowth of their economic
activities, and are particularly favoured by the older, illiterate
traders for whom commerce is a way of life.

Women consistently report slightly fewer friends than men, and married
women have fewer friends than the single, widowed or divorced. Young,
single girls have no difficulty leading an active social life if their
parents or guardians permit it. Most people agree that a single person
has more time for socialising and especially for institutionalised
recreation than married people, and there is sufficient shortage of
single women in most towns to ensure their popularity. Divorced women
sometimes migrate to towns to support themselves and find another husband,
and unmarried girls think of towns as providing social opportunities for
meeting a rich husband. Recreation with members of the opposite sex -
parties, drinking, dancing - is more common among young, single people
than in other sectors of the population (as in Europe), because the

CHANGING SOCIAL STRUCTURE IN GHANA

former have the time and inclination for such activities. Married women are too busy, and the norms of the community limit them largely to informal recreation with their husbands at home or with other women. Since recreation is customarily segregated by sex, spouses seldom go out together except to church. This reflects working class as opposed to middle or upper class practice in Europe , but characterises all levels of West African society, with a few elite exceptions.

When asked about acquaintances, women who were widowed or divorced were most likely to claim to greet a large number of neighbours and to know many of them well. Single women and the monogamously married often greet many of their neighbours, but are less likely to claim to known many of them well. Women living separately from their husbands and those in polygynous marriages are least likely to greet many people on the street, but more of them than of the others consider that they known many of their neighbours well. This may indicate a longer period of residence in the neighbourhood, or the fact that these women are mostly traders and thus see neighbours passing and talk with them. While data from Ghana suggest that marriage does not limit the range of contacts, the Nigerian data indicate that this is true for monogamous but not for polygynous marriages. Women in polygynous marriages consistently report fewer friends than other women. They may have less need to make friends in the community because their households tend to be large and self-sufficient. They can take turns going out for water or shopping rather than having to go every day themselves. They often find sufficient companionship among their co-wives.

Women are more likely than men to report friends among their co-tenants and neighbours, an indication of the greater concentration of their activities in and around the house. Many women trade or practise their craft at home, so even those who are economically active may have little opportunity to meet people living in other parts of the town. Apparently employment affects the composition of the friendship network rather than its size. There is no difference between housewives and employed women in the proportion having three or more friends or in the proportion who had friends they met at home or in the town, though of course working women also had friends they had met at work. However, working women are slightly more likely than housewives to see all of their friends daily. A woman sitting in the market or on the door step is probably more available for visiting than a woman busy in the compound. Her friends know where to find her, and may get into the habit of stopping for a chat.

CONCLUSION

The data indicates that participation in the labour force is a more important factor in a woman's marital than in her social adjustment, and that continuing customs of various ethnic groups are a more important influence on women's economic activity and the societal response to it than urbanisation or other factors of social change. The Ibo, who have only become active traders in this century, still feel guilty about neglecting their husbands and children. The Yoruba, among whom the practice is older, appear to have no qualms. This helps to explain the limited participation of Irish women in the labour force (Fogarty *et al*

FEMALE ROLES IN WEST AFRICAN TOWNS 89

1971:111) and may indicate the length of time it will take for American
and European women to fully adapt a norm of working outside the home.
Satisfactory adjustment to a career in addition to marriage is not just
a question of supportive services, important as these may be; it also
relies on societal attitudes, on both men's and women's concept of the
woman's role.

The hypotheses are only partially confirmed. A woman's participation
in domestic decision making is related to her own definition of her role
as wife and to her relative contribution to household expenses. By their
economic activities, women obtain increased power within the household
(Clignet 1970). But unlike the situation in the West Indies (Smith 1956),
in West Africa this does not appear to be associated with increased
marginality of men in the domestic situation. Occasionally, a woman
has to take over household support because her husband is ill or unemployed for a long period, but she usually continues to defer to him
in other than economic matters. He is still head of the household.
Women able to support their standard of living are often autonomous
in economic decisions, but tend to defer to their husbands for migration
decisions and to expect their husbands to take responsibility when
various problems arise. Many people prefer to leave troublesome
decisions to others; most women want a husband to lean on, who will
support them emotionally and physically even if financial support is
unnecessary. Therefore, urban women are demanding, and often getting,
a higher status, but usually not at the expense of their husband's
status. Women who are economically independent usually willingly
exchange deference for the status of wife and mother, a highly valued
one in these societies. This deference is, of course, supportive of
the husband's role as authority in the household and helps to stabili e
the marriage. The woman who prefers greater autonomy generally divorces
her husband or welcomes a polygynous marriage in which domestic duties
can be shared. Therefore, this improved position of women does not
necessarily lead to nuclear families or stronger emotional ties between
spouses (as forecast by Goode 1963), because traditional relationships
may prove just as functional and require less change on the part of the
actors.

Elite women in West Africa are like most married women in developed
countries in that they share their husband's status rather than taking
their status from their own achievements. They may prefer a companionate
or syncratic marriage, which they have been told is the European norm,
but often find themselves in an authoritarian one because they cannot
sustain an elite way of life without their husband's salary. There is
insufficient data to indicate whether this lowers the divorce rate in
the elite sector of these societies.

Husbands do appear to show greater dominance early in marriage than
later, but it is difficult to trace the relationship between this and
women's greater economic activity later in life. Older women may re-
enter the labour force because of economic necessity, disillusionment
with marriage, a desire for greater independence, or just custom. They
are more likely than young women to have polygynous husbands or to be
widowed or divorced, and hence free for active trading. Data on
occupational and marital careers suggest that increased trading activity

90   *CHANGING SOCIAL STRUCTURE IN GHANA*

is more often a result than a cause of a loosening of the conjugal tie.

Finally, the average urban woman in West Africa has a satisfying, if quiet, social life; there are few signs of maladjustment or anomie. Most women lack the education which might make institutionalised recreation more attractive. A woman interacts less with kinsmen in town than she would at home, and some would count this as a benefit of urban living. The limited contacts with relatives (compared to men) may be due to lack of time resulting from the combination of career and marriage, but this is also affected by the transfer for natal lineage to husband's lineage which is symbolised by the marriage ceremony. In European society, where kinship is counted equally on both sides, marriage does not create this break.

Since West African cities are for most residents more like huge villages than something generically different, they do not find urbanisation a threat to their familiar way of life. Women's roles are not greatly changed by living in such cities. They participate in much the same sort of social and occupational life as they would have at home (though the occupation may be trading rather than farming and they may have more free time thanks to urban amenities) while enjoying the wider range of contacts which the town provides. Being a wife and mother is still of paramount importance, even though being a good wife and mother often means being a successful trader as well.

NOTES

1. I am grateful to the S.S.R.C. (Grant HR1527/1) and the Birmingham University Centre of West African Studies for supporting data collection in Nigeria and Ghana respectively. This paper was presented at the World Congress of the International Sociological Association in Toronto, Canada in August, 1974.

2. Grandmaison (1973:196) provides no total figure for the adult female population of Dakar, but estimates that only 6870 women were employed in 1965, 53% of them in wage employment. A quarter of the latter were domestics and 22% worked in factories. Most of the self-employed were traders.

RELIGION, SOCIAL CHANGE AND THE SOCIOLOGY OF CONVERSION

JACK GOODY

An oft-held view of the technologically less developed societies holds them to be marked by faith rather than rationality, custom rather than behaviour, by culture rather than society. Their commitment to norms is thought to be more intense, their solidarity more mechanical, their statuses more ascribed than in the contemporary West.

This characterisation has some smell of truth, though one must reject utterly the implication, upon which social anthropology, both of the professional and amateur variety, often insists, that such differences have anything to do with an entity, mode or process one might call primitive mentality or savage thought. Were this so, the rapid and radical changes that have taken place in Africa over the last two generations would have been impossible. Comments on the thought of other peoples are comments upon pan-human processes. The broad differences lie primarily, we suggest, on the level of the technology of the intellect, of the means of communication (J. Goody and Watt 1963).

In this paper Watt and I argued that the introduction of literacy increases, potentially at least, the role of scepticism. In the first place the recording in writing of myths, genealogies, and the names of saints makes it difficult for them to slip out of the cultural universe when they have done their job; they have to stay and be accounted for. We are cluttered with the debris of beliefs and customs of past ages, and cannot but be aware of the fact that the world was not always as it is. Secondly, when sceptical thoughts are fixed in writing, they become a starting point for further speculation on the nature of the universe, the objects of good government, the validity of a particular cure. Literacy is virtually the precondition for dissent groups, for revolution as distinct from mere rebellion.

But scepticism, while it can never be cumulative in the same way, is not absent from oral cultures. Nadel gives an example of such an attitude among the Nupe of Northern Nigeria when he is discussing the activities of masked dancers: 'This orthodox belief (that the mask is a spirit) is perhaps not shared equally by everybody. There is no doubt that there are sceptics among the onlookers, people who "know better", and who look down or pretend to look down on the ceremony as an obsolete and slightly ridiculous hocus-pocus. But once the mask comes near to them and bends its huge body over them, all scepticism seems gone, and they run away as fast as they can - they laugh, some of them at least, but they run nevertheless. And when I tried to test the seriousness with which they regarded this make-believe of masks and spirits, and offered food to the dancer in the mask (whom I knew very well), everybody at once commented on my *faux pas*, and was anxious to inform me that, as I ought to have known by then, "spirits don't eat"' (1935:437-8).

The Nupe lie on the fringes of the Islamic world and are certainly influenced by literate means of communication. But other observers have made similar comments about the societies in which they have worked, including Fortes on the Tallensi of Northern Ghana and Douglas on the Lele

92   *CHANGING SOCIAL STRUCTURE IN GHANA*

of Kasai (1963:256).

Scepticism is not a frame of mind, an intellectual reaction, that is confined to advanced societies. Indeed, it is not a frame of mind at all, but rather an attitude towards particular issues. A man may be sceptical about one aspect of the set of cultural beliefs he has inherited, and not at all about the rest of his intellectual capital. This is indeed the state of most of us most of the time. But sceptical attitudes come most to the fore in connection with magico-religious practices and beliefs. Even some of the great religious works contained within their pages seeds of doubt. In his book entitled The Sceptics of the Old Testament, E.J. Dillon wrote: "'Agur' Job ' and 'Koheleth' had outgrown the intellectual husks which a narrow, inadequate and erroneous account of God's dealings with man had caused to form around the minds of their countrymen, and they had the moral courage to put their words into harmony with their thoughts. Clearly perceiving that, whatever the sacerdotal class might say to the contrary, the political strength of the Hebrew people was spent and its religious ideas exploded, they sought to shift the centre of gravity from speculative theology to practical morality" (1895;ix-x). Were scepticism not common, the phenomena of conversion, apostasy, withdrawal and religious change, would not be as widespread as they are.

Scepticism, then, is not found only in modern society, despite the general idea that non-Europeans, 'primitive cultures', 'exotic societies', call them by what periphrasis you wish, are marked by magic, superstition and the rigidity of belief. Shrines are evaluated, among other things, for what they can and cannot do, in terms of their strength and weakness, the degree of power or efficacy. In many cases, no contradiction appears between claims and results, because both are phrased in ways which are incapable of being subjected to critical judgment; it is difficult to evaluate the efficacy of prayer when the aims are specified in vague terms of well-being and happiness. But in simpler as in more complex societies, much communication with supernatural agencies relates to concerns of a more specific kind, the fertility of a particular woman, the sickness of a particular child, the success of particular ventures, with one's own most pressing needs. In these affairs, judgments concerning the efficacy of the request (or of those aspects of a ritual that constitute such a request) are certainly subject to confirmation and disconfirmation in any society at any time; it does not require any special attitude or mentality to see where and when failure occurred.

The result of such disconfirmation is often the adoption of new rites, new cults, new gods. I do not wish to maintain here that all religion is always in a state of flux, instability, change, that there are no permanent or even semi-permanent forms. Indeed I am not even sure how one would establish such a proposition. But I would argue, as I have done for Ashanti (1957) and would do for LoDagaa, and to some extent for the Gonja, that there is an area of religious behaviour which allows for disconfirmation; it allows for this because it has to, and this accounts (though it is only one possible way of accounting) for the search for new cults; anyhow the willingness to accept them should they appear on the scene.

Ashanti is a clear case. Not only did Islamic practices come in from the North, which was the main trade outlet for the external trade but also a whole variety of fetishistic imports. In addition to the imports them-

RELIGION AND THE SOCIOLOGY OF CONVERSION

93

selves, there was a process of continuous creation of gods (*obosom*)
going on within Ashanti itself. Of course, the actors themselves often
saw the process of creation as one of revelation; it was indeed the
discovery of some agency of which they had not previously been aware,
whether it came from outside or inside.

Meyerowitz has an interesting account of one such act of creation,
initially abortive, in her book, At the Court of an African King (1962).
It was at the time of the *Apo* ceremony, the local spring festival, that
the author met the Chief of Techiman about to set off to the village
of Akrofrom to witness, he said, 'the birth of a god' (1962:96).....'he
explained to me that a priest had recently been possessed by the
spirit of a god, who wished to be worshipped on earth and have a shrine
at Akrofrom. But the god's spirit had first to be called down from the
sky by the priest, an event which had been predicted to take place on
Friday or Saturday'. On Friday everyone assembled at the village;
the priest of the new god appeared in a variety of symbolic objects that
constitute the customary paraphernalia of priesthood in Ashanti;
> 'The spears, knives and daggers symbolized his god as a giver of
> life and death, the *nkotoba* (the clubs of authority of the gods),
> his power to kill trangressors, above all witches, and in war,
> the enemy. The python skin was the symbol of the god's renewal.
> The Akan gods of this type called *obosom*, of which there are
> scores, are believed to be the sons of the Supreme Being and act
> as intermediaries and deputies of the deity. They are the 'little
> gods' but each is treated in daily practice as though he were
> omnipotent, omniscient and omnipresent'.

On this occasion, although the priest appeared in his full regalia,
nothing happened; the god did not manifest itself in any recognisable
way. As time passed, the crowd became first impatient, then cross
and eventually dispersed, only to reassemble on another occasion. For
the god was bound to manifest itself in the end, since a large, well-
built hut had already been built, in the traditional style of a
sanctuary with the conical thatch extending right down to the ground.
The costs of the operation had topped £3U0, but it was reckoned to be
worth the investment. 'Do you not see,' remarked Mrs. Meyerowitz's
companion,
> 'the village will get all that and more through the god, if he proves
> to be powerful? For he will heal the sick and punish the witches
> and his fame will travel, and many people from all over the Gold
> Coast will come and be treated by the priest and will spend their
> money here. And then a school or dispensary can be built and many
> fine houses all around' (99).

The unfortunate priest had no luck that day and was a sorry sight;
Mrs. Meyerowitz describes him as 'obviously a case for the psychiatrist...
He was out for power and money to compensate an inferiority complex which
evident'. Despite the encouragement of priests from other and more
established shrines, nothing materialised. Indeed 'it took the priest
many more weeks and a whole month's assistance by Taa Kese's High-priest
before the god, Dimankoma ('creator of the world'), descended to earth'.
From then on the priest and the village did not look back.

94   *CHANGING SOCIAL STRUCTURE IN GHANA*

Thus the search for new deities, whether generated by scepticism or by the prospect of gain, may lead to the replacement of one cult by another of a rather similar, but nevertheless somewhat different kind. Variety and innovation creep in and consequently the religions of these societies are often the most changing features of their culture, although, unlike technological changes, there may be few repercussions for the rest of social life.

The processes at work are difficult to observe and analyse. They are difficult partly because the changes do not happen overnight, but only over the longer term. But they are not impossible to make out because not only does one encounter the process of invention at work, but there may also be official documents of various kinds bearing upon the recent history of these cults, enabling one to extend the time span over which even a non-literate society can be examined.

To illustrate one of these processes of invention, I turn to the LoDogaa. My friend Betchaara was talented in the verbal arts and at the same time a man who was rather isolated from the fellow members of his lineage in Birifu. But he travelled widely and had a reputation as a man well-informed on supernatural affairs. Down by the River Volta, where he kept a canoe to cross people over to the Upper Volta, he had a number of shrines which were neither 'ancestral' nor 'purchased' but 'created'. He got to know about these shrines from the *kontome*, the hill and water sprites, the beings of the wild, the so-called fairies or dwarfs that appear in most African cultures throughout the world. These creatures are themselves innovators in a real sense, at least as far as man is concerned. For the LoDagaa (at least in the Bagre myth) it was they who taught mankind, in the shape of the Younger One *(to ble)*, how to make a boat, cook food, make iron, shoot with a bow and arrow, indeed taught mankind all the attributes of culture, except one thing alone, the way to procreate. The process of creation was first carried out by God, the High God, but man, or rather woman, became acquainted with human techniques by observing the natural world, in fact, the copulation of snakes. But then procreation may be said to fall within the domain of nature rather than culture.

The beings of the wild, then, are innovators. For the LoDagaa themselves it would be as difficult to assess the extent to which they were acting independently of God, as it would be for a Christian trying to assess the relative contribution of God and man to the invention, say, of penicillin (to take an invention with which God can unambiguously indentify himself) or a set of events such as the evacuation of the British Army from Dunkirk (to take a national example that partakes of the same qualities). Nevertheless they were the specific mediators of these innovations; they brought them to man, and revealed them to the first human being while he was lost in the woods, in the wild places uninhabited by man. For in LoDagaa religious thought, it is the Earth shrine that is specifically connected with the cultivated land and the *kontome* who are associated with the hills, rivers and trees that lie beyond. However, it would be a mistake to make this attractive (and, I think, recognised) dichotomy, too bald, too rigid. Even here the oppositions are more shaded, more subtle than many 'structural' models of binary classifications allow; indeed altogether more like the thought of modern man (the receptor

RELIGION AND THE SOCIOLOGY OF CONVERSION   95

apparatus is after all the same) than the oppositions of the neo-
Durkheimians would suggest. The ritual area of each Earth shrine extends
in fact into the wilds, for all land is conceptually under the aegis of
such an altar. Moreover, the location of the Earth shrine is usually quite
easy to single out in the densely populated countryside of the LoDagaa, for
it consists of a clump of trees and bushes, an uncultivated grove which
during the dry season stands out in stark contrast to the reddish-brown
soil of the cultivated fields. Equally the beings of the wild encroach
upon the human habitat; indeed in the rooms of a large number of LoWiili
men and women, the most prominent features are the mud figures of the
shrine to these beings, whose eyes of cowrie shells flicker in the half-
light of the cooking fires. And in some cases special houses are built
outside the main compound for these beings, which is also done, it should
be noted, for those dead animals that continue to trouble the hunter.
Building a house for such 'black' animals can be interpreted as bringing
them into the world of men, taming them by association with the cultivated
land, with house and home, with the ritual area. The same may well be true
of the beings of the wild, but I am unsure how much comments of this kind,
though beloved by anthropologists, add to the original statement, since it
is difficult to see how else man could bring supernatural agencies under
control other than by this process of domestication.

In part, then, these beings of the wild are innovators because they
are distinct from human society; they are the importers of new messages,
new techniques from the outside world. But the messages they import are
not only about hunting game or sowing seed; they are also about the outside world generally, at least in its non-human aspects. In the process
of getting lost in the woods, men have revealed to them new shrines, new
rituals. The rites of the Bagre society came in just this way. So, too,
according to Betchaara, did the shrines he had set up near the River
Volta. While these beings are often helpful to man, they are in many ways
suspect, often behaving like more serious versions of Puck and deceiving
man into misguided actions. Nonetheless they are one of the means by
which men discover a kind of 'truth' *(yil miong)*. In particular, it is
the *kontome*, the beings of the wild, who enable a diviner to comprehend
the dreams and problems his clients bring him and to indicate the supernatural solutions for the ills of mankind. Since in many cases such
'solutions' signally fail to solve the problems of the diviner's clients,
the possibility of scepticism at once raises its head. In some cases the
diviner himself can provide an answer by supplying, through a further
divining session, the name of another agency to be appeased, for a
particular trouble may have a multiplicity of causes, one of which may
be masking another. Alternatively, and more usually, the client will
turn to another diviner, possibly a distant specialist in another village,
possibly one that practises a different form of divination, anyhow one
where an element of 'distance", of difference, is present. In this case
the client may attribute the failure of the first consultation to the
diviner's inability to interpret the signs, to the means which he is
employing to discover the truth, or to the trickery of the beings are
advising him.

The scepticism of oral man, which arises in the context of the inevitable element of disconfirmation in magico-religious solutions to specific
problems, often results in a search after new diviners, new types of

96 *CHANGING SOCIAL STRUCTURE IN GHANA*

divination or, more usually, new deities to replace the God that failed. What is true of solutions for diseases, infertility and the failure of crops is also true for witchcraft. Witchcraft is ever-present as a means of explaining sickness or death, though it has no monopoly of evil, as some accounts have tended to suggest. Men seek protection against attack by the use of such mystical powers, but witchcraft and sorcery constantly reappear, even when one resorts to witchcraft in an attempt to combat witchcraft. The Gonja place some trust in the powers of chiefs to ward off attacks by members of their political community, but nevertheless outbreaks occur and individuals are accused (E. Goody 1970). But such accusations, cathartic as they may be from many standpoints, do not banish the threat of witchcraft from the community, any more than the healing churches succeed in vanquishing, at least in a material sense, the range of diseases known to man. Hence when any cult is heard of that gives hope of banishing witchcraft, or at least of modifying its effects, it is likely to receive a warm welcome, even though it is of foreign extraction and carries with it theological and conceptual aspects that do not altogether conform to local custom and belief, to the world view of the hosts.

A cult of just such a kind was the cult of Na-angminle, that spread through the Upper Volta and the north-west of Ghana in 1952. The spread of Na-angminle was a 'non-processual' event *par excellence*. Its advent into the Upper Volta achieved a success that alarmed the French authorities, who in their turn warned their English neighbours in what was then the Gold Coast; at this time, when independence was in the air, there was a certain community of interest among administrators against plagues, natural and supernatural, that were perceived as common threats, though the two parties had been at war with one another a few years earlier and even now rejoiced at each other's misfortunes in dealing with the local inhabitants, attributing their failures to the policies (direct as against indirect rule, integration with the metropolitan culture as against local development, forced labour as against taxes) which their neighbours were intent upon pursuing.

The news of this cult reached the Lawra district in September, 1952. It was spread by travellers, who brought surprising tales of miraculous cures. Soon the chiefs and headmen of most villages were involved in organising lorries to take themselves and their people to the Upper Volta in order to be purged and protected. The Chief of Birifu, who attended primary school, had become a dispenser in a clinic, and was a local leader of the revolutionary Convention Peoples Party (CPP) that was taking the country to independence, led truckloads of his men the hundred miles or so to Tumu, just south of the northern border of Ghana. There he stayed the night with his paternal half-brother Kumboono, who was prominent in the party that opposed the CPP. Using Tumu as a base, he took his people across the border to have their sins washed away and their futures made secure.

The rush for 'the little God' began in September, 1952. When I arrived in Tom on October 2nd, 1952, Nibe, the headman of Zendagon had already gone to 'the town of the little God', the Sisala village of Najo in the Upper Volta, accompanied by two paternal half-brothers and a brother's son. On the following day, the Chief of Tom set out and other chiefs and headmen in the Jirapa, Duuri, Birifu and Zambor areas followed, together with

RELIGION AND THE SOCIOLOGY OF CONVERSION   97

contingents from their villages   (J. Goody 1952:L2421).

After five days Nibe returned. The reason he and other chiefs had
gone was to acquire protection against possible vengeance by mystical
means. In the old days, chiefs took people's cattle, explained Nibe,
and this new shrine *(tiib)* protects you against the vengeance of the
dispossessed. But before the medicine associated with the shrine could
be effective, a man had to rid himself of the animals wrongfully acquired
by driving them into the woods - as an act of 'confession' similar to
that a witch had to undergo in order to get the protection she needed
against counter-measures.

The chiefs to which Nibe referred were 'the white man's chiefs'
(nasaal na), appointed by the administration. In the pre-colonial period
this area had known only 'men of influence', though they too might become
rich by successful seizure. It is important to realise that the LoDogaa
would differentiate between seizure *(faa)* and theft *(zu)*; thieving was
in secret, from kin, seizure was open and from outsiders. ˙ Theft was
always punished, but seizure was usually seen as retaliation, as a way
of reclaiming a 'debt', recognised by both parties.

The new chiefs had many duties to perform on behalf of the government,
for they were an essential link in the political organisation. The handful of British administrators and the small number of police and soldiers
could control the country from a military point of view largely because
of machine guns which had enabled them to conquer the country in the first
place. But they could do little to administer it without local collaboration
and an indigenous chain of command.

Apart from his function of receiving complaints from his people and
orders from the District Commissioner, a chief's main tasks were to settle
trouble cases and collect taxes. Both could be profitable undertakings
and indeed the 'new' chiefs of small areas in Northern Ghana, like Kayaani
of Tugu, Boiyong of Kwonyukwo, Gandaa of Birifu, Karbo of Lawra, all these
men became much wealthier in wives and cattle than the traditional chiefs
of the centralised states. As the former rose, the latter fell. For
example, when Gandaa died in 1950 he left 35 widows; at that time the
chief of Lawra was said to have 65 wives. I knew no-one in the long-
established state of Gonja with holdings in either women or cattle of
anything like the same extent. The largest 'harem' I knew of was that
of the Chief of Busunu, a man of comparable age to Gandaa and one who had
fought against Samori in 1897; it consisted of 13 wives. Compared with
the compound of this important sub-divisional chief of an ancient kingdom,
the dwellings of Kayaani, Gandaa and Karbo were vast palaces, though being
of mud they would fall down with their founder. And their investments in
cattle were immensely greater than those of their counterparts in Gonja.

The reasons for this great disparity were several. The centralised
states lived on trade, taxes and booty; for the chiefly estate, farming
was an occupation for slaves. Consequently when raiding and slaves were
suppressed, trade taken over by the Europeans, Syrians, Yoruba and Ashanti,
and taxation channelled into local treasuries, the traditional chiefs
found it difficult to maintain their status. Meanwhile, the acephalous
peoples, who had never been anything but farmers, were now able to produce
a certain surplus for sale and go off to work in the South for wages;

CHANGING SOCIAL STRUCTURE IN GHANA

their standard of living rose as that of Gonja fell, and with it rose the income of their chiefs, whom their people saw as offering some kind of protection against the outside world.

Secondly, the traditional chiefs had definite duties as well as rights. They could exact farmwork but had to give out hospitality. Moreover, out of their income they had to maintain a staff of advisers, drummers, followers of various kinds, who constituted not only an expense but also a series of partial checks against autocratic behaviour. The new chiefs had no such expenses. They copied their centralised neighbours in making demands upon the labour of their subjects; some of them contrived to make a good thing out of shrines, [2] others out of tax-collecting and court cases. But they had few restraints, traditional or otherwise, on their behaviour.

The position that had been built up by the 'new men' was threatened by political developments in the Gold Coast. Firstly, the post-war administration was staffed by younger men, ex-officers from the services, University graduates, men who were able, physically and temperamentally, to exercise more supervision than their predecessors, if only because they had cars and roads. Secondly, and more importantly, pressure from below and above was leading to a democrati ation of national and local government. The Native Authorities, composed entirely of chiefs, were giving way to Local Councils, with a majority of elected members. The first elections in Lawra were held in 1952; at these it was the young 'clerks' *(krachi)* who were returned to power, not the elders. Many of the chiefs felt their position threatened by the ballot, which could be seen as a possible instrument of retaliation in the hand of the aggrieved. [3]

During this period Na-angminle spread like wildfire. It soon had its own song in Dagaari:

Maa wo, maa wo, maa wo, n ma wooi
Confess, confess, confess, I don't confess,
Na-angminle ny sie nyhang nu puɔ
The little God catches a witch in his hand,
ko woro
And he confesses.

In many villages I visited at that time, people knew of it, joked about it, and told grave tales of what it had caused to happen. The 'mad' boy in Bonyiri's house was offered a protective bracelet associated with the cult: 'Ill have to ask my fellow witches,' he was said to have replied. My cook laughed quietly when he heard that the chief of Birifu and his senior headmen had become ill on their return from the shrine; 'There's something there', he noted. Down to earth comments were frequently heard about the chiefs who were rushing off to get absolution and protection.

It was difficult to 'place' the shrine of Na-angminle in terms of the traditional religion. Some said it was an old shrine which had been rediscovered. But certainly its effects were 'new', the mass pilgrimage, the sudden appeal, the destruction of property, the new norms. Some of these latter were of the traditional kind, but had a new twist to them. Men were forbidden to work on a Monday and women on Saturday, thus carefully avoiding the Christian Sunday and the Muslim Friday, but at the same time recognising the general shift from a six to a seven day week

RELIGION AND THE SOCIOLOGY OF CONVERSION   99

that has resulted from opportunities for wage employment and more generally
from the advent of a Mediterranean system for the social organisation of
time.

There were other prohibitions that were less consequential. When a
woman collected the shea-nuts she needed to make fat (shea-nut butter),
she had to put them straight in a basket, not pile them up on the ground
first and go on collecting. Otherwise, when she returned to the pile,
the nuts would change into cowrie shells and the woman would die. Firewood,
too, could not be piled up, but had to be cut and carried straight home.
These prohibitions clearly involved some measure of hardship, and in view
of the anti-witchcraft role of this shrine it is significant that they
bore on women rather than men. Just as it is significant that all cust-
odians of these shrines were men; it was they who gave a pejorative
meaning to the act of piling together, which was not, to the best of my
knowledge, present before. But otherwise the element of innovation in
these particular taboos was not great.

However, in some other respects, the shrine did herald, or confirm,
a change in morality. In the first place, it got rid of witches and
wizards, [4] and hence cleared the community of one major source of evil.
Many tales went around about its effectiveness. The headman, Nibe, told
me how three women had confessed to killing 80 people, and how one
supplicant had gone to have her fowl filled and it refused (i.e. it
fell on its belly). She became mad, went outside the room and shouted
hulloos. The custodian called everybody together and the woman confessed
to eating 24 people. She was sent home and told never to harm anyone
again.

Another woman was said to have left a half eaten corpse on her way
to the shrine and when the custodian accused her of this, she confessed.
He ordered her never to go back to that place, but she disobeyed him and
died when trying to touch the flesh ('meat').

While the anti-witchcraft element in these cults is 'new' in one
sense, it is so only because the problem of dealing with witches always
reappears and new means have to be evolved to combat it. The process is
in one respect cyclical, though each cult institutes some norms of its own.
In one way, however, the taboos of the 'little God' brought with it
elements of new moral behaviour. One injunction ran: 'If you steal
anything without asking, it will punish (catch) you.' Injunctions against
theft are not in themselves new; they characterise earlier shrines in
the area as firmly as they did the Ten Commandments of incoming Christianity. But, as we have seen, the new tenet appears to apply to 'seizure'
as well as 'theft', and hence to recognise the changes in local government
and social control that have emerged in the recent past. The new shrine
elaborates a new morality to cope with the changing situation.

In her account of the spread of Kabenga-benga among the Lele of the
Congo, Mary Douglas makes a similar point about the way in which the
cult was adopted. She remarks upon its rapid spread and upon the great
changes in ritual action that followed. Similar cults had risen and
fallen in the country, ten in the last fifty years. Their incidence
may certainly have increased owing to the suppression by the colonial

CHANGING SOCIAL STRUCTURE IN GHANA

authorities of the poison ordeal; a similar situation seems to have occurred in West Africa owing to a prohibition on the carrying of the corpse as a means of post-mortem divination. And certainly such cults do display signs of reaction to colonial rule. But they are not to be thought of only in terms of the 'new' situation created by recent culture contact; they are part of the traditional African scene, and an innovating element at that. They are part of a continuing struggle to deal with human problems and are not simply a manifestation of the colonial interchange.

The factors behind these cults are well brought out in Douglas' study of Kabenga-benga. She points to their financial aspects and how the original importers rapidly increase their investment if the cult catches on, but rightly, I think, see the internal pressures as the dominant ones. She writes: 'Certainly the Lele were not brought to adopt their cults from a childish, irrational credulity which swallowed the most wildly unlikely claims. They found themselves tempted to adopt it, in spite of a lively scepticism, from strong practical motives ... its interest to the Lele was its solution to pressing internal problems (1963:256-7).

Like the cargo cults of Melanesia, anti-witchcraft movement of this kind have often been regarded as arising out of the new situation that followed colonial over-rule, as a response to a rapidly changing situation. Many of the features of cargo cults and other such movements are indeed syncretistic in the sense that they incorporate elements from the colonial society with which they are in contact. But it would be most extraordinary if things were otherwise, that is, if new cults failed to incorporate in this manner. However, their 'newness' does not derive simply from the colonial situation. In the first place cultures throughout the world have been in constant contact with others, during the whole history of mankind, and even contact with literate cultures is no new thing for large areas of the globe. But in any case, as I have argued elsewhere (1961), the internal contradictions of much religious activity drive the actors to invent new cults, or to import them from outside, or to collect them by the kind of pagan pilgrimage that existed, for example, in many parts of northern Ghana, to Burukung in the Chiare hills, to the Dente shrine of Kratchi, to Senyon Kupo in Western Goja, to the Tong Hills of the Tallensi, to Nako Tong among the LoDagaa of the Upper Volta, and to a multitude of similar shrines scattered through the length and breadth of the region.

I would add that in accepting such a cult one is not simply accepting an identical addition to a supernatural array, A (1), A (2), A (N), and A (N other). For each shrine carries with it certain norms, which might vary from a limited prohibition, such as the avoidance of the meat of a certain animal, to a precept of a much more radical kind, such as 'All persons who die on Friday are witches and must be treated as such'. Consequently every new shrine that came into the community meant the introduction of some new behavioural norms, of greater or lesser significance. And it would also require some adaptation of the cosmological scheme; for such shrines are not just reduplications of each other; they do not necessarily fit neatly into a gap left by the departure of some unsuccessful cult; indeed the existing cult may be the subject of some quite violent take-over bid.

This interpretation of cults must call in question the view that religion is necessarily the most preserving, static and reactionary element

RELIGION AND THE SOCIOLOGY OF CONVERSION 101

in the social structure, the opiate of rulers and people alike. Certain aspects of religion are certainly conservative in this sense, but others are dynamic, innovatory; indeed in simple, relatively isolated societies, changes in the social system are perhaps more related to religious practice than to anything else, apart from the response to ecological changes and external attack.

These changes, then, are not simply of the cyclical kind that occur within domestic groups as individuals die and are replaced by others, as families expand and then contract (Fortes 1958). There is something of this aspect about these movements; they appear to be a regular feature certainly of West African religions. But while they are regular, they can also be instruments of change, of structural as well as organisational change.[5]

I have spoken of the religious changes that occur in non-literate societies, certainly those of West Africa, and of the internal dynamics of magico-religious systems which lead people to seek new cultural forms. It is the same impetus that led the Ashanti towards Islam (Wilks 1961) as led them to adopt new shrines from both outside and inside, though there were additional attractions behind Islam. But while the factors leading men to adopt Islam (or later Christianity) were similar, the results were very different. For the kinds of change that Islam introduces seem to derive largely, though not exclusively, from the fact that it is a religion of the book.

I will illustrate the role of literate (i.e. 'world' or 'universalistic') from the recent history of religious change among the LoDagaa. It was in 1906 that the White Fathers first moved south over the border from the Upper Volta and established themselves in the very north of the Gold Coast at the settlement of Navrongo in country inhabited by the Kassena and Nankanne peoples. They had moved south because they feared that their status in the French colonies might be upset as the result of the election of a secularly oriented government in France. A base in the British colony would allow them to supervise work in the Upper Volta as well as to extend their activities into new territories. The administration in the Northern Territories had been established only for a few years and was still largely military in tone and personnel. Civilians were not altogether welcome, particularly when they represented something of a challenge to the policies of the administration in that area. The Government had to start any new enterprises that needed to be initiated. It was in fact the army who, with local labour, built the roads, constructed the telephone system, erected the first hospitals, established administrative buildings and made the first halting efforts to provide schools. They even organised shops in Gambaga and Wa at which cloth and other imported items were sold to the people at large. Their policies were 'statist' and at times opposed to private enterprise. Not only did they prefer to run things their way, but they were particularly suspicious of missionaries. They had no desire for the north to become a battle ground between various Christian denominations, as had happened elsewhere in Africa.

Consequently, the White Fathers had little encouragement from the administration despite their introduction of English speaking priests. Nor did they receive much more encouragement from the inhabitants, and it

CHANGING SOCIAL STRUCTURE IN GHANA

was only slowly that they extended their following. The great breakthrough came in the early 1930's in the Dagarti (Dagaba) country in the north west. A small mission had been established at Jirap in the Gold Coast in November 1929. At first the mission had a limited following; suddenly there was a mass conversion. The process of religious change is often seen in terms of Paul's conversion on the road to Damascus, the illuminating vision of another supernatural order, the rejection of earlier beliefs, the radical re-ordering of one's existence. The reality is very different, save in the exceptional case.

In Jirapa in August of 1930 an old and moribund man was admitted to the hospital they had set up. Since he appeared to have some inclination towards the faith, he was baptised and given a medal. He was also given an injection of caffeine and much to everyone's surprise soon recovered, and the news of this miraculous cure spread rapidly around the neighbourhood. By June of the following year, there were 500 postulants. Then in September came the drought. There is often a dry spell in the middle of the farming season, and each year the LoDagaa consult diviners, sacrifice to shrines, seek various ways of bringing the rain. This year the usual remedies had failed and the Earth priest himself (according to one authority, at the suggestion of the old man who had come back to life) approached the missionaries to see if they could help. The White Fathers invited the delegation to pray to God, and it was as they were returning home that their fields were inundated with rain.[6]

Again the news sped around the countryside. In October, 2,240 persons arrived at the mission to seek help and acquire medals. By the end of the year, 7,000 individuals were being taught the catechism. During 1932, there were sometimes 10,000 people squatting around the mission building, and soon after other missions were established, in Kaleo (1932), Dissin (Upper Volta, 1932) and Nandom (1933).

Initially at least, there was no sudden shift in the world view of the LoDagaa involved. When the missionary prayed with them for rain, he explained that it was God (*Na-angmin*, that is, their God) who wanted them to turn to him and away from other agencies, a theme which is thoroughly in keeping with one theme in LoDagaa thought, as is brought out in the Bagre myth discussed below. Indeed for the LoDagaa or the Ashanti, the pull of Christianity or Islam is not a matter of converting the whole of one's religious beliefs from one set into another of a totally different order.

The diagram provided by I.M. Lewis in his introduction to Islam in Africa makes the point very clearly. Each level of supernatural agency has its counterpart in the 'pagan' religion (1966:66).

Traditional Categories and Cults	Islam
(Otiose) High God ----------------------> Allah
Ancestors (particularly where seen as part of High God hierarchy) --> The prophet, angels, saints, jinns
Nature, fertility and possession of spirits --> jinns, devils
Witchcraft, oracles, magic, divination ----> the same: *sihr*, etc.

RELIGION AND SOCIOLOGY OF CONVERSION   103

Most of the categories of existing beliefs are also present in Islam.
Moreover, the parallelism is based upon the actor's frame of reference;
I know of no society in West Africa which does not make an automatic
identification of their own High God with the Allah of the Muslims and
the Jehovah of the Christians. This process is not a matter of conversion
but of identification. Nevertheless, it prepares the ground for change,
here as elsewhere. For it is by the same process that Hinduism has spread
in India. 'By the technique of indentification each local or regional
apotheosis is equated with some more universal deity of the great tradition
.... Identification is perhaps the premier technique of the more inclusive
process which Srinivas has called 'Sanskritisation' (Marriott 1955:215).

The relative ease with which people move from one concept of the High
God to another is, I suggest, indicative of the possibility that such a
shift can take place not only between religions, as in conversion, but
also within religions. Indeed I have endeavored to show that in the
situation with which we are dealing, there is not as much difference as
one might suppose. The LoDagaa did not initially think of the acceptance
of Christianity as conversion, because the introduction of a new cult does
not involve a displacement of other gods. It is only when a religion says,
'Thou shalt have no other Gods but me', when it becomes exclusive, that
the problem of conversion arises, and this I suggest happens only with
literate religions.

The movement within religions that I am talking about is seen in
Meyerowitz's account of the 'birth of a god' which we examined earlier.
Here the new god actually takes on the name of the High God whom the
Ashanti usually think of as 'otiose', - in narrative terms, as driven
skywards by the pestles of women thrown high in the air as they pound their
yams (Rattray 1915:20). In this local manifestation, at least, the High
God becomes active rather than 'otiose'; he is able to kill and to cure
and does not simply create man and then sit on the sidelines. The same
is true of the shrine of Na-angminle whom the LoDagaa patronised so
vigorously in 1952. For Na-angmin (*le* is the diminutive) is the name of
the High God, normally so withdrawn from the universe he created (J. Goody
1962:209). Yet here again in the local manifestation he has become active
on a person to person basis, even curing witchcraft itself.

On the face of it, this Na-angminle cult is difficult to understand,
for the High God among the LoDagaa is usually far removed from man, the
Final Cause, the Heavens, Fate. The LoDagaa say you cannot kill a fowl
to God; he has no altar and there is no way of communicating with him.
But in the Na-angminle cult, they did kill fowl and make material objects
(e.g. bangles) associated with the shrine. I therefore tended to ascribe
this apparent change of role to syncretistic tendencies, to culture contact,
for did not the worship itself contain new ingredients derived from the
colonial situation? Here I fell into the same error as those who see in
cargo cults nothing more than a response to change. I mistakenly saw
LoDagaa religion as a static phenomenon and attributed the dynamic elements
in the religious sytem to contact with the outside.

The true situation became apparent to me only when I looked more closely
at the Bagre myth I had recorded (J. Goody 1972). For here quite a
different emphasis was placed upon the High God than emerged from other
LoDagaa religious practices which I had witnessed. There, as I have said,
God played a relatively unimportant part in the cosmology, in sacrifice

104   *CHANGING SOCIAL STRUCTURE IN GHANA*

and in prayer. But in the myth of the Black Bagre he played a central
role throughout and it is clear that, as in Ashanti religion, he is
seen as creating not only man but supernatural agencies as well (Rattray
1923:41). The whole content of the myth was much more theistic than was
the case in other ritual contexts. In the myth the intervention upon earth
of God the creator is always conceivable; but mostly he keeps clear of
humanity, as indeed the Final Cause must keep clear lest he be deemed to
have failed mankind. The dilemma is clearly revealed in the White Bagre
when God explains why he did not come down to earth.

> (the neophytes) said, 'Now,
> does God
> know about Bagre?'
> They asked
> and he replied, 'Yes,
> It was God
> who created us.
> Everything
> we say,
> he hears.
> Everything we do,
> he sees.
> Because
> he created us
> and knows all about us.
> And God
> told us
> he would have come
> for all to see,
> but the reason was,
> that if he came here,
> he could not do his work.
> For if anyone's kinsman
> were about to die,
> he would ask,
> 'Why does God kill (my) kinsman?'
> If someone's kinsman died,
> he would come
> and ask me to revive him.
> If someone was ill,
> they would come and ask me
> to cure the sickness.
> If someone
> is struck by another,
> he will come and say,
> 'Kill the man who struck me'.
> That is why,
> God
> doesn't want us
> to see him.
> He is near
> and yet far.
> That is why
> he said, 'Well,

RELIGION AND THE SOCIOLOGY OF CONVERSION   105

he would send a person
to come
who is more powerful than us all' (1972:197-8).

Thus the position of God among the LoDagaa reflects a dilemma of
which theistic theologians are as well aware as the rest of mankind.
Why does an all-powerful God not put everything to rights? From time
to time, a solution is sought; among other shrines and cults, there
arises one which claims that closer communion with God will expel demons,
cure sickness, perform miracles, just as Christ and Mahomet did. But
after a while mankind becomes disillusioned with this cult and turns to
another in an attempt to heal its wounds and solve its problems.[8] In
the swing between the active and the otiose lies an important dynamic
of religion; in the ambiguity of the creator God lies the possibility
of change.

The swing to Islam or Christianity can be seen as part of this process
of introducing a new cult and at the same time as bringing God into a more
active role. But having swung in that direction, there is less chance of
swinging back, because the priesthood (resting on literacy and higher
productivity) requires a rejection of alternatives. One cannot now place
one's faith directly in God's many creatures, only in God and his prophet
- though in both religions the saints leave some room for manoeuvre and
indeed provide an approximate equivalent to the polytheistic pantheon.
But there is always the Book, the Holy Scriptures, the Word of God, which
places limitations on the amount of play; though it does not totally
eliminate religious innovation, it does tend to confine it.

Religious systems, then, are less tightly structured than is often
supposed. Scepticism is not absent from traditional societies, though it
is literacy that makes it incremental. The failure of prediction, or the
advent of new problems, may lead to the rejection of old cults and the
adoption of new ones. The turnover of cults means the introduction of
new precepts, some of which can be regarded simply as replacements or
additions, whereas others may involve important changes in moral norms,
symbolic thought or ritual action.

Recent movements of this kind are not just a reaction to the advent
of Europeans, though they may have been influenced by such contact both in
content and in frequency. Rather they represent one solution to a constant
problem of religious systems, the failure of prediction. The initial
acceptance of world religions is often part of the open-endedness of non-
literate systems; it is only after this acceptance that the literate religion
attempts to impose a rejection of other cults and other forms of worship,
and that 'conversion' takes place.

A further factor making for the adoption of new cults is the ambiguous position of the otiose creator God, who is potentially able to
intervene in the world. New cults may claim to be able to approach him
directly to bring him back into the world. The advent of the world religions
falls into this pattern and the identification is easily made. But once
again, literacy prevents, or at least constrains, the return to more plural-
istic concepts, to a more flexible cosmology.

106 *CHANGING SOCIAL STRUCTURE IN GHANA*

A final and more general point. My discussion has concentrated upon religion in Ghana. But it has wider implications for the study of cargo cults, of conversion and incorporation (e.g. Sanskritisation) and of the implications of literacy. It implies too, that religious systems, that is, the totality of cosmology, supernatural agencies, forms of divination and worship, are not structured into some tightly formal pattern; there is more ambiguity, more flexibility, than the structuralist straight-jacket allows. Otherwise how would we account for the phenomenon of change which, as far as religion is concerned, can be found in traditional as well as in modern contexts, a function of *la pensée sauvage* as well as *la pensée domestiquée*.

NOTES

1. The Tong Na of the Tallensi is another such example (Fortes 1945:250ff); see also Eyre-Smith (1933).

2. e.g. The Glibdaana of the Tallensi and Gandaa, the chief of Birifu.

3. It should be added that both these pressures towards democratisation were largely external to the district, the pressure from below being mainly in Southern Ghana and that from above coming from the Colonial Office. The young 'clerks' received support because they were seen as the proper persons to deal with an essentially literate form of government. This at least was my impression as a Returning Officer in these elections.

4. I use the term wizard not for a male witch but, following Kluckhohn (1944), for a person supposed to be making mystical use of projectiles.

5. I do not wish to imply that there is any neat dichotomy between the two, but the distinction sometimes has a heuristic value as a signpost.

6. There are two published sources for the early history of the conversion of the LoDagaa, both in French and therefore mainly concerned with the establishment of the first mission among the LoDagaa in the Upper Volta, at Dissin in 1932. These publications are: J. Lesourd, Un peuple marche vers la lumière: les Dagari, Paris, 1939, and M. Paternot, Lumière sur la Volta, chez les Dagari, Paris, 1953. Both are written by White Fathers associated with the founding of the mission; both have introductions by Paul Claudel; the first is more factual, the second more imaginative. For a more recent treatment of the problem, see Albert A. Kuuire, The Christian Faith in the Dagarti Culture, Dissertion for the Licence in Catechetics and Pastoral Theology, presented at the Institute Lumen Vitae, Catholic University of Louvain, 1972.

7. Busia states that 'a god is but the mouthpiece of the Supreme Being' (1954:193).

8. Rattray quotes an old Ashanti priest, who put the situation with great clarity. 'We in Ashanti dare not worship the Sky God alone, or the Earth Goddess alone, or only one spirit. We have to protect ourselves against, and use when we can, the spirits of all things in the Sky and upon Earth' (1923:150).

ON THE SPREAD OF ANTI-WITCHCRAFT
CULTS IN MODERN ASANTE

M A L C O L M   Mc L E O D

A wide dissemination and proliferation of religious movements has been taken as characteristic of West African societies. Such movements, often spreading rapidly across tribal, political and linguistic boundaries, have received considerable, though sporadic attention in the literature (Morton-Williams 1956; Haliburton 1971); in this paper I wish to consider some of the factors involved in the spread of anti-witchcraft movements into modern (i.e. post-1896) Asante and to touch upon the relationship of these cults to wider aspects of social change.

Two broad theories have been put forward to explain the form, chronology and function of a number of movements reported from modern Asante which offered principally to protect their adherents from witchcraft and bad medicine and which specialised in catching witches. Ward and Fortes (to some extent supported by Tooth, Field and Debrunner)[1] have argued that such cults are 'new' (seemingly post-1930) and have principally arisen to meet needs generated by strains in the local matrilineage (*abusua*). Such strains, expressed in terms of witchcraft fears, accusations and confessions, are brought about by varying responses to colonial economic and social opportunities: old values of sharing and cooperation within the lineage becoming increasingly difficult to uphold. Goody rejects this view (J.R. Goody 1957), claims that strain and insecurity are not inevitable in colonial circumstances and suggests that the cults may be replacements for older methods of witchfinding. He also argues that the cults go far back into the pre-colonial period and that their recent efflorescence may be largely due to the extra time and money now available for 'religious' activities.

Before closer analysis can be made of these cults in relation to change, it is necessary to establish briefly the broad pattern of pre-colonial Asante religion. Traditionally Asante accepted that apart from lineage associated ancestors, there were three broad categories or levels of non-human powers beneath Nyame, the withdrawn Creator-God: the *abosom* ('gods'),*suman*, and *aduro*. The *abosom* were free ranging divinities who were thought to put themselves into contact with man from time to time by possessing individuals. In this way communication could be established between man and god and the wishes of each be made known to the other. Before this could be done fully and easily the seized man or woman had to be trained by established priests to become an *okomfo*: a possession priest. Such training was traditionally supposed to take seven years. Gods, and to some extent their *akomfo*, were associated with the wild bush which surrounded every Asante village and it was generally believed that *abosom* were both greedy and capricious beings, eager for the food of sacrificial offerings and likely to break off contact with men either on the death of a priest (instead of possessing a successor) or at any time during the priest's or priestess' life.

108 *CHANGING SOCIAL STRUCTURE IN GHANA*

The groups who sought aid and advice from these gods were not restricted in any definite way: individuals, kin groups, villages or even states might week aid from any *bosom* they wished and the fame of some of these free divinities drew supplicants from all over Asante and even from Coastal Akan areas. Equally allegiance could be transferred from one god to another at any time an individual wished.

The *suman* was an entity of a far lower level for, beside lacking the power of divining (because it did not possess people) it could be bought and sold, reproduced or destroyed at the will of its human owners. *Suman* ranged in power and cost from simple Koranic charms to complex conglomerations of materia mystica which were thought, when combined in the correct way, to have the power to effect definite but limited ends. Each *suman* was created or copied for specific purposes, e.g. to prevent theft, guard against cutlass wounds or protect a farm from wild beasts. Many *suman* also had names, although it was and is not unusual to find different types of *suman* made for different tasks bearing identical names(Rattray 1927;12)[2]. Most *suman* were activated and occasionally 'strengthened' by small sacrifices, e.g. of an egg.

Aduro, medicines, were and are the lowest level of this scale of power: the term covers both Western medicines (aspirin, penicillin, etc.) and herbal or arboreal preparations. Medicines, like *suman*, are acquired for money, or rather the secret of their preparation can be passed on in return for a monetary counter-prestation. Unlike *abosom* and most *suman*, they carry with them no associated prohibitions (*akyiwadie*), and require no offerings to be made to them.

As Goody suggests, there is fairly acceptable evidence to show that powers of some description, be they gods, *suman* or medicines, have long circulated within Asante and have also moved between the Northern savannah (the source of most recent anti-witchcraft cults) and the Akan forest areas. This itself is a phenomenon of some importance, serving to re-emphasise, if such re-emphasis is needed, that it is misleading to study the societies of this area in isolation. Yet neither Goody nor Ward is specific about the type of the powers they are discussing and this needs clarification. Firstly it is clear that many of the powers Goody notes as circulating in pre-colonial Asante were *abosom,*[3] although, as he stresses, minor *suman* and medicines have long been used as a money-making device by Northerners, especially Moslems, in Central Asante. Yet the 'new' powers, the anti-witchcraft powers like Tigari, Nana Tongo, Bosuana, do not fall easily into any of these categories. Such powers are made up of both a central *suman* and medicines (often sanctified kola nuts) which are eaten or drunk by those placing themselves under the cult's protection. Yet the central *suman* is ascribed a character of especial power, it is often personalised, believed to go about in a human form, often in Northern dress, and to catch witches. Sometimes it is said to possess its priests and it has limited power of foretelling the future. Such powers thus seem to differ in character from those discussed by Goody.

It is clear that the actual date of the appearance in Asante of these powers is of crucial importance to the interpretation to be placed on them. Although neither Goody nor Ward presents very many data to establish the basic chronology on which both their arguments turn, there is nevertheless a considerable amount of evidence available from both written and oral sources. I give this in extremely summary form below.

The first anti-witchcraft movement for which there is irrefutably clear

ANTI-WITCHCRAFT CULTS IN MODERN ASANTE 109

evidence was Abirewa (lit: 'the Old Woman') which sprang to sudden prominence in Asante in 1906 and was suppressed by the Colonial Government a short time later.[4] Spreading in a roughly North-South direction Abirewa (and linked Brogya and Bungulu cults) promised to protect those who took its medicine from witches and users of bad medicine. Its adherents had to keep a set of rules stressing cooperation with fellow-villagers and the leading of a virtuous life. Attacking witches or rule breakers were 'caught' by being made ill or killed. The movement quickly spread through almost all Asante and down to coastal Akan areas. Villages paid substantial sums to import the Abirewa *suman*, its associated medicines and to learn the correct rituals. There is some evidence that the cult was deliberately touted and spread by small groups of non-office holders (*mmerante*) and that some of the senior chiefs feared and opposed its introduction into their areas.

The missionary bodies then active in Asante saw this new 'religion' as a successful rival to their own proselytising which was at that date making very slow headway. They exerted pressure on the Colonial Administration and produced reports of torture and extortion in cases where 'witches' had been caught. They also brought to light the fact that 'slain' witches were mutilated and their bodies thrown into shallow graves. The administration fearing that such a pan-Asante movement, coming so soon after the Yaa Asantewaa war might take on anti-white features, quickly suppressed the new cult and destroyed its paraphernalia and shrines.

This suppression was everywhere effective, but the next 50 or 60 years in Asante saw the continual reappearance of very similar movements. At first the white Administration saw these as direct revivals of Abirewa which they closely resembled both in form and operation. Thus the cult Fwemso ('Watch over me'), active in the 1920's and several other cults were suppressed by Orders in Council on the grounds of extortion and torture (and because, of course, it was also considered that 'witchcraft' did not exist). Later cults like Tigari, Bosuana and Nana Tongo, all originating outside Asante, which managed to modify their procedure so as not to give offence in this way, were allowed to continue although closely watched and even licensed by both District Commissioners and Omanhene. They continue to be introduced into Asante today and they still operate by offering protection to those who eat or drink their medicine and by catching witches and other malefactors who, on becoming seriously ill, confess their misdeeds and are cleansed of them.

Thus it can be firmly established that the cults described by Ward as being 'new' in 1956 had, at that date, at least 50 years of history behind them. Individual cults may have been new, but we have to note that they represent a tradition going back at least until 1906. It therefore becomes difficult to ascribe these cults in any simple way to economic or lineage strains brought about by colonialism. We have either to argue that such strain was widespread and serious (or conceived by the Asante as serious) within less than ten years of the establishment of continuous British rule, or that other factors are involved. To support the simple strain hypothesis we would also, of course, have to argue that the strain was contained or channelled in some way after the suppression of Abirewa, burst out again in the 1920's and has continued at much the same level ever since.

The question remains as to whether these anti-witchcraft cults are a purely post-conquest phenomenon. A few scraps of evidence and a few vague oral traditions suggest that there may have been some sort of anti-Kumasi witchfinding movement active in the rather chaotic decades of the nineteenth

110 *CHANGING SOCIAL STRUCTURE IN GHANA*

century but the truth is obscure at this distance. Today the Yaa Asantewaa War marks the limit of direct human memory for present day Asante
and suppressed or decayed cults are not usually incorporated into formal
oral tradition in the way that chiefly-centred political events are.
Moreover the absence of a continuous succession of office holders for
most shrines and the deliberate suppression of knowledge of past witchcraft cases in Asante means that there is constantly a loss of knowledge
of these cults over the years.

Yet it is clear that to some extent these cults initially did provide
a substitute for earlier methods of witchfinding which had, by 1906, been
proscribed by the colonial government. Two methods of witchfinding are
recorded from the pre-white period. The first turned upon the chewing or
drinking a decoction of poisonuous *odum* bark (E. Guineense): if the poison
was vomited this was taken as a sign of innocence.[5] This was a formalised
procedure apparently controlled by chiefs. The second method, corpse-
carrying, seems to have occurred during situations of intense emotion at
the burial rites for a dead person.[6] The corpse itself, or hair and nail
clippings from it, were carried around the deceased's village on the heads
of bearers. The spirit (?sunsum) of the dead person possessed these bearers
and through them pointed out who was responsible for the dead. Both processes were suppressed by the white government and, although a few cases of
corpse-carrying were reported into the 1920's, this suppression seems to
have been well under way by the time of Abirewa's appearance. By that time
too, witchcraft had ceased to be recognised as a capital offence under the
new dispensation and the mere act of accusing someone of witchcraft was
considered an indictable offence by some District Commissioners.

It is difficult not to accept that Abirewa was to some extent a substitute
for earlier and abolished methods of witchfinding. Yet its rapid spread and
wide acceptance must also be linked with another feature of the early years
of British control: the deliberate weakening of the Asante political hierarchy.
Before 1896 Omanhene seem to have exercised, or tried to exercise, a degree
of control over the activities of *akomfo* and to have restricted the importation of new powers or medicines into their areas. In the same way they
seem to have restricted the free movement of medicine owners and sellers within and between states. These controlling powers, along with chiefship itself,
were weakened after 1896. The British kidnapped, deported, exiled, impris-
oned and outlawed many major and experienced political figures. In their
place they substituted their own deeply resented and inexperienced nominees,
most of whom had no right to the offices they accepted. Abirewa seem to
have been actively spread by non-office holders who seized the new opportunities for personal initiative in this field. Some chiefs seems to have
ineffectually tried to combat the movement which further reduced their power.
The opening up of communication between states, the weakening of chiefly
power and the abolition of earlier methods of witchfinding and the fact that
witchcraft was no longer considered an offence under colonial law, all these
created in 1906 a situation favourable to the rapid spread of Abirewa, a cult
which not only stressed traditional rules of amity and cooperation, but which
also brought considerable wealth to those who spread and owned it.

But changes in political control and investigatory procedure may create
a situation in which such cults might occur: they do not on their own explain
either why these cults originate outside the Asante area, or the mode of their
individual operations. While it is quite clear that these modern *suman*, such
as Abirewa, Nana Tongo, (the Tallensi Tong Naab), Tigari (from the Wa-Bole area),

ANTI-WITCHCRAFT CULTS IN MODERN ASANTE

Senyon Kupo (from Senyon near Bole), and other such movements are part of the common heritage of forest-savannah ritual cooperation outlined by Goody, were still have to account for the readiness of the Asante to accept powers from these areas and, further, to ascribe to them a character they do not have in their home land, and especially why lineage or general aid powers should take on such a predominantly anti-witchcraft role once imported into Asante.

In a broad sense it is clear that in a highly structured social order like Asante the prime source of new powers must mainly lie outside society and its accepted, formal boundaries. In the Asante case the unsocialised bush was clearly believed to be the place from which many new medicines and *abosom* originated, and the temples and priests of the latter were both, in their way, in some sense marginal to society: the former at the actual edge of villages, the latter free to behave in ways which violated many of the basic social and sexual rules of Asante. But to understand the crucial position of extra-Asante powers in combatting witchcraft, one has to understand both the relationship of witchcraft to the ideology of the local descent group and the whole order of the Asante universe: a universe in which the Asante conceive of themselves as occupying the central point.

A witch in Asante (*obayifo*, male and female, *bonsam*, male) is a person possessed of *bayi*, a non-material power which allows destructive attacks upon matrikin. Witches are thought to operate in companies (*fekuo*) organised on the hierarchy of ranks found in the Asante political system. These companies meet together periodically in tall trees at the edge of the bush to share victims which each member brings in turn. A witch can only kill and eat close matrikin, but can indirectly slay people from other groups by arranging an exchange with a witch from that lineage. Witches are thought to be mainly concerned with devouring 'blood' (*mogya*), with killing women and children, or causing miscarriages, abortions, and both male and female sterility. They may also be inspired by envy or jealousy to prevent people accumulating money, or to turn them into drunkards. The majority of witches are said to be women, although these are less destructive than the rarer type of male witch. Such female witches are said also to attack their own fertility and to kill their own children. The majority of people who confess to witchcraft at anti-witchcraft shrines are in fact women (about 7:1) and they mainly claim the sort of activities and desires outlined above. Witches are said to go about upside down, fly out or are carried at great speed on their *bayi* (which turns into a bush animal for this purpose), and betray their character by lumps, swellings and growths on their bodies and by unnatural facial hair in the case of women. The *bayi* is usually acquired as a gift, (often from a maternal or paternal grandmother) after birth, or picked up unwittingly in a bead or coin found lying in the pathway.

It is clear that the Asante concept of the witch includes several obvious elements of both physical and behavioral inversion: the *bayifo* walks upside down, goes out at night, moves about naked and consorts with wild bush animals rather than moving and behaving in the manner which all normal persons are supposed to do. But intertwined with these features are elements directly related to more specifically Asante values. It is clear that the prime characteristic ascribed to *abayifo* is their desire for blood and their related attacks on human reproduction. 'Blood' (*mogya*) in Asante thought has two aspects: the term refers both to the physical substance and to a particular and central set of social relations conceived of in terms of this substance. Blood is transmitted from women to child and matrilineally

112   *CHANGING SOCIAL STRUCTURE IN GHANA*

related groups are conceived of and referred to in terms of the transmission of this single blood. There is great formal emphasis placed on the need to continue the transmission of blood: girl children are valued far more highly than boys because they have the potential for continuing this transmission. The central characteristic of Asante witches is thus focussed on feminine fertility and the crucial importance of this to the matrilineal group. The strong links between witchcraft and feminine fertility can be also seen in the idea that *bayi* are most often kept in a woman's belly or vagina, the bodily areas associated with reproduction, or in her waist beads (*toma*) which support the red pubic cover cloth (*etam*) and are inextricably linked with female sexuality. Witches thus attack the very group on which they depend for their existence and to whom they are most closely tied. They thus reverse what is conceived as the most basic and vital bond in Asante social life: the matrilineal transmission of blood.

This intra-lineage maleficence, Asante believe, can only be combatted by imported and almost entirely Northern-based cults, which not only offer to catch witches (as did the earlier ordeals) but to protect those who subscribe to them from the activity of witches. Why should such powers as these be so continuously attributed to Northern *suman* during the last sixty or more years? It is a widely accepted stereotype in Asante that Northern societies are almost totally free from witchcraft and that this is ultimately due to their possession of powers like Senyon Kupo, Tigari, Bosuana, Nana Tongo etc. - even though these may be powers that have nothing to do with combatting witchcraft in their native areas.

It seems reasonable to relate these Asante beliefs to the position that the Northern grasslands (*serem*) hold in their cosmology and this, in turn, to the general Asante experience of the North. It is clear that there is an almost blatant and unavoidable contrast between the physical and social situation of the North and the central forest areas. The dry, open savannah contrasts strongly with the luxuriant, close-packed forest, and Northerners, with their entirely non-Akan languages, their facial scarifications, smock clothing, living in dispersed and often fortified settlements and having mainly patrilineal descent systems, represent to the Asante a type of society which differs from their own in almost every way they consider important. In the past Northerners were recruited as slaves for work in Asante and for sale on the Coast. Nowadays they provide nearly all the day or period labour for the jobs the Asante see as too menial or filthy to perform themselves. In allocating them such places in their society, the Asante are clearly treating them as less that fully human; they are despised and scorned and given tasks which no Asante will do. Yet this ascription is also part of the Asante willingness to ascribe to Northerners a freedom from witchcraft which they do not always have in practice. Witchcraft in Asante is directly and inextricably linked with the most highly rated values, even the basic premises of society. Witchcraft, all Asante acknowledge, is something which is liable to operate within the local matrilineal group. The correlate of this seems to be that Asante are willing to ascribe a lack of witchcraft to those societies which they see as being most different from their own - for if witchcraft centres around particular values and groupings of Asante life, then societies which lack these features should also lack witchcraft.

This attitude is sedulously encouraged and built upon by Northern immigrants who treat their eager Asante hosts and employers to elaborate tales of the power and efficacy of their gods, powers and medicines. There is thus a broad correlation on the one hand between the actual and social distance, the degree of perceived difference and political and social subjection to Asante, and, on the other hand, the mystical situations which Asante are willing to ascribe to the peoples concerned. While in the last two hundred years Asante has expanded militarily, politically, and economically at the expense of the savannah people, the latter have at the same time carried out a sort of reverse religious colonisation and exploitation of the forest. But such an exploitation can only be maintained so long as Asante knowledge of the North is sporadic, brief and kept on the level of stereotypes. Once direct experience increases and there develops a perception of Northerners as having comparable types of problem to those of the Asante, and even of all men living in society, then this attribution of special powers to their gods is weakened. Thus as the ease and regularity of travel increases, and with it direct and prolonged knowledge of the North, then so the Asante move further and further afield to seek new and untried medicines and powers from as yet scarcely known peoples. By the early 1960's anti-witchcraft powers were being sought and imported from as far away as the area to the north of Wogadougou, or even from Gao.

Thus beliefs about witchcraft and the ways it can be combatted are related both to the form and structure of Asante society and the derivative categorisation and evaluation of other social systems. Ordinary witchcraft is concerned with the supposed centre of each person's life, the lineage of which he is part, while the socially distinct North provides powers whereby it may be fought.

The importation and utilisation of these anti-witchcraft powers thus turns on a set of basic Asante attitudes. But particular cases also depend on actual contact between individual Asante and Northerners. These Northerners are almost always seasonal immigrants who year by year travel south to work on Asante farms or to seek menial jobs in the cities and towns of the forest region. Those who work on cocoa and other sorts of farms usually lodge with the same Asante families or in the same villages each year and it is in this way that they first make contact with Asante who are seeking mystical aid and reinforcement for their individual position. Thus the broad lines of the spread of these Northern-based cults, as Ward saw, loosely follow the pattern of new economic enterprises to the extent that these attract the largest numbers of immigrant workers purveying new powers. In the immigrant situation Northerners have few or no resources apart from their physical strength, their native wit and the chance to trade upon the firm Asante belief in their efficacy of the powers of their distant homeland. They enter a society eager to believe and whatever they may tell their avid listeners is, by definition, largely beyond contradiction or even doubt.

The history of one such cult based about six miles from Kumasi is typical of many such movements. A group of three brothers, all aged between thirty and forty, developed in the late 1940's a cocoa farm in the Brong Ahafo area. Within a year two died, neither having shown any earlier signs of illness or disease. The third brother feared that witches within his lineage were attacking him for the now prospering farm, and sought the advice of one of his labourers. This man claimed that the people of his home village near Wa possessed powers which could protect those who used them from all sorts of mystical and physical attacks. The surviving brother waited till the cocoa season was over and, taking 100 of his profit, was escorted to the North by the labourer. During a stay of about one week there he underwent a number of ritual treatments involving bathing in medicines and eating a number of special preparations. He was also instructed in the basic rules and prohibitions of the *suman* he was to be given and finally presented with this carefully wrapped in a white calico cover which he was forbidden to loose. When he arrived back at his home he carefully secreted this *suman* in his room near the top of his bed and allowed nobody else to approach it. As when anyone travels North to seek medicine in this way, the news of his journey and return quickly spread through the village and the whole neighbourhood. He was treated with the special mixture of fear, respect and circumspection reserved for such travellers: as nobody can be quite sure where they have been or whether the power they have fetched is good or bad, protective or destructive, it becomes general policy to go carefully and see how they themselves prosper or fail. The owner of the new power was himself clearly aware of this general new attitude towards him and interpreted it as showing the power of his new *suman* to spread a protective shield about him.

Many powers are imported in this way but social and personal circumstances allow few to develop into full-scale anti-witchcraft movements. In the case here discussed, as in many others, the key event did not come until several months later when many people in the village had begun to forget about the new *suman*. At that date a young woman fell ill and despite both hospital and local herbal treatment her illness continued and even increased in severity. She began to have great difficulty in walking and complaining of intermittent pains in her joints and belly. After about two months when her family had begun to suggest to her that there must be some deeper cause of her affliction, she began to say that she was a witch and that she had dreamed of seeing a giant Northerner in an iron smock chasing her with a club; it was the beating she had received from this club which was giving her the pains with which her body was now racked. The local villagers began to interpret these confessions as pointing to the new *suman* which they declared was the Northerner whom she had seen. She was taken to the *suman's* owner who said that all this was quite possible, even likely, and who demanded a small sum, some schnapps and a red dog to sacrifice to the *suman* so that she might beg forgiveness and be cleansed. Shortly after having made a full public confession, taking upon herself the responsibility for three recent deaths in her lineage, she recovered.

Tales of such events spread rapidly in the neighbourhood and soon friends and acquaintances of the *suman's* owner were coming to him to beg to be given to eat protective medicine derived from the *suman*. This he quickly produced by leaving cola nuts close to it over night and then handing them out to supplicants while at the same time telling them a list of basic moral rules that they must keep. In return they each gave him a prestation of a few shillings. As each person came to take this medicine and learn the rules and prohibitions of the power they greatly enlarged the potential number of those who, on falling ill, might interpret (or be made to interpret) their illness as being due to being attacked by this new *suman* for wishing harm to those under its protection. For a while a large proportion of local illnesses were attributed to the activities of the new power which now began to be talked about as a great figure which went about at night catching witches and other evil-doers. The

ANTI-WITCHCRAFT CULTS IN MODERN ASANTE 115

2 shilling charge for drinking the medicine began to bring in larger
and larger sums each week and a small circular temple (the shape Asante
feel is typical of Northern houses) was erected at the edge of the
village to house the new *sumán*. The village elders decided that as
outsiders were being attracted in increasing numbers to eat the medicine
and be cleansed of their offences against the shrine's subscribers, it
was only proper for the town as a whole to take a greater part in
running the cult and sharing its profits. They made a suitable arrangement with its original importer and sent a delegation on behalf of the
whole village to inform the Omanhene that a new power was active in his
area. Money was also subscribed by several of the richer cocoa-farmers
to send the importer and a companion to the North to fetch additional
'strengthening' powers. These men later took a proportionate share of
the profits, and each year a small percentage was put on one side for
the village stool.

The presence in the area of the new power, (now occasionally referred
to as a *'bosom'* for politeness sake and because it had begun to be seen
as a living, individual force) served to crystalise and bring into the
open several long-standing but submerged disputes and rivalries. The
owner, a staunch U.P. supporter, found that many C.P.P. followers, on
falling sick, came to him and confessed that they had long planned his
downfall and had initially derided and planned to spoil the power he had
brought in believing that it was aimed at their destruction. The availability of new protective medicines in the area also served to bring to the
mind of individuals the various dangers they might be faced with and to
drive them to take this cheap form of protection, the mere public subs-
cription to the cult serving as notice to those around them that they
were aware of particular threats to their position and to warn these
people that illnesses which might befall them could be laid at the door
of the new power. Illnesses which previously might have been shrugged
off or borne without too much disturbance were now quickly interpreted
as the results of misdoings, and confessions were made. The fame of the
shrine spread wider with each confession and the villagers found themselves coping with a daily influx of strangers seeking protection or
prolonged treatment at the shrine around which a row of visitors' huts
was soon being constructed.

It is fame of this type which gives rise to the second method whereby
such cults are disseminated. When the males of a local lineage, a group
of male friends or even a whole village hears that a particular power is
proving efficacious in catching witches (and money) they may decide to band
together to obtain the same power for themselves rather than merely eating
the medicine provided by its local shrine. They therefore collect together
money and set off for its reputed home in the North. Because of the large
sums involved (frequently 100 or more) such journeys are consciously
considered and financed enterprises which are expected to show a profit
as well as to provide protection to those involved. Competition to board
the bandwagon of profitable cults sometimes leads to deliberate deception
among both Asante and Northerners: when Asante reach the North and set
about contacting the owners of the original power they seek, they may find
themselves confronted by several rival claimants each swearing that theirs
is the only, true and original version. Equally when Asante arrive at an
unfamiliar area of their own country seeking the shrine they have heard so
much about, they may be misled into believing that a village's newly acquired
power is the older-established one they are searching for.

116 *CHANGING SOCIAL STRUCTURE IN GHANA*

While such spreading of a power's fame and importance is going on in the forest area the Northerners who are associated with the home village maintain an active interest in its operations. Each year they will send someone south to check that its rules and prohibitions are being obeyed and to collect a percentage, often a tenth, of its year's profits. When a particular shrine shows signs of declining trade they will generally advise that the local witches have managed to 'spoil' it and advise that additional powers be sought at the usual cost from the North. Such itinerant inspectors may also act as mediators in cases where two rival shrines from the same ultimate source are in dispute. There thus develops a symbiotic relationship between a family or village in the North and several families or villages in Asante which may be continued and elaborated over a number of years.

Although such cults occur and recur in Asante life each has but a limited existence. To some extent their power is the sort usually associated with chain letters or pyramid-selling: they can only continue by involving more and more people in their operations. So long as people are willing to place themselves under the protection of a -particular shrine then those people with whom they interact regularly and closely will look to the cult as the cause of illness and some types of misfortune. The more that do this the more there will be, within the limits of travel and convenience, who will also turn to the cult for protection. But, as in all Asante witchcraft cases, the remedies provided by the cult are never effective in permanently reimposing ideal patterns of behaviour. After a while people will begin to find newer cults more hopeful and turn to these, restarting the whole cycle. Few cult owners or leaders ever manage to pass on their leadership to successors and most cults disappear with the death or the establishment of the prosperity of the original importer.

While it is clear that these cults have modified their procedure over the last 60 years their basic character and operations remain much the same. The breakdown of political control in Asante and the suppression of older anti-witchcraft powers gave 'youngmen' the chance to import and profit from Abirewa in 1906 but the roots of these cults lie still earlier and deeper in the basic Asante conceptualisation and evaluation of the universe. Such cults require no long and arduous apprenticeship (as did the older *abosom*) and they still provide one avenue to wealth and power for men. Today there is no simple correlation between those who use or run them and participation in 'modern' economic activities: sometimes it is only after making money in this way that men will start cocoa-farms or buy lorries. The essence of each cult lies in the opportunities it gives to individuals to reimpose some sort of consonance between individual physical health or sickness and the ideal moral order which is expressed in terms of lineage values. But by and large illhealth and misfortune do not occur in direct proportion to the degree which individuals uphold moral values and the remedies effected by the cults are at best temporary. Individual cults are quickly forgotten and new onesare seen as offering unique opportunities for protection and salvation. In this sense witchcraft is always on the increase, cults are always new, as Ward was so firmly told by her Asante informants, because witchcraft in Asante(and all the activities which go with it)is essentially conservative. People are continually falling below the ideal standards of their society and potentially new medicines are always available to connect these failures with the largely random incidence of physical illness.

NOTES

1. H. Debrunner (1959); M.J. Field (1958 and 1960); M. Fortes (1948); B. Ward (1956); and G. Tooth (1950).

2. Thus it is dangerous to identify without more evidence the various cults and *suman* called Kankamea, Kankam, Kunkumba, etc., as all coming from Birifu,as Goody suggests.

3. The use of Akomfo Anokye by Goody as a support for his thesis is a dangerous one. None of the early literary sources mention Anokyein association with either the Golden Stool or Osei Tutu and he only begins to appear in the literature towards the start of the present century. He may well have existed but all the sources for him are derived from a time when the political power of Asante rulers was on the decline and when rumours and myths of religious powers seemed to have been increasingly elaborated.

4. For the most easily accessible sources on Abirewa see: A.Ffoulkes (1908-9: 387-97); F. Fuller (1921: 221-2); J.G. Christaller (1933: 309); H. Debrunner (1959: 124); and R.S. Rattray (1927: 31). For possible earlier cults towards the coast see: Bohner, Im Lande des Fetisch quoted in H. Debrunner (1959: 106); and D. Kemp (1898: 131).

5. See W. Bosman (1967: 124); T.E. Bowdich (1872: 163); A.B. Ellis (1887: 200); W. Hutton (1821: 88); B. Cruikshank (1853: 287); Ramseyer and Kuhne (1875: 105); and R.S. Rattray (1929: 392-5).

6. Corpse carrying:for an early account of coastal practices see W. Bosman (1967: 220). Also B. Cruikshank (1853: 133-5); and R.S. Rattray (1916: 53) and(1927: 167-70).

THE WEST AFRICAN FARMING HOUSEHOLD

POLLY HILL

Outside the cities and the largest towns, most West African men, and many women, are primarily engaged in farming and my main purpose in this chapter is to analyse the structure and organisation of the West African farming household. Although my material relates only to various societies in Nigeria, Ghana and the Ivory Coast, as well as to Bamenda (formerly in the British Cameroons) and to the Hausa in the Niger Republic, many of my observations have general application to West Africa south of the sahel zone.

Polygyny

Polygyny is the rule in West Africa in the statistical sense that the average number of wives per husband at any point of time, in any locality, usually stands well above 1.0. This does not, of course, mean that at any moment most husbands have more than one wife - but rather that most men (especially older men) aspire to have two or three wives. As divorce rates, as well as death rates for adults in the prime of life, are high, the pattern of distribution of wives among husbands undergoes constant change. Accordingly, it is inappropriate to refer to certain husbands as polygynists, to others as monogamists, for it may easily happen that a man has two wives today and one tomorrow: it is the society itself which is polygynous. Polygyny, then, is from one angle a system which permits a substantial proportion of husbands to gratify their desire, if only at some stage of their lives, of having more than one wife.

It is not as a rule any imbalance between the sexes which allows of polygyny, but the fact that young men contract their first marriages several years later than young women. In some half dozen different localities in rural Nigerian Hausaland, I have found that the average number of wives per husband tends to be of the order of 1.2 to 1.4; and statistics for northern Ghana, cited by J.R. Goody (1973), indicate the same orders of magnitude. Given these ratios, it may be that at any point of time, some 70% of married men have one wife, some 25% have two wives - the proportion with three or more wives always being small[1].

In rural Hausaland (and maybe in many other societies, though statistics are generally lacking) the average number of wives per husband is closely related to the husband's age and wealth - two factors which are not independent variables. In Dorayi (a rural locality of dispersed settlement near Kano city[2]) where the overall ratio of wives per husband was 1.4, the corresponding ratio for the richest men was 2.1, for the oldest men (over sixty-five or so) 1.8: therefore, insofar as high marriage payments delay first-marriage, they are obviously to the advantage of the rich and the old. Elderly Dorayi men cannot tolerate widowhood, and only one of the 53 oldest men in the community was wifeless; there, as elsewhere, elderly men commonly marry young women. As the capacity of individual men

120 *CHANGING SOCIAL STRUCTURE IN GHANA*

to attract and retain more than one wife is so variable the "incidence of polygyny" as measured by the overall ration, is a rather uninteresting figure.

In fact, with short intervals between marriages, the married state is normal for all West African men who have ever been married, except in some cases of severe ill health. Rural women under the age of (say) fifty are also invariably married[3] - though there may be conventional waiting time between marriages. Indeed, polygyny may be regarded as a system which effectively 'guarantees' every woman under (say) fifty years the 'right' of being married. When older women are widowed or divorced they may or may not remarry: if they do not, they often elect to live with a married son or daughter.

Accordingly, there are five possible categories of adult in West African farming households headed by men: household heads, married sons (if they continue to work on their father's farms after marriage), young unmarried sons, wives and older widows (or divorcees). To simplify matters, I am excluding from household membership all those male co-residents (and their dependants) who farm independently of the household head; and I am ignoring the fact that married sons who work on their father's farm may sometimes live in separate houses. As, nowadays, brothers seldom farm together, West African farming households are here regarded as excluding co-resident brothers as well as married sons who farm independently of their fathers.

In patrilineal and bilateral societies it is the rule in the country-side (although not necessarily in the towns[4]) for husbands and wives to be co-resident. In matrilineal societies, however, as Fortes's work on Ashanti cocoa-farmers has shown[5], there is sometimes a tendency, though possibly only in older-established cocoa areas, for some wives to remain resident with their matrikin (more particularly their mothers) after marriage - though even then co-residence of spouses is more usual. However, long-established Ashanti cocoa-farmers are probably unrepresentative rural dwellers owing to their strong preference for living in what may be termed 'towns', rather than in villages or dispersedly[6]. So I think that it is reasonable to assume that in rural West Africa generally most husbands live with their wives[7] - and that most farming household are headed by men.

Perhaps divorce rates tend to be higher in polygynous than in monogamous societies, if only because a woman's virtual right to remarry is the better assured? However this may be, the statistics relating to the incidence of divorce in polygynous rural West Africa are so meagre as to contribute nothing to the debate. For present purposes it is sufficient to note that incidences (however measured) appear to be generally high ; that a high regard for the married state as such is often associated with a low regard for the stability of any particular union; and that (nevertheless) life-long unions are everywhere fairly common - irrespective of whether the husband has a succession of other wives. Although divorce is frequently sought by wives[8], they often suffer more from the severance than their husbands. Men are not apt to become detached from their land as a result of divorce; on the other hand, as will be seen, women commonly (though not necessarily) lose all their farming rights. In Muslim savannah societies men have a sole right of control over their children and, irrespective of the circumstances of the divorce, divorced women are commonly obliged to relinquish their children (Hill 1972); on the other hand, in matrilineal societies children tend to adhere to their matrikin.

THE WEST AFRICAN FARMING HOUSEHOLD   121

Men's and women's farming

In the last resort the terms 'urban' versus 'rural' are hard to define, especially as many city men (notably in Yorubaland) are primarily farmers and as some rural men are not primarily engaged in detailed crop production. However, in most rural communities every man is best denoted a 'farmer'[9], and this quite irrespective of whether he employs labourers[10], or has a remunerative non-farming occupation - as most farmers do (Skinner 1964b). The varying responsibility and functions of the heads of farming households are best examined in relation to those of their wives.

It has recently been suggested by Goody and Buckley (1973) that the role of women in African agriculture, especially in forest country, is much more significant than in Europe and Asia, owing to the relative unimportance of the plough which is widespread in Eurasia and necessarily operated by men. However, such speculation does not explain the very great variations in the roles of women within the West African forest zone, where tsetse infestation altogether prevents the use of the plough. Why is it that in matrilineal Akan country, in the forests of southern Ghana and Ashanti, food crops are mainly cultivated by wives who are obliged to work on the farmland cleared by their husbands - and this irrespective of whether they cultivate farms of their own - whereas in (mainly patrilineal) Yorubaland a high proportion of women concentrate almost exclusively on trading[11]. It is often thought of as 'natural' that the obligations of Akan women should extent both backwards from the household into the fields and forwards into the rural periodic market-places, which are largely female institutions. Why, then, do Yoruba men do most of the food farming, while most of the trading is the responsibility of their wives? The situation is not explicable in terms of land tenure, for the evidence (such as it is) suggests that in both regions foodstuffs are mainly produced on the husband's land. Nor do Akan men necessarily enjoy superior opportunities so far as non-farming occupations are concerned - thus Akan women traders in southern Ghana are even more dominant than their Yoruba counterparts[12]. As for cocoa-farming, all the evidence suggests that development in southern Ghana proceeded so rapidly in the twenty years before 1914 because men were free to devote all their time to this work. Many Akan men find it positively beneath their dignity to do any weeding. The elderly Adontenhene of Akwapim was referring to the traditional situation when he told me in 1961 that 'the men are attached to the land, they own it and clear it; the women are attached to the food, they grow it, process it, cook it and sell it.'

One obvious reason for the contrasting situations in Akan and Yoruba country is the special nature of Yoruba urbanism, which involves many men in short-distance migration, out of the cities, for farming. I suggest that another explanation might be the relative unimportance of yams, during this century at least[13], in Akan country - though cause is indistinguishable from effect. In most, though not in all, regions, yam-mounds are invariably dug by men. Then, as men disdain the task of food-carrying (women and children being the rural beasts of burden, except in those savannah regions where the humble donkey prevails[14]), such bulky and easily-cultivated crops as cocoyams and plantains might happen to be the special concern of women - the Akan being more reliant on these crops than the Yoruba. Possibly, though again this is mere surmise, regional variations in women's roles within Yorubaland might be partly explicable in terms of the balance of

122   *CHANGING SOCIAL STRUCTURE IN GHANA*

different crops.

Moving eastward through the Nigerian forests to Benin (Mid-Western State), the scanty information indicates that yam-mounding there may usually be men's work, though women undertake all the weeding and planting; all other crops are always planted, tended and harvested by women, who also control their use (Bradbury, 1957). Again in the three south-eastern States, a distinction is commonly made between yams and other food crops, though women, as well as men, sometimes cultivate yams. The general principle is that wives bear the main responsibility for provisioning their households and are regarded as "owning" such crops as cocoyam and plantain - as well as cassava, which tends to increase in importance as population densities increase. It is the husband's duty to see that each of his wives has sufficient farmland for her own and her children's needs[15]; and the wives may be expected to meet any shortfall that arises by purchasing food from their own resources. An excellent account of the division of labour between men and women is given by Daryll Forde in <u>Yakö Studies</u> (1964). The Yakö[16] are largely dependent on yams which are grown on land allocated to married men by the patrilineal descent group. While the division of tasks is applicable to the farm as a whole, yet the husbands' and wives' yams (which are grown on the same farm) are planted and dug separately, incised with distinctive marks and tied on separate groups of sticks in the storage shed. A wife receives her first seed-yams after marriage from both her father and her mother, the latter providing her with the early type which always belongs to women. While most of the yams are owned by men, women are the main cultivators: they are even responsible for the heavy mounding work, though they may sometimes be assisted by male labourers[17]. The husband undertakes the clearing of the forest, often working co-operatively with other men of his descent group, and takes part in the yam planting, after which the work devolves almost entirely on his wives. Elaborate conventions dictate the extent to which husbands' and wives' yams are used for family consumption at different seasons.

Turning now to the intermediate zone between forest and savannah, where both grains and roots are staples, Phyllis Kaberry's detailed study (1952) of the economic position of women in Bamenda (a region which is now in Cameroon) is quite unrivalled in West Africa. All agricultural activities, other than the clearing of trees and heavy bush, are there undertaken by women. Although this is so, a wife's obligations to feed her husband are such that he may usually claim the harvest in the event of divorce. However, women are not necessarily deprived of land as a result of divorce, for their usufructural rights over lineage land throughout their life span are equal to those of men: so in the light of my assertion regarding the security provided to women by the polygynous system it is interesting that polygyny in Bamenda "is limited to a very small section of the population". (Ibid:87)

Two other societies in the intermediate zone for which detailed material on the sexual division of farm-tasks is available are the Gouro of the Ivory Coast[18] and the Tiv (Bohannan, 1968) of the Nigerian Middle Belt. In Tiv country, where the intricate allocation is such that few tasks are performed by either men or women, and where men refuse to do any weeding, and the simple rule on crop-ownership is that guinea corn and yams belong to women (although men dig the yam-mounds) and millet

THE WEST AFRICAN FARMING HOUSEHOLD

123

belongs to men. So a man must obtain his wife's permission to sell yams; and if a profligate wife sells yams required by the family it is still the husband's duty to provide the additional money or food required. As for land rights, whereas a woman's rights always depend on residence and marriage, those of a man are determined by birth - 'to be without land is to be without kin' (Ibid: 87).

While yams are grown in parts of the southern savannah, the basic food crops throughout the vast savannah zone are grains (mainly millet and guinea corn - not maize), which are supplemented by groundnuts (consumed mainly as oil and the residual cake) and cowpeas (a kind of bean). In many societies most hoe-cultivation, and in particular the ridging with a heavy hoe[19], is men's work, though women may help with the sowing and harvesting. In rural Nigerian Hausaland where Muslim wife-seclusion (purdah) has become almost universal during the past few decades[20], the wives in most localities are unable to leave their houses during the course of a normal day, so that all the hoe cultivation, including the weeding, has to be done by men. However, even in former times when most wives enjoyed some freedom of movement, it was commonly thought that farm-work was beneath the dignity of women of free-descent, being proper only for women slaves, who may have comprised nearly a half of the servile farm labour force. But among the rural Hausa of the Niger Republic, who practise little rural wife-seclusion, wives do much farming on their own husbands' farms[21]. As for the Kanuri of Borno (in north-eastern Nigeria) it has been reported [22]that wives play a major part in crop-production. Certainly the conclusion must be that even within the Muslim savannah there is very great variation in women's roles.

One of the most detailed accounts of food in the domestic economy relates to the Tallensi of north-eastern Ghana (Fortes, 1937). Although the most arduous farming labour falls on men, women have many functions: the raw materials for conversion into food are 'produced and otherwise brought into the compound by the joint efforts of man, woman and child '[23]. Here, as so commonly elsewhere, the small vegetables (such as pepper, tomatoes, okro) which are essential ingredients of the sauces, which are served with the basic porridge, are mainly grown by women, in manured plots close to their houses.

It is abundantly clear from this survey that West African husbands and wives seldom form a unified production unit - comparable, for instance, with the Hausa *gandu* in Nigeria, which is such that fathers and sons form a work-team [24]. Furthermore, although (as we have seen) it is very commonly the husband who controls the land on which food crops are grown, wives are no more apt to work under his direct authority when cultivating the crops than when doing the cooking. Vast and heterogeneous (both culturally and ecologically) though West Africa is, individual wives (other than those who are very young) invariably enjoy a large measure of economic autonomy: nor do wives have any more need than husbands for the jealous guarding of their rights, which are equally inherent and no more subject to erosion. Indeed in those societies where land is increasingly alienated by sale, women's rights over land are tending to increase[25], so that it is their husbands who should beware.

Of course this is not to deny that there is much mutual dependence and complementarity, as well as autonomy, within the household. 'In the

124   *CHANGING SOCIAL STRUCTURE IN GHANA*

domestic economy of food' wrote Meyer Fortes of the Tallensi 'every unit in the system is completely autonomous in some respects and dependent upon a more comprehensive unit in others' (1bid: 240). But, when things are going badly and the farming household is suffering from lack of food, women often have as much responsibility as men, and maybe as much power, to remedy the situation. However, when death or divorce intervenes, the wife's position tends to be more precarious than the husband's in most (though not in all) societies, owing both to her relative lack of land rights and to her dependence on others for land clearance. Polygyny effectively guarantees every younger woman the right of remarriage: it is an essential social security system for West African women.

This is one reason why I am sure that the time is not yet ripe to analyse, whether statistically or otherwise,the'incidence' of polygyny in different rural societies in relation to the varying economic roles of women. The recent spate of literature on this subject is male-biassed: the men are presumed to be the operators, the women the tools. If older, richer men tend to have more wives than the average, who knows whether this may not mainly reflect the women's choice?[26] It is because of their right to remarry, that women can risk extricating themselves from a union by seeking divorce: given this freedom, as well as their economic autonomy, women can often avoid being ground down by an exceptionally improverished husband[27].

The fact that West African marriage bears so little resemblance to European marriage, in terms both of the domestic economy of the household, and of day to day social activities, receives insufficient emphasis in the literature. Spouses usually enjoy little everyday companionship except, perhaps, when they grow old: they rarely sit and converse; they eat separately; they tend to have separate ceremonial and recreational activities. Considering that they are rarely seen walking down a path together, it is no wonder that they seldom work jointly to produce crops which either party may sell, or toil alongside each other on the fields.

Perhaps, however, the staunch independence of individuals, *qua* individuals, is best illustrated by co-wives: even when secluded co-wives are obliged to endure each other's company throughtout their working hours, as they are in rural Hausaland, their remunerative food-processing and trading occupations are always pursued independently, even when they both have the same occupation, such as the production of groundnut oil for sale. Furthermore, this Hausa example shows that women sustain their inherent autonomy even when locked up[28] in purdah. It is my contention (Hill, 1969) that the bulk of grain sold to final consumers in rural Hausaland is retailed by secluded women, whose separate houses are linked by children, and not in open market-places which are the province of men.

Members of West African households have a far less emotive attitude to intra-household monetary transactions than their counterparts in developed conutries. Thus with the rural Hausa -

> 'Cash is a positive good, and there is no reason why personal relationship should create any inhibitions about giving or receiving it. A woman who makes groundnut oil for sale is in business on her own account and there is nothing immodest about buying oil from herself with her "housekeeping money" '. (Hill, 1972)

Then, a mother may give a son money to buy food, rather than cooking it

THE WEST AFRICAN FARMING HOUSEHOLD 125

herself - there is a flourishing trade in cooked meals (not mere snacks) in many rural Hausa communities. Many other examples could be given, but I conclude by mentioning that Yoruba husbands commonly give their wives cash commissions on the food they sell on behalf of them.

Unmarried sons

Unmarried sons (of the age range of (say) 16 to 25 years, according to places and circumstances) are usually an important element of the total work force - in rural Hausaland, where women do no farming, they may account for as much as a quarter of the entire working population[30]. Such sons are seldom independent farmers and such plots as may be given to them by their fathers are always small. In many rural societies unmarried sons are necessarily in an unpleasant transitional state, lacking freedom as well as clearly defined rights, and dependent on their father's willingness or ability to contribute to their marriage expenses: I am sure that their restlessness is, and always has been, inevitable, and should not necessarily be attributed to expanded education and urbanisation. In rural Hausaland young men, and even pre-pubertal boys, are often unable to sleep in the family house or to partake of food there. Insofar as marriage expenses are rising faster than the general level of prices - as they certainly are in some regions - a brake is applied to the world-wide tendency for earlier first-marriage for men.

Married sons

In societies where married sons tend to continue working on their father's farms after marriage, their contribution to the total household labour force may exceed that of unmarried sons. To simplify this discussion on the position of such married sons, I confine myself to patrilineal and bilateral societies - thus, for instance, avoiding the question of the extent to which in matrilineal societies maternal kinsmen of the younger generation are 'son-substitutes'. Owing to the surprising lack of material on what amounts to an important aspect of land tenure, I am obliged to offer various surmises regarding the processes by which sons establish themselves as independent farmers after marriage.

My first presumption is that in most societies where land is not the limiting productive factor, most sons, and/or their wives, start cultivating some basic food crops, for self consumption and possibly for sale, soon after marriage, either on farmland which has been formally alloted to them (by their fathers, or by the local community or descent group, as the case may be), or on uncultivated bush land which is freely available to all members of the community. My second presumption is that the process of separation from the father is seldom completed immediately on marriage (unless, of course, the son migrates), but usually takes some years[31]. Indeed a father may gradually shed his farmland over his lifetime until, when he is old, he may have none left[32].

The Mbembe of south-eastern Nigeria are an interesting case of a society where, as yams are considered scarcer than land, a young man cannot get married unless he can provide his wife with sufficient seed-yams from his personal farm to make her a shared farm of reasonable

CHANGING SOCIAL STRUCTURE IN GHANA

size (Harris, 1965). Both husband and wife receive further yams from their parents on marriage, and the couple slowly build up their yam stock until a peak is reached when the man is in his forties. In general, in this society, an endeavour is made to match each man's supplies of land and seed-yams. Many elderly couples have fewer yams than the newly married.

As for the situation where land is the principal scarce factor, my presumption is that in many societies fathers, and/or land-controlling groups or authorities, feel a general obligation to make farmland available to the newly-wed. Indeed, as with the Afikpo (Ottenberg, 1968) (who now lack virgin land), the right to use the land of a major patrilineage (or matrilineage) may apply to any adult male - in the former case to any male lineage member who is an initiate of the village secret society. Before each season opens the Afikpo farmland is divided according to relationship, age (the older the man the larger the share), and willingness to use the land.

West African population density maps are often very patchy so that married sons may only have to migrate short distances to find sufficient unoccupied land. Whether or not such migration involves a change of residence, it may not involve a complete severance of economic links with the father, who may expect some help from his son. Longer distance migration for farming is not usually feasible for younger married sons, who lack both the necessary finance and sons of working age to assist them: they are the men with a particular incentive to migrate to urban areas or for non-farming work.

So in most West African societies it is to be presumed that it is the son's first marriage, not his father's death, which is the crucial event that launches him on an independent career as a farmer - in which case (see, also below) there should be less emphasis on the dangers of land-fragmentation on death, and more on the life-time process of departure. However, there are some societies, of which the Hausa are much the most notable example, in which it is usual for sons to continue working on their father's farms for a quite indefinite period[33] after marriage, maybe until the father's death.

The complex network of rights and obligations linking fathers and sons under the Hausa system known as *gandu* has been dealt with elsewhere (Hill, 1972:ch.3). Although such factors as family pride, duty and sentiment are often responsible for maintaining the relationship, the matter of economic security is always important to both parties, unless the father is very poor. The father has a ready-made family labour force available to him at a moment's notice[34]; the son is entitled to a share of the crop and/or food and ought to be able to rely on his father to give him a personal plot (on which he is free to work at certain times, as well as when his father does not require his services) and to meet his community tax, as well as various forms of conventional or ceremonial expenditure connected with marriage and birth. Although *gandu* is entirely voluntary, so that sons may set up as independent farmers at any time, and do not necessarily suffer as a result, sons-in-*gandu* are definitely subordinate to their fathers who may even sell[35] the *gandu* farmland against their wishes, and who are always free to sell the *gandu* grain: it therefore follows that *gandu* is not a variety of co-operative farming (for which one always searches in vain) but rather a species of contract, with limited obligations on both sides.

Gandu is an old system: in the days of farm-slavery (which ended but

THE WEST AFRICAN FARMING HOUSEHOLD   127

half a century ago) the slaves and the sons were in *gandu* together.
Although a rudimentary farm-labouring system (under which younger,
poorer, farmers and farmers' sons work for daily wages on other men's
farms) has partially replaced farm-slavery, the greatly increased
incidence of wife seclusion during the past quarter century has meant
that household heads have become ever more dependent on their sons. The
main reasons for the willingness of enterprising sons, in this day and
age, to tolerate their subservience to their fathers are firstly that
they are usually allotted sufficient time to devote to the expansion of
their own farming and non-farming work (sons-in-*gandu* may employ farm
labourers on their personal farms); secondly that sensible elderly
fathers hand over more and more responsibilities to their sons, maybe
ultimately reversing their roles, or dividing their farmland between
their sons in their lifetimes; and thirdly the high degree of respect
accorded to older men in Hausaland[36]. However, nowadays men are seldom
prepared to remain subordinate to their eldest brother (except, occasionally, when there is a large age-gap), so that when the father dies the
gandu usually collapses quite soon, each son taking a share of the farmland: twenty or thirty years ago fraternal *gandu* was quite common (Smith, 1955).

The development and eventual dissolution of the farming household

It is my aim to treat 'inheritance' (in the broad sense) as

> 'an ongoing process by means of which individual members
> of the family are allocated definite rights and obligations
> with regard to control, ownership and exploitation of resources
> and goods; and in such a manner that as the position of an
> individual in the family changes concurrently with events such
> as births, marriages and deaths, his mode of attachment to the
> family estate shifts accordingly; the element in this process
> which is relatively constant being a firm and continuous attach-
> ment of the whole family group to the natural resources which
> sustain it.'[37]

As we have seen, the most crucial factor affecting the longer-term development of farming households in the extent   to which married sons remain
farming with their fathers. If few sons hive off, if the area of cultivated
farmland increases *pari passu* with the growth of the household, then the
fortunes of the farming household may tend to improve until the father dies
- in which case the notion of the standard domestic cycle, such as has three
different phases, the last being the phase of replacement of father's family
by son's family, is not applicable (Hill,1972: 165 ff). However, even if
married sons are prone to depart, the polygynous system may sufficiently
favour old men as to ensure that many of them 'replace' their married sons.
But in those societies where the sons leave fairly quickly and where, for
one reason or another, young women seldom marry old men, the peak of fortune
may be reached when the household head is in his forties - as with the Mbembe,
whose wealth is measured in yams.

Before turning to consider inheritance in the limited sense of 'what
happens to productive resources (mainly farmland) on death', it is necessary to examine the nature of the land rights exercised by the living.
The labour of clearing virgin (or thickly afforested) land in the forest
zone is so great that it is often undertaken by groups of men which establish

128 CHANGING SOCIAL STRUCTURE IN GHANA

permanent rights. While these rights ultimately reside in the group (and its successors), crop-cultivation is undertaken by individuals on separate plots. Unless orchard crops, such as cocoa, are established, these plots are commonly cultivated for a few years only and are then fallowed; before cultivation is resumed, the bush must be cleared, either by individual farmers, or (as initially) by a group. In either event, there is the question of whether individuals should resume cultivation of their old plots, or whether reallocation should occur. If a system of reallocation which takes no account of the previous ownership pattern is the rule, then men may be said to have no permanent rights over parti-cular portions - in which case farmland is effectively non-inheritable. A situation approaching this extreme case may sometimes exist with the Yoruba, though more often, perhaps, sons have preferential rights over their father's land, provided they exercise them in due time (Lloyd,1965: 151).

In fact, irrespective of whether the land is ultimately vested in a (patrilineal or matrilineal) descent group or in a residential commu-nity, there is usually a strong element of long-term, i.e. transmittable, rights over land which is regularly cultivated and fallowed.

> 'The ascription of the ownership of land to the community or village is only accurate if viewed as a social aggregate. For even with the community of the village, actual occupation and control are decentralised, so to speak; the family, rather than the community or village, in fact exercises acts of owner-ship. The chief interest of the community or village in the land is the purely social and political one of maintaining group solidarity.' (Elias, 1951:91)

But even in the forest zone the labour of first-clearing is not necessarily undertaken by a group. Thus individual migrant cocoa-farmers in southern Ghana themselves cleared the virgin land they had bought; even when, as a member of a land-purchasing 'company'(Hill, 1963b), a man had combined with others to buy a block of land, clearance was his individual concern.

In the forest zone there is often a definite modal size of farm (i.e. farm plot) of some half to two acres and I suggest that this has some correspondence to the area which may be cultivated by one man or woman in a season[38]. This I noted in southern Ghana, in localities where indigenous (not stranger) farmers owned the cocoa farms[39], and it has also been reported from Yorubaland and elsewhere[40]. Although there is some tendency for richer farmers to own larger plots, the main difference between rich and poor is in the number of plots owned. Most farmers own several separate plots and when a farmer dies there is often no need to subdivide the individual plots, which may be shared out between the inheritors like a pack of cards.

Turning to the savannah zone, as the act of first clearance is far less arduous than in the forest, communal clearing is much less common there. Nor is there so strong a tendency for farmers to resume working their original plots after they have been fallowed. Except in very densely populated dis-tricts, there is usually a kind of reserve of farmland, or bush, which is available to any member of the community or, less commonly, to members of a descent group, and specific rights over such land are not usually heritable. But in the neighbourhood of farmsteads or settlements, individual farmers often establish permanent, heritable rights, especially if the land is

THE WEST AFRICAN FARMING HOUSEHOLD   129

regularly manured; and the higher the population density (after a certain threshold has been passed) the greater the ratio of heritable land.

However, the rural Hausa are a special case for, irrespective of population density, a high proportion of all cultivated farmland, except in newly settled areas, falls into this category of heritable manured farmland, farmers having a positive preference for this agronomic system (Hill,1972). Although this system was common in certain districts in pre-colonial times - notably in the large close-settled zone around Kano city - the proportion of heritable manured farmland has increased greatly in recent decades.

In the savannah, as in the forest, the ordinary farmer's farm-holding usually consists of several farm-plots, which are likely to have been established at different times (Ibid:22). However, it is observable that there is much more variation in the size of plots (Ibid:233), both within and between localities, than in the forest zone - one explanation for which is the relative lack of land-allocation systems.

Given this background I now attempt a few rash generalisations about the redistribution of farmland that is apt to occur on the household head's death:

(1) Under matrilineal systems, which are more common in the forest zone than in the savannah, inheritance is impartible - there is a sole heir. Although such an heir may well be entitled to retain a large proportion of the farmland for his own personal use, he also has an obligation to grant usufructural rights to such members of his matrilineage as require them, and in practice such rights may tend to be heritable, even though the land is inalienable. If the deceased has younger brothers of the same mother, then nowadays the farmland usually passes successively to them, until the youngest is dead when it is usually transmitted to a sister's son.

(2) In patrilineal societies there are nowadays effectively[41] two basic inheritance systems such that the farmland is divided, more or less equally, either between all the sons or between the sets of sons[42], of each mother. Under the latter system (which may be informally known as 'division between wives', or formally as *per stirpes*) a son with (say) three full brothers gets only a quarter of the share of a son with no full brothers; while this system is fairly common in the forest zone[43], I think it may be unusual in the savannah[44].

(3) In bilateral (cognatic) societies, which are more common in savannah than forest, daughters as well as sons may receive a share of the farmland. Although according to the strict interpretation of the law they ought to do so in Muslim societies, such as Hausaland, they often waive these rights in favour of their brothers, or sell them the land on easy terms, this being especially likely to occur when they had removed elsewhere on marriage[45].

(4) It would seem to be a general rule that following the death of the household head individual members of farming households in patrilineal and bilateral societies, are seldom worse off, in terms of their access to land, than they had been before, except in some cases where 'division between wives' is practised. Although in some societies, including Hausa-land, men have an increased propensity to migrate following their father's

130 *CHANGING SOCIAL STRUCTURE IN GHANA*

death, this is due rather to their increased sense of freedom, or to their ability to finance their migration by farm-selling, than to worsened living standards.

(5) In matrilineal societies, on the other hand, a son's position may deteriorate sharply following his father's death if he had previously been enjoying rights within his father's farmland which then pass to the matrilineage (Hill, 1972:165 ff). However, there may have been a beneficial turning-point for the son earlier in his carrer when he first claimed his matrilineal rights.

(6) On the matter of the 'fragmentation'of farmland on the death of the household head, I think there are a number of reasons why this is a much less serious problem than is often supposed - and that declining standards of living in localities with high and rapidly increasing population densities are usually mainly due to population pressure as such, not to inheritance systems. Among my numerous justifications for this bold assertion are:

(a) Under matrilineal systems, the sole-heir system may be such that, as time goes by, too much land becomes concentrated in the hands of those who happen to be inheritors[46].

(b) In those patrilineal societies where sons gradually establish themselves as independent farmers after marriage, maybe with the help of land transferred to them by their fathers, inheritance is anticipated in an orderly way, so that if the father dies when he is old little redistribution of land remains to be effected.

(c) For numerous reasons, brothers are often quite differently situated at the time of their father's death, especially if they are of very varying ages: thus the eldest sons of a prosperous Hausa farmer may have evolved into successful farmers on their own account (while continuing to shelter under their father's wing in *gandu*), although the youngest may still be entirely dependent on their fathers (Hill,1965: 165 ff). Accordingly (as already noted), the brothers may be little concerned with equal division of their father's farmland, merely sharing out the separate plots (as such) between themselves. Statistical evidence for both the migrant cocoa-farmers of southern Ghana and the Hausa[47], indicates that farmers are often aware of the danger of overmuch subdivision on death.

(d) As we have seen, in some societies and circumstances farmland is not heritable on death, though this may not, for example, prevent one of the sons from casually continuing to cultivate his father's bush farm.

(e) So long as most farm-tools continue to be traditional types manufactured by local blacksmiths[48], there will be little relationship between the size of farm-plots (provided they are not really small) and productivity.

(f) While 'division between wives' may be most rigid (Lloyd, 1962:

THE WEST AFRICAN FARMING HOUSEHOLD

131

281,297), that between the children of any wife may not occur, or be quite informal.

(g) Cocoa-farms are often considered as indivisible as heads of cattle - for the profits from working the plot, rather than the plot itself, may be shared[49].

(h) Finally, the tendency for self-acquired (individualised) property, such as cocoa-farms, to be converted into lineage property on death, tends to put a brake on subdivision[50]; it must not be too lightly assumed that land which has been extricated by individuals (maybe by purchase) from a communal melting pot is necessarily a new category of 'permanently individualised land'.

(7) Although it is true that the introduction of new orchard crops, such as cocoa, is always likely to result in some changes in land tenure and inheritance systems, the example that has just been given suggests that, in the longer run, these changes are not necessarily so radical as is sometimes supposed. In matrilineal cocoa-growing societies the most extraordinary change, so far as sedentary (non-migrant) cocoa farmers are concerned, is in the extent to which women evolve into independent (cocoa) farmers on their own account. Before examining this further, a few notes on women's inheritance systems must be made. In general, the sets of rules governing the inheritance of men's and women's property in any society are quite distinct; furthermore, with the exception of small livestock (which are commonly owned by either sex), farmland (insofar as women enjoy heritable rights, which most non-cocoa-farmers do not) and stored crops, women's property tends to be of different types from men's. Although the inheritance of women's cocoa-farms has been little studied, I think it is safe to say that their farms much more often pass (often intact) to their daughters than to their sons, and that women seldom inherit farms from men, unless there is no suitable male heir[51]; as husbands very seldom clear cocoa-farms for their wives, or give them land, they are usually entirely devoid of rights over their wives' farms.

A note on women cocoa-farmers

As we have seen, women are seldom the outright owners of the food-farms they cultivate, so the degree of security resulting from women's ownership of cocoa-farms in certain matrilineal societies[52], in southern Ghana, Ashanti and in the southern Ivory Coast, is quite remarkable. Statistics show that in some of these societies women cocoa farmers may be nearly as numerous as men[53], but their farm-plots (though not necessarily their holdings) tend to be smaller[54]. It is not known whether wives' obligations to cultivate food crops for their husbands and other household members have diminished as a result of their cocoa work. Perhaps, in the longer run, more middle-aged women cocoa farmers will eschew the married state: certainly the Akim women I interviewed aroung 1957-8 constantly emphasised that cocoa-farm ownership was a new and most welcome form of insurance against poverty arising from divorce.

132   *CHANGING SOCIAL STRUCTURE IN GHANA*

CONCLUSION

Readers may be puzzled by the inclusion of this chapter in a book
concerned with changing social structure. I therefore want to conclude
by expressing the hope that this type of comparative analysis, which is
as much concerned with diversity as with uniformity, may do something to
assist consideration of the varying effects on West African farming households:(1) of such foreseeable changes as increasing population density,
longer life expectancies, reduced age of first marriage for men, increased
farm selling; (2) of such uncertainties as increasing or decreasing tendencies towards inegalitarianism as farming techniques improve; and (3) of
such unprogressive Muslim trends as more rigorous wife-seclusion and low-
ered age of first-marriage for girls.

NOTES

1. These statistics relate to all the husbands and wives in a farming area,
    with a total population of about 3,500, which lies just south of Kano
    city, in the close-settled zone, where I did fieldwork in 1971-72: it
    is an area of dispersed settlement which I arbitrarily called Dorayi.
    See Hill, 1974, for further particulars of Dorayi.

2. See Note 1.

3. Few prostitutes reside in rural areas.

4. As with the Ga of Accra.

5. See 'Time and Social Structure: As Ashanti Case Study' in Fortes.

6. Dispersed residence is nowadays very common in many West African
    forest and savannah regions, as it was in pre-colonial times.

7. In circumstances where the household maintains more than one house - as
    frequently with the migrant cocoa-farmers of southern Ghana, see Hill,
    1963 - then a husband's wives may be distributed between the houses.

8. The incidence is usually impossible of estimation, as husbands often
    require their wives to divorce them. However, Forde states that among
    the Yakö (Forde, 1964:126) divorces usually arise from the voluntary
    departure of the wife.

9. Official censuses always reflect this, as men nearly always have some
    responsibility for farming, and regard this as their primary occupation.
    This lack of differentiation is among the more important reasons for
    holding that as all rural West African men are farmers, it is unneces-
    sary, as well as politically misleading, to refer to them as peasants.
    (See Mintz (1973): in West Africa it is not true that 'However total
    a peasant society may appear to be, its members rarely - if ever - may
    be said to compose the entire fabric of rural life', p; 94)

10. Labourers are commonly employed to supplement, not to replace, family
    labour,including that of the household head. See Hill,1956,1963 and 1972.

11. According to Fadipe (1970, but based on a thesis written in 1939), in

THE WEST AFRICAN FARMING HOUSEHOLD 133

pre-colonial times women were expected only to harvest crops. See also Guyer (1972) and Mintz (1971).

12. I base this assertion on my own research in southern Ghana in the early nineteen-sixties, which revealed that nearly all the men traders in the market-places were non-Akan.

13. It is curious fact that although present-day maps always show the 'yam zone' as including the forests of southern Ghana and Ashanti, there is no significant commercial production of yams there, supplies being 'imported' from further north. Given the importance of present day yam festivals and the fact that Bowdich (1819: 325) recorded that yams were grown in Ashanti by slave-labour on plantations resembling hop gardens, it can only be presumed that yams were formerly far more important.

14. Such rigid wife seclusion as prevails in Hausaland today would be impossible without the ubiquitous donkey.

15. See, for example, Ottenberg (1968:180). See also Harris (1965).

16. The Yakö live near the Cross River, just east of certain Ibo.

17. It is interesting that among the Mbembe, whose neighbours are the Yakö, yam-mounding is performed almost entirely by North-Eastern Ibo labourers who come to the area primarily for this work (Harris 1965: 102).

18. Meillassoux (1964). As Gouro country straddles between forest and savannah, the greater importance of women's work in the forest may be noted.

19. Such as the traditional *galma* of Hausaland - see Hill (1972). Forde (in Ottenberg, 1960, p.126) distinguished between those savannah peoples, with an inferior technology, who merely 'scratched the soil with light hoes' and those, including the Hausa, who practised deep hoeing and ridging: presumably men usually wielded the heavy hoe in the latter case.

20. This extraordinary development may mean that rural seclusion in Hausaland is stricter, and more widespread, than anywhere else in the Muslim world. (Most curiously, there are still some accessible pockets of Muslim Hausaland - I am not referring to the pagan Maguzawa - where most women are free to enter the farmland, though nobody knows why this should be: however, such women do not necessarily cultivate the soil.)

21. The numerous publications of Guy Nicolas, of which a long list is given in Hill (1972) relate to these people. See, in particular, Nicolas (1964).

22. See Cohen (1967). However this book provides little material on farming communities.

23. Family structure thus represents (p.240) "a compromise between strong centralizing or integrating tendencies and powerful differen-

134 *CHANGING SOCIAL STRUCTURE IN GHANA*

tiating tendencies'.

24. See p... below. Among the Hausa in the Niger Republic, on the other hand, wives may work in *gandu* with their husbands and do not necessarily have personal plots. (Personal communication from Guy Nicolas.)

25. Limited space precludes a discussion of the effect on household organisation of increased land alienation in some societies.

26. Older wives, in particular, often urge their husbands to acquire additional wives.

27. I here venture the assertion (which I shall hope to justify elsewhere) that all the evidence suggests that West African rural societies are inherently inegalitarian, the poorest households always tending to be short of food at certain seasons.

28. The Hausa word for purdah is *kulle*, which literally means 'locked'.

29. Nor is this anything new - see Fadipe (1970).

30. Moreover, as they are sometimes more inclined to work as farm-labourers than married men, their proportionate contribution, so far as the community is concerned, may be greater.

31. As with the Tallensi: a newly married son 'has a small degree of autonomy which increases from year to year.' Fortes (1937: 239). See, also, Forde (1964: 18).

32. This is the situation of some Yoruba fathers. See Lloyd in Derrett (p.150).

33. Whereas fathers in many societies feel entitled to demand informal assistance from their married sons, maybe in return for a share of the produce, as with the Tallensi - see Fortes (1937: 244), these demands are liable to lapse as time goes by, whereas with the Hausa the contract tends to strengthen.

34. Sudden changes in weather often make labour requirements quite unpredictable.

35. Farm-selling is an old practice in rural Hausaland, where there are no land-owning lineage, having been common in many localities in pre-colonial days.

36. This is in daily life: office-holders, such as Village Heads, are often surprisingly young.

37. Gray and Gulliver (1964). (Unfortunately none of the societies examined in this excellent book are in West Africa).

38. It is less likely to be related to the area which an individual might clear, both because of the possibility of communal clearing and because clearing can be carried out over varying periods in the off-season. (The matter of farm-division on death is dealt

THE WEST AFRICAN FARMING HOUSEHOLD   135

with below).

39. Thus in Asafo, in Akim Abuakwa, in 1959, 54% of a sample of cocoa-farms owned by male native (non-migrant) farmers were between ½ and 2 acres, as many as 30% being between ½ and 1 acre. (See, also, fn 54).

40. See Forde (1964: 15). Statistics on the sizes of farms, and holdings are generally fragmentary and misleading, owing to the lack of cadastral surveys and to dangerously unreliable agricultural censuses.

41. While in certain societies, such as Mbembe, the eldest brother has authority over the land when his father dies, it is likely to be he 'who must share out year by year any of the father's land which remained unallotted at his death' and who makes provision for his younger brothers as they marry - Harris in Derrett (1965: 110). In societies where younger brothers inherit, there is everywhere a general tendency for certain types of property to pass directly to sons.

42. In Yorubaland division may be between all children - see Lloyd in Derrett (1965).

43. See, for instance, Lloyd in Derrett (1965); Obi (1963) on the Ibo; and Hill (1963: Appendix IV.3). (There is generally a good deal of ambiguity about the position of unmarried sons.)

44. However, in Hausaland when a man dies without sons, only his full brothers inherit, although the original division on the father's death had not been *per stirpes*.

45. See Hill (1972). When a Hausa woman retains an inherited farm it is usually (though not necessarily) cultivated by her husband.

46. This has become a serious matter with certain migrant farmers in southern Ghana who own vast acreages of land - see Hill (1963).

47. With the exception of two of the many ethnic groups involved, the migrant farmers refrain from dividing strip-farms of less than a certain width - see Hill (1963); as for Hausaland, see Hill (1972: 233), regarding the very small proportion of farms under one acre which had been divided on the death of the present owner.

48. While the plough is an important innovation in certain savannah areas (including parts of Hausaland), most West African farmers use no manufactured steel tools, apart from the matchet which has long been in great demand in the forest zone, and possibly the axe.

49. For a Yoruba example, see Lloyd (1965: 162).

50. According to Lloyd (Ibid: 120), a man's self-acquired cocoa-farms (i.e. those which he had established himself) 'pass corporately to all his children', and not to his junior siblings. In the case of patrilineal migrant cocoa-farmers (see Hill 1963), self-acquired

136   *CHANGING SOCIAL STRUCTURE IN GHANA*

farms are often formally divided between sons, though seldom between grandsons.

51. My enquiries in Akim Abuakwa (north of Accra) suggested that as men sometimes give cocoa-farms to women (who may also inherit from men in the absence of a male heir), there is a general tendency for an increasing proportion of cocoa land to become concentrated in the hands of women, who always prefer women heirs - younger sisters, rather than daughters, sometimes inherit.

52. Whereas Lloyd's work (1962 and 1965) showns that in Yorubaland (where societies are patrilineal or bilateral) women cocoa-farmers sometimes inherit farms from men, no writer has indicated the relative numbers of men and women farmers. Using the 1960 Ghana census I have estimated, see Hill (1970), that about 38% of all those who were recorded as being cocoa-farmers (as distinct from *abusa* labourers, with whom they were confused in the census) were women; the ratio was high for all major cocoa-growing areas, including Brong-Ahafo.

53. In Akim Abuakwa (see fn 51) reliable statistics relating to 1,338 cocoa-farms owned by native (non-migrant) farmers showed that 37% of them were owned by women, who owned 30% of the total acreage. In 1932-35 in Akokoaso (further north) it was found (see Beckett 1944) that 39% of 'independent' cocoa-farmers were women. Among the matrilineal Agni of the southern Ivory Coast there are many women cocoa-farmers - see Dupire (1960:190). In Asokore in Ashanti, in 1945-6, 30 out of 200 adult males were cocoa-farmers compared with 44 out of 246 adult women - Fortes *et al* (1947: 163).

54. As many women are assisted by their sons and/or labourers in establishing cocoa farms (and in harvesting cocoa), I was surprised to find that in Akim Abuakwa and New Juaben the modal size of women's farms was consistently somewhere lower than that of men's farms. Thus, in Oyoko, north of Koforidua, data for 692 cocoa-farms showed that percentages under 1 acre were 51% for men and 60% for women. A sample of 22 Oyoko women owned as many as 154 cocoa-farms - 17 of them owning 6 or more farms.

DELEGATION OF PARENTAL ROLES IN WEST AFRICA AND THE WEST INDIES

ESTHER GOODY

The ethnographic literature on West Africa contains many references to the sending of children to kin to grow up away from their own parents (Skinner 1964; Oppong 1965; Cohen 1969; Azu 1974; E. Goody 1961, 1966, 1969, 1971a, 1973; Goody and Muir 1972). A number of 'explanations' have been offered for this widespread practice which can never be seen solely as an economic, micro-political, or kinship institution, and often seems to share aspects of all these. In all the societies for which it is reported, the fostering of children by kin also provides proxy parents in cases where the family or orientation has been scattered by death or divorce of the parents. Such a rescue operation may be termed *crisis fostering* to distinguish it from *purposive fostering* arranged while the family is intact, which is entered into with the intention of securing some benefit to the child, his parents, the foster parents, or perhaps to all.

Many reports on West Indian domestic and kinship organisation also include a reference to sending children to kin to be looked after. Typically an infant goes to his mother's mother or perhaps to a mother's sister and is often brought up to regard this foster mother as his mother, using 'mother' as a term of address for her, and calling his own mother by whatever term of address her siblings use (see R.T. Smith, 1956:143; E. Clarke, 1966:142, 179; T. Spens, 1969:278 ff.). These accounts suggest that the rearing of children by kin in the West Indies tends to be the result of the inability of the parents to provide proper care (whether because they have no joint home, or because the mother must work full time), a situation that I have called crisis fostering in discussing the West African material. However, there are also hints of purposive fostering in the West Indies; Clarke speaks of 'schoolchildren' who are ostensibly taken into a household to help in exchange for food, clothing and a chance to go to school. One such child she encountered was treated much like the other children in the house - all of whom helped with chores - but she alone did not go to school (Clarke, 1966:177). Among the Black Carib of Guatamala Gonzalez describes the sending of young boys to families in town where they take an increasing share of jobs around the house, and learn both literate skills and town ways (Gonzalez, 1969:54ff.). Again, Horowitz in his study of Martinique refers more than once to children staying with kin in cases where their parents are living together (1967:49). But on the whole the picture is one of fostering as a means of coping with children of dissolved or non-residential unions. Indeed, M.G. Smith (1962b:80) writes as though this was the only circumstance under which children would be sent to be reared by kin, and treats fostering in the way he does household composition, as a reflex of the mating forms.

In both West Africa and the West Indies, then, children are sent to be reared by kin when the family of orientation cannot, for some reason, manage. And in both areas, fostering is used as a means of widening the

138 *CHANGING SOCIAL STRUCTURE IN GHANA*

education of a child, of providing relatives with companionship and assistance, and of strengthening ties with kin who are relatively well-off. In the West Indies it appears to be crisis fostering which is most prominent, while in West Africa purposive fostering is probably more important.

The question of whether the West Indian institution is a 'survival' from West Africa via the slaves brought to Caribbean plantations is not relevant at this point. I am concerned with analysing the present constraints and supports of behaviour, whatever its origin.

Although people from these two regions seem to have very similar institutions in respect of the rearing of children by kin, they behave very differently when they come as immigrants to the United Kingdom. In a recent study in four London boroughs, we have documented the very high percentage of West African children sent to English foster parents (Goody and Muir, 1972). Less direct information from several sources indicates that West Indians virtually never send their children to English foster parents (though the local authority may occasionally place children of disturbed or broken homes with their own foster parents as a welfare measure). Instead, West Indian mothers prefer to send their young children to a 'nanny' who takes several children into her home from early morning until six in the evening. Payment is either on an hourly or a weekly basis and the mother is expected to do all laundry for the child and often must provide food. These women are also known as 'daily minders'. Probably the large majority of women who do daily minding are themselves West Indian and it appears likely (though reliable figures are not available) that the majority of children sent to them are also West Indian.

The problem I wish to pose here is this - why should two groups with apparently similar institutions at home for coping with children outside the natal family **of** orientation react in such different ways to the constraints of living in an urban environment abroad? In order to be able to answer such a question, we must look more closely at both traditional and contemporary fostering in these two areas, as well as at the circumstances of life in London for both groups of immigrants. It may be that the parents of each group are seeking different goals in coming to England, and more immediately, have different reasons for delegating the care of their children to others. Or the choice between forms of child care may simply be one of economics: one mode or the other may be more expensive and require more resources. Or it may be that we have been over-hasty in seeing the traditional forms as they appear in West Africa and the **West Indies as essentially** similar. **Perhaps they function rather differently at a basic level, and in the immigrant situation this difference gives rise to the variations in adaptations to the new environment which** we have found.

Fostering in West Africa

Despite the relatively small number of West African societies for which there is detailed, numerical data on frequency and distribution of foster children, it is becoming clear that this is a pan-West African phenomenon for which no locally appropriate functional explanation will

PARENTAL ROLES IN W. AFRICA AND W. INDIES 139

suffice. While it is perfectly true that fostering 'fits' stratified
societies such as the Hausa and Bornu bacause it is one avenue for the
establishment of clientship relationships, it also appears between
commoners in Gonja and among the relatively egalitarian Ga. Similarly,
where wives are kept in seclusion by well-to-do Muslims, the need to
have a child as a link between households and with the market is pressing, and neatly met for those without children of their own by taking a
foster child. But fostering is also common among pagan ana Christian
Yoruba, where no such explanation is appropriate. Or again, in contemporary towns and cities, one often comes across children staying with
kin, helping in the house and attending school. But African fostering
cannot have arisen as a means of avoiding expensive boarding school fees.
I myself first came upon fostering among the Gonja of northern Ghana, in
a town with no school, and where indeed few children in the kingdom, and
scarcely any adults, had had a chance to attend one. The Dagomba, also
of northern Ghana, make use of fostering to train a daughter's child in
the traditional skill of the paternal *dang* (Oppong: 1965). The neighbouring Gonja have many of the same skills, and a high incidence of
fostering, but only rarely do they use the institution as the basis of
apprenticeship. In the west of the kingdom, the Gonja do, however, see
the sending of a son to grow up with his mother's brother as one form
of arranging for the mother's care when she eventually returns in old
age to her natal kin. The son already there can give her a home and can
farm for her, in addition to the support which her brother is morally
obliged to contribute. The spatial distribution of marriages is narrower
in eastern Gonja, and a wife's 'retirement' less likely to mean her
departure to a distant village. Perhaps for this reason, the fostering
of a son with his mother's brother is much less common in the eastern
divisions.

One could go on citing similarities and differences between local
variations of fostering in West Africa. The general point should be
clear - there are a wide range of specific 'reasons' or 'functions'
each of which makes excellent sense in its own context, but no one (or
indeed several) of which can be made to 'account' for the widespread
occurrence of institutionalised fostering of children by kin in West Africa.

Yet if one considers other culture areas, this practice is strange
enough to warrant some kind of 'explanation'[1]. Few Europeans or Americans
would readily take a sibling's or cousin's child into their home for
several years, or send their own son or daughter to an aunt or grandparent
from the age of five until they were grown up. Purposive fostering, the
placing of children with kin to fulfil one's obligations and at the
same time gain for them the opportunity to grow up in a different family,
often in a different town, does not seem to occur in Indo-European societies. There are partial equivalents of a functional kind (*compadrazgo*,
and other forms of fictional kinship) but not the actual removal of a boy
or girl for the whole of childhood and adolescence, as we commonly find
in West African societies.

Why is there this very general difference between the two sets of
societies? What kind of underlying factor is common to all the various
West African groups which have different particular reasons for fostering
their children?[2] It must be a very general factor, because these groups
differ widely in language, social structure, political organisation

140 *CHANGING SOCIAL STRUCTURE IN GHANA*

and religious institutions. The simple answer is that fostering reflects the claims, rights and obligations, of members of an extended kin group. Given the norm that kin have to share rights and obligations over resources, the fostering of children becomes only a special case of such sharing.

This is entirely explicit for the Gonja of Northern Ghana. Rights of siblings over one another's children are expressed in two models. One model allocates the first daughter of a marriage to the father's sister as a foster daughter, in recognition of her role in establishing the bride in her new home. The father's sister will be informed of the birth of this first daughter, should send kola to the naming ceremony, and provide waist beads for the little girl. When the child has reached the 'age of sense' (*e kø kinyesheng*), the father's sister comes with a gift of cloth for the mother and for the child, and takes the little girl home with her. She will remain with her aunt until she is ready to marry, suitors paying their respects both to the foster mother and the true parents. There is a term of reference for female foster parent, *tchepe*, but the child uses the term for father's sister in addressing her.[3] She never calls the father's sister 'mother' nor ceases to call her own mother by the familiar *maa* form for mother.

The other model for Gonja fostering designates the second or third son as a foster child of the mother's brother. A man who wishes to ensure his rights over a sister's son may insist on paying the expenses of the naming ceremony which takes place seven days after birth. Otherwise he will come to 'beg' for the child some time during its infancy or early childhood. As with a female foster child, the boy does not join his foster parent until he is considered old enough to 'have sense', which means around the age of 6 or 7. Once a boy has joined his foster father he should remain until old enough to marry, learning from him the skills of farming, hunting and house building which are necessary for all adult men. The foster father ought to help the youth to marry, or he may offer him a horse or a gun rather than a wife. Thereafter the boy may either remain with his mother's brother or return to his father; among Muslims and members of the ruling estate, men virtually always return in the end to their father's town, but commoners may opt to remain with a mother's brother. The term of reference for male foster parent is *nyinipe*, but the appropriate kinship term is used in address, and not the term for father, which continues to be applied to the real father.

In practice, a wide range of relatives serve as foster parents in Gonja, but these two models are the stated forms that act as charters for other claims. Siblings all say that they 'own' (*wø*) each other's children, which means both that they are responsible for them, and that they have claims over them. Unless there is some reason why the parents cannot manage their children, perhaps through poverty, lack of discipline, or the break-up of the natal family of orientation, the initiative in arranging fostering is usually left to the would-be foster parent. Only when he or she presses their rightful claim will the child actually be sent. Occasionally, a child is sent to an office holder or to a Koranic teacher. In these cases it is more likely to be the ends of the parent which are the critical factors.

It is characteristic of West African societies that the 'sibling group' is not thought of as confined to children of the same mother and father. This inclusiveness is usually reflected in the terminology, which designates the children of sisters (in matrilineal systems) or brothers (in patrilineal systems) or of brothers and sisters (among the bilateral Gonja) as themselves siblings. For instance, Fortes writes of Tallensi brothers (*sunzø*) as in some contexts including all male members of the agnatic lineage of a man's own generation. In Gonja, *all* of a person's relatives of the same generation are either 'older sibling' or 'younger sibling'. Claims on the children of classificatory siblings are also successfully made in Gonja, though only rarely when the relationship is more distant than that of first cousins. It would seem to be in those cases where the terminology is open-ended, and the norms of siblings' rights and obligations very generally phrased, that the recognition of claims over children serves to define the limits of effective obligation. Rearing a sibling's child has this function because, in addition to the formal moral obligation of kinship, the fostering relationship itself creates what I have elsewhere called the 'reciprocities of rearing' (E. Goody 1971b). That is, specific, reciprocal, obligations of care and support are built up during childhood; the foster parent is seen as looking after the child, feeding and training it, and these acts create a debt which the child must later be prepared to repay. Thus where second or third order relationships might cease to be considered binding in and of themselves, when they are reinforced by fostering a second set of obligations comes into play which is compelling in its own rights. Furthermore, the fostered child grows up in a household of classificatory siblings (the foster parents' children) with whom he or she is on effective terms of full sibship, rather than the more distant relationship which exists between distant kin who meet only occasionally.

In traditional West African societies, then, fostering depended on claims made against, and honoured by, kin. At the same time the sending of foster children between elementary families served to strengthen the bonds between kin by superimposing specific claims on the more general ones which tend to define the roles of distant relatives. An illuminating comparison might be with systematically practised cross-cousin marriage; indeed the diagram Yalman uses to indicate the claims of cross-cousin marriage in a Kandyan Ceylonese village would serve equally well to illustrate the claims of fostering. As with cross-cousin marriage, it would be a mistake to expect that fostering will always occur between the children of primary kin (see E; Goody 1973).

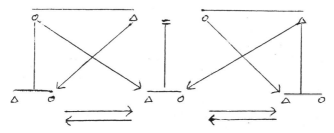

The interconnection and lateral extension of claims for cross-cousin marriage: Kandyan Sinalese. (Figure 14, N. Yalman. *Under the Bo Tree*, 1967: 154)

142   *CHANGING SOCIAL STRUCTURE IN GHANA*

Recent fostering in northern Ghana

In Table 3 data on relationship of foster parent are given from four different studies, representing in all seven communities from eastern, central and western Gonja. The sex of the fostered child is given in brackets for each study. Several points emerge from these figures. First, in all the studies, a very substantial proportion of foster parents come from the parental generation (between 39% and 59%). This should be borne in mind for comparison with the West Indian pattern of fostering. Next, if we compare the proportion of male and female foster children resident with a grandparent (real or classificatory), we find that it is the girls who are much more likely to be sent to someone in their grandparents' generation (50%), while for boys this happened 20% of the time only. This same pattern is found in some of the southern Ghana samples. The sending of girls to a 'grandmother' fits with their training in a domestic role, for they are expected to take over household tasks as well as provide companionship for the old women. Old men, on the other hand, are fed and looked after by their daughters or daughters-in-law, and a boy cannot be expected to fill a man's economic role. Finally, only in the men's marriage survey (sample 4) were there children sent to foster parents who were not kin. Indeed, only in two of the three communities represented in the men's marriage survey did this occur. These boys went either to join the household of a chief (6 cases) or to a Koranic teacher (5 cases, all in western Gonja). No girls went to non-kin in any of the communities studied.

Fostering in southern Ghana

I must stress at the outset that most of my own work in West Africa has been with a relatively remote group, the Gonja on whom the industrial age has hardly begun to make an impact. The coastal peoples to the south have, on the other hand, been within the orbit of European trade and all that this implies since the beginning of the sea-borne trade with Europe in the late 15th Century. I have been able to do little work directly with coastal peoples apart from making brief surveys in four communities representing three different language groups in southern Ghana. The following remarks draw on these surveys as well as interviews with West Africans in London, and on two books published in 1974: Dr. C. Oppong's *Marriage in a Matrilineal Elite* and Gladys Azu's *The Ga Family and Social Change*. Although the documentation for the coastal areas is incomplete, the picture is fairly clear.

Briefly, there appears to be a tendency to shift from fostering by kin to the arrangement of 'fostering' with strangers who can provide either training in modern skills, or a chance to gain familiarity with urban, western ways. In the Ewe, Krobo and Fanti communities I looked at briefly in southern Ghana, daughters were sent to live with and 'serve' women who baked bread for sale, seamstresses and traders; sons went to fishermen, carpenters, fitters and masons. Where such teachers were available within the kin group they were selected for preference, but in a number of cases they were not, and an arrangement was made with a friend or someone of good reputation who could train the child. My impression was that availability of a suitable 'master' could determine the choice of skill to which the child would be apprenticed.

PARENTAL ROLES IN W. AFRICA AND W. INDIES   143

Table 3

Gonja (northern Ghana): Generation of foster-parent
for four samples

Foster Parent is of:

Data from:	Grand-parents' Generation	Parents' Generation	Child's Generation	Not Kin	Total N=
1. Buipe census[a] (children, m and f)	13 (38%)	20 (50%)	1 (3%)	0	34
2. Kpembe core[b] sample (children, m and f)	15 (48%)	12 (39%)	4 (13%)	0	31
3. Bole/Daboya[c] sample (adults, f)	39 (51%)	35 (45%)	3 (4%)	0	77
4. Men's marriage[d] survey (adults, m)	13 (20%)	37 (57%)	4 (6%)	11 (17%)	65
	80 (39%)	104 (50%)	12 (6%)	11 (5%)	207 (100%)

a. Old Buipe: 1956.

b. These are all the fostered children in two sections of the
divisional capital of Kpembe (eastern Gonja): 1964.

c. The Bole sample consisted of all adult women in randomly
selected compounds in the western Gonja divisional capital
of Bole; the Daboya sample consisted of all the adult women
in nine selected compounds in the central Gonja divisional
capital of Daboya: 1965.

d. This survey was carried out in three divisional capitals of
eastern, central and western Gonja, and surrounding villages.
The informants were all adult men in selected compounds: 1966.

144   *CHANGING SOCIAL STRUCTURE IN GHANA*

For Ga boys, there appears to be a similar pattern of choice between a kinsmen or a local expert of good repute (Azu 1974).

For girls, in addition to skills in sewing, baking and trading, there has evolved the institution of the 'housemaid'. I say evolved, because there does not appear to have been anything similar in the traditional societies of West Africa, with the possible exception of girls who were lent to a creditor as surety for a debt.[4] These children (they might also be boys, though apparently this was less common) are referred to in the classical ethnographic literature as having been 'pawned', and there seems to be a word in many if not all of the West African languages to distinguish this practice.[5] Such pawns worked in the household of the creditor until the debt was redeemed. There might ultimately be an agreement to let the girl be married there in exchange for cancelling the debt, but casual sexual relations between the girl and her master were usually specifically forbidden.

The modern housemaid may be a relative of her master or mistress. This is preferred and is common (Oppong 1974). However, many appear to be unrelated, and to come for a sum of a few pounds paid monthly or annually, to the parents of a young girl,[6] or when she is older, to the girl herself. Such girls tend to stay only a few years, and then either marry, or move on to some form of more remunerative employment, perhaps to an apprenticeship where they can learn a more saleable skill than housekeeping. There is a definite pattern of recruiting girls in rural areas to work as 'housemaids' in the cities of Ghana.

It would seem that as the skills and experiences which parents desire for their children become more diversified, they begin to look beyond their kin to find someone to train them. Fostering by kin is gradually transformed into various forms of apprenticeship and domestic service. At the same time that kin are proving less able to meet these needs, there is a movement towards limiting the acknowledgement of kinship claims by those whose own education has led to a standard of living far above that of most of their relatives. While there is evidence that parents and full siblings still successfully request assistance in regular and substantial amounts, among the educated elite there is no longer the same pattern of honouring the claims of distant kin, even when made according to traditional norms (Oppong 1969b).

Recent fostering in southern Ghana

The data in Tables 4 and 5 come from three very brief surveys in southern Ghana. The purpose of the surveys was to discover whether the Gonja were unusual in giving such weight to fostering by kin in the rearing of their children, or whether similar practices might be found in other West African societies. Time and resources did not allow me to spend more than a few days in either the Ewe or the Fanti community, while the Krobo survey was conducted through local assistants after I had returned to England. The main weakness of the material lies in its narrow focus. The interviews with Ewe and Fanti were necessarily conducted through an interpreter, and the central question, once the constitution of the informant's sibling group had been established, was 'Who reared ..... (each sibling in turn)?' Although this was further broken

PARENTAL ROLES IN W. AFRICA AND W. INDIES   145

down by periods in infancy, childhood and adolescence, a full exploration
of the rearing situation was not possible. I am persuaded that the Krobo
interviewers confined themselves almost entirely to the formal interview
schedule. Informants were adults, and the information thus refers to
childhood of from 20 to 60 years ago (1972). What I did not anticipate
in planning these surveys was the shift from kinship to non-kin fostering.
Hence when exploring the vocabulary of childrearing in the vernacular in
order to standardise the questions prior to interviewing, I did not ask
about how such apprentice-fostering was referred to. The figures in Table
4 particularly, on the non-kin fostering of boys, do not fit with observations on the sending of boys to learn such skills as carpentry, driving,
'fitting' (automotive mechanics) and so on. While this may be a very
recent pattern, it seems more likely that informants did not consider
these apprenticeships as 'rearing' when the 'master' was not a kinsman.
Those few cases which do appear in Table 4 may be the ones in which a
change of residence occurred in the context of apprenticeship, thus more
closely approximating the kinship fostering pattern, in which the foster
parent expects to have the domestic services of the child as part of the
relationship.

In these southern Ghana samples a substantially higher proportion of
girls than boys is sent to non-kin foster parents. Some of these girls
are learning trades like baking or sewing, while others are acting as
'housemaids'. The fact that they were considered as being 'reared' by
their mistresses may be related to the domestic nature of the skills
they were learning, and the undoubted fact that their training involves
helping their mistress in her household work as well as also in some
cases learning a particular skill.

Both boys and girls in the southern Ghana samples are sent relatively
infrequently to grandparents to rear. The contrast with the figures for
Gonja (northern Ghana) is pronounced, and the difference between this
pattern and that of the West Indian samples is extreme (see below). There
are some differences between the different southern Ghana samples in frequency of fostering by the grandparental generation on which I cannot
comment here. There is a regular tendency for girls in all samples to
go more frequently to their grandmothers than boys to their grandfathers.
This, as I suggested in discussing the Gonja data, seems likely to be
related to the domestic nature of the fostered girl's training.

The great majority of the boys in the southern Ghana samples went to
a 'sibling' of either the father or the mother (73%). This preference
for a foster parent of the parental generation appeared in some of the
Gonja samples, and it is much clearer here. For the girls in the southern Ghana sample also, the parental generation provided by far the largest class of foster parents (53%), with the next largest group being
unrelated (19%). A substantial minority of both boys and girls (18%
and 16% respectively) went to an elder sibling (own or classificatory).
These proportions are much higher than the 6% average for the Gonja
samples and probably reflect the fact that older siblings who are
educated or have learned a trade are more likely to be seen as able to
contribute to a child's development than older siblings in the pre-
industrial, pre-bureaucratic world of northern Ghana in the first half
of the 20th century.

146   *CHANGING SOCIAL STRUCTURE IN GHANA*

Table 4

Relationship between child and foster parent in three [a]
southern Ghana societies: Boys

Societies

Foster Parent is of:	Fanti	Ewe	Krobo	Total
Grandparental generation	0 -	2 (18%)	1 (1%)	3 (2%)
Parental generation	39 (75%)	7 (64%)	53 (74%)	99 (73%)
Child's generation	11 (21%)	2 (18%)	11 (15%)	24 (18%)
Not Kin	2 (4%)	0 -	7 (10%)	9 (7%)
	52 (100%)	11 (100%)	72 (100%)	135 (100%)

Table 5

Relationship between child and foster parent in three[a]
southern Ghana societies: Girls

Societies

Foster Parent is of:	Fanti	Ewe	Krobo	Total
Grandparental generation	8 (17%)	6 (23%)	2 (3%)	16 (11%)
Parental generation	26 (54%)	10 (38%)	41 (60%)	77 (53%)
Child's generation	6 (12%)	7 (27%)	10 (14%)	23 (16%)
Not Kin	8 (17%)	3 (12%)	17 (24%)	28 (19%)
	48 (100%)	26 (100%)	70 (101%)	144 (99%)

[a]These data are based on interviews in which the rearing
histories of all members of the informant's full sibling
group were recorded. In Ewe and Fanti communities the
informants were selected from people known to my sponsors,
and form what can only be described as an arbitrary sample.
The Krobo sample consists of all adults in every tenth
compound on selected streets of the two largest Krobo towns.
The figures exclude 56 cases in which the generation of the
foster parent could not be determined, although he or she
was stated to be a relative.

PARENTAL ROLES IN W. AFRICA AND W. INDIES

Table 6

Generation of foster parent: comparison
of northern and southern Ghana: (combined
samples)

	Grandparents' Generation	Parents' Generation	Child's Generation	Not Kin	Total N=
Gonja	80 (39%)	104 (50%)	12 (6%)	11 (5%)	207 (100%)
Southern Ghana	19 (7%)	176 (63%)	47 (17%)	37 (13%)	279 (100%)

While both southern and northern Ghanaian samples reflect a
preference for selecting foster parents from the parents' own generation, there is a relatively greater emphasis in the north on sending
a child to a grandparent, and in the south on making use of siblings
and unrelated foster parents. At the time these children were being
fostered, between 1910 and 1950, northern Ghana scarcely participated
in the economic differentiation and educational stratification of
modern society. The south, on the other hand, had begun to enter the
age of technology with all that this involves. In seeking to understand the shift away from grandparents as foster parents in favour of
siblings and strangers, the critical factor is the balance between
fostering as a reflection of rights vested in kinship roles, and
fostering as a mode of education. Both these aspects coexist in
traditional Gonja fostering (see E. Goody 1973). However, with a
shift to sibling and non-kin fostering the element of kinship rights
becomes secondary to the educational functions of fostering. A child
is not sent to an elder sibling (and certainly not to a stranger)
because they have a *right* to a lien on its labour and companionship.
On the other hand, this was a significant element in the request for
a foster child in traditional Gonja. It would appear that in the
modern world of southern Ghana, rights vested in kinship roles have
become less compelling than the need to help children to make their
way in the new occupational and social milieu. Indeed, the shift
probably reflects the diminishing role played by the senior generation
in helping youth to become established in the adult world. Instead of
age in itself leading to positions of importance, relatively restricted
skills, especially those based on advanced education, become the critical factor. In all the Ghanaian samples there is a pronounced emphasis
on fostering by parents' siblings. This emphasis reflects reciprocal
rights and obligations acknowledged between both full and classificatory
siblings.

I have argued thus far that traditional fostering by kin, while it
fulfilled many specific functions which varied with the form of each
society, also reflected the strength of claims which members of a kin
group could successfully make on one another. As the skills demanded
for full participation in an increasingly diversified economy grow more
complex, with success in school of growing importance on the one hand,
and many new crafts on the other, it is no longer possible for just
any adult to provide the model and the training which are necessary for

148   *CHANGING SOCIAL STRUCTURE IN GHANA*

the child to take his place in society. Where no kinsman is available, an arrangement for the child's education must be made on another basis. The usual pattern is that the child's labour over a period of several years pays for the training he receives, though a lump sum may be given to the teacher at the beginning or at the end of the training period. In this transformation of the traditional institutions of fostering we see two aspects emphasised: the experience is sought for the child as a way of helping prepare him for a more successful adulthood: the labour of the child is a major part of the recompense for the training received, but money may pass either to the 'teacher', or to the parents, in lieu of the kinship obligation which would once have sufficed. If there is a highly educated member of the family, a teacher or a clergyman, or one who is in another kind of important job, he will often be asked to take on children, since it is felt that he is in a position to give them a better training than others would be; it is not only specific skills which are sought, but a facility with the written and spoken word and with westernised ways.

Fostering by West Africans in London

How is all this related to the fostering of children by West Africans in London? There are many practical reasons why fostering might appeal to this group: they often live in cramped conditions, and do not have room for small children; the mother may need to work full time to help support the father's studies; often, the mother is herself trying to train in addition to her job, and thus needs to be free in the evenings; the father is usually studying as well as working, and needs a quiet home in which to read; many mothers are training as nurses, and need to be free for night duty, or even to live in hospital. Yet English or American parents in a similar situation would simply not consider fostering a child with strangers as an appropriate solution. It should be made clear that West African parents are often distressed to have to part with their very young children to foster parents, and they take elaborate pains to ensure that the families to whom they go are clean and kind, and that they feed and care for them properly. But basic assumptions of the two cultures differ. A cultural paradigm as to the appropriateness of delegating child rearing underlies West African thinking on this subject which, though there is evidence that Europe once shared at least some of the same ideas[7], has ceased with the writings of psychologists from Freud to Bowlby to seem credible to the west. One part of the explanation of the high incidence of fostering by West Africans in London, then, is that parents who are trying to fill several other roles as well, share a cultural view of parenthood which approves of delegating certain aspects of this role.

Another part of the explanation lies in the traditional definition of fostering as character building, an educational process. This educational side of fostering has been increasingly emphasised in recent years as the institution has been adapted to modern conditions. When faced with a child care problem in England, the West African parent asks, how can I arrange both for the care and for the education of my child? Since it is very young children who constitute the main problem,[8] language and domestic culture are the main things the child is expected to learn. A number of parents in our intensive study commented explicitly on the advantage they hoped their children would gain at school from having spoken English as a first language. A different sort of light is shed

PARENTAL ROLES IN W. AFRICA AND W. INDIES   149

on this aspect of fostering in England by a question which we asked
the parents on the extensive survey. 'If you were living in West
Africa now, or when you go back, would you consider fostering your
child?' While some parents replied that they would have to do so
if a relative was in need, the great majority said that there were
no circumstances under which they would do this. And much the most
common reason given was 'there is no one there better able to rear
him than we are'. That is, relative to their kin and the people
they knew, these budding elites did not feel there was anyone who
could train their children any better than they could themselves.
Yet this judgement apparently does not apply in the United Kingdom,
for while living in London, fifty per cent of this sample of nearly
300 couples had either previously fostered a child with an English
family (25%) or were currently doing so (25%). Their firm rejection
of fostering in West Africa ostensibly included 'all circumstances'
and thus ought to be comparable with the situation of very real
objective strain under which many lived in London. But even allowing
for a certain amount of idealisation, it is clear that West African
parents feel they are getting something of worth through fostering
their children with English parents, which fostering in West Africa
would not secure. This is mainly seen as greater facility with the
language and a greater ease with western institutions, both of prime
importance to a highly upwardly mobile group.

West African fostering in different contexts

I have very briefly considered the distribution of children in
fosterage in three very different West African contexts: first, we
saw that in Gonja society, where education and occupational differentiation are very little affected by industrialisation, children go
almost always to kin. Exceptions are found only among boys, who sometimes are sent to Koranic teachers and occasionally to office-holders.
Forty per cent of the children go to a foster parent of the grandparental
generation, while about half go to kin of the parental generation - that
is, to a parent's real or classificatory sibling.

The second context was contemporary southern Ghana where apprentice
fostering is becoming important. Here 'masters' are still sought among
kin for preference, but differentiation of skills may make this impossible. Apprentice fostering affects both boys and girls, but exists side-
by-side with fostering for more diffuse objectives. Children are also
sent to educated relatives in the hope that they may receive both an
improved education and perhaps advantages in securing work later. Here
foster parents are seldom of the grandparental generation, and children
most often go to a 'sibling' of the parent, or in a substantial number
of cases, to non-kin.

The final situation in which we have found fostering of children
by West African parents is among the temporary immigrants to London.
Here the children are much younger, reflecting the absence of domestic
help or relatives in the household to assist with the care or infants
and toddlers. There are no relatives available to serve as foster
parents in London[9] and children all go to strangers, and indeed to
non-West African couples who care for them in exchange for a weekly
payment.

Table 7

Children in three Jamaican communities living with
neither parent; Percent living with kin and with
non-kin; Percent of all children living with foster
parents.(Clarke 1966: Appendix 5.)

	FOSTERED CHILDREN LIVING WITH:				TOTAL FOSTERED CHILDREN	TOTAL CHILDREN IN COMMUNITY	PERCENT ALL CHILDREN FOSTERED*	PERCENT ALL CHILDREN FOSTERED by NON-KIN
	Kin		Non-kin					
	No.	%	No.	%				
Orange Grove	20	90%	2	10%	22	296	7%	1%
Sugar Town	65	72%	25	28%	90	318	28%	8%
Mocca	14	54%	12	46%	26	133	19%	9%
ALL THREE COMMUNITIES	99	72%	39	28%	138	747	18%	6%

*It is not clear from Appendix 5 whether the children enumerated are
those in each community or all the children born to adults living in
each community. I nevertheless include the comparison to give some
indication of the proportions of children being reared by relatives
and non-kin.

PARENTAL ROLES IN W. AFRICA AND W. INDIES   151

These data reflect a clear progression from fostering by kin to fostering by strangers which shows a close similarity to apprenticeship. They also suggest a decreasing reliance on the grandparental generation in situations in which fostering is viewed as a means of securing skills or advantage for the child. Admittedly the situation of immigrants to London is an extreme one, but perhaps all the more revealing for that, especially when contrasted with the response of West Indians to objectively similar circumstances.

Fostering in the West Indies

There are a few references in the ethnographic literature on the West Indies to the sending of children to live with kin even though their natal family of orientation is still intact and forms a residential unit. Gonzalez writes of the 'loaning' of children between compounds as sometimes being based on kinship ties and this seems to include children of intact families (1969:52-3). Sanford also refers to 'loaning' of children and it seems likely that in some of these cases the parents are living together (1971:100). Horowitz specifically mentions that parents may send a child to a relative from an intact conjugal household (1967:49). There are also clear indications that children are sent to stay with non-kin who are in a position to offer them a better start in life than their own parents. Edith Clarke's data from three very different communities in Jamaica show a substantial proportion of children living with neither parent; over the three communities the average is 18% (see Table 7). Nearly one-third of these fostered children are living with non-relatives. In the poorest community (Mocca) almost half the fostered children are with non-kin, while nearly all those from prosperous Orange Grove are with relatives. But although Orange Grove children are seldom sent out to live with non-kin, Clarke reports that more unrelated children come to live in Orange Grove homes than was the case in the other communities studied (1966:178).

The sending of children to middle and upper-class white and Creole families in the hopes that they will receive an education and assistance in finding a secure occupational niche is also reported by Gonzalez for the Black Caribs of Guatemala (1969: 53ff.) and Sanford for the Carib and Creole population of a British Honduras community (1971: 94-5).

Yet despite these references, purposive fostering with kin and with strangers seems to account for a relatively small proportion of the children who are reared apart from both their parents in the Caribbean area. Again from Sanford's figures, 59% of her instances of 'child keeping ' (205 cases) I would classify as crisis fostering, with another 13% (46 cases) as probable crisis fostering. If we include the latter group, then something like 72% of her cases were due to the inability of the parents to rear the child themselves (Sanford 1971: 82). As Sanford points out, this classification is based on reasons given 'after the fact' and cannot but represent bias of some sort. Unfortunately there are few figures of which I am aware which enable a distinction to be drawn between crisis and voluntary fostering in the Caribbean area[10].

Although additional figures are lacking, the burden of the descriptive material in the West Indian area is clearly that children are most often placed with a pro-parent because their parents have no home in

152   *CHANGING SOCIAL STRUCTURE IN GHANA*

which to care for them. These may be children of transient unions, 'outside' children whose presence in a conjugal household is not welcome, or children whose parent or parents must work in a city or abroad, and cannot care for them as well; but for some such reason the parents cannot cope and some pro-parental figure has to be found.

The multi-functional quality of fostering in the West Indies is precisely what we find in traditional West African societies, and the adaptations in West Africa to western industrial changes are echoed in those described for the Caribbean. Yet the working out of the pattern is subtly different. Not only does a relatively higher proportion of crisis fostering seem to characterise this area, but fostering among kin seems more likely to mean the rearing of a child by a parent's own parent rather than, as in West Africa, by a wide range of classificatory relatives, particularly parent's siblings.

It is in societies based on cognatic descent systems, or with weak unilineal descent groups that fostering appears to flourish in West Africa. West Indian societies are cognatic, with a few weakly unilineal (e.g. M.G. Smith, 1962a). Despite this similarity, the range of kin which participates is wider in West Africa than in the West Indies. What is interesting for the comparison of fostering in the two areas is that these collateral kin are, in West Africa, seen as having a claim on children to foster. Furthermore, they are ready to acknowledge requests to take children which are phrased in terms of kinship ties.

Sanford refers to anxiety over dependability of kinship bonds among the Creole and Carib peoples of British Honduras (1971: 108). But the bonds of which she is speaking are those linking primary kin, that is, full and half-siblings and parents and children. And given the dispersal of half-siblings in different households in the town, and extended absence of fathers and the periodic absence of many mothers, this is not perhaps surprising. It is a case of a despersed core, with very little in the way of backing-up institutions. The comparable situation in West Africa finds the paternal half-siblings usually located in a single compound (this will be the case with maternal half-siblings in a matrilineal system like Ashanti). The same compounds contain a number of elementary families, linked by senior members of a kin group who usually recognise one person as their formal head. This person in turn represents the compound to the community, acting on behalf of the individual members on such public occasions as life crisis rituals or serious litigation.[11] Should the child's own family of orientation break up, there is a double safety net - on the one hand there are the two on-going residential groups in which the parents have birth status rights, into either of which he will be welcomed, and on the other there are the kinsfolk living elsewhere who have a claim on him, and an obligation to care for him if this becomes necessary. Fostering does sometimes occur within a residential complex of several domestic groups. In Gonja, this happens most often when an elderly mother is assigned one of her granddaughters as a companion and a runner-of-errands. But on the whole fostering occurs between compounds, and very often between villages. By this I mean that the parents are living in a different compound or village from that of the foster parent,

PARENTAL ROLES IN W. AFRICA AND W. INDIES

and that these are their regular homes. In Gonja, and I believe in other West African societies too, the fostered child moves between fixed points (domestic groups, though not necessarily based on a conjugal unit), and these fixed points are embedded in a nexus of wider institutions, kinship, jural, ritual, political, into which the child is introduced in a systematic way, and as a member of his residential group.

To an outsider, it seems as though the fostered child in the West Indies has only his foster home as a secure base.[12] And further, that however strong the bonds between parent, child, and foster parent, this is in effect an isolated unit. Even where domestic groups are gathered into larger aggregates, as among Black Caribs in Guatemala (Gonzalez 1969), there is not the pattern of extra-domestic institutions into which these larger groups are integrated.

Thus fostering in West Africa leads the child out from the domestic and local group of the parents, but this remains his primary base and he (or she) remains the child of this compound, of this village, of these particular parents. One minor index of this continuity in Gonja is that kinship terminology does not alter with fostering. The child and the foster parent use the same kin terms as before, and the child continues to call only his own parents by the fond terms for 'mother' and 'father'. The major index of the lack of change in status through fostering is that a man is eligible for no new offices by virtues of residence with his foster parent, and remains eligible for whatever offices were open to him in his natal community; inheritance is not altered by fostering relationships, though a fond foster parent may give gifts *inter vivos* to a foster child.

In contrast, there seem to be two themes in West Indian fostering. First, the child may be sent 'outside' to unrelated foster parents, usually in a quasi-servant role, but with the intention that he learns urban middle class ways and gets an education. If this is successful, then as an adult he will be in a good position to support his parents. There may be a breaking of ties with natal kin, and an attempt to 'pass' into middle class society. If the child fails to secure an education or effective occupational skills, he will be thrown back onto his own kin and class. The second theme is the fostering grandmother. Here the child is returned to the mother's home, which may or may not still be her primary base. If the mother has established a separate conjugal household, it is likely to be with a man who is not the child's father, and the majority of writers on the West Indies seem to agree that 'outside' children are not welcome in the conjugal home (see especially Clarke 1966: 174). If, as in Sanford's community in British Honduras, the parents are both away working, there *is* no conjugal home to which the child can relate. The result appears to be a very strong relationship with the fostering mother. Several authorities have noted that she is apt to be called 'mother' while the real mother is referred to by her name, and treated as a 'sister'. Sanford suggests that it can go much farther than this. Writing of a woman who reared a younger brother and sister, she says:

> 'This woman receives from her younger siblings the reverence and the regular acquiescence to her authority over them that a mother would receive. .... Their attitudes are almost a caricature of the respect for authority which is a strongly

154   *CHANGING SOCIAL STRUCTURE IN GHANA*

evidence characteristic of social relations in Stann Creek.
No matter that they are both quite old and responsible themselves, their sister is the elder and she is loved, feared,
and obeyed in all respects as if they were children. She is
their psychic mother (133-4).'

Yet Sanford insists that the 'keeping' of children by Creole
and Carib peoples in British Honduras is not a form of adoption,
and gives as evidence the fact that the mother's right to reclaim
her child is recognised as over-riding any promise she might have
made to the fostering parent (1971: 92-4, 125). Interestingly
enough this is discussed in the context of the treatment of parent
and foster parent by the grown foster child. A girl who sent gifts
only to her foster mother and not to her real mother was criticised
for forgetting the woman who bore her and looked after her in infancy.
Sanford remarks that she would not have been able to withstand these
criticisms if she had been living in the community, but as she was
working abroad they did not affect her. Another woman affirmed that
if either of the two boys she had reared should turn out well (i.e.
become well-off), she would see to it that the mother shared in her
good fortune. As these examples suggest, it appears to be the fostering mother in the first instance who benefits from the assistance of
grown children, but the mother is seen as having a residual claim,
though this may be difficult to enforce, and may depend on the good-
will of the foster parent.

Such dual responsibility can be seen as arising, on the one hand,
from the moral obligation which links genetrix (and genitor) and offspring,regardless of their subsequent relationship, and on the other
from the reciprocities of rearing which arise from the dependency of
infancy and childhood, and the emotional and moral claims this makes on
the child in adulthood. The same dual obligations exist for the West
African foster child, but there are two important differences in their
form. First, the moral obligations towards his biological parents are
augmented by the fact that they also provide him with his place in adult
society, since this is (or was in traditional times) implicit in birth
status. This very strong pull back to one's natal kin is recognised by
the Gonja who say that a son will always return eventually to live with
his father. Anyone could provide instances of this happening, even in
middle age. The rights and obligations arising out of bestowal of birth
status may be seen as *status reciprocities*.

Secondly, there seems to be much less emphasis on children as a
form of security in old age in West Africa. With Sanford, I suspect
that this may be because of the insecurity of the West Indian situation,
rather than because West African parents do not look to their children
for comfort in old age. But in the African context there is a wider
range of relatives with whom one may find support, and perhaps more
important, old age in many societies is a time when both men and women
are highly respected **for** their wisdom and skill.[13] Nor, in most traditional societies were adult sons likely to disappear regularly for the
major part of their working lives. In the West Indies both the migration of young adults out of the country, or to distant centres of
employment, and the absence of a strong extended kin group, leave the
older folk without a sure means of support and companionship in old age.

PARENTAL ROLES IN W. AFRICA AND W. INDIES   155

In the West Indies, then, the fostering of children appears to be associated with a narrower range of kin ties; the foster child is often without an alternative home and grows up very strongly identified with his foster mother. Her home is his home; there is little to pull the foster child back to his own parents, although he owes them respect and support too; and finally, adults, particularly women, may depend very greatly in old age on the support of their youngest 'child', who is very likely to be a foster child. Indeed, it would seem that by fostering her daughters' children, a woman can effectively so extend her own period of child-rearing that it lasts not until middle age, but through to old age. Sanford speaks of women 'building their empires as mothers' by appropriating their daughters' children (1971: 99; see also Clarke 1966: 180-1).

The importance of the grandmother as foster parent in the West Indies can be seen in Table 8. The figures for British Honduras and Jamaica also reflect the pattern of sending children to non-kin, presumably in apprentice fostering.

Table 8

West Indian Fostering Relationships: Generation

	Foster Parent is of:				
	Grand-parental generation	Parents' generation	Child's generation	Not kin	Total N=
Dominican rural village[a]	130 (89%)	10 (7%)	---	6 (4%)	146 (100%)
British Hondural coastal village[b]	156 (55%)	34 (12%)	6 (2%)	89 (31%)	285 (100%)
Three Jamaican communities[c]	74 (54%)	21 (15%)	2 (1%)	39 (29%)	136 (99%)

a. From M.T. Spens (1969) <u>Family Structure in a Dominican Village</u>

b. From M. Sanford (1971) <u>Disruption of the Mother-Child Relationship in Conjunction with Matrifocality</u>. I have omitted category 'other kin' (N=64) in calculating percentages, as this could not be assigned to any generation. The figures in above table thus represent percentages of those classifiable by generation from Sanford's data.

c. From E. Clarke (1966) <u>My Mother who Fathered Me</u>, Appendix 5. I have considered only children living with neither parent. Two cases have been omitted as they could not be classified by generation.

156 *CHANGING SOCIAL STRUCTURE IN GHANA*

The other point to note from Table 8 is the very low proportion of foster parents of the parents' own generation. There are some cases in each sample, but the figures are very low in comparison with those for grandparents.

West Indians in London

These comments are based on a pilot study carried out with Dr. T. Spens and a West Indian (Dominican) assistant in a London suburb where there is a small Dominican enclave. They draw also on reading of West Indian ethnography, and on Dr. Spens' close knowledge of Dominica. They must, however, be considered as tentative findings rather than as the results of a full-scale study.

The trip to England is in a sense but a further extension of the emigration in search of work which takes West Indians from the farm to the local sugar plantation, on to the towns and cities, or perhaps to the fruit, tobacco or sugar estates on other islands or the mainland of central America. Puerto Ricans holding US passports go to the United States in search of work. Those from the ex-British colonies come, or used to come, to England. Many, both men and women, leave a child behind with a mother or sister, and some men come promising to bring over wives and children. Those who reunite their families in England often add to them, while others find a spouse and start a family. The jobs they are able to get are those which English workers avoid, such as industrial cleaning, railwaymen, bus conductors, unskilled and semi-skilled factory work - jobs which pay poorly and require few skills. Since both husband and wife are almost certainly committed to sending money home regularly, both must work.

The pattern of illegitimate first (and often second) pregnancies is very clear among the families in the pilot study. Seven out of nine women had borne their first child before marriage, and three were still not married several years later. Illegitimacy among first-born is not equally characteristic of all Dominican women, however. Again and again these women explain that they came to England because they had a child (or several children) to support and they could not do this successfully on the island. Thus emigrants to London appear to be selected from those who have difficulty in meeting their responsibilities under the conditions of low wages and high unemployment on Dominica. Mothers of illegitimate children are prominent in this group, and probably account for the large majority of single women who come to work in England. All those in the pilot sample had left their illegitimate children with kin in Dominica. One of the women had come with her husband, but again for much the same reason - to work and earn a better standard of living. This couple left their first child behind with the wife's mother so that they could both work full time. This is exactly the reasoning given by single women for leaving a child with its grandmother: 'If I had to look after the child I couldn't work so much, and that is why I came to England'.

But for the single woman with a child to support, work has an added meaning: she must send money to the woman in whose care she has left the child. This person is almost always the mother's mother. The money is seen as fulfilling two obligations. In the first place, the care of

PARENTAL ROLES IN W. AFRICA AND W. INDIES   157

her child places an extra burden on the grandmother. And secondly,
the daughter feels responsible for helping the mother herself with
cash if she possibly can. There is, however, a subtler pressure on
a woman to contribute to her child's support: if she is the one who
provides money for daily necessities and for such extra expenses as
the clothes and celebration of First Communion, then she has a much
clearer claim to the child's affection and loyalty later on. She has
been a proper mother, even though circumstances forced her to leave
the child to be reared by others. This is of very great importance
in the mother's eyes. One woman whose mother died just before she
left for England had left her daughter with the child's godmother.
She did this very reluctantly, and insists that she has always
continued to send money for her support, because the godmother would
like to adopt the girl, and she does not want to lose her. In another
case the mother had sent money for the maintenance of her son while
he was being looked after by his father's mother. She was careful to
continue these payments in order to retain her rights in the child,
and later was able to take him to live with her.

A woman feels differently about the child she has left with her
own mother. My impression is that this is usually a temporary arrangement in the beginning, 'until I am able to send for the child in
England'. Whether the grandmother views it in this way is unclear.
Significantly, two of the women in our sample had encountered serious
resistance from their mothers when seeking to bring to England the
child left in their care. Both had left the child for some time longer,
and one ended by having to return to the West Indies to resolve the
matter there. Thus the mothers do not from the first consider that
they are turning a child over to its grandmother 'for good'. However,
this is often the outcome of fostering by the maternal grandmother,
either because she effectively resists returning the child, or because
the mother is never in a position to send for it.

The grandmother's position is very much strengthened by the fact
that a child left with her in infancy grows up knowing her as its mother
and calling her 'Mama', while calling its own mother by her first name
and often treating her like an older sibling. Interestingly enough,
this even happens when the mother is present in the household. One of
the London women had lived with her mother after the birth of her first
child, going out to work while the grandmother looked after the baby.
The child grew up calling the grandmother 'Mama' as its mother did, and
calling the mother by her first name, as the grandmother did. The mother
describes the situation as 'like I was the big sister'. It didn't worry
her at the time, and after some years she left her son with his grandmother to come to England where she married and had two more children.
When the boy joined her in England he still refused to call her 'Mama'
and at this time she minded very much and tried unsuccessfully to change
the pattern which had been established in his infancy. There is another
instance in our small pilot sample of this same pattern - a son who grew
up calling his grandmother 'Mama' and who in this case refused to admit
that his own mother *was* his mother.

Women are very ambivalent about 'losing' a child to their mother in
this way. On the one hand they feel extremely grateful that the grandmother was able to care for the child at a time when they could not do so.
This places the mother doubly in her own mother's debt: firstly, there are

158   *CHANGING SOCIAL STRUCTURE IN GHANA*

the reciprocities of rearing built up during her own infancy and childhood; now there is a second set which links child, mother and grandmother. In this situation the continued residence of the child with its grandmother in adolescence and adulthood is seen as one way of looking after the grandmother in her old age, one way of fulfilling the obligation felt towards her. One of the women in the pilot study, still unmarried with four children, said that she sometimes regrets having had so many children, as 'No man will marry you with four children. They are scared of the responsibility'. However she went on to say that whenever she thinks like this, she remembers her mother and how she needs the children, and what a help they are to her. The eldest boy is now 17 and has a job, and in addition makes a vegetable garden for his grandmother. The others fetch wood and water and run errands. She expects them to look after her mother in her old age. So she is glad she had the children, since her mother needs them. 'But,' she added, 'they must also give me some sort of respect as well'.

And here is the crux of the matter. A child who feels primary obligations towards his grandmother and treats his mother 'like a big sister', cannot be depended on by the mother in her later years in the same way as one she has reared herself. The reciprocities of rearing are laid down between child and grandparent, not between parent and child. And concern about whether children will care for their parents in old age is very real[14]. Mrs. M's first child was born in Dominica, and acknowledged by the father who could not marry the mother as her family was 'lower' than his. The girl has been raised by a sister of Mrs. M's mother, and even now is staying with her since Mrs. M's husband does not want the child in their home. Mrs. M. is pleased that her daughter shows great fondness and respect for her foster mother, but she only hopes 'that R---- will not neglect me in my old age, when she is bigger and able to help herself'. The Dominican interviewer comments that in her opinion the girl will not let Mrs. M. down because she is conscious of her mother's goodness towards her. The interviewer is here referring to the fact that Mrs. M. has always sent money to help with her daughter's maintenance and kept in touch with her.

The concern over whether a child will feel obliged to care for a parent in old age when reared by someone else is most clearly seen when the foster parent is not the maternal grandmother. This is probably because the mother feels a strong obligation towards her own mother, which she can fulfil through her child, and also because the bond between mother and grandmother is close enough that the child identifies the two and can reasonably be expected to give the mother too 'some respect when she is old'. But when the foster parent is a step-mother or godmother, then women become really anxious that they will lose their right to the child's sense of obligation in old age. In one of the sample families, the husband and wife had virtually separated but still occupied the same house. The mother was determined to try and maintain this arrangement as otherwise she feared she would lose her children. She wants to look after them when they are small so that they can care for her when she is old. She thinks they will do this, except perhaps the eldest girl who is against her.

None of the West Indian children in the pilot study had been sent to English foster parents, and indeed London informants specifically

PARENTAL ROLES IN W. AFRICA AND W. INDIES   159

deny that they would ever do this. Sending very young children to a 'nanny', that is a woman who looks after them locally during the day, is a fairly common practice. Ideally woman prefer to stay at home when their children are very young, but this is not always possible. Some who must work manage by taking an evening job when the husband can be at home with the children. Others make use of either West Indian or English daily minders ('nannies') with whom they leave the children from early in the morning to 5 or 6 in the evening. School-age children are often 'latchkey' children who return to an empty house and may even be expected to start the supper for a working mother.

Economic aspects of fostering and daily minding in London

To what extent is the preference of West Indian parents for daily minding rather than fostering with English families a matter of economic necessity? The range of costs for daily minding in London (at 1970 prices) starts below that for fostering, but there is an area of overlap. The less expensive foster parents charge no more than the more expensive daily minders. There are additional costs in both forms of care: for daily minding, food (usually supplied by the parents) , laundry, and twice-daily fares on bus or underground, and of course clothing; for fostering, occasional lump sums of clothes, new shoes, etc. and the expense of visits.

It is worth noting that although the West Africans in London are on the whole much better educated than the West Indians, the jobs they are able to find are very often the same. Both tend to take unskilled or semi-skilled jobs in transport,the post office, or factories. Hence many West Africans are not materially better off than West Indians. Although virtually *all* West Africans are in London as students only 11% of the extensive sample were mainly supported by either loans, student grants or money from home. The families in one of the two groups in the intensive phase of the West African Immigrants study, the Ibo, were receiving no money from home and were instead trying to send money to kin who had lost homes and jobs as a result of the Biafran war. Overall the Ibo families tended to delegate their parental roles less frequently than the others, but this applies equally to fostering and daily minding. Despite their financial straits, there were Ibo families who fostered their children in English homes.

When discussing the relative advantages of fostering and daily minding with West Africans the choice generally turned on factors other than expense. Daily minding was preferred because parents could check up on the minder's standard of care, and for convenience if there was a good minder near the mother's place of work. It was disliked because of crowded conditions, poor care and constant travel. Fostering was disliked due to difficulty of checking on the foster parent's care of the children (parents are expected to give notice of visits beforehand), and because of the difficulty and expense of frequent visits. Fostering was preferred to daily minding because of the 'home atmosphere' - the children were thought to get more attention and be treated more like own children by a foster parent; there was no need to take and fetch the children **every** day (often in the dark and cold); and the mother was free in the evening to study or work the night shift.

160   *CHANGING SOCIAL STRUCTURE IN GHANA*

Fostering can be considerably more expensive than daily minding, and a few West African **families** are undoubtedly better off than virtually all West Indians. Yet these differences do leave a considerable area of overlap, where there are West Africans who are as hard up as the typical West Indian family, but who still prefer to foster their children rather than send them to a daily minder. While there is probably an economic element in the choice between the two modes of care, impoverished West African parents do foster their children. Nor can this factor account for the explicit rejection of English foster homes by West Indian parents.

Comparison of contemporary patterns of fostering in West Africa and the West Indies

We noted that there were two themes, one dominant and one subordinate, in West Indian fostering. The main theme is the caring for a child by the maternal grandmother when the mother is for some reason unable to do so herself. The secondary theme is the sending of a child to non-relatives in apprentice fosterage. Both are reflected in the summary figures for the West Indies in Table 9 (drawn from the totals of Tables 6 and 8), where by far the majority of foster parents are found in the grandparental generation, while the next largest category consists of non-kin. This pattern contrasts strongly with the relative lack of emphasis on the mother-daughter-grand daughter chain in West Africa. If we take the southern Ghana situation as reflecting a degree of occupational and social differentiation roughly equivalent to that in the West Indies,[15] we find that the great majority of related foster parents are in the parents' generation, that is, they are collateral rather than lineal kin. While the figures suggest that the resort to non-kin in apprentice fosterage is less pronounced in the Ghanaian samples, observations do not entirely support this finding. This may be because non-kin fostering is increasing rapidly at present, while the figures refer to the childhood of informants who were adults in the mid 1960's. Fostering by non-kin is definitely more common in southern Ghana than in the north where several samples had no instances, and the overall incidence is substantially below that in the south, and markedly lower than the figures for the West Indies. We have suggested that this is probably related to the greater occupational and social differentiation in the south, itself a response to increasing urbanisation and industrialisation.

But why should there be such a striking contrast between the West Indian preference for fostering by maternal grandmothers and the West African pattern of sending children to collateral kin of both parents? The analysis of West Indian material has indicated that two factors are critical in accounting for this bias. On the one hand, mothers are very often in need of someone to care for an infant while they work or establish a stable conjugal union. The woman on whom a mother has the strongest claim for such service is her own mother. On the other hand, older women are extremely anxious about what will become of them in old age, and one kind of provision they can make is to continue 'mothering' children after their own period of childbearing has ended. The children they have the strongest claim to are pre-marital children of the daughters (and less often, of their sons). Finally, the needs of daughter and mother coincide: the former is seeking to gain an additional child, the latter to delegate the care of an infant.

PARENTAL ROLES IN W. AFRICA AND W. INDIES 161

Table 9

Comparison of northern Ghana, southern Ghana and
West Indian fostering relationships, by generation
of foster parent. (From totals of Tables 6 and 8)

Foster Parent is of:

Population	Grand-parents' Generation	Parents' Generation	Child's Generation	Not Kin	Total N=
Northern Ghana	80 (39%)	104 (50%)	12 (6%)	11 (5%)	207 (100%)
Southern Ghana	19 (7%)	176 (63%)	47 (17%)	37 (13%)	279 (100%)
West Indies	360 (64%)	65 (11%)	8 (1%)	134 (24%)	567 (100%)

The dynamics behind the sending of children to be reared by their
parents' siblings in West Africa are entirely different. Parents believe
that they are likely to spoil their own child, while a relative will be
more demanding. The purpose of (non-crisis) fostering is the education
of the child as well as the fulfilment of kinship obligations which are
recognised between full and often between classificatory siblings. To
the extent that foster parents in the grandparental generation are seeking domestic services rather than supplying training in adult skills[16],
then the preference for collateral kin also reflects the educational
aspect of fosterage.

Finally, it should be emphasised that only very rarely are men
stipulated as foster parents (or 'keepers') in the West Indies, while
the West African data show a rough balance between male and female
foster parents. This I take to reflect the essentially *nurturant* role
of West Indian fosterage except where older children are sent to non-
kin. The utilisation of male foster parents in West Africa corresponds
to their function in training boys both in adult skills, and manly virtues.

The differences reflected in Table 9 result in a distinctive 'shape'
to fostering in West Africa and in the West Indies which may be summarised
as follows:

West Africa	West Indies
Strong element of purposive fostering by kin	Emphasis on crisis fostering by kin, purposive fostering by non-kin
Most foster parents are in parents' generation (i.e. collateral kin)	Most foster parents are in grandparental generation (i.e. lineal kin)
Male foster parents common	Male foster parents rare

162 *CHANGING SOCIAL STRUCTURE IN GHANA*

West Africa	West Indies
Model of fostering stresses the claims of foster parent	Model of fostering stresses the needs of parent and child
Fostering kin are not necessarily primary kin of parents	Fostering kin tend to be primary kin of parents
Fostering links siblings' children (lateral linkage)	Fostering links generations (lineal linkage merging mother and her siblings with their children)
Fostering does not change birth status identity; status reciprocities unaltered	Fostering may change birth status identity informally; no status reciprocities operate

Comparison of child care arrangements by West Africans and West Indians in London

What then can we say about the observed difference between West Indians who refuse to consider placing their children with English foster parents while in England, and the West Africans who favour this form of arrangement? We have seen that both groups must make some arrangements for their young children to allow them to pursue the goals for which they have come so far. And while economic factors would favour a higher incidence of fostering among West Africans than among West Indians, these factors are not sufficient to account for the complete rejection of English foster parents by the latter group. Further, it is clear that both groups share the premiss that delegation of some aspects of the parents' roles may be in the best interests of both parent and child.

I would suggest that the difference lies in the cultural meaning of fostering to the two groups. For West Indians, the rearing of a young child by another women involves the transfer of at least some (if not all) aspects of 'motherhood', with all the loyalties and obligations that arise out of child-care in the early years. So long as this transfer is used to reinforce the ties between a woman and her own mother, it is tolerated as necessary, though we have seen that feelings here may also be ambivalent. But to risk the loss of a child to a complete stranger - which is the implication of sending it to live with another family - this is simply unthinkable. The care offered by English foster parents is not seen as offering any advantages to compensate for the threat to ties which the child will feel obliged to honour as an adult.

For West Africans, the meaning of fostering is different. Traditionally children were not sent away as infants, and a foster parent is not seen as a substitute mother, but rather as providing character training and instruction. Where fostering occurs between kin, it is recognised as fulfilling (and creating) rights and obligations, but these in turn

PARENTAL ROLES IN W. AFRICA AND W. INDIES 163

reinforce existing ties of a secondary nature rather than create a new set of primary ties (as happens between the West Indian child and the foster parent who becomes a 'psychic mother'). The delay of fostering in West Africa until the child 'has sense' at six or seven is consistent with this pattern of augmenting existing ties rather than creating a new set of primary bonds. Early rearing reciprocities are already established between the mother and child, and reinforced by status reciprocities linking the child to both parents. Only the later reciprocities of rearing based on training in adult skills remain as a basis of bonding. When the parental roles are under strain in an immigrant situation, the West African response is also consistent with the traditional pattern. The roles of father and mother are seen as firmly established and not as liable to threat in a caretaking situation. The fostering experience is perceived as providing a service to parents and their children, and as being primarily educational and custodial in function (since no kinship obligations are involved in fostering by strangers).

CONCLUSION

In West Africa, kinship fostering is evolving into apprenticeship on the one hand, and residential formal education on the other. To end with a speculation, I suggest that much the same pattern may have occurred in Western Europe with the development of a more complex division of labour. The relevant factor in occupational differentiation is that it becomes increasingly difficult to find a master of the required trade among one's kin. Apprenticeship then becomes an obvious alternative and is clearly associated with movement into the city and away from kin. Where trades are restricted to a closed group, especially a kin group, the picture would obviously be altered, and information from caste-based societies would be critical here. Again, the centralising of advanced literate skills in religious foundations which exclude family life (and hence cannot supply their own recruits) is another critical case which would reward study in the context of educational fostering. Like apprenticeship, formal education takes over some of the functions of fostering in less complex societies, functions which themselves include the provision of a link between the nuclear family and wider structures beyond.

NOTES

1. Though by no means unique, see studies of fostering and adoption in Eastern Oceania in V. Carroll (ed.) 1970, as well as the Caribbean material.

2. There is another, equally important question, with which I am not concerned here: What accounts for the fact that fostering is institutionalised in some West African societies, while it appears to be absent from others? This question is more difficult than might appear, because our work in London suggests that even those groups which do not foster in West Africa are prepared to do so in the U.K. In other words, the underlying factor is present in these ostensibly non-fostering groups too, but there appears to be some alternative institution which takes the place of fostering within the traditional system. But all the pre-requisites are there, in both types of West African society.

164 *CHANGING SOCIAL STRUCTURE IN GHANA*

3. Or, if with another relative, the kin term ordinarily used for that person.

4. A further possible exception may have occurred in traditional Yoruba society. Informants on the London Survey sometimes distinguished between a relative sent as a foster child (*alagbato*) and an unrelated child (*omodo*) who was considered of inferior status. This was likened by a few informants to a slave.

5. In *Gbanyito* the verb is *terma*, while the verb which applies to fostering is *belo*, 'to rear, or bring up'.

6. Ages can only be very roughly guessed from Busia 1950, my main source on this point. The youngest girls may be 10 or 12.

7. Morgan, in writing about the Puritan family in 17th century New England, records the placing of daughters in the houses of relatives and friends to learn housecraft, while apprenticeship began at 11 or 12 and lasted for a minimum of seven years, with the master having complete control over the movements of the youth, in and out of working hours (1944). See also P. Ariès on the prevalence of sending children out to wet nurses in France in the 17th century (1962: 374). Systematic searching would almost certainly reveal many more examples from a period when the boundaries of the family were not yet so tightly drawn as they are in our society today.

8. See Muir and Goody 1972, and Goody and Muir 1972 for a discussion of the developmental cycle of West African immigrant families, and the resulting high incidence of births among student parents.

9. In fact a surprising number of West African couples do have one or two relatives in the U.K., but as they are also here in order to study and must work to support themselves, they are not available as foster parents.

10. To do so on the basis of whether or not the child's parents are living together at the time of enquiry is not satisfactory, since in at least some cases the family of orientation is likely to have dispersed following the fostering arrangement.

11. See Fortes 1969: Chapters IX and X for an especially clear account of the compound as a mediating structure in Ashanti.

12. This is partly a function of the age of which a child is sent to foster parents. In West Africa this tends to be around 5 to 7, often referred to as the time when a child begins to 'have sense'. In the West Indies, on the other hand, the pattern seems to be to place an infant with a foster mother in order that the mother can work to support herself and the child, and be free to try and form a stable union. In the latter case, the child knows no other home than that of the foster parent, though the mother may visit it regularly.

13. The coming of western technology and education is altering this rapidly. When wisdom is learned at school, the elders are at an increasing disadvantage.

PARENTAL ROLES IN W. AFRICA AND W. INDIES   165

14. It was Dr. Spens who made me realise the depth of this.

15. Southern Ghana lacks, of course, the racial differentiation which plays such a central part in West Indian stratification. I would not wish to imply that this is not of great importance in determining the available avenues of social mobility in the two culture areas, but the West Indian data come from black and coloured populations, and thus the discussion is necessarily limited to this stratum.

16. This assumption is only partly warranted in a West African context. A father's father may still be relatively young and actively engaged in his trade. On the other hand, many grandparents are sent foster children to provide companionship and small services when they become old and infirm.

ECONOMICS AND KINSHIP IN MULTI-ETHNIC DWELLINGS

E N I D   S C H I L D K R O U T

Introduction

The establishment of new communities through migration, resettlement, or the arbitrary delimitation of boundaries around territorial or political units leads, perhaps inevitably, to the development of new concepts of communal identity. Precisely what identities emerge as new polities are created, the extent of conflict involved in the process, and the conditions under which new identities emerge are all matters for empirical investigation. Drawing boundaries around nations or regions, or even observer labelled units such as 'tribes' or ethnic groups does not in itself predicate the emergence of corresponding cultural identities at these levels. Nor does rural urban migration necessarily lead to the abandonment of traditional customs and values in favour of the adoption of any pre-specified non-traditional value system: westernisation and urbanisation are not synonymous; scale and values do not necessarily co-vary. Although this may now seem obvious, we have few descriptions of how new identities actually emerge, of what factors generate value consensus in new polities. In this paper, I intend to describe some of the factors which lead to the emergence of a sense of communal identity among urban immigrants from many ethnic communities living together in the section of Kumasi known as the zongo. In this ethnographic setting the emergence of such a sense of communal identity may be observed very clearly in the domestic context since immigrants from many different ethnic groups, both kin and non-kin, actually reside together in large multi-celled dwellings. This residential pattern makes the domestic context a crucial arena for social and cultural integration. This phenomenon is itself due to the particular economic constraints which affect domestic organisation and residence patterns is Kumasi. Thus, while this paper is concerned with processes of socio-cultural integration, they can only be understood as the consequences of certain underlying economic patterns of urban immigrant life. More specifically, I describe the way in which economic factors lead to residential heterogeneity, both in terms of the kinship and the ethnic composition of domestic groups. The major focus is on the socio-cultural consequences of these processes, and on the specific ways in which economic factors lead to particular patterns of domestic organisation which in turn create new identities and values.

In speaking of the emergence of a new culture or sense of communal identity among urban immigrants, I refer to the consequences of their incorporation into a community which has a distinct set of values. Individuals identify with this community when they feel that social relationships with others in the community are based on premises which do not operate in relationships with outsiders. This identity can develop only when people understand each others' behaviour because it

168 *CHANGING SOCIAL STRUCTURE IN GHANA*

is predictable and because they recognise that they are likely to behave similarly in like circumstances. Once this sense is what might be called 'value empathy' exists, we can speak of a culture and a corresponding sense of communal identity. Outside pressures may contribute to the development of such an identity, in that they may help people to perceive common interests, but for the purposes of this paper I choose to concentrate on the internal processes which lead to the emergence of common values.

In contexts of social opposition this communal identity may appear to be 'ethnic'. I prefer, however, to restrict the term ethnic to identities based on an ideology of kinship, provenance, and a sense of distinctiveness. Communal identities may also be ethnic identities if the primary (although not the only) means of recruitment is through a kinship tie, if the members of a category distinguish themselves or are distinguished from others by their or their ancestors' place of origin, and if they have some sense of distinctiveness in terms of common interests, political status, values or anything else. Ethnic categories and groups are always parts of societies, while communities may be coterminous with societies. Communal identities are based on the existence of a common set of values, that is on a common culture. Members of the same ethnic category need not have a common and distinct culture (Schildkrout 1973a), so that ethnic boundaries may be social, and symbolic, but need not be cultural.

Social life in the ethnically heterogeneous immigrant community in Kumasi known as the zongo[1] is largely governed by a value system which specifies sanctions, norms and ideals which influence behaviour. The presence of such an identifiable normative system makes it possible to speak of the zongo community in Kumasi, although within this there are many sub-communities based on ethnic identity. The zongo value system differs from the traditional value systems of rural-born immigrants. It has developed in Kumasi as a result of various processes of social integration occurring in many behavioural fields: when interaction is frequent or necessary between immigrants of different ethnic backgrounds, some accommodation and adjustment of traditional values invariably take place. This process may be observed in the economic field, for example, as people carry on transactions involving the exchange of goods and services; in the political field, when groups and individuals carry on transactions involving power and prestige; and in ritual, where Islamic ideology acts as a catalyst of socio-cultural integration. It may also be observed in the domestic context where day to day adjustments are made as individuals from varied cultural backgrounds learn to live together, accept their differences,and discover their common interests.

The domestic context, as I am defining it, includes all social relationships and interactions which occur between individuals who are co-resident in or interact in a house. These relationships may include political and economic transactions as well as relationships of kinship, affinity, clientship and friendhip. The house, like the neighbourhood, is a spatial unit. It is not therefore conceptually equivalent to the abstractly defined fields of interaction which we may label as political, economic, ritual and so on. All of these kinds of transaction occur in the domestic context, so that by focussing on the house as context in which interaction takes place, one is able to consider how all these various types of transaction lead to socio-cultural integration.

ECONOMICS IN MULTI-ETHNIC DWELLINGS 169

In Kumasi zongo the domestic context is perhaps the msot important social setting, fostering the emergence of a common set of values among immigrants. The house, and secondarily the neighbourhood, is the primary locus of interaction for many immigrants and their children. Although socialisation is not discussed directly here, the importance of the processes of integration I describe should be evaluated in terms of their effect on urban-born immigrants who grow up in this setting. Thus, the primary culture of urban-born immigrants is zongo culture, and although the urban-born may assume an ethnic identity as well, based generally on the father's place of origin, his or her culture is that of Kumasi zongo, not that of the ethnic community. Values are learned in the domestic context, so that, for the urban-born, ethnicity has few, if any, cultural correlates.

The economic basis of house ownership

In Kumasi the term zongo refers both to a neighbourhood where Muslim immigrants from the northern savannah region first settled in the beginning of this century, and to the community of immigrants. Many of these are of northern Ghanaian origin and others are 'aliens' in terms of national citizenship. After the British conquered Asante in 1896, migrants from northern Gold Coast, Upper Volta, Nigeria, Dahomey, Togo, Niger and Mali began to come to Kumasi in large numbers. Many settled permanently in Kumasi, as they consolidated control over the north-south trade in cattle, kola nuts, manufactured goods and other items. Their numbers were increased by an influx of northern migrants who sought employment in the city or who passed through Kumasi on their way to Asanti-owned cocoa farms. By 1960 this stranger community constituted between one third and one half of the town's population of 212,000, depending on how its boundaries are calculated.[2]

The British clearly encouraged the growth of this community by leasing plots of land to the strangers at lower rentals than were offered to the indigenous, but recently vanquished, Asante. There was never any official or even *de facto* ethnic zoning in Kumasi, so that, as the stranger community expanded, the immigrants moved into many other sections of the rapidly growing city. Many built homes to accommodate their families and new migrants, while others lived in Asante houses. But regardless of the actual neighbourhood of their residence, Muslim immigrants from northern Ghana and the surrounding countries and their offspring continued to be viewed as strangers and to define themselves as members of the zongo community.

Thus although the immigrants come from many culturally and linguistically different societies, they are united in Kumasi by their common status vis-à-vis the Asante. They also constitute a distinct community because of their participation in particular sectors of the economy, and because of increasing social, political and religious integration in the community itself. In economic terms most zongo immigrants, rural- or urban-born, are either self-employed entrepreneurs - mainly traders and landlords - or are wage labourers who occupy the unskilled and semi-skilled rungs of the occupational ladder. The distribution of occupations varies somewhat according to the ethnic identity and associated migratory pattern of first generation immigrants, and according to generation of urban

170   *CHANGING SOCIAL STRUCTURE IN GHANA*

residence. Nevertheless, in general, northerners and other Muslim immigrants[3] in the zongo who are in wage employment are in the poorest-paying jobs, while those who are engaged in private entrepreneurial activity are able to earn high incomes. This pertains particularly to the category of landlords who will be discussed in more detail below. Within the zongo, a prestige scale based on wealth and Islamic education exists and is related to internal political power. But in the urban economy as a whole neither the zongo traders and landlords nor the wage labourers are able to enter highpaying salaried employment because few of them are literate in English. Many are proficient in Arabic, but this does not enable them to enter the high levels of an occupational status scale which is defined according to Western values and which emphasises skills which the immigrants do not generally develop. Thus neither the very wealthy nor the poorest northern immigrants can advance in that sector of the economy in which status or 'class' is defined according to Western values. Islam, however, provides an alternative status scale in which wealth, gained through entrepreneurial activity, and Islamic education and orthodoxy are the defining criteria. Insofar as Islam encourages Arabic rather than English literacy, it also limits the possibility of the immigrants' entry into those managerial and professional occupations which are linked to political control and prestige in Ghana and in Kumasi as a whole. Economic and cultural, and hence political, encapsulation of the zongo does not, then, always imply poverty, but it clearly restricts the ways in which Muslim immigrants and northerners can advance[4]. This accounts for the very high value placed on the economic aspects of house ownership. Landlordism and other forms of entrepreneurial activity provide opportunities which in some ways defy the structural limitations imposed on the immigrants in the urban and national economy, insofar as this economic system is defined by the formal wage structure and by skills and values which the immigrants do not choose to develop. Thus while entrepreneurs are limited in the prestige scale reflected in the wage structure, they are nevertheless able to advance dramatically within the context of the zongo. Since zongos are trading communities as well as pools of cheap labour, they link major centres throughout Ghana and West Africa. Consequently the opportunities open to immigrants are not as limited as it might appear if one examined their position in the wage scale alone. This has important implications for an analysis of class structure, for although we may place immigrants and indigenous Ghanaians on one scale of wealth, there are at least two scales of prestige (the Western and the Islamic) operating in two different economic sectors (the wage sector and the entrepreneurial sector). The fact remains that because of the importance of Western values and associated skills in defining prestige and 'class' in the wage sector, economic advancement for these Muslim immigrants is entirely dependent on entrepreneurial activity. Prestige and wealth gained in the immigrant community through such activity may be converted into political power within the context of the zongo, but it may not easily be transferred outside.

This, then, is the setting in which one must examine the economic aspects of house ownership and residential choice. Immigrants in the zongo are all tied into the urban economy, that is, into an economy in which the primary source of subsistence and income derives from wage labour and entrepreneurial activity - trade and landlordism - not from agriculture. Although kinsmen sometimes cooperate in joint enterprises, the prevailing pattern is one of individualism. Patron-client relationships

ECONOMICS IN MULTI-ETHNIC DWELLINGS

rather than joint kinship enterprises are the most common form of cooperation. This has been the predominant pattern of economic life in the zongo since the community began. Thus from the early days of settlement in Kumasi, house ownership has been of crucial economic and political importance for the immigrants. Most migrants came to Kumasi alone, often without close kin. House owners, known by the Hausa term *masugida* (sing. *maigida*) became patrons to new migrants. They provided housing, jobs, and sometimes even wives for those new migrants who became their clients. They acted as brokers, or middle-men, in long distance trading operations by accommodating itinerant traders and receiving commissions on trade. Asantes and Europeans seeking migrant labour for cocoa farms, industries and commercial concerns also turned to the *masugida* for employees.

Immigrants who became landlords were thus able to use their investments in many different ways. Houses were sources of regular income in the form of monthly rents, since most migrants became tenants. Houses were a means of attracting clients: in return for free accommo-dation, the landlord could acquire a client who would work in the land-lords' trading enterprise. Itinerant traders could be accommodated and commissions could be received on trade; and finally the landlord could house his own family which, as a result of his economic circumstances, usually expanded more quickly than the families of wage-labourers. Landlords and other entrepreneurs most often have two to four wives, while wage labourers typically can afford only one.

Since house-ownership is the safest and one of the most lucrative capital investments a migrant can make, many who began as wage labourers try to turn their earnings into this form of capital. Women traders also often become successful landlords in their own right. Both male and female landlords are able to convert their investments in housing into political authority, although the spheres of male and female autho-rity remain differentiated - women acquire authority in their own kin group and in the women's community; men can more easily convert the profits of landlordism into general political authority in the zongo as a whole. Most, but not all, titled political offices in numerous zongo associations are reserved for men, but only for men whose reputations are backed by capital assets, most commonly in the form of houses. Tenants and clients, a direct consequence of this form of investment, are important sources of political support. It is not surprising, then, that a person's status is often described in terms of the number of houses he or she owns. Important leaders in the zongo have been known to own as many as thirty houses, each consisting of from fifteen to twenty-five rooms. Both men and women attempt to build as many houses as possible, and since the zongo has been continually expanding, this has been a predictably profitable and safe form of investment.

The importance of the house as an economic investment is reflected in its physical structure. In all of the neighbourhoods where northern immigrants live, even in two areas built as government projects, houses are large rectangular structures with rooms opening onto a central courtyard. Most houses are one story high, but some of the wealthiest owners have built two, three and four story dwellings. Other landlords augment their investments by building outside rooms onto the original rectangular structure.

172   *CHANGING SOCIAL STRUCTURE IN GHANA*

Individual rooms are small, usually no more than ten feet by ten feet, and little time is spent in them during the day. When they are not in the market, women and children spend much of their time working, talking and playing in the courtyard. In this area one can observe a great deal of cooperation in child care, house cleaning, cooking, and preparing food or other products for sale in the market. Almost everyone eats in this courtyard, even if they belong to different households, that is, food purchasing and consuming units. Thus, despite the separate and numerous relationships which residents have with people living in other houses, there is a great deal of interaction and cooperation among co-residents, whether or not they are members of the same household, in the sense defined above.

Ethnicity and kinship in household composition

The significance of the physical structure of the house becomes apparent when one examines its composition. One can then appreciate the heterogeneity of the residents who are interacting in this context. The statistics presented here on house composition come from a census I conducted in four neighbourhoods in 1966. The sample consisted of eighty-nine houses containing approximately 2500 residents. Although all of these houses were owned by Mossi landlords, only fifty percent of the residents were Mossi. This reflects the prevailing pattern of ethnic heterogeneity characteristic of the houses owned by most zongo landlords, whatever their ethnic identity. Although owned by members of a single ethnic community, these houses were, I suspect, similar to houses owned by members of most ethnic groups. Even if a broader survey were to show differences in the composition of Mossi and non-Mossi owned houses, the fact that the Mossi owned houses are dispersed within each neighbourhood indicates that there is no pattern of ethnic clustering in the neighbourhoods as a whole.

There are a number of factors which lead to heterogeneity in house composition. It is clear that houses are not built primarily to accommodate kin. In the entire sample only one house consisted entirely of kin. In all houses only thirty-six percent of the residents were consanguineal kin or affines of the house owners and many of these (thirty-nine percent) were wives, husbands and children. This is both because kin groups can sometimes be too small to fill a house (particularly in the newly built neighbourhoods) and because adult siblings and children have a tendency to disperse into different houses and neighbourhoods. From the point of view of a landlord, relatives can be more of an economic liability than an asset. When siblings and children are not engaged in a joint economic venture with the owner they are encouraged to find their own accommodation. Given the nature of the urban economy, except in those cases where they are cooperating in trade, this is often the case. When a sibling or married child works for the owner in a trading enterprise, taking care of strangers, selling, teaching in an Arabic school, driving a lorry, or the like, he (or she) is likely to remain in the owner's house exactly as if he were an unrelated client. Thus married sons may be accommodated for some time out of a father's moral obligation to support his children, but as soon as they have separate incomes they are encouraged to move out. When some form of economic cooperation outside the domestic context does not exist between adult kin, they usually separate in terms of residence. It is very difficult to accept

ECONOMICS IN MULTI-ETHNIC DWELLINGS   173

rent from a relative, so if he does not become the equivalent of a client, exchanging services or income for rent, he is encouraged to move. When economically independent adult kin do not move out, conflict often develops, since the house owner usually feels some obligation to provide food for resident kin, but resents this when they make no contribution to his income.

Another factor which encourages the dispersal of kin is the inheritance system. In Kumasi zongo, where Maliki Muslim law is followed, a person's property is divided between all of his or her children, men inheriting twice as much as women. When houses are divided, individual rooms are the units of inheritance. This gives rise in second, third and subsequent generations, to jointly owned houses. In those cases where the number of rooms can be neatly divided among the heirs, the resulting pattern of ownership, although complicated, is clear. Each heir has rights over particular rooms, and he or she may reside in them, sell them, or rent them out. When the number of heirs exceeds the number of rooms, there is an increasing reliance on the cash equivalent of shares. In some cases heirs sell their shares to one another, or to outsiders (sometimes to members of other ethnic groups), so that at least some of the heirs have entire rooms in which they can live if they choose to do so. In other cases most of the heirs live elsewhere, rent out the property, and divide the income according to the size of each share. Unless an individual owns at least one whole room, or unless he pays the other owner's rent, he is unable to occupy the room. Consequently after several generations from the time a house was built, many owners do not live in their own houses. Absentee landlords are also found among rural-born immigrants who build more than one house, but they are increasingly common in the second and third generations.

In terms of the domestic cycle we find that, although urban kinship networks expand as the rural-born migrant marries and has children and grandchildren, residence groups do not necessarily expand as kinship units, even though there may be plenty of space in a dwelling. When a person builds or buys a house, he or she usually occupies it with his or her spouse and unmarried children. Children attempt to build their own houses, and if they do not work for their parents as adults, they tend to move out when they marry or sometimes earlier. Women usually go to live with their husbands, except when they own property and their husbands do not. Thus when an owner dies and the inheritance is divided, a number of different residential patterns may emerge, depending upon the ratio of houses and rooms to heirs and on many other factors including the other economic assets of the heirs and their spouses. In some cases siblings or the children of siblings become co-residents and rent out whatever rooms they do not occupy. In other cases, when the room/heir ratio is low, some or all of the heirs may live elsewhere, rent out the house, and divide the cash income. In all of these patterns it is clear that the desire to collect rent on valuable property prevails over the desire to live with kin. There are, for example, individuals who move out of the houses they own and rent rooms for themselves in less desirable and cheaper neighbourhoods (ranked in terms of such things as proximity to the central mosque, the market, and so on), while they rent their inherited property in the more valuable areas near the original zongo neighbourhood. This choice is seen not so much as a means of avoiding friction between kin as

174   *CHANGING SOCIAL STRUCTURE IN GHANA*

of realising the economic advantages attached to the ownership of particular properties.

Since individuals can keep effective rights in property without tying this to residence, the fragmentation of the kinship unit as a residential unit does not mean that all economic relationships among kin cease. However, among urban-born immigrants many of the bonds that are established among kin are contractual: they are of the same kind as those occurring between non-kin. Because rooms may be sold outside the kinship group, joint owners of a single house may consist, for example, of three siblings and a fourth unrelated person who may even belong to another ethnic group. The economic relationships between siblings, as joint heirs, are identical to the relationship each of them has with the fourth owner. All own individual shares in a piece of property that just happens to consist of a single house.

So far the fragmentation of kinship groups among the families of landlords has been discussed. Such fragmentation also occurs among immigrants who do not own houses, but for slightly different reasons. The older neighbourhoods are the most crowded, yet because they are closest to the city centre and the market, they are the most desirable areas. Kinship networks of course expand, but it is very difficult to rent several rooms in a single house to keep up with this expansion. As a result, polygynous men often have wives in different houses and sometimes in different neighbourhoods; adult children rarely live with their parents, and adult siblings who do not own property in the same house very rarely reside together.

Despite this residential dispersion not all social obligations and relationships between kin lapse. However, the extent to which domestic economies (households) are merged, even in the cases of residential separation, depends upon the types of economic and conjugal relationships binding kin and affines. Households do not necessarily coincide with residential units[5]. This is obvious in the case of men with several wives. If the man is affluent enough to have a separate room of his own, his wives, even if they have rooms in other houses, come to him several nights a week to cook and sleep. If he does not have a separate room, the husband sleeps in his various wives' rooms, which may be in different houses, on the nights that each wife cooks. In other cases, junior wives cook in the house of the senior wife, regardless of where they sleep, but this arrangement is not favoured among Kumasi women who value their independence. Whatever arrangement is followed, the husband is responsible for providing each wife with money or food for at least the evening meal. This is so, no matter what the wife's own income is. If a married son moves out but at the same time maintains some extra-domestic economic link with his father, the son and his immediate family may return to the father's house in the evening to eat. Since they will sleep elsewhere, the father gains income by renting the rooms his son and his son's immediate family would otherwise occupy. As long as the son works for or with his father, the father must provide the evening meal, although the son's wife or wives will often cook, in deference to the seniority of their father-in-law's wives.

The range of these different possible arrangements is very great due to the large number of variables involved. This means that there

ECONOMICS IN MULTI-ETHNIC DWELLINGS 175

is no necessary or even typical coincidence between kinship groups, domestic groups (households), and residential groups. An analysis of the domestic cycle, and even merely of the composition of residential units, involves an analysis of the variables involved and their possible permutations and combinations. Some of the variables which have been discussed so far and which must be considered in analysing specific cases include the ratio between the size of property and the number of owners, the marital status of the owners and their kin, the economic relationships between kin, and individual choice as to place of residence and the use of economic assets.

As a general pattern it is clear that as kin move out, rooms become vacant and may be rented to non-kin, often to members of different ethnic groups. This has been made possible by a continual influx of migrants into Kunasi since the beginning of the century, and by a high degree of residential mobility among urban residents. As immigration to Kumasi slows down, as it did in the early 1970s due to the government's policy of restricting the entry of African aliens, it can be expected that kinship and domestic groupings will more nearly coincide. However, as long as Kumasi remains a major market centre for long distance trade and a centre for the dispersal of northern labourers to rural cocoa farms, the economic value of houses and rooms will be maintained and kin may be expected to disperse as tenants move in.

The ethnic heterogeneity of houses is due mainly to the prevalence of non-kin in them. Due to inter-ethnic marriage, of course, not all of the owners' kin are members of the same ethnic community. In the sample of eighty-nine house, fifteen percent of the Mossi owners' kin were not Mossi. The large number of non-Mossi residents in these houses (fifty percent) was due therefore to a tendency on the part of landlords to rent rooms to non-kin who were members of other ethnic communities. Only one-third of the residents who were not kin of the owners were Mossi. Members of the owners' own group, like kin, are often seen as economic liabilities, in that one cannot easily apply sanctions to them to redeem debts. Should a landlord attempt to evict a member of his own ethnic community for non-payment of rent, he is urged by the leaders of the community to reach a settlement which may not be economically advantageous. Tenants from other ethnic groups can more easily be evicted or brought to court.

For these reasons, no house in the sample was ethnically homogeneous. The Mossi were one of thirty-six ethnic communities represented, and in each house there were between two and fifteen groups represented. Besides the Mossi other residents fell in the following categories: northern Ghanaians (18%); others from Upper Volta (11%), Nigerians (11%), people from Togo, Dahomey, Niger and Mali (4%), Akans and southern Ghanaians (6%). Many of these people have little in common with the Mossi in terms of traditional culture and language. While there seems to be some clustering of other Voltaics and northern Ghanaians, others who are culturally more distant are not excluded. Moreover, in situations where ethnicity is relevant, differences between culturally related groups can become as significant as differences between culturally distant group.

176   *CHANGING SOCIAL STRUCTURE IN GHANA*

Incorporation and integration in the domestic context

If one looks at the domestic cycle, not from the point of view
of the developing and dispersing kinship group, but rather within the
framework of the dwelling unit itself, one must note the processes and
the extent to which unrelated tenants are incorporated. It is true, of
course, that the dispersal of kin leads to social integration on an
inter-house and inter-neighbourhood basis, since kinship relationships
are highly valued and are maintained even when they are not associated
with joint economic activities and co-residence. The aspect of integration which is of interest for this paper, however, is that which occurs
within the structure of the house. This is a process that is complementary to the dispersal of kin, since this dispersal is what makes the
co-residence of non-kin possible. While one would expect to find non-kin
in the large houses of rural-born migrants who have few relatives in
Kumasi, it is important to note that the *continuous* dispersal of kin over
several generations implies that this is not a pragmatic response to migration, but is rather a highly valued form of residence. The economic
value of accommodating non-kin has already been discussed, and we may now
turn to other social consequences of these residence patterns.

The fact that co-residence often coincides with ties of clientage
between landlord and tenant has been noted. Clients do not pay rent,
but perform extra-domestic services for their patrons. These relationships occur frequently between members of the same ethnic community but
sometimes also develop among immigrants from different ethnic groups.
Such relationships, based initially on an exchange of services, often
develop into kinship and affinal ties just as kinship and affinal links
can often become ties of clientage, when a kinsman works for and is
housed by another. It is significant that in Kumasi fictive kinship
ties, usually evolving out of both clientage and co-residence, become
'real' after several generations, exactly as if adoption had occurred.
When a person calls a *maigida* or another tenant by a term for 'father'
or 'older brother' to demonstrate deference and respect, and when this
is correlated with the assumption of obligations and claims that are
believed to characterise kinship relations, the children of these
individuals often continue to use kinship terms and to fulfil the
obligations of kin. The major difference between such fictive kin
ties and biologically based kin relationships is that the fictive kin
relationships are voluntarily contracted. As long as the expectations
entailed in kinship relationships are met, the kinship idiom will be
used. When these roles are assumed for several generations, the sense
of obligation becomes a moral imperative, and the fact that the tie
grew out of clientage and co-residence rather than birth may be forgotten or denied and a genealogical claim may be added to the jural content
of the relationship.

The importance and prevalence of fictive kinship in Kumasi is related
both to the consequences of migration, in that many migrants come to the
city without the kin they need, and to the economic system, in which so
many activities involve patron-client ties. The use of the kinship idiom
does not minimise the economic aspect of patron-client ties; it simply
justifies the attribution of many other obligations to these relationships.
House owners find wives and pay bridewealth for their client-tenants as if
they were fulfilling the obligations of a lineage head. The clients later

ECONOMICS IN MULTI-ETHNIC DWELLINGS 177

reciprocate by giving a child of the marriage to the house owner who then may give a child as a bride to one of his sons. Fictive kinship relationships also develop between tenants who are not in patron/client relationships. They sometimes foster each others' children, establishing a kind of co-parenthood relationship which is regarded as a sibling relationship, since siblings in many of these West African societies traditionally have some jural responsibility over each others' children (see Schildkrout: 1973b and E. Goody: 1966).

Thus although houses contain many unrelated people, very close relationships develop which become the jural equivalents of kinship and which are conceptualised in this way by the zongo residents. This is particularly important for first generation immigrants who have few biological kin in Kumasi. Nevertheless these relationships persist over several generations and although urban-born immigrants rarely contract new fictive kin ties, they usually maintain the relationships developed by their rural-born parents and grandparents. This attests to the great importance of kinship relationships which should not be ignored in view of the residential dispersal which occurs. In the long run, this dispersal leads to the augmentation of kinship networks since biological ties are supplemented by fictive ones. Fictive kin, like biological kin, are encouraged to disperse so that the economic value of property can be maintained.

Fictive kinship is one way in which the social integration occurring in the domestic context is expressed. Another striking consequence of the residential pattern just described is the cultural homogeneity, or value consensus, found among urban-born immigrants. Although patrifiliation confers ethnic identity, and although adolescents and adults form recreational, political and religious associations on an ethnic basis, among urban-born immigrants ethnicity has no cultural correlates. Many urban-born immigrants speak only Hausa, the lingua franca in the zongo, and many know little or nothing about the traditional cultures associated with their ethnic identity. Until the age of at least seven most children are unaware of ethnicity, even though this may become quite important to them as adults, when it may be used as one of a number of bases for defining social relationships.

The multi-ethnic composition of all these houses means that some elements of a common culture most evolve. Women and children cooperate constantly in the house, and they develop many 'common understandings'. The effort first-generation immigrants expend to get along with each other in the domestic context pays off in the second generation, where one finds an increasing rate of inter-ethnic marriage (despite more equal sex ratios), a large number of multi-ethnic social, religious, recreational and political associations, and considerable economic and political cooperation among immigrants from different ethnic communities. Urban-born immigrants speak of Kumasi customs; they consciously recognise that a zongo culture has evolved and that this is the only culture they know. This does not prevent them from using common ethnicity as a basis for association on particular occasions, but it does very significantly limit the degree to which ethnic differences can prevent communication and understanding. Moreover, the many cross-ethnic relationships which develop, support the cultural integration which occurs.

The processes of social and cultural integration seem to have gone

178 CHANGING SOCIAL STRUCTURE IN GHANA

further in Kumasi zongo than in many other heterogeneous urban environments precisely because interaction and cooperation are necessitated by the kinds of residential groupings migrants encounter. If interaction between migrants of different ethnic groups were restricted to the market place or to the Mosque, for example, integration would be considerably slower and less complete. If this were the case, second and third generation immigrants would probably still retain their parents' languages and might be cognisant of many other aspects of traditional culture. Their identity would be symbolised by culturally specific ways of behaving, not by such things as printed membership cards in formally constituted associations. Traditional enmities and alliances might be preserved much more than they are; and social status, or rank, insofar as it is associated with ethnicity would depend upon the valuations which one group traditionally made of another. But among town-born immigrants these things do not occur. Prestige depends upon Islamic education and wealth, and conflicts rarely follow ethnic divisions entirely. On many occasions the Islamic ideology of brotherhood is used to express an inclusive level of identity which supersedes that associated with the identity conferred through patrifiliation. Islam does not in itself cause this integration, but its ideology expresses the process of socio-cultural integration which occurs in the domestic context.

CONCLUSION

In this paper I have first tried to show how economic factors affect the composition of residence units in a particular urban context. I have then examined some of the consequences of these economic factors in terms of socio-cultural integration. I have discussed factors which lead to the dispersal of kin and members of the same ethnic community into different houses and different neighbourhoods. This leads to social integration on a community-wide level since residential separation in no way implies the abandonment of all effective and jural ties between these people. Complementary to the integration which is achieved on an inter-house and inter-neighbourhood basis is the resultant integration which occurs within the context of the house. This is both social and cultural, in that it involves immigrants who come to Kumasi with very different backgrounds. Through the recurrent process of kin dispersal, and the residential incorporation of non-kin, migrants of different generations of urban residence and immigrants with different ethnic backgrounds become co-residents. This prevents the encapsulation and isolation of ethnic communities or new migrants in the urban setting. This may be why one notices the degree to which the immigrant community in Kumasi, the zongo, has developed a distinct culture which overrides the ethnic divisions within it, but which also polarises the stranger community as a whole, in cultural terms at least, against the indigenous Asante population. Social and cultural integration occurs within the domestic context in the zongo, through the mechanisms of patron/client relationships, the development of fictive kinship, and the simple necessity of day to day cooperation and interaction. Although differences in wealth clearly exist between landlords and tenants, since these are co-resident, and since co-residence so often implies clientage and kinship,

ECONOMICS IN MULTI-ETHNIC DWELLINGS

179

the domestic context is also important in preventing the emergence of
'class' cleavages or conflicts within the zongo community. For these
reasons, therefore, the domestic context is crucial in generating a
new level of communal identity among Muslim immigrants in Kumasi. In
hindsight, this could be taken as an example of 'fortuitous' urban
planning. On the one hand, it militates against internal conflict in
the zongo; on the other, it intensifies the 'encapsulation' of immigrants.

NOTES

1. Zongo is a Hausa term meaning stranger's quarter or caravan site,
   and is used for trading communities in all of   Hausa-speaking
   West Africa.

2. In fact, in 1960, 60% of the population were Akan (Asante, Fante
   and others); 8% were non-Akan southern Ghanaians; approximately
   15% were northern Ghanaians; and approximately 15% were non-
   Ghanaian Africans from the surrounding countries. These figures
   are no more than approximations based on the 1960 Ghana Census.

3. Not all northerners are Muslims. Insofar as the zongo is defined
   as a stranger community, as it often is by outsiders, it contains
   all northerners in Kumasi. As a Muslim community, however, it
   does not, but many non-Muslim northerners, particularly the traders,
   convert in order to advance within the zongo. The term northerner
   is commonly used to refer to savannah people as opposed to forest
   people (Asante and others) or coastal people, and is often used
   interchangeably with the term zongo despite these distinctions.

4. The question of intentionality arises here. One can argue that the
   indigenous and colonial authorities encouraged encapsulation in order
   to maintain a pool of cheap labour. However, since entrepreneurial
   activity was not a the same time limited, this encapsulation became
   a matter of choice, particularly for those who engaged in trade
   rather than wage labour. It was not until the Busia government that
   any attempt was made to close the loophole left open by a long-standing
   policy of laissez-faire capitalism in regard to internal West African
   trade.

5. For the purpose of the survey of Mossi-owned houses, a person was
   counted as a resident if he or she regularly slept in the house,
   even though this may not have meant seven days a week.

A STUDY OF DOMESTIC CONTINUITY AND CHANGE:

AKAN SENIOR SERVICE FAMILIES IN ACCRA

C H R I S T I N E   O P P O N G

The problem

The controlled comparison of data collected from communities in Ghana practising matrilineal and patrilineal reckoning of descent and inheritance has on several occasions proved to be a fruitful procedure in the anthropological study of the domestic domain of social life in Ghana. By this means considerable light has been shed upon such matters as the nature of incest and adultery (J.R. Goody 1956), household residence patterns and resources management (J.R. Goody 1958) and the mother's brother/sister's son relationship (J.R. Goody 1959). In the study discussed in this paper a similar procedure was adopted of selecting homogeneous, non-representative samples of respondents including matrilineal Akan, patrilineal Ewe and 'mixed' Ga, with a view to examining certain aspects of continuity and change in conjugal family relationships among a section of the Akan urban elite. The aspects selected were the conjugal division of labour (or what has been termed the *jointness* or *segregation* of the conjugal roles) and the functional individuation of the conjugal family (or the extent to which it forms a *closed* or *open* domestic unit for various types of activities)[1]. These two dimensions have been the subject of study in a number of recent discussions on urban family living[2].

The population examined in the present study consists of samples of highly educated men from the Akan, Ewe and Ga areas of Ghana, but with the main body of material being collected from Akan men and their wives working in the senior ranks of government service in the capital, Accra. Supporting data has been taken from a survey of undergraduates in the two coastal universities of Legon and Cape Coast. These people form part of the country's socially and spatially mobile elite. Being heterogeneous from the ethnic standpoint and yet homogeneous from the point of view of occupation and education, these samples provide a suitable basis for the exploration of a number of hypotheses concerning the continuity of domestic life, as well as the causes and correlates of innovation in the elite household of the towns[3]. I have elsewhere discussed a number of such issues including the education of the children of relatives (1969a), domestic budgeting (1970a), decision-making (1970b, 1973) and the changes in both domestic norms and behaviour which tend to occur in the wake of successive generations with their increasing levels of formal education (1972a,b,c).

Here I want to take a further look at two issues central to discussions of continuity and change in the urban family. The first is the widespread observation that traditional domestic behaviour continues

CHANGING SOCIAL STRUCTURE IN GHANA

among the educated, many of whom are living at a distance from most
of their kin, not simply in the continued exchange of customary goods
and services between the new suburbs and the home areas (Oppong 1969a)
but also in the context of the relationships between members of the
conjugal family themselves (Gutkind 1965:59). It was moreover hypothesised that if traditional behaviour persists, then this will differ
according to ethnic origin. Significantly, a number of those interviewed were conscious of ethnic differences in domestic behaviour and
expectations, noting that these often persisted among the educated
elite. Such comments are what Merton calls the 'anomalous strategic-
data' which played an important part in the initial formulation of the
research design. The comments made by both men and women pointed to the
belief that Akan husbands and wives living in Accra were likely to be
comparatively segregated in two major respects, financially through the
influence of persisting matrilineal inheritance as well as in the performance of domestic chores and the care of children. It was considered
that Akan men do not like to help in the house and that among the Ewe
the conjugal tie was somewhat 'closer'; commenting on the Ga system one
Akan wife considered it to lie somewhere between the Akan and the Ewe.

The second issue to be considered is the general direction of
change - its causes and correlates, particularly the part played by
education. Again it was assumed among some of the more sophisticated
actors in the population studied that the marriage relationships among
Akan couples with two or three generations of educated forebears (that
is, mainly coastal Fanti) were 'closer' than those among the newcomers
to the ranks of the educated (often Akan from the interior Ashanti and
Brong areas) and that kin among the former were not so close to the
married couple and their children. Clearly these observations are in
line with some virtually universal trends, documented by Goode (1963)
and others.

The research design

The initial difficulty encountered in the study was conceptual,
that of conceiving a framework within which to organise an array of
different kinds of data relating to several areas of domestic activity.
Since the main concerns were the type of conjugal roles and the extent
to which the conjugal family formed a distinct unit, it was decided to
employ the two dimensions, *joint/segregated* and *open/closed*. The first
refers to the extent to which husband and wife together assume rights
and responsibilities and perform tasks together (or in place of each
other). The second refers to the extension of spouse/parent roles
beyond the boundary of the nuclear family. Both are concerned with the
substitution of actors in the domestic domain. Using these two dimensions, the allocation or rights and duties between the spouses themselves
and between spouses and their kin, four types of conjugal role system
may be distinguished with regard to any particular area of activity -
joint/open, segregated/open, joint/closed and segregated/closed[4].

In collecting data, both macro and micro approaches were employed;
use was made of both surveys and case studies. At the same time information was gathered on both norms and behaviour. The research was
designed not simply to obtain representative samples of individuals in
order to describe features of family life or attitudes to family living

DOMESTIC CONTINUITY AND CHANGE IN ACCRA

among the educated section of the total population. Rather the aim was to explain how and why individuals, couples and larger groups of people differed from each other in their behaviour or ideas, and to explore a number of suggested correlations between features of the traditional kinship systems, such as descent, inheritance and residence patterns on the one hand and aspects of conjugal and kin ties on the other. Thus analytical types of survey were designed which made use of short, self-administered questionnaires. In each case two sets of data were collected; the first related to the independent variables crucial to the study, such as ethnicity and level of forebear's education, while the second aimed at obtaining quantifiable information regarding the dependent variables in the study, namely, the degrees of jointness and closure. This meant that the production of scales or indices incorporating the responses of actors about their behaviour or norms which could be used to compare these degrees.

The attempt to devise indices of social behaviour phenomena has been the constant problem of research from Durkheim (1895:55-8) to Merton (1957:16,115) and continues to play a central part. The lack of satisfactory definition surrounding the use of the phrase 'conjugal role segregation' so strikingly used by Bott (1957), and the difficulty of employing this notion in specific studies has been brought out by writers such as Harrell Bond (1967) and Platt (1969). In the study reported here a number of indices and scales were devised to show the extent to which husband or wife performed a task jointly with the other. Scores were then constructed to indicate the extent to which the wife and husband jointly provided for the family's financial needs, the extent to which husband and wife jointly managed their financial resources (including such matters as spending, saving and ownership) and the extent to which the husband assisted with household tasks and the care of children (Oppong 1970). Similarly the closure of the conjugal family in financial affairs could be assessed by the amounts of money spent on assisting kin and by the numbers of relatives educated. For attitudes, scales were devised to show degrees of the respondents' approval both of jointness in financial matters and of the closure of the conjugal family (Oppong 1972c). Using these several indicators people could be classified and allocated to contrasting sets on the basis of the number and kinds of characteristics they were found to possess.

We may now briefly consider some of the family norms in the societies from which our respondents originate before going on to describe their conjugal system in Accra. This will be followed by an examination of some of the cultural differences which appears to persist between members of the different ethnic groups and then a discussion of the general changes which seem to be taking place.

Traditional norms

The Akan (Fortes 1950), the Ga (Field 1940; Azu 1974; Kilson 1967) and Ewe (Nukunya 1969) each have a distinctive system of kinship, marriage and domestic organisation. Common to them all, however, are the reckoning of membership of property holding lineage on the basis of unilineal descent and the corporate functioning of these groups in family activities, such as domestic decision-making, child-rearing, inheritance and

184 *CHANGING SOCIAL STRUCTURE IN GHANA*

management of property. In each case marriage is potentially polygynous and involves two kin groups in the negotiations. In traditional families the conjugal pair is not isolated from kin after marriage. The husband and wife live in the same compound or next door to their relatives, and so kinsfolk are invariably on hand to cooperate in both male and female tasks inside and outside the house. Certain crucial differences exist, however, in the structure and the functioning of the three systems, which can be seen in relationships between husband and wife in the three ethnic groups. One of the most striking differences in traditional domestic organisation is that frequently among the Akan and the Ga but not among the Ewe we find a pattern of duo-local residence of spouses. Among the Akan and the Ga it is consanguines who traditionally reside together, not spouses (at least in the densely settled communities) so that children seldom live throughout childhood with both of their parents. Among the Ewe, however, the conjugal family is normally the basic unit in the household, which is seldom very large in size (unlike the traditional lineage compounds found in Ga and Akan communities). In urban Ga compounds of traditional type the men live quite separately from women in monosexual households, adult men living with their older sons, women living with their mothers, sisters and small children. In the typical Akan case, matrikin of both sexes live together.

What of the domestic division of labour in both earning the living and housekeeping? All southern Ghanaian women (Akan, Ga and Ewe), like their counterparts in many regions of Africa, have long been recognised as playing a vital role in providing for the material needs of themselves and their children. Indeed southern Ghana is one of those characterised by a 'female farming system' (Boserup 1970). The majority of women in all the three ethnic groups are actively engaged in farming for food, growing cash crops or trading (Gil, Aryee and Ghansah 1964:110,122). Numerous observers have commented upon this state of affairs (Fortes 1948:163; Field 1960:30; McCall 1961:297; Hill 1963; Nukunya 1969). As the 1960 Census of Ghana showed, less than a quarter of the women in the three main groups in the south were simply classified as 'housewives' (Gil, Aryee and Ghansah 1964:103). This pattern of female participation in the labour force, coupled with the provision of part or all of the material needs for themselves and their dependents, continues in the urban environments where women supplement and sometimes provide the daily budget (Acquah 1950:49; Busia 1950:20; Caldwell 1969).

On the other hand we have little evidence of massive male participation in domestic chores, such as cooking, cleaning and child-care, either in southern Ghana or anywhere else in Africa. Men's roles have been predominantly those of hunters, warriors, farmers and fishermen, especially as these require speed, strength and endurance. Moreover, while census returns include data on female employment in various capacities outside the home, they do not include parallel information about the extent to which men play housekeeping roles. We are forced to rely for the most part upon observers' comments. Nukunya's description of the Ewe situation is similar to that reported from many communities. It stresses the complementary aspect of the division of labour:

'Though the home is run by the combined efforts of all its members, between men and women there is a clear and complementary division of labour. Certain tasks are performed by one sex, while others fall exclusively within the domain of the

DOMESTIC CONTINUITY AND CHANGE IN ACCRA

185

other. The man generally does the work which demands
great physical strength, such as clearing the bush,
constructing the woodwork in the building of a house,
making fences and cutting roads from the home to farm'
(1969:155).

While we have descriptive statements, we lack comparative quantified
data from the several regions. Indeed the kind of data we require
for comparison is more difficult to collect than statistics on female
employment on the farm, in the market or in the factory. The husband's
role inside the home is obviously a much less visible one. Only
detailed questioning or intimate observation can enable one to assess
a man's part in child-rearing or in domestic chores. However, we may
assume that among rural communities, just as the extent of the participation of women in the agricultural labour force varies, so too does
the extent to which husbands assist wives with these chores. Indeed
such variations in the male domestic role do emerge from a close
scrutiny of the available sources.

The composition of the household obviously places definite limits
upon the categories of kin and affines who may regularly cooperate in
the performance of domestic tasks. Certain basic similarities are
clear: in all three societies women do the cooking as well as the bulk
of other domestic chores. They are helped to a considerable extent by
children; and wives cooperate with other women in their households.
In the households in which women live separately from their husbands
they cook for them and send the food by their children. But what of the
husband/father's role in domestic affairs? Obviously among the Ga and
Akan, where the husband lives in a different household, he is not in a
position to be called upon to help his wife in any domestic tasks. She
is typically living with her mother and sisters, who are the people most
likely to provide her with assistance. The Ewe case is somewhat different, for husband and wife are living together, often without any other
adults in the home, and the husband is in a position where he may well
be needed to give assistance to a sick or overworked wife. In fact
certain domestic tasks such as cleaning fish for cooking or chopping
wood lie in his recognised sphere of activities. Thus although the
division of labour might be roughly described as complementary in all
three societies, the Ewe husband is in quite a different domestic position from his Ga or Akan conterpart who lives with his own lineage kin
and is spatially separated from the processes of child-care and cooking
that his wife is carrying out on his behalf. Detailed enquiries among
selected populations dependent upon fishing and farming may reveal
further differences of this kind.

The next point, which concerns the management of domestic financial
resources rather than the expenditure of time and energy, relates to
matrilineal descent and inheritance prevalent among the Akan and a section
of the Ga. Since Bosman observed in 1704 that, on the death of an Akan
husband or wife, the relatives come and immediately sweep away all, leaving the widow or widower without anything, several writers have discussed
the kinds of economic rights and obligations that exist between kin,
spouses and affines in Akan society; the legal and social implications
have been discussed by Sarbah (1897), Danquah (1922, 1928), Rattray (1923,
1929) and Fortes (1948, 1950, 1963, 1970, 1973). Though the social and

186 *CHANGING SOCIAL STRUCTURE IN GHANA*

economic system has been constantly subject to change, many basic features have endured. For example, Sarbah's work is still the authority referred to in cases subject to customary law when the legal rights and duties of Akan husbands, wives and kin are in dispute.

Because of the right of matrikin to inherit the property of the deceased to the exclusion of the spouse, and in the case of a man the exclusion of his children, married people customarily have no community of goods. Each traditionally retains his or her own property and when it comes to making provision for the domestic budget, man and wife (or wives) share the costs (Sarbah 1903:16). Even when a wife labours to help her husband to acquire and maintain property such as a house or farm, it is legally the sole possession of the husband (Sarbah 1903:60). The economic rights of the wife and children consist essentially in maintenance from his property, both during his lifetime and after his death. At death the responsibility devolves upon his heir, who inherits the care of the widow and her children together with the property. The children may only receive a share of the husband's or father's property if a will or gift *inter vivos* is recognised by the husband's matrikin. Only one category of wives and children of Akan husbands have a right to inherit a portion, should the husband die intestate, namely, those subject to the provisions of the Marriage Ordinance of 1884, whereby a widow is entitled to two-ninths of her deceased husband's estate.

Because of this lack of economic security in their husband's households and because of their enduring matrilineage rights, it is said that at the time of their marriage Akan women are told by their matrikin to take their property to their maternal homes and their debts to their husbands'. An Akan saying states that one does not get rich from another person's matrilineage, which is a warning to wives not to expect to benefit from the family property of their husbands.

In contrast to the matrilineal system of the Akan, the Ewe practise a system of patrilineal inheritance whereby a man's children are included among his heirs. Thus although a woman may herself have no customary rights to inherit a portion of her husband's property, the rights of her children are assured. We are still told however that the Anlo Ewe conjugal family cannot be said to cooperate in a joint economic venture, and that the far reaching economic independence of the spouses makes close marital union difficult (Nukunya 1969:156-7).

The Ga system, which has been variously called cognatic, bilineal, patrilineal and matrilineal, includes both types of inheritance. For present purposes it may be classified as mixed and therefore as standing somewhat between the Akan and the Ewe[5]. In the Ga case too, husbands and wives customarily have separate property interests (Azu 1974).

In the three systems then, husband and wife usually share some of the tasks of rearing and providing for the financial needs of the children, but the performance of houshold jobs and the management of material resources tend to be separate spheres of activity. In every kind of

DOMESTIC CONTINUITY AND CHANGE IN ACCRA

activity the conjugal family tends to be an open group with filial, conjugal and parental rights and duties stretching across it boundaries.

However, the major differences in traditional family relationships, that is, in residence, descent and inheritance, suggest a greater tendency towards jointness in the conjugal roles among the Ewe. Does the same obtain among the elite?

Families of the urban elite

Most of the civil servants in the survey were Akan, Ga and Ewe, who came from southern Ghanaian towns and village, and included administrators, doctors, lawyers, accountants and teachers. About half had travelled abroad in the course of their education. About a third had illiterate parents; over half of the rest had educated fathers and the remainder had educated grandparents as well.

The Senior Civil Service from which these respondents were selected forms a significant part of the new educated 'elite' in modern Ghana (de Graft Johnson 1966; Tiger 1967). Only a few of them come from the 'old elite' families, such as the Brews of Cape Coast described by Priestly (1969). They occupy a high place in the overall prestige structure of the country and enjoy an array of material privileges similar to those discussed by Lloyd (1967a) for their Nigerian counterparts. Smythe and Smythe (1960), also writing of Nigeria, have described in great detail the kinds of houses in which they live, many of them built for their expatriate predecessors; while Caldwell (1968) has outlined some of the demographic and residential aspects of their domestic lives.

Such men are often among the first in their families to reach such levels of employment and to depend for their livelihood on a high, independently earned income. But their wives too are often employed so that a number of decisions have to be taken over the allocation of this income, as well as living space and time, between the married couple themselves and sometimes among conflicting claimants outside the conjugal family. To understand this process, let us consider the development of a conjugal family over time, the organisation of the family budget and the internal division of labour.

When a civil servant marries, he can choose one or more ways of contracting the union, including by customary rites or by registration according to the Marriage Ordinance. Usually an expensive wedding either civil or church, is followed quickly, or even preceded by, the birth of a child. More than half the couples had their first child in the same twelve month period as the marriage. Indeed, in nearly one in three cases conception preceded the marriage, while 11% of the marriages were only registered after the birth of one or more children. By the age of thirty the wife is likely to have had three or four children. Four is the ideal number desired by the majority of highly educated women, but husbands tend to want significantly more; in the event the average completed size of educated urban families is six (Caldwell 1968).

188   *CHANGING SOCIAL STRUCTURE IN GHANA*

However, childbirth and the rearing of infants have a minimum effect upon the employment of wives, the majority of whom are earning incomes. Seldom does childbirth interrupt their work for more than a few months; when there is a baby or toddler in the house, a resident maid servant or relative become indispensable to the educated housewife. Since the wife's work is seldom of such a kind that she can take her child along with her (as can women farmers or traders) she is compelled to find a helper to assume some of her maternal responsibilities. So women delegate much of their baby minding and child-care to nurse girls or to relatives. When they are only two years old the children are often sent to a local nursery school (of which there are many in Accra). During crisis periods of travel abroad, sickness or job transfer, children may be sent to stay with close relatives for up to several years. If the parents are studying abroad, the children are occasionally sent to foster parents in that country. For couples whose higher education has been a protracted process, these alternative provisions for the care of children sometimes mean that it is several years before they live together in a household with their own children.

Mr. and Mrs. Anum are an example of such a family. They were married in the early sixties by customary rites and the wife continued to stay with her mother till after the birth of her first baby. Several months later the husband won a scholarship to study in England. When the baby was a year old, the wife went to join her husband, leaving the baby with her mother. Over two years later they registered their marriage in London where Mrs. Anum continued to work and her husband to study. His course lasted for five years and in the middle of it his wife had another baby. After a few months they decided to take the child to the wife's mother, finding that the care given by the foster mother in England was unsatisfactory. After spending a few months with her mother and two sons in Accra, the wife returned to her husband in London where she again worked in an office until they both came home together. It was six years after the marriage before the couple set up a household with their children and Mrs. Anum admitted that these had considerable difficulty in getting adjusted to live with their own parents.

This case is an extreme example of the kind of separation of nuclear families and the rearing of children by relatives that sometimes results from prolonged education and from transfers with in the civil service. What is significant is that such incidents are not merely anomalies, exceptions to a general pattern, but that the substitution of the maternal role is considered normal. Indeed, many educated people completely reject the idea that a mother should give up work outside the home when she has children under five years old[6]. Although women with three or more children are less likely to work outside the home, the majority still do so. The general pattern is for the wife to continue working as long as she can during pregnancy and then to combine her annual leave of one month with her three months maternity leave. The baby can be three or four months old before she goes back to work; in the meantime she hopes to have a relative in the house or to have trained a responsible maid. This pattern, usually repeated four or more times during the first few years of marriage, seems to be the generally accepted solution to the problem of women's two roles. If there is public controversy, it appears to centre upon

DOMESTIC CONTINUITY AND CHANGE IN ACCRA 189

the minor aspects of the system, not upon the system itself. There are complaints from employers that some working girls receive too frequent benefits from maternity leave pay and on the other hand complaints from women that they do not get full pay during their leave[7]. Moreover, mothers are often concerned about leaving a baby to the physical care of a nursemaid; they worry whether the girl will feed the baby properly during their absence, whether she will change it often enough and whether she will keep a watchful eye on it at the crawling stage. But little mention is made of the possible dangers of mental or emotional deprivation arising from the mother's absence and the frequent turnover of child-minders. Wives who have younger sisters and nieces to come and stay with them are more fortunate than those who change maids every few weeks and are at their wits' end how to fulfil their responsibilities as mothers and continue working. Few choose to stay at home and care for the baby and the house themselves; even when they do, they are seldom alone but have someone to whom to delegate a number of tasks.

The extent to which the husband takes an active part in child care seems to vary very much from couple to couple and according to their circumstances at the time. Wives whose husbands take an enthusiastic and active part in the care of young children are of course very pleased and praise them highly, but they consider their husbands to be worthy exceptions to the general rule. Resposibility for care of the pre-school child appears to rest mainly upon the wife, with husbands playing varying parts. The norm is for the wife to delegate many of her responsibilities in this area to relatives or employees. A point to emphasise is that this openness in the parent-child relationship is a continuation of a traditional practice, though in the modern urban situation a number of factors make it more difficult to maintain the same degree of security and continuity in the delegation of maternal roles. The problem for the wife in finding suitable people to assume some of her responsibilities is seen in the main as practical, not psychological or moral, that is, as connected with the nature of urban employment and the increasing difficulty of finding cheap female labour and unemployed relatives able to fill the demanding task of nursemaid. To the observer, educated couples are sometimes seen as abusing the system by turning to their own advantage the economic   dependence of other families and using small children as lowly paid servants, at the very time when these should be attending school. The way such children are treated in the house manifests the wide cultural and economic gap often existing between urban and rural kin (as well as the unrelated) living in the same household. However, the intention of the parents of children sent to such homes is presumably to lessen the gap.

Just as in the case of infant care, the task area of household chores is remarkable for the fact that it is scarcely ever carried out by the husband, wife and children alone, in fact there are many cases in which they play a relatively small part[8]. Chores can be ranked with some consistency according to the likelihood of the wife's doing them herself. At the bottom of the list are the cleaning jobs (the sweeping, window cleaning and dish-washing) which she is not likely to do unaided. Again, few do the laundry themselves; some employ washermen, others have maids to do it[9].

190 *CHANGING SOCIAL STRUCTURE IN GHANA*

There are a number of other tasks which a wife may carry out with her husband (though there are wide variations in the amount and types of tasks individual husbands do); these include shopping at stores and washing the car but men are unlikely to give much help with making beds, washing up, setting the table and cooking.

The urban salaried man is also distiguished from most of his rural brothers by the ownership and use of property. For the majority of the elite, whatever they own is owned individually. Those who do own property jointly with other individuals are twice as likely to own it jointly with kin as with their wives. Not all of the properties owned jointly with kin are inherited; some are new farms and building projects entered into with brothers and parents where a portion of the salary is invested. A few build town houses and put them in the joint names of themselves and their wives or children. Virtually all give some financial help to relatives and much of this money is sent to kin in the form of regular monthly remittances. About half.send over five pounds a month, besides all the other amounts they spend on education, gifts, funerals and other expenses. Many wives, too, have calls for financial help made upon them. Younger siblings want money to go to secondary school, elderly aunts want money for funeral clothes. A large item of expenditure is the cost of educating the children of relatives up to secondary school level or higher, the majority of such children being either younger siblings or nephews and nieces (Oppong 1969).

As in other parts of West Africa, the rearing and educating of children by non-parental kin, both in rural and urban situations, is widely practised and considered the normal continuation of customary usage. While it is accepted as being beneficial to the children of needy parents, there is a growing feeling among the educated that couples should only be expected to finance the education of their own children[10]. Sometimes resentment is expressed at being asked to pay school fees for yet another relative, and sometimes there is adamant refusal to accept this responsibility. The decision whether to take on another such financial burden often rests upon an estimate of the financial position of the child's father, the closeness of the kinship tie and the sense of personal obligation for past benefits received from the child's relatives. Thus Mr. Yaw, whose father died soon after he was born and whose school fees were paid by his mother's brothers, feels a special obligation to help his own sister's children. He looks after his sister's son who is at college and for several years he paid about £35 a year to help meet his expenses. He has also helped other younger maternal nephews and nieces with small amounts; if it proves necessary he will offer similar help in future, for he recognises the extent to which his own career depended upon the benevolence of his maternal uncles in the early stages. So that, despite widespread feeling to the contrary, the outcome of a variety of claims and decisions means that a large proportion of educated couples (wives as well as husbands) take on responsibilities for educating and rearing other people's children. A few even pay for the education of three to six children other than their own over a considerable number of years.

DOMESTIC CONTINUITY AND CHANGE IN ACCRA   191

Thus it is normal both for parents to delegate some of their parental responsibilities to others and for educated couples to care for other people's children, looking after them temporarily while the parents are abroad, sending them to school and accommodating them when their parents are in need. However, the lot of the distantly related or unrelated child sent to stay with an elite family is less happy; the child has to carry out domestic duties rather than being provided with a formal education.

In these several ways the burdens of child-care are distributed amongst different households both rural and urban, rich and poor, educated and illiterate, related and unrelated. Even within a single household the tasks are delegated and shared. Presumably while the process of delegation and the exchange of money or service continues, both the rural and urban families can have a number of children without undue strain being put upon their resources. If the social and economic life of women is little hampered by child-birth and child-care, they may continue to reproduce large families of six or more even when they are in a position to limit their family sizes at will. The entire domestic burden of rearing her own young has not yet been thrust upon the wife, just as the full economic burden of providing for every material want of wife and children has not been thrust upon most husbands. In fact this burden may never be carried if women are able to continue as full-time workers. However, if domestic services become less easy and cheap to obtain, the women's role in the economy will presumably diminish, unless the already growing nursery service is expanded at an even greater rate. Certainly few educated women at present seem prepared to play the role of full-time housewife and mother, with the economic dependence on the husband and the other changes in the conjugal relationship it entails[11].

As we have seen, financial provision for the household is broadly a joint, shared area, in which some 75% of wives and virtually all husbands contribute their share. The husband usually contributes the most, since his salary is generally much higher, and he usually pays all the large bills such as rent, television, car, fridge and so on (Oppong 1971a). However, financial management (as distinct from provision) is a less joint process: the mode in which money is saved and property acquired contrasts with the job of providing money for current expenditure by working outside or inside the home. In the first place, it is only the minority of salaried wives who are reported to spend their money jointly with their husbands. A large number of husbands have no idea how their wives spend their money and the opposite is also true. Very few couples actually maintain joint bank accounts with their spouses, though many think it is a good thing in principle. For the domestic budget, then, there is general agreement (in ideal and in action) about the joint responsibility of spouses for financial provision for the household. But the management of resources is mainly carried out separately.

Some of the norms of domestic activity can now be seen in terms of our earlier categories. The performance of household tasks and child-care may be designated as relatively open and segregated, with kin or employees playing an active part and few couples acting interchangeably; that is to say, few husbands ever assume the majority of

CHANGING SOCIAL STRUCTURE IN GHANA

Figure 4

Chores and Child Care

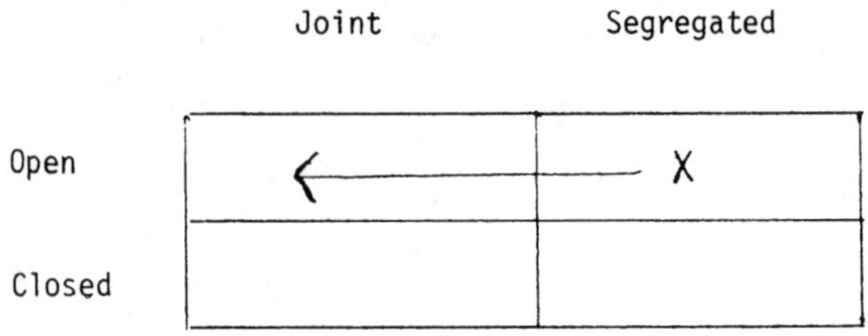

Joint   Segregated

Open

Closed

Figure 5

Financial Provision

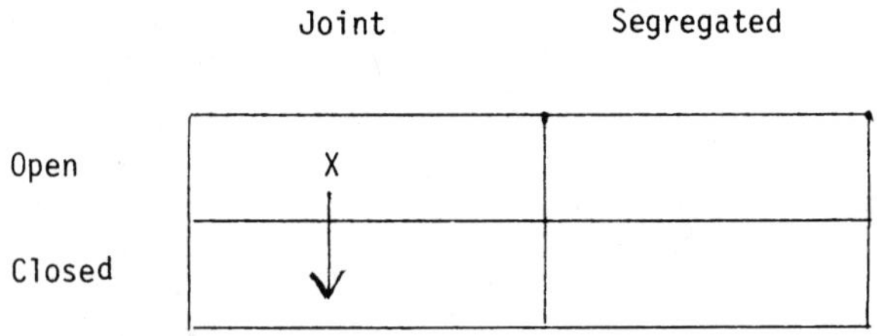

Joint   Segregated

Open

Closed

Figure 6

Financial Management

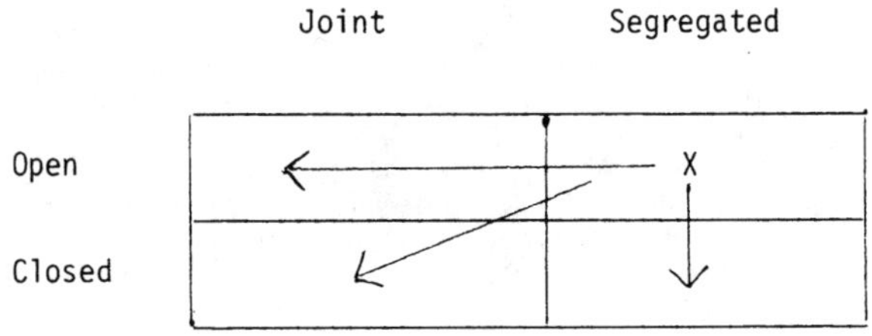

Joint   Segregated

Open

Closed

X   =   Location of majority of population

=   Desired directions of change

DOMESTIC CONTINUITY AND CHANGE IN ACCRA   193

responsibilities in this sphere. Financial provision may be categorised as open and joint; both husbands and wives contribute and a considerable proportion of their income is used to support other kin. Financial management is frequently open and segregated, since few couples own and manage joint resources and a considerable number share interests in family properties. From this generalised standpoint we can see that much that is traditional in family organisation is seen to continue, although often in a new guise in the urban setting. However, subtle and far-reaching changes are also taking place, as is shown by the symptoms of strain, tension and conflict found during close observation of individual families.

This was expressed by those wives who did not receive what they considered to be adequate help in carrying out their daily child-care and household tasks from their husbands, their kin, or from others; a number of wives were pressing for their husbands to give more help. Meanwhile husbands expressed a feeling of strain at the pressure to give a lot of financial aid to kin; to relieve this feeling, they either refused the requests of relatives or tried to persuade their wives to increase their contribution to the upkeep of the joint household. The area of financial provision and management appeared to be the one in which tension and open conflict were most frequently expressed. Spouses were pressing each other to be more generous in their contributions to the household budget. At the same time some were objecting to the claims of other kin. In other words, there was pressure for greater jointness and closure in financial matters. In Figures 4,5, and 6 I have attempted to show in diagrammatic form the directions in which people subject to strain, dissatisfaction and conflict were trying to move, as well as the situation with respect to the two dimensions of openness and jointness in the major activity areas studied.

When the allocation of time and money and the modes of decision-making were examined in detail in a small number of household, the relations of two kinds of couples were comparatively tensionless and stable; firstly there were those husband-dominated couples where conjugal relationships were relatively segregated and where the division of labour was complementary, with the husband providing the money and the wife providing the domestic skills; secondly there are those couples in which decision-making regarding the use of money and time were relatively joint and closed. The kinds of relation most unstable and conflict-prone were either those in which the couples attempted to be joint in making decisions over the use of time and money but were frustrated by outsiders, mainly the husband's kin; or else those in which decisions were taken autonomously and relations were segregated in each activity area (Oppong 1973). We may now turn to examine the variations resulting from continuity of customary norms and the changes geared towards the adaptation to urban circustances, which may result in the reduction of domestic tension and the maintenance of stable, viable family units in the new urban environment.

Table 10

Couples jointly participating in financial activities, by ethnic origin

Ethnic[1] origin	Financial[2] provision	Financial[3] management	N
Akan	44	46	61
Ga	35	50	40
Ewe	44	62	32

Notes

1. In this and table 12, N = 133 ethnically homogeneous couples. The Akan include mainly Akwapim, Kwawu, Fante and Ashanti. The Ewe category includes a number of couples from other ethnic groups in which patriliny and virilocal marriage are the norm.

2. The wife scored high on a financial provision index calculated according to the relative contributions made to a number of domestic expenses, including clothes, food, rent, school fees, fuel, domestic service and transport.

3. The couple scored 1-4 on an index showing whether they spent, saved or owned property jointly.

DOMESTIC CONTINUITY AND CHANGE IN ACCRA   195

Table 11

Male students' attitudes to the husband's financial responsibilities by ethnic origin

Percent in absolute agreement with the statement that 'A man's sole continuing financial responsibility is to his wife and children. His relatives should not expect to get anything more than occasional gifts and help from him.'

Ethnic origin	%	N
Akan*	39	89
Ga	54	82
Ewe	50	107

* In this and Table 13, the Akan include Akwapim, Kwahu and Akim.

196 *CHANGING SOCIAL STRUCTURE IN GHANA*

Table 12

Husbands performing household tasks,
by ethnic origin

Ethnic origin	Unskilled[1] chores	'Male'[2] tasks	Child[3] care	Overall[4] chore score	N
Akan	38	39	28	66	61
Ga	38	35	32	67	40
Ewe	56	59	44	91	32

Notes

1. Husband reports he has done all the following tasks: making beds, setting the table, washing up, tidying up.

2. Gardening, mending fuses, washing car, household repairs.

3. Bathing children, dressing children, mixing baby food.

4. Husband scores high on an index of frequency of participation in all types of chore.

Table 13

Men students' attitudes to housework, by ethnic origin

Percent in absolute agreement with the statement, 'In general, men should leave housework to women.'

Ethnic origin	%	N
Akan	22	89
Ga	23	82
Ewe	14	107

198 *CHANGING SOCIAL STRUCTURE IN GHANA*

Ethnic Variations

The first task is to enquire whether the Akan, who come from communities with matrilineal descent and the duolocal **residence** of husband and wife do in fact exhibit a greater tendency to segregation in their conjugal relationships in the modern urban setting than the Ewe with a traditionally patrilineal background. As regards joint provision for the households' financial needs, Table 10 shows no difference between the two. In the case of financial management, however, their relationships are more segregated. The actors themselves see this segregation as being partly a result of the feelings of insecurity and distrust generated by fears concerning matrilineal inheritance and the financial relationships husbands maintain with their kin (Oppong 1970). That Ewe men place a greater stress on their financial responsibilities as husbands and fathers than their Akan counterparts is indicated by Table 11. In this the Ga, who are mainly patrilineal, are seen to resemble the Ewe.

As regards the sharing of household tasks and child-care, the Ewe husbands once more disclose a greater tendency towards jointness of conjugal roles than their colleagues (Table 12). In this matter the Ga resemble the Akan. Furthermore, Ewe men are less likely than the Akan and Ga to consider that chores are women's work (Table 13). Thus in the three major areas of financial management, the performance of chores and child-care there is support for the hypothesis that the Ewe will have a more joint conjugal role relationship than the Ga and Akan (where duolocality is present).

Direction of change

Finally, I give a brief review of the situation regarding change, firstly with regard to extra-familial kin, secondly with regard to the husband and wife themselves. Financial obligations to kin outside the conjugal family are being cut down. In each ethnic group there is a decrease in the numbers of children of kin educated with each successive generation of education. Men with educated grandparents bear an appreciably lighter burden than those from families that have more recently entered the educated elite (Oppong 1969b; 1970). Similarly fewer financial demands are made upon the resources of those with educated parents and the joint ownership of property with kin is less common (Oppong 1972c). The observed trend is towards financial closure.

For the conjugal pair there is evidence of an increase in jointness in both behaviour and norms associated with increasing levels and generations of education. For instance, couples in which the wives have a higher education are more likely to have joint financial arrangements and to make decisions together (Oppong 1970;1972). The couples among whom such changes towards jointness are most marked are those in which the husbands are from the third educated generation and the wives have had a higher education (Oppong 1970).

To summarise, the aim of the study described here was to analyse the elements of both continuity and change in the domestic relationships of a sector of the Ghanaian urban elite and to determine whether differences were related to different traditional backgrounds. A conceptual

DOMESTIC CONTINUITY AND CHANGE IN ACCRA 199

framework was adopted that gave two dimensions of conjugal family relations, both concerned with the substitution of actors in the domestic domain, namely, jointness/segregation and openness/closure. The basic areas of domestic activity examined for jointness and closure were three: financial provision and management, the performance of chores and child-care. To make this comparison, a number of measures were used to group the material collected, which included both case studies and survey responses from relatively small and homogeneous samples. By means of these measures it was possible to test a number of widely held hypotheses, including those concerning matriliny and the segregation of the conjugal role relationship (e.g. Schneider 1961) as well as those concerning greater jointness and closure in conjugal family ties consequent upon changes in the relations of individuals to their sources of livelihood. Levels of education and the numbers of educated generations were found to be crucial indicators of such changes. Our findings were comparable to those of Gough (1952; 1961) who twenty years ago reported on the domestic relations of the matrilineal Nayar, noting especially the dwindling of kinship obligations and the gradual emergence of the conjugal family as the significant group.

NOTES

1. Early users of the concept of jointness in conjugal role relationships include Herbert (1952, 1954) and Bott (1957). Farber (1966) adopted the terms 'open' and 'closed' in describing the conjugal family from Weber (1962) and Redfield (1947).

2. Examples include studies such as that of Rainwater (1965) who examined jointness of conjugal role relationships with regard to family size and Talmon Garber who discussed changing family structure in Israel (1962).

3. The value of testing relationships among variables of the homogeneous and non-representative sample is well known in sociological research carried out in urban societies as well as in the study of small scale rural communities.

4. For further discussion of the utility of this framework see Oppong (1971).

5. See Woodman (1969) for a recent discussion of the Ga system of inheritance.

6. Responses of both men and women students on this issue indicate how normal a working wife is felt to be by the educated. Thus in the student survey 95% of men and 92% of the women were in absolute or partial agreement with the statement that 'a married woman has the duty of helping her husband to earn a living for the family' (Oppong 1972b).

7. Since 1971 women employed in government institutions receive full pay during maternity leave.

200   *CHANGING SOCIAL STRUCTURE IN GHANA*

8.   For a detailed account of the performance of household chores by task and frequency, see Oppong (1972).

9.   In an enquiry carried out among 123 primary school children from elite families, 42% indicated that their mothers did the cooking unaided; 10% that they did the laundry; 2% that they did the dish washing and window cleaning, and 1% the floor cleaning.

10.   In the student survey, 57% of men and 58% of women were in absolute agreement that 'a person should only be expected to educate his or her own children'.

11.   For a discussion of the ways in which women's work and wage earning enhance their position in domestic decision-making, see Oppong (1970).

RESETTLEMENT AND REHOUSING: UNINTENDED CONSEQUENCES

AMONG THE NCHUMURU

D. P A U L L U M S D E N

Introduction

Numerous studies have been carried out and much ink has been spilt in the West by sociologists, social workers, town planners and public health officials in their attempts to assess the effects of the 'housing environment' on man, attempts at teasing out any direct or indirect relationship between housing quality and the occurrence of juvenile delinquency, between crowded living conditions and the presence of ill-health, between moving house and the onset of mental disorders, between poor housing and family disorganisation, and so on[1]. Several writers, then, have made general comments on the topic of housing and 'family life'; for example, Rosser and Harris (1965:65), on the basis of their research in Wales, have written that the 'type and availability of housing are fundamental factors in family behaviour'. More recently, Madge (1968:516) has asserted that,

> 'There is...a close interrelationship between housing and family organisation. In all cultures and at all times the type of housing has corresponded in some way to the organisation of the family and has in turn sustained and reinforced existing forms of family organisation'.

Certain social anthropologists had already commented on this matter on the basis of their knowledge of Ghanaian house construction and 'dwelling groups' (Fortes 1949a:48; J. Goody 1956:41 and 1958:80). Of especial relevance for my paper are the remarks made by Professor Fortes at a symposium on Trans-cultural Psychiatry. There he declared (1965:128,132; foreshadowed in 1945:207) that:

> 'It is an interesting observation that in most sedentary African societies there is no word for family which is not also the word for house; the concepts of family and house are regarded as the same... Here the house, the external integument of the family, *is* the family, and the family is being lived through in terms of its interaction with its external integument, the house.'

> '...In sedentary Africa the dwelling is not just a spatial boundary, it is also an objective symbol of the identity of the family; this is 'we' in a very special sense...'

It is with the above quotations in mind that I wish to discuss some aspects of the impact of a new 'housing environment' on the domestic life (or 'domain') of members of one small Ghanaian ethnic group, some of the

202 *CHANGING SOCIAL STRUCTURE IN GHANA*

unplanned consequences of planned social change. In so doing, I will be discussing (a) the effects of an increase in social 'scale', and of mass overcrowding and a pervasive lack of 'privacy', (b) the 'warping', so to speak, of the customary developmental cycle of the domestic group amongst this people, (c) the nature and meaning of the term 'household', and (d) the social indicators of the permanence of the stay of resettled villagers at a 'new town'. First, however, a word must be said about both the project and the people concerned.

The project and the people

One of the truly impressive development schemes in recent times has been Ghana's Volta River Hydroelectric and Resettlement Project, about which much has already been written (see Moxon 1969; Chambers 1970; and Lumsden 1973). With the sealing of the Akosombo dam in 1964, Lake Volta began to form, becoming the world's largest man-made lake to date in terms of its vast surface area: some 3,275 square miles. Approximately 80,000 persons had to be resettled because of this project, these coming from some 740 affected villages; the bulk of the resettlers was rehoused in 52 town-sites planned, built and supervised by the government and its agencies. It was fondly hoped that, as President Nkrumah's dictum had it, no one would be left worse off because of the project; indeed, various planners came to view the resettlement exercise as a tremendous opportunity for 'transforming' the rural heartland. As the then Chief Resettlement Officer viewed the exercise (Kalitsi, in Chambers 1970:225), it was 'the country's finest opportunity to introduce into society cells of change (i.e., the 'new towns') to activate the whole rural population of Ghana'.

As part of this 'transformation', and partly too because time was too short for a self-help resettlement programme to be carried out, each 'entitled' household head was provided with a new style of housing at one of these resettlement sites. Each such person received a 'core-' or 'nuclear-house' in one of three standardised styles; each house allocated usually consisted (in phase one) of but one completed room with a roofed-over area for a second room (Chambers 1970: chapters 6 and 7), no matter what the size and complexity of the head's household might be. This one-room house of landcrete blocks and metal roofing was the sole compensation received by most resettlers, no matter how many rooms their old house of swish and thatch had had.

Inevitably, an undertaking of such magnitude ran into many problems, and received many complaints. The Volta Resettlement Authority (V.R.A.), to its credit, accomplished a great deal and did so under enormous pressure. However, on the basis of my own research, I am convinced that the V.R.A. tried to do too much, in too short a period of time, and with too few trained staff on the scene to handle the 'rejection symptoms' of the transplanted communities. Moreover, as we shall shortly see, the constraints set up by the V.R.A. on what the resettlers could and could not do in the new towns simply exacerbated adjustment problems, and themselves caused real economic loss and social difficulties. This is the all-too-familiar story of the sometimes tragic disparity between the manifest and the latent consequences of social planning, between the intended and the unintended.

Figure 7

Krachi District Today, Showing the Major Nchumuru Villages and the Amount of Land Lost to the New Lake Volta in that District Alone.

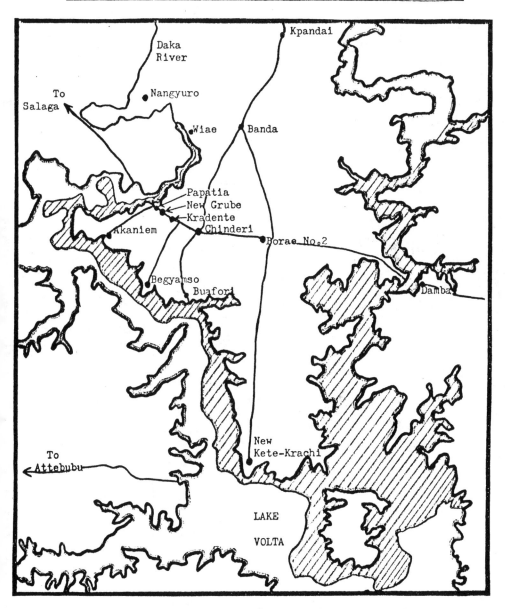

Adapted from Preparatory Commission,1956,Vol.2:108;Scale = 1:500,000.

Figure 8

Diagram (1): A Block of D-type V.R.A. Houses (Phase I).

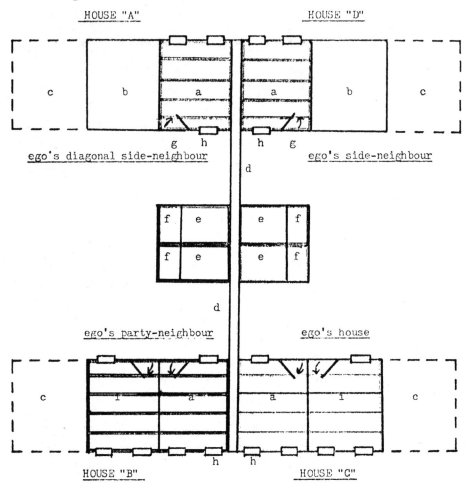

-KEY-

a=one completely enclosed V.R.A. room measuring 10 ft. by 12 ft.
b=incomplete V.R.A. second-room
c=area reserved for a third room
d=party-wall
e=kitchen or storage area
f=bath-stall & urinal
g=doorway
h=window(wood shutter only)
i=completely enclosed second-room

RESETTLEMENT AND REHOUSING AMONG THE NCHUMURU   203

It was partly in order to examine and assess the impact of this project at the local level that field research was carried out amongst the *N'Chumbulung*, or, to adopt the usage favoured by literate members for both the singular and plural forms of their name, the *Nchumuru* people. Enumerated in the 1960 Census as consisting of some 13,500 persons in all, the Nchumuru mainly live today in both Eastern Gonja and Krachi Administrative Districts, in the orchard savannah on both sides of the Daka river, from the Salaga area over to the region of Dambai on the Oti river. Their tonal and unwritten language, also called 'Nchumuru', is one of the northern dialects of the Guang cluster (Manoukian 1951:8, Painter 1967:75); most are also fluent in Twi; a few speak Gonja too. They use a Hawaiian type of cousin terminology; property is inherited by a system of homogeneous transmission (Goody 1962:Ch.15); the residence pattern is noted below. The primary occupation of 85.7% of the household heads surveyed is farming, with yam being the most important cash crop for the men; the women plant and sell condiments, and are heavily involved in petty trading (e.g., smoked-fish, firewood). These people are not to be confused with the 'Ntshumuru' in the Nkonya area of the Volta Region (Asante 1886:22).

Regrettably, I do not have the space adequately to discuss their history and social organisation here. Suffice it to say that there are two leading Chiefs, one for the Nchumuru in each Administrative District and based at Nangyuro and Begyamso; the whole people is divided into six 'sections'(*nsuro*) or phratries, each with its own name, Chief and Stool. Each *kasuro* consists of a number of related villages; the effective core of each village consists of at least one *kabuno* (pl.,*mbuno*), the local, corporate, multifunctional and patrilineal descent group. The *kabuno* (meaning 'a courtyard') has a name, a male head, 'secrets' and other property; marriage sometimes takes place within this unit; its adult male members should have their houses in the same area of a village. A hierarchy of segments may be analytically distinguished within the *kabuno*; the minimal segment is that called the *lungno* (pl., *elungno*). This term is used by Nchumuru to refer to both the elementary family and the household; however, as anticipated by Fortes in the quotation above, the term is closely related to that for the house itself (*lung*).

My study was carried out mainly in four villages in 'the little land of Ntshumuru' (Asante 1886:25; see map 13 in Mähly 1885:914), near the former confluence of the Volta and Daka rivers in what is now called Krachi Administrative District. Here, Nchumuru roots are deep; archaeological findings suggest that Nchumuru have lived in this area since some time in the 17th century (Mathewson 1967a, 1967b, and personal communication 1968). The four villages together had a total Nchumuru population of 1,457 in late 1969, plus some 'strangers'. One can arrange these villages along a continuum of 'disruption', from the least affected to the most affected by the Volta project, as follows (see Fig.7):(1) Kradente, (2) Akaniem, (3) the self-resettled village of Papatia, and (4) the V.R.A. resettlement town of New Grube, which houses the members of five formerly separate Nchumuru villages - these 'village-groups' being Panda Grube, Dentemanso, Grube, Krukruba and Tankrenku. Further information on the four sites is given elsewhere (Lumsden 1973); it is by comparing and contrasting the social life, structure, and 'housing environment' at, and the survey responses from these four sites that one can best appreciate the full impact of the Volta project. However, the rest of this paper is concerned primarily with the New Grube situation alone.

204   *CHANGING SOCIAL STRUCTURE IN GHANA*

<u>The new Grube 'housing environment'</u>

New Grube is one of the two V.R.A. sites in all of Krachi Administration District whose population consists mainly of Nchumuru people. The total Nchumuru population there is 665 persons, and these live in 117 households; in addition, there are various government and V.R.A. personnel, teachers, and 'strangers' living there, for an overall total site population of 785. As built, New Grube is one of the smaller of the 52 V.R.A. resettlement sites; however, the original plans called for the construction of a larger town, the assumption then being that Akaniem and Papatia people would also be rehoused there: 264 houses were to have been built, but only 152 were constructed. On three sides, the bush encroaches, though it is riddled with the many pathways to the yam farms, and several small clearings in it, near the houses, hold the stone altar-shrines of the 'imported' gods Kunde and Tigare; the major Nchumuru 'fetish', Nana Kosoe, now 'resides' there. The town-clearing itself, with its rows of grey white houses and glinting metal roofs, is kept clean by the daily dawn brushings of the womenfolk's brooms and by the men's sometimes weekly communal weeding sessions.

The resettlers at New Grube, most of whom arrived there in the period from September, 1965, to late 1967, have been subject to a number of constraints; for example, they must live with the presence and under the scrutiny of three junior officials of the V.R.A.; moreover, the resettlers were told that they could not bring their many domestic animals with them to the site, the intention of the planners here being to avoid anything which might make 'their' new towns look unsightly. The consequence of this policy has been that the resettlers had to leave behind or dispose of their valuable goats, sheep, and pigs; many of these have since been lost or stolen, and so the resettlers have suffered a rather heavy economic loss, without any compensation. The other key constraint has been that on one's ability to enlarge one's V.R.S. 'core-house' to meet one's household's needs.

The 'D'-type house provided at New Grube, the 'smallest' of the three standardised types (see its architect's drawing and comments, in Chambers 1970:169,170), consisted of one completed room measuring 10 ft. by 12 ft.; the almost flat metal roofing covered this room and extended out to cover a second room, which also had a cement floor but had no walls. Each house has a landcrete kitchen area and bath-stall facing the room area and connected to it by a high wall, this structure being covered by a sloping metal roof. Four such 'houses' were built joined together in a block, two to a side on roughly an east-west axis; thus, one can speak of each house's occupants as having 'party-neighbours', the people living on the other side of the party-wall, and 'side-neighbours', those living in the house next door in the same block of houses but in the other pair (see Fig. 8 : cf. Hole 1959:173, fn. 14). It is most easy to interact socially with one's side-neighbour, while one's most private moments can be overheard by one's party-neighbour.

Thanks to the wooden louvres set in the door and the three window openings, to the 3-inch gap between the walls and the roof, and to the gap under the door, each room easily admits dust-laden winds, rain, malarial mosquitoes, scorpions, and the occasional tsetse fly, while delightful small

RESETTLEMENT AND REHOUSING AMONG THE NCHUMURU 205

small lizards populate the roof beams--for all of which I can vouch. With no second ceiling in the houses, the metal roof aids in turning the interior of each room into an unbearable oven in the daytime, especially in the hot season; furthermore, when it rains, the water beating down on the metal sheets produces such an uproar that conversation (and interviewing!) is almost impossible. Despite all this, most of the people like the fact that the house is built of materials which are a prestige item in the area, particularly the metal roofing. However, insufficient room-space is the key complaint, and it is at this point that the constraint noted above operates.

From the early 1960's to 1968, official V.R.A. policy held that one could only add rooms onto one's core-house if one built them of landcrete blocks and metal roofing; partly this policy was intended to preserve the neat, model-town image of the V.R.A. sites; partly the requiring of metal roofing was to give protection against fire - and bush fires are a threat in this area. In 1968 this policy was softened to allow the use of swish for walls, but metal roofing must still be used. The consequence of both policies at New Grube has been to prevent or inhibit house-expansion, for most resettlers could not afford the expense of the required materials; moreover, many are unaware of the softening of the original policy. In December, 1957, the V.R.A. decided to re-assume responsibility, one given up in May, 1966, for completing all core-houses to the second phase; starting in the summer of 1968, the V.R.A. sent cement, doors and window-frames to New Grube, and work started on the completing of the second room of each house: in theory, the resettlers must repay the V.R.A. for these materials over a five-year period. In April, 1969, a ten-man crew of V.R.A. masons and carpenters arrived to speed up this process. Completion of the second room has eased some of the households' space problems; however, despite this fact, and despite the facts that households needing extra space in some cases were able to use houses allocated to absentee 'owners', and that a few men are beginning to build swish and thatch houses near to, but off of, the V.R.A. site, the important point is that real physical overcrowding still persists amongst three of the five village-groups resettled there: some households have endured physical overcrowding for 2-3 years. The constraint on roofing material, and metal roofing's expense, will continue to inhibit householders from adding a third or (at maximum) a fourth room onto the core-house.

What, then, have been the consequences of such a housing situation for Nchumuru social and domestic life in New Grube?

Some consequences

(i) Social scales

The resettlement of the members of five formerly separate villages into the one small site has meant that there has been an *increase in 'social scale'* for the people there: there has been an increase in 'the number of people in relation and the intensity of those relations' (G.& M. Wilson 1945:25). Thus one finds that elders and members of the other village-groups are invited to attend and take part in one's own group's religious rites and court cases; part of the wedding *'fufu* of the bride' is sent to some elders of the other village-groups, while some of their womenfolk visit related new mothers in the other groups and receive some of the special food served on such occasions. Physical separation alone inhibited such activity before the resettlement. Most striking to the people themselves has been the change in funeral observances; now even those not related to the deceased and his group stop their farmwork and gather for the duration of the funeral 'custom' (*kali*), the men of each village-group sitting together as a group, and their women also sitting together in groups but apart from the men; this happens now even for the funeral of a non-Nchumuru resident. This means that more people attend funerals now than did so before; thus, more drink must be bought and distributed by the bereaved group; the expenses are greater but then too the amount gathered on the day of contribution (*nsuwa*) is also greater, and usually meets all major expenses.

At New Grube too, one now has more people to 'greet' and share drink with; for the young people, there are more dances held in the one place for one to attend and at which to stalk and cajole a comely partner for the night. The larger and more easily accessible population there provides an eager consumer demand for the goods of traders and drink-sellers from surrounding hamlets, while New Grube women themselves have been encouraged to participate as sellers in the market there, and in the smoked-fish exchange system (*kuchari*) with nearby 'battor' (Ewe) fishermen. It is said that some Nchumuru women have learned how to make and sell *gari* (fried cassava) since the resettlement, learning this from women of the other village-groups there.

But there is an uncomfortable aspect to this increase in social scale as well. One is no longer in everyday interaction solely with one's own village mates, presenting one's homely self to close kinsfolk alone. One must now 'behave' or 'act' in front of a much larger and more critical audience. Thus, some women complain that women of other village-groups mock them if they do not have good clothes to wear around the V.R.A. site, while some of the men note that they can no longer sit around in their dusty and ragged farm-clothes at the end of the day but must dress-up instead - partly, this also reflects the fact that the V.R.A. compounds are open to the eyes of all passers-by. Furthermore, for those men married to women from the other village-groups at New Grube (this accounting for 12.9% or 12 of the 93 marriages there), resettlement has meant that they are now more under the scrutiny of their in-laws than they were formerly, while for the wives of these men it has meant that they can now more easily visit their kin.

There is also the feeling that, because they are more exposed to the wider world of strangers, by being beside a main road, there is a falling-away of the practice of what one informant rather primly called 'Nchumuru women's cultural songs', these being songs gloriously bawdy in word and deed, sung by a circle of hand-clapping women. Only once during my stay at New Grube was this activity spontaneously indulged in, whereas it would seem to be reasonably frequent in occurrence at the more hidden sites of Begyamso and Akaniem. A similar reason is given by a few Papatia people for what they say is now a more restrained approach to 'carrying the corpse' there; however, it is still the rule for the New Grube people that, despite on-looking strangers, the container carrying the corpse swings and sways with its two bearers, being moved by the spirit of the

RESETTLEMENT AND REHOUSING AMONG THE NCHUMURU

deceased, while one may also see there the woman possessed by the deceased mutely wandering through the site to give the deceased's last farewell. Tradition lives on in its new setting.

(ii) Overcrowding and privacy

Some of the foregoing relates to the matter of 'privacy', and it is to this topic of the effects of overcrowding and of the lack of privacy that I now turn. Of his elementary family's having to sleep in one room, the late chief of Grube remarked to me in early 1969 that they were 'just like mice driven by a bush fire into one 'hole'. But it has not been simply a matter of physical overcrowding; many different activities have had to take place in the same room, so there has been what Chapin (1938:753-54,756) would term 'use overcrowding', and what Loring (1956:166:168) would speak of in terms of 'role-density' rather than of simple physical density. What have been the consequences of this potentially stressful situation?

First, it might be noted that resettlement has affected one's ability to be a hospitable 'landlord' (a valued role) to any visitors one might receive from far-off villages, for one does not have the room to put them up. At Akaniem, 76.4% of the male household heads said that they had enough space in their house to entertain friends, as did 92.3% of those at Papatia; but, at New Grube, only 42.1% felt they had enough space, the need for taking care of visitors being particularly keenly felt at the time of the festival in honour of the god Kosoe. Each *odikro* (village chief) there no longer has his special reception hall for visitors. Similarly, some New Grube men have had trouble finding a place for their more permanent non-Nchumuru farm-labourers to stay. Second, what of the impact on the elementary family? Much interest has centred on the impact of crowded living conditions on the developing child. Plant (1937) in particular has dealt with this topic; he has argued that overcrowding would inhibit the development of a child's feelings of individuality and self-sufficiency, feelings which 'without doubt' are 'fostered by opportunities for privacy'. Plant further suggests that crowding 'prevents the building of illusions about sex', that children from 'crowded families' would be more 'realistic' about other people, and that they would exhibit such signs of a general fatigue or 'mental strain' as 'irritable outbursts of temper'. This is certainly applicable in some degree to the Nchumuru case but strikes one as being somewhat overdrawn, given the space available to the child in the daytime - but it is at night-time that both physical and use over-crowding become most salient: a diachronic study is needed properly to assess this impact on the child. It is true that the absence of a reasonably private study area in the compound is likely to affect negatively the performance of school-children (cf. Lumsden 1971).

Studies of the rehousing of overcrowded, working-class families in Britain (e.g., Nogey 1955; Harrington 1965) have indicated that a more 'companionship type' of conjugal unit might emerge, and suggest that the husband might become more involved in domestic affairs and in the care of the children than was the case before when space was limited. But in the Nchumuru case, whether in the resettlement site or not, and whether the elementary family is crowded or uncrowded, the husband traditionally takes an interest in the children's upbringing, plays with the babies after work, and will even stay at home and away from his farm-

CHANGING SOCIAL STRUCTURE IN GHANA

work for several days until a sick child (of either sex) has recovered. Parents at New Grube indicated that the experience of resettlement and rehousing had not affected the way in which they were rearing their children[2]; however, it remains my hypothesis that there is less permissiveness shown towards children's behaviour in a situation of overcrowding, where they are more 'underfoot', than would otherwise be the case: only at New Grube did I see a few cases of parents clouting youngsters, though this may partly reflect my more frequent residence in that site than in the other sites surveyed (cf. Harrington 1965:118,136).

Nchumuru traditional practice does provide a mechanism whereby overcrowding could be resolved in a particular elementary family, this being by the 'fostering out' of one or more of one's children. Both as 'a help' to them and as a token of respect and affection, or in order to learn a trade, a young boy may be sent to stay with a 'care-taker', the *nyampe* (e.g. father's senior brother, father's father), and a young girl to a *chipe* (e.g. father's sister, father's mother, or even a mother's sister[3]). However, no such New Grube head explicitly gave overcrowding as a reason for fostering-out a child or for taking one in, instead; the 'traditional' reasons (old age of relative, barrenness, etc.) were given. The Census Survey located only one possible case of fostering at Kradente, and no current cases at Akaniem[4]; at least 11 cases are known as involving household heads at Papatia, and 26 are known involving New Grube ones. The evidence for overcrowding being a factor in fostering at New Grube is thus at best only suggestive, not conclusive.

It seemed likely that there would be a differential impact of the new house-type according to sex; it was hypothesised that this impact would be greater on women, in their role not just of wife but of 'housewife', than it would be on the men (cf. Wilner *et al.* 1962:204; Harrington 1965:117; Fortes 1949a:47, and 1965:132). Though they say that they have not had to take on any new house-keeping duties because of the Volta Project, the womenfolk have felt the impact of the shortage and overcrowding of rooms keenly. Amongst the Nchumuru, a menstruating woman must not enter a room in which a man is keeping his 'jujus' (*asibeng*) and medicines, for if she did so the man's religious objects would lose their power. Thus, if that household only has one completed room, the woman must find somewhere else to spend the requisite one week (six days) until she is once again 'clean'. Furthermore, thanks to the lack of room-space, most wives have been unable to indulge in the Nchumuru woman's customary ostentatious display in her own room of several stacks of various types of clay pots set in a specially arranged row; besides being for display, some are intended as replacements for damaged pots, and one or more act as a hiding-place for the wife's money. Many wives also lacked a room of their own, this being in a sense a blow to their status as wife (cf. Fortes 1949a:59) and their self-respect, and a blow to that of the husband, for traditionally he ought to provide one room for each of his wives. One gathers that this lack, remedied to some extent by the V.R.A.'s 1969 room-completion programme at New Grube, might well affect the 'image' and organisation of the elementary family in the society, if Fortes and Mayer (1969:37) are correct in their assessment of the significance of 'the mother's room'; this, they say, 'both in reality and in the imagery and conceptualisation of family structure, is the heart of the family'. I will return to this matter of 'image' shortly.

RESETTLEMENT AND REHOUSING AMONG THE NCHUMURU

There is some evidence to confirm my hypothesis that overcrowding would foster and promote the occurrence of domestic quarrels at New Grube. Thus in a systematic sample survey of male household heads (T=40), 45% of those at New Grube stated that domestic quarrels had been happening more frequently in recent years than they had occurred four years before, when they were living at their old village sites. In contrast, only 5% of those surveyed on this at Akaniem and Papatia combined said such quarrels were more frequent now than they had been four years before, while 75% at these two non-V.R.A. sites said such quarrels were now occurring 'less frequently'. Amusingly, one Dentemanso elder said that domestic quarrels are more frequent at New Grube because, 'Here the women have come to see many things and different characters from the men that when compared to their husbands annoy them to seek divorces'. On the other hand, a Grube young man claimed that such quarrels are less frequent at the V.R.A. site because the men would not like the people of the other village-groups there to be hearing them 'shouting all the time'.

Domestic conflict is particularly likely to occur when two women must share the same room (and perhaps the same cooking facilities as well); quarrelling between co-wives is felt by Nchumuru males to be a major drawback of polygynous marriage even when each wife has her own room, as is her right; how much more delicate, then, is the situation for the households of polygynists at New Grube. In addition, it must be realised in this connection that in the Nchumuru view of 'sex and temperament' women are 'naturally' more given to feel and express anger than are men[5] and on the basis of my observations of some New Grube fights one might be tempted to agree!

The new housing has also had an effect on sexual relationships at New Grube. The shortage of rooms has been an annoyance to young people for not only does one need privacy at such a time but also one needs a room. For one to engage in sexual intercourse out of doors, in the bush, is forbidden, for to do so would profane (heat-up) the Earth and would in consequence delay the coming of the rains needed by the farmer: an expiatory sacrifice was made at New Grube in April, 1969, when the rains were late, on the presumption that such an act had occurred. Of the married male household heads living in New Grube, 49.4% (or 39 of 79) indicated that their sexual activities with their wife (or wives) had been negatively affected by the lack of privacy afforded by the V.R.A. rooms. They complained of the presence of too many children (and that of some children of too advanced age) in the room, or, more frequently (17 of 39), that their particular party-neighbour could overhear whatever they were doing in it. Indeed, the Tankrenku 'linguist' went so far as to claim that New Grube people were no longer having babies because of this lack of privacy. This claim, however, is somewhat exaggerated for almost two dozen babies were born during my stay at New Grube.

Given Fortes' statement about the house being 'an objective symbol of the identity of the family' (1965), and given the fact that overcrowding exists at New Grube, one would hypothesise that there might be a change in the 'image' of the 'family' held amongst the Nchumuru there (cf. Mead 1955:283). It was thought that the resettlers, especially the young people, would now consider it advisable (a) for a couple to have fewer children, and/or (b) for a man to have only one

210 CHANGING SOCIAL STRUCTURE IN GHANA

wife at a time. All male household heads were asked whether they agreed more with the opinion that a man and his wife should limit the number of children to be born so that they could take better care of those they already had, or with the opinion that such limitation is wrong[6]. Overall, 32.3% of the 201 men said that they would favour limitation, while 67.7% said they would not; the replies by village are of more interest. At Kradente, 16.7% of the male household heads said they would favour limitation; at Akaniem, only 3.6% agreed with limitation, as did 17.9% of these men at Papatia. However, at New Grube 56.8% of the male household heads (or 54 of 95) agreed with the statement favouring the limiting of the number of children. These same men were also asked their opinion of how many children would be the best number for the same man and same woman to bring forth. At Akaniem, 34.5% of these men suggested various numbers of children which fell within the category of '10 and under' as being the best number of children for one set of parents to have. At Papatia, 38.5% of the replies fell within the '10 and under' category, while at New Grube, 47.4% of the replies were within this category.

A total of 40 male household heads, in a systematic sample survey, were asked for their opinion as to the number of wives a man should have 'at any one time nowadays'. For Akaniem and Papatia combined, 55% of the 20 men involved felt one wife or one after the other (serial monogamy) was the desirable number, whereas at New Grube, 70% of the 20 men interviewed there gave this reply. At Akaniem and Papatia combined, 40% of the men interviewed suggested two wives or 'about' two would be desirable, while only 20% of the New Grube men gave this reply. These results give a certain plausibility to my hypothesis.

However, what are the views of Nchumuru youths on these questions, most of whom have not yet fathered children nor taken a wife? Seventy-six youths, ranging from 17 to 26 years of age inclusive, were interviewed on this matter, 26 of these coming from Akaniem and Papatia, and 50 coming from New Grube. When asked their opinion about how many children a man should have, 61.5% of the resulting replies from Akaniem and Papatia, and 60% of those from New Grube, indicated that 10 and (in most cases) less than 10 children would be desirable: there is little difference between the sites. However, there is a difference if one looks at replies suggesting that well over 10 children per man is the desirable number; only at New Grube, and in Tankrenku in particular, do youths mention 20, 30 and even 60 children. One Tankrenku lad who said 30 children would be desirable, explained that 'more children make the town feel happy', while another Tankrenku youth, who aspired to having 80 children, remarked in a somewhat mercenary vein that this was because 'the more children you get, the more things you get' (i.e., 'dashes' from them in later life).

When asked their opinion as to how many wives a man should have, again there is no support for my hypothesis: 73.1% of the Akaniem and Papatia youths suggest one wife, while 54% of those at New Grube give this reply; 15.4% of the Akaniem and Papatia youths speak of two wives as being desirable, while 30% give this reply at New Grube.

RESETTLEMENT AND REHOUSING AMONG THE NCHUMURU   211

In sum, the replies of the male household heads at New Grube, with their indication of the desirability of having fewer children and only one wife at a time, do accord with my hypothesis, though overcrowding is unlikely to be the sole reason for such replies. However, the replies of New Grube youths to similar questions do not support the hypothesis. Partly this disconfirmation may reflect the fact that the younger of the 50 youths concerned (the 17 and 18 years olds) are not yet of the age when a youth is likely to have fathered a child nor old enough to get married, and so some of these may not be fully aware of the additional problems created by the shortage of rooms for such events. Partly too, their replies may indicate their feeling that the room-shortage is unlikely still to exist when they do wish to get married, or their comfortable expectation that their father or father's brother will find a place for them somehow.

(iii) The developmental cycle

In the introduction, I spoke of the 'warping' of aspects of the customary developmental cycle of the domestic group by the Volta project and its consequences; it is to this topic, to that of the 'changes', to use a less evaluative term, in the developmental cycle and the domestic group, that I now turn, focussing on residence, marriage, spouse roles and household composition.

Speaking in very general and ideal terms, one may say that a young child sleeps during its first few years in its mother's room; the mother goes to her husband's room for the exercise of sexual rights, taking her turn every other 3-day period if she is a co-wife, or the husband may go to the junior wife's room if he shares one with the senior wife; her husband moves into her room for the duration if he should have a male guest (his 'stranger') visiting him and room-space is limited. As more children are born to the couple and these mature, a room is provided in the father's compound for the young girls and one for the young boys; as indicated earlier, one or more of these children may be fostered-out for a few years, the 'care-taker' in many cases living in the same village as the child's parents so that the child in some cases may sleep at its father's house and spend only the daytime with its *nyampe* or *chipe*[7]. If space is limited in the father's compound or if the child has a close friend elsewhere in the village, the young boy (or, seemingly to a lesser extent, a young girl) may temporarily bunk down at a friend's or relative's house where space is available. Shortly after a girl reveals that she has menstruated for the first time, she undergoes a brief 'putting-on of womanhood' rite and is then of marriageable age; in the olden days of infant bet-rothal and arranged marriage, reportedly, that same day or a few days after this rite the girl would be 'sent' in procession to her groom's house. There is no puberty rite for males; the boy continues to help his father on the latter's farm; when the boy reaches his mid-teens, his father ought to provide the boy with his own room in the father's compound, though this may have to be shared with another adolescent male. To this room quietly at night, the boy may bring his **girl** friends.

By his late teens the boy will probably be farming on his own, his father or father's brother having supplied him with some yam seed-lings; he remains at his father's house, though if his behaviour displeases

212   *CHANGING SOCIAL STRUCTURE IN GHANA*

his *kabuno*, he may go to live and farm at his mother's brother's
village (cf. J. Goody 1956:58). Nowadays, by his mid-twenties the
boy will commence his first marriage, this being marked by the presentation to and acceptance by the girl's parents of two or three bottles
of 'akpetishie' liquor and a small sum of money (the customary amount
of both varying from village to village); officially it is the boy's
father who pays for and sends this drink thereby symbolising his
authority over his son, though the boy himself seems actually to be
the one to buy it; with the acceptance of this prestation, the boy
acquires exclusive sexual rights in the girl, but not full domestic
rights--she is not yet his 'full wife'. After the presentation of
the drink, the boy is likely to remain living in his room in his
father's compound; the girl now may openly go to the boy's room at
night and and may also visit him during the daytime but otherwise
she remains at her father's house, where she might prepare some
food for the boy at times. Theoretically, she ought to stay at her
father's house, perhaps for a few months or years, until the boy,
having acquired sufficient funds and goods and acting through his
elders and an old woman, 'begs' her *kabuno* to allow the girl to be
formally sent to his room. However, it does sometimes happen today
that the girl's parents may allow her to go and stay with the boy,
after the drink has been given, without a formal 'sending of the
bride' rite if, for example, the boy has no sisters to do his cooking
and sewing for him, or he has a lucrative job in a distant town.
Moreover, not all men do perform the complete rite (the 'fufu of the
bride' or a payment of 15 new cedis) for their wife, though it is
regarded as being somewhat shameful to neglect to do so[8]; the formal
'sending' may be delayed simply because the wife, for so she is
called, gives birth, thus necessitating the man's having to present
her with a large number of gifts in return; informants state that a
man would not be able to afford to pay for both these pregnancy gifts
and the 'sending of the bride' in the one year. In fact, a girl may
'bring forth' even before the boy has presented the drink for her[9];
this means that a child may spend its first few months or a year or
so at its mother's parents' compound.

    In his early twenties, the boy will probably wish to build his
own house, especially if he intends to get married soon. It is
definitely not Nchumuru custom for the boy to remain living in his
father's compound once he has his wife with him regularly in the
daytime; informants from different villages all agreed that this
was rarely done simply because the boy's new wife and his father's
wife would be bound to quarrel if they lived in the same compound:
in only 12 (or 4.9%) of the 244 households surveyed was there another
married couple in the household in addition to the head's own marriage,
some of these being junior brothers to the head (and their wives); only
4 of these 12 cases were in New Grube.

    The boy's house ought to be built in his father's village and
in his *kabuno's* area within that village, and ideally would be near
the father's own house. One should build at least two rooms in constructing one's first house, a bedroom for each spouse, perhaps with
a kitchen-space in between. Thus established, the boy's own domestic
group expands over time, with children being born into it - and then
themselves maturing to the point of setting out on their own, with
perhaps another wife or two being added on, or, in later years, with

RESETTELEMENT AND REHOUSING AMONG THE NCHUMURU   213

the addition of a foster-child, or a divorced sister. Eventually this domestic group dissolves; the head achieves ancestorhood, only to be reborn later on and to recommence the cycle outlined here. How has the shortage of room-space in New Grube affected this developmental cycle?

I have noted that even in the pre- or non-resettlement situation a child may sleep elsewhere in the village because of a lack of space in the parental home; this trait has been forcibly accentuated in New Grube by the lack of sufficient protected sleeping space there such that, prior to the 1969 V.R.A. room-completion programme, there was, especially in Dentemanso and Tankrenku village-groups, what one might term almost a 'free-floating' mass of 'small boys' who spent each night wherever space, friendship and the weather allowed. This was also a worry to their mothers; cried one Dentemanso woman, 'is it good to leave one's child outside whilst you sleep in a room?'

When a systematic sample of male household heads was asked how easy they thought it to be for their sons or other youths to get their own rooms at that site, 65% of the 20 men at Akaniem and Papatia combined stated that it was not easy at all, while 95% of the 20 men at New Grube gave this reply (and did so even though the V.R.A. programme was almost complete by the time of the survey); 20% of those at Akaniem and Papatia stated that it was very easy for their sons to do so, while no one at New Grube gave this optimistic reply. The large number of men giving a 'not easy at all' reply at the non-V.R.A. sites arises from the transient situation at Akaniem where not enough rooms have yet been built in the new area[10] to compensate for those rendered uninhabitable by the heightened water table's undermining of their foundations; at Papatia, the men giving this reply simply emphasised what a hard and expensive task it was to build rooms. The New Grube replies of 'not easy at all' note, as one would expect, that the parents cannot afford to expand their V.R.A. houses. The new style of housing there does not have the 'elasticity' of the old swish style, and this fact, together with the existence of V.R.A. house-expansion regulations, means that many fathers simply are not able to provide their adolescent sons with their own rooms, nor are 'young men' able to build near their own father's house in their particular *kabuno's* area: thus patrilocality is inhibited. Those youths fortunate enough to have a place to stay would, of course, be encouraged by their own inability to build within the V.R.A. site to remain at that place beyond the period considered customary; the father's domestic group's phase of dispersion or fission might thus be dampened and delayed.

How has marriage been affected? These same 40 men were asked how easy they thought it to be for a young man to present drink for a girl at their site nowadays. Twelve men at Akaniem and Papatia combined and 12 at New Grube felt it to be easy to do so since the cost is not that prohibitive (e.g. 2 new cedis and 20 pesewas); besides, as a Grube man remarked, whether it is easy or hard to get the money for this does not matter, 'since you love the girl'. Eight men at Akaniem and Papatia combined and 8 at New Grube felt that there was some difficulty with the drink presentation; as a Banda Grube men phrased it, 'it is not very easy to get the money, but the most (difficult) thing is how to get the (girl's) parents to accept it'. The resettlement has not affected the presentation of drink, aside from providing the New Grube (and nearby Papatia) youths with more candidates close at hand and more opportunities (dances, etc.) than before to meet them; it has also allowed the prospective parents-in-law to scrutinise more easily and continuously the behaviour and 'character' of suitors from the other village-groups.

214 *CHANGING SOCIAL STRUCTURE IN GHANA*

These men were also asked for their opinion as to how easy it was to perform the 'full custom' (the 'sending' and attendant rites) for a girl at their site nowadays. Sixteen men at Akaniem and Papatia combined and 16 of the 20 at New Grube agreed that it was 'not easy at all' (i.e., 80% of the 40 men), most of these drawing attention to the great expense of performing the rites: figures mentioned range from 14 new cedis to over 60 cedis, with one man mentioning 150 new cedis. As an Akaniem man put it, 'To get 15 cedis is a problem and so people keep long in performing the full custom here. Some even don't perform (it) before they die'. However, the replies of the Tankrenku men to this question, to which all 7 gave the 'not easy at all' answer, do reflect the impact of the Volta Project; they complain that the performance of the 'full custom' was easier when they were living at their old village where the local fields, game and streams freely provided much of the needed foodstuffs: 'here (at New Grube) you have to buy everything, but at old site, not everything that you have to buy'. In fact, only once during my stay was a 'bride' formally 'sent' to her husband at New Grube, this being in Tankrenku village-group in May, 1969; this was also the first time the 'custom' had ever been done there; a second such performance took place shortly after my departure.

Of special interest are the replies of those most directly concerned with the topic, the replies of 76 youths (those aged 17-26 inclusive); these were asked simply whether they considered it to be 'easy' or 'hard' to get married at their particular site. At Akaniem, 46.2% (6 of 13) of the youths felt that it is hard to get married there, the rest claiming that it would be easy since so much of the necessary foodstuffs could easily be got there; one of these youths, aged 18, commented that marriage was easy 'because since we are all from the same town, it will be very easy to marry from here. Only accommodation is very necessary'. At Papatia, 92.3% (12 of 13) of the youths gave the 'hard' response, as did 86% (43 of 50) of those surveyed at New Grube. At all three sites, the reason given for the 'hard' reply was the great expense of the necessary foodstuffs, pieces of cloth, etc., for the 'sending of the bride' - however, as a Krukruba youth, aged 24, wisely remarked, 'To take good care of her is the problem. To marry her is just a little thing'. Again, the Tankrenku replies, from all 24 such youths, most clearly reveal the impact of the Volta Project; they speak of the generally greater cost of living in the new environment, of the necessity now to buy fish whereas before one could get fish freely from one's *kabuno's* streams, now flooded for ever, and of the lack of work other than farming whereby a lad could make the money for the rite in this area. Furthermore, one 20-year old clearly articulated the uncomfortable aspect of the increase in social scale I mentioned earlier; it is hard to get married at New Grube because 'if you could not do it well here, people will laugh at you. But for old town, we are just one group'.

Marriage also has been affected by the shortage of room-space at New Grube. If a young men does have the room-space, then it is likely that his girl will be allowed to go and stay with him sooner than might otherwise have been the case, if she is also from a New Grube village-group, simply in order to alleviate the overcrowding that is likely to exist in her father's house. If a young man does not have adequate room-space, then his girl's coming is likely to be delayed longer than they both may desire; moreover, it seems likely that this state of affairs would mean that more children would be born prior to any performance of the 'begging' rite, and more would live in their mother's parents' household at New Grube, than would ordinarily

RESETTLEMENT AND REHOUSING AMONG THE NCHUMURU   215

have been the case. This situation was somewhat ameliorated by the V.R.A.'s 1969 house-expansion programme, but was not totally alleviated. The impact of the shortage of room-space has also keenly felt by polygynists.

Of a total of 204 male household heads for all four sites surveyed, 27 (or 13.2%) are polygynously married (a 28th case lives in his enfeebled father's compound in Kradente), two of these being in the process of acquiring a third wife; of these 204 men, 166 (or 81.4%) are currently married, and polygynists account for 16.3% of this last figure; fourteen polygynists live at New Grube. When these 14 were asked to comment on how the resettlement exercise had affected their household's way of life, 8 (or 57.1%) mentioned as the first item the lack of sufficient living space, while 12 of the 14 (or 85.7%) mentioned the shortage of room-space at some point in their reply; on this matter of concern, they are not different from the other male household heads. They do, however, have the extra problems of finding a room for their junior wife or wives, and of preventing quarrels between the co-wives; here we may briefly consider the topics of sleeping arrangements, cooking arrangements, and of the husband's 'control' over his wives.

The two main forms of sleeping-room arrangements for such spouses at all sites are either (a) for the husband and each of his wives to have their room in the one compound, or (b) for the husband to share a room with his senior wife while his junior wife has her own room in the same compound, in which the younger children also stay. Both forms of arrangement occur at New Grube, with the second form being somewhat more accentuated; it is harder there not only for a man to provide each wife with a room to herself but also for him to provide such sleeping space within the same compound or even the same block of houses. Tankrenku polygynists report that one wife had had to sleep in the kitchen-area or with a relative when it was the other wife's turn to join the husband in the one completed V.R.A. room, this taking place during the long period prior to the 1969 house-expansion programme. At all sites, co-wives take turns sleeping with the husband, with a 3-day or 1-week period apiece being the customary arrangements, though in two Papatia cases the co-wives each sleep with the husband every other night. The resettlement, except for the matter of the lack of privacy discussed earlier, has not affected these customary sleeping arrangements much, although a few men must walk a bit further to reach their second wife's room.

As for cooking arrangements, in theory each co-wife ought to pound 'fufu' and prepare food for the whole household in turn, and a few do take turns every other day; in one Grube case, in which the household is split up between two houses located in different blocks, the one house-using group gathers at the other house when it is that wife's turn to cook for all. It is most common,however, for each wife to prepare food separately for her own children and for each also to send food to the husband, so that he receives two dishes of food at each meal; some informants claimed that if each cowife was cooking separately, then this indicated that the husband had lost his 'control' over them, but in most if not all cases this occurence of two cooking groups or units of consumption within the one household simply reflects the fact that there are more children in that household, too many hungry bellies for the one wife to cope with; it indicates that that domestic group is well into the developmental cycle's phase of expansion. There are 8 such cases reported, 7 of them within New Grube; in addition, in two Akaniem cases each wife cooks separately but the husband eats only of the

216 *CHANGING SOCIAL STRUCTURE IN GHANA*

food prepared by the wife whose turn it is to sleep with him.

It is clear that in those New Grube cases in which the co-wives and their respective clusters of children are no longer able to live in the same compound, as they once did, nor even to dwell in adjacent houses, there are opportunities for each wife, and perhaps for the junior wife especially, to act more autonomously, being less under the direct scrutiny of the husband and/or that of the senior wife. In two cases the distance between the two houses used by each household is particularly great, as much as 100 yards separating the rooms of the senior and junior wives between which the husband in each case migrates; here especially there exists the potential for a more matrifocal emphasis in the domestic organisation than would ordinarily be the case. Nevertheless, as has already been shown, the youths at New Grube do aspire to being plurally married at some point in their marital career, despite the shortage of appropriate room-space there.

The housing situation at New Grube has affected the performance of spouse roles, whether the male head is a monogamist or polygynist. Changes and readjustments in sleeping and cooking arrangements have been indicated above; moreover, the wife in most cases need no longer perform her duty to pound the earthen floors of swish rooms, but provides various other domestic services as usual; the husband need no longer perform his duty to cut the grass used in thatch-roofing, but continues to perform his duties to seek out and provide medicines if his wife should become ill, to pay for fines she may incur and to give her 'dashes' at times (e.g., on her bringing forth children). However, the husband has undergone what I term 'role impoverishment'; i.e., the satisfactory performance of certain of his duties as husband and father, which performance custom decrees and he desires, has been inhibited by external constraints - in this case by V.R.A. house-expansion regulations: many cannot supply their growing sons and their wives with their own rooms near his. There is no evidence, however, that this state of affairs has led to any lessening of sons' respect for their father; but, has the resettlement and rehousing exercise lessened the husband's authority over his wife - has marital stability been undermined?

I have already noted that domestic tension has been fostered and promoted by the overcrowding at New Grube, and that for some women it is galling to see other women wearing fine clothes or getting other items from the local stores and market, which they themselves or their husbands cannot afford - in this last, unsatisfied cravings and a feeling of relative deprivation are at work; both features put a strain on the conjugal tie, such as it is considering that men and women by custom ordinarily eat and sit apart and have other social separatenesses. It is clear also that the potential does exist for either the husband or wife to meet someone new and more interesting, or someone with more money perhaps, than their current spouse from amongst the members of the other village-groups there or perhaps from amongst the visitors to the New Grube market. The Nchumuru are not unaware of the potential for adultery (provided one can find a room for one's assignation!) and divorce at the V.R.A. site, a divorce which either spouse may initiate. A Krukruba man commented that 'because of poverty, the women now seek more divorces than the men'; a Tankrenku polygynist argued, however, that husbands at New Grube were aware of the dangers and so were minimising or trying to prevent causes for divorce: 'Because when we came here their husbands look after them more than (they did in) old town'.

RESETTLEMENT AND REHOUSING AMONG THE NCHUMURU   217

In fact, only 25% of the 20 male household heads interviewed there on this topic, in a systematic sample survey, felt that divorces were more frequent now than they had been 4 or 5 years earlier, before the resettlement; 40% felt the frequency was about the same and 20% felt the frequency was less; by comparison of the 20 men surveyed on this at Akaniem and Papatia combined, 20% felt divorce was now more frequent, only 5% felt it was about the same, and 65% felt the frequency was less. An Akaniem man commenting on this claimed lessening in divorce frequency there: 'Men are now very careful with their wives, as there are only a few women in this town'; another remarked that it was 'because some of the women get whatever they need through trading and so they do not divorce their husbands'. Nevertheless, the potential does exist at New Grube for determining the conjugal bond, excluding here the case of the customary and expected 'terminal separation' (E.Goody, 1960) for old women, but this has not, at least so far, been actualised to any extent. It should also be noted that if domestic difficulties do arise between spouses, thanks to the resettlement exercise in most cases the husband can now easily locate, within the same site, a close relative of his wife's to come and give an 'advice' to her and thus help to settle the matter quickly; obviously too, the wife would not have far to go to seek kin support for her stand.

I earlier noted that some women have been encouraged to involve themselves in petty trading, or to do so more regularly and deeply since their resettlement; it is clear that some of the New Grube men are worried by this development. All male household heads at all sites were asked for their opinion as to whether a wife should engage in trading activities or should concern herself only with household duties. Overall, 57.2% of these 201 men felt that a wife, or one of one's wives, should go into trading in order, for example, to buy clothes or other items she might want; but, a hefty 38.8% felt that a wife should concern herself only with household duties, this feeling being very strongly expressed in Akaniem (81.8%) and in New Grube (28.4%),though less so there. Most of this last group of men would agree with the Akaniem man who commented that 'her conduct will become worse if she goes into trading activities'. At New Grube, 15.8% of the 95 male household heads (coming from all 5 village-groups) explicitly stated their fear that if a wife engaged in trading she might leave the husband for another man; thus a Banda Grube man remarked that, 'She will see better men and follow them, and will not mind the husband'; a Grube informant testified as follows: 'My wife was selling porridge every morning; now where is she? She is gone to Ashanti'. This explicit statement of a fear that the wife would leave the husband was made by only 8.3% of the men at Kradente, 1.8% of those at Akaniem, and 5.1% of those at Papatia. Thus, by promoting women's involvement in trading activities, the Volta Project's occurrence may bode ill for some marriages - but again, a diachronic study is needed to assess this aspect properly.

As with the case of co-wives, so too with the provision of room-space for divorced sisters or, more especially, for widowed or 'divorced' father's elderly sisters and one's mother; whereas in the pre-resettlement situation such women would return to dwell in a brother's compound, at New Grube they are put wherever one can acquire space for them. In a situation of physical and use overcrowding for the elementary family, the presence of such aged female relatives might be expected to be felt as a burden, but I found no sign that one's duty to look after such women was being shirked: 7 households

218   *CHANGING SOCIAL STRUCTURE IN GHANA*

at New Grube included the head's mother, 4 others included a father's sister, and another one even included a mother's sister. In addition, where one's mother had returned to dwell in her natal village in old age and this village was now resettled with one's own in New Grube, resettlement has made it easier for a few men to visit and keep an eye on their mother. As for 'terminal separation' in New Grube itself, the shortage of room-space would also affect its occurrence, perhaps inhibiting it for those women whose natal village is also now there but whose kin have not the room for her as yet; their building of a swish room for her immediately outside the V.R.A. site is another available option.

(iv) The nature and meaning of 'household'

Lack of space prevents me from presenting here a detailed picture and discussion of Nchumuru household composition; however, the number of persons enumerated in each of the 244 households surveyed is given in Table 14. Note that this particular table gives the household sizes frozen at one point in their individual progression through the phases of the developmental cycle; clearly, those households currently well into the phase of expansion will have more members than will those well into the phase of dispersion or fission.

It will be noted that the average number of persons per household for all five New Grube village-groups combined is lower than the corresponding figure for any of the other three sites; this reflects at least in part the shaping of households there by the amount of room-space allocated to and acquired by each village-group. The average number of persons per household for these village-groups ranges from 4.2 persons in Krukruba to 6.4 persons per household in Dentemanso.

When one examines a Nchumuru dwelling and those who use it, the 'house-using group', so to speak, one may analytically distinguish between (a) the person who owns the dwelling - and the owner may be a female, (b) those who use it, and, for some purposes, (c) the person who may inherit it (e.g., father's junior 'brother'); most importantly, within the general class of house-users, one must distinguish between (i) those persons who both eat and sleep at the dwelling, (ii) those who eat there but who sleep elsewhere, on a regular basis, and (iii) those who sleep there but who eat elsewhere. These last distinctions must be made in examining Nchumuru household composition. For example, the figures for the number of households at each site in which all members regularly both eat and sleep at the head's compound are: 31.3% (5 of 16) of those at Kradente, 65.2% (45 pf 69) of those at Akaniem, 38.1% (16 of 42) of those at Papatia, and only 29.9% (35 of 117) of all households at New Grube. In addition, the figures for the number of households at each site in which some persons regularly eat as members but sleep elsewhere are: at Kradente, 50% (8 of 16), 15.9% (11 of 69) at Akaniem, 28.6% (12 of 42) at Papatia, and a hefty 35.0% (41 of 117) of all the households at New Grube.

These figures reflect not only the effect of the factor of availability of room-space, but also reflect the ordinary flow of persons for reasons of friendship and the relationship between residence and phase of one's marital career I noted above; for example, in 5 (or 2.1%) of the 244 households it is reported that 1 or more members go off to sleep elsewhere with friends.

Table 14

Size of 244 Nchumuru households, as of Sept., 1969

	Villages		Number of persons									Total	Average number of persons in household
			1	2	3-5	6-8	9-11	12-14	15-17	18-20	27		
(1)	Kradente households	N %	3 18.8	1 6.2	4 25.0	4 25.0	1 6.2	1 6.2	2 12.6	-- --	- -	16 100.0	6.3
(2)	Akaniəm	N %	4 5.8	9 13.0	18 26.1	21 30.4	11 15.9	4 5.8	1 1.5	--	1 1.5	69 100.0	6.3
(3)	Papatia	N %	2 4.8	2 4.8	11 26.1	20 47.6	5 11.9	2 4.8	-- --	-- --	- -	42 100.0	6.2
(4)	New Grube	N %	13 11.1	9 7.7	43 36.8	33 28.2	10 8.5	5 4.3	2 1.7	2 1.7	- -	117 100.0	5.7
	Overall Total	N %	22 9.0	21 8.6	76 31.1	78 32.0	27 11.1	12 4.9	5 2.1	2 0.8	1 0.4	244 100.0	6.0

Table 15

Number of houses involved in each household Sept., 1969

Villages		One house/1 Compound	Two Houses	Three Houses	Four Houses	Use Part of 1 House Only	Total Households
(1) Kradente	N	16	--	--	--	--	16
	%	100.0	--	--	--	--	100.0
(2) Akaniem	N	68	1	--	--	--	69
	%	98.6	1.4	--	--	--	100.0
(3) Papatia	N	36	--	--	--	6	42
	%	85.7	--	--	--	14.3	100.0
(4) New Grube	N	89	15	3	1	9	117
	%	76.1	12.8	2.6	0.8	7.7	100.0
Overall Total	N	209	16	3	1	15	244
	%	85.7	6.6	1.2	0.4	6.1	100.0

RESETTLEMENT AND REHOUSING AMONG THE NCHUMURU
221

In the case of 7.2% (5 of 69) of the Akaniem households, 16.7% (7 of 42) of the Papatia ones, and 6.8% (8 of 117) of those at New Grube, these each include one or more women who regularly eat at their father's or other relative's house and then go to sleep at their respective husband's /boyfriend's room, for the 'begging' and the 'sending' rites have not yet been done for them.

It must also be noted that the households I have been discussing are not always contained by one house or compound; this is particularly true in New Grube, where the lack of room-space has forced a dispersion of a household's members to wherever sleeping space may be available. This situation is shown in Table 15, but it must be remembered that the data in the Table present the situation in New Grube near the end of the V.R.A. house-expansion programme, prior to which there would have been more 'multiple-dwelling households' shown. Furthermore, not all of these other houses used by the individual households are contiguous one to the other.

Alland (1963), in his study of the Abron of the Ivory Coast, found it necessary to accept the folk-distinction between 'residence' and 'domicile', between where one has a place to sleep and, structurally far more important for the Abron, where one goes to eat. Exceptions to the ideal rules of residence and domicile, on which no figures are given, are dismissed (ibid:278) as being 'merely the result of certain kinds of marriage, or simply of housing shortages in some families, and (as being) not themselves important to an understanding of the social structure'. The Nchumuru case in New Grube, where for many households' adult members a physical distinction between one's regular eating and sleeping places is something new and bothersome, and which threatens for some to become the rule rather than being a mere and transient exception, cannot be so lightly dismissed. Instead, it leads one to ask what is the meaning of the term 'household', and, is co-residence a necessary criterion for membership in a household?

Analytically, of course, a household and the elementary family are different things, though the Nchumuru would use the same word, *lungno*, for both concepts without distinguishing between them. For my own census survey, the 1969 Ghana Trial Census Survey definition of a 'household' was used, this being quite similar to Fortes' classic definition of the 'domestic group' (1958:8):'The domestic group is essentially a household-ing and housekeeping unit organised to provide the material and cultural resources needed to maintain and bring up its members'. Indeed, through-out this paper I have used the terms 'household' and 'domestic group' interchangeably (as does R.T.Smith 1968:302; also cf. Bender 1971:236; J. Goody 1958:67, and Leach 1968). However, recently, Stacey (1969:37, 48 49,50,52) has argued that the Fortesian domestic group is 'analytically distinct' from the household, the latter having 'no such (developmental) cycle, its methods of renewal being quite'different' (ibid:47) from the former units. In my opinion she has insufficiently taken into account the wide latitude Fortes(1958:8) allows to membership in the domestic group; however, I accept her point that a 'household' entirely composed of wholly unrelated persons should be kept in a separate category from one in which some or all the members are somehow related, or are linked to the elementary family which Fortes(1958) sees as 'the reproductive nucleus of the domestic domain...the nucleus of the group'. Such a distinction would be of use in the urban and industrial milieu, less so

222   *CHANGING SOCIAL STRUCTURE IN GHANA*

in 'kinship-based' societies or milieux; in fact, of all the Nchumuru households I have been discussing, none would fall into a 'wholly unrelated membership' category (cf. also E. Goody 1960:28,39) and accordingly I speak of the developmental cycle of the household or of the domestic group. But is the household or domestic group necessarily a co-residential unit?

Radcliffe-Brown (1950:5) E. Goody (1960:39,212), Gonzalez (1960:106), Bohannan (1963:36) R.T. Smith (1968:302), and even Bender (1971:223), and no doubt many others, have all argued that co-residence is integral to the defining of a unit as being a household or domestic group; they assume this is so everywhere, under any circumstances. Stacey's statement (1969: 34) that a *'household* is based upon the principle of commensality: the group of people who normally eat together, or who share a common larder and accounts', is, I would suggest, a less limiting definition and one of more use for comparative sociology than are the criteria proposed by the writers noted above - even though Stacey herself (1969:49) later uses co-residence in her definition of the domestic group. Of greater interest and pertinence, however, is Bender's 'refinement of the concept of household' (1967:495). As he phrases it:

> 'One is dealing, then, not with two distinct social phenomena - families and households - but with three distinct social phenomena: families, co-residential groups, and domestic functions. All three frequently correspond, both ideally and in fact... The three also can and sometimes do vary independently'.

What has happened at New Grube is that formerly co-residential households, because of the shortage of adequate and appropriately located room-space, have become 'dispersed households' or 'multiple-dwelling households'; one could also speak of (a) contiguous multiple-dwelling households, and (b) non-contiguous multiple-dwelling households (cf. Bender 1971:228,236), though the physical separation is not great enough (New Grube is, after all, but a small town) to make this a crucial distinction in practice except in the case of the households of two polygynists, and perhaps a few other cases. However, these are still viable households and are rightly so designated; the dispersion has revealed the critical importance the Nchumuru attach to the performance of domestic functions by the household - this being more important than the mere co-residence of members, for such performance continues in the absence of complete co-residence. Even though Nchumuru ordinarily sit apart in groups by sex and relative age to eat food from the one cooking group, it is where one has one's food prepared and other domestic services performed that seems to be the locus of one's prime allegiance: home is where **the** hearth is. One may say that the resettled household is still largely 'holding onto' its pre-resettlement membership, with due regard for its progression, where not constrained, further along its developmental cycle; there is also a jural element to this retention, a tacit agreement to remain together, to remain under the authority of, and to accord respect to, the pre-resettlement head (cf. Bender 1971:224); as the Nchumuru phrase the jural status of the household head with respect to its members, they are 'in his hands'.

It is this jural aspect which persuades me to classify as being one household even those Akaniem cases of polygyny in which each wife forms a separate cooking group *and* only sends food to the husband when it is also

RESETTLEMENT AND REHOUSING AMONG THE NCHUMURU

her turn to be sleeping with him (*contra* E. Goody 1960:30), and the
New Grube cases where the husband is markedly physically separated
from his junior wife. Finally, I have tried to indicate how housing,
or rather the lack and inadequacy thereof, in the New Grube situation
has become a moulding or even determining factor in the developmental
cycle of the customary Nchumuru domestic group in a way unparallelled
in the pre-resettlement and the non-V.R.A. milieux. The New Grube data
reveal one way by which social change and readjustments enter into and
take place within the developmental cycle, stemming from an exogenous
input or 'stressor' from outside of the society's own politico-jural
domain, and suggest how a new form of domestic group, or perhaps a
change in the cycle's customary rhythm, may occur within the unending
series of phases: expansion, fission, and replacement.

(v) Signs of permanence

One final question remains to be answered, and that is, what of
the future? In 1965 the then Chief Resettlement Officer could remark
that the 'spectre of a ghost town hangs over every settlement we have
built' (in Chambers 1970:225); will the Nchumuru stay in New Grube?
All 117 household heads there (of both sexes) were asked how long they
intended to stay at the site; 75.2% stated that they intended to stay
there for the rest of their life, 22.2% expressed some uncertainty by
giving a 'don't know' response, while only three of the 117 persons
(1 in Dentemanso and 2 in Grube village-group), or a mere 2.6%, stated
that they intended to leave in under two years' time. This response
pattern might gratify the planners, but a mere statement of intention
to stay is not sufficient for our purposes; one needs some definite,
visible and preferably quantifiable social indicator, some concrete
expression, of this intention. I would suggest that there are several
such indicators of the intention of the vast majority of Nchumuru to
stay at New Grube, the housing problems notwithstanding.

The most important index of the sincerity of a person's intention
to stay is whether or not that person has planted any trees at the site,
trees such as mango and silk cotton which will produce revenue in future
and ownership of which a man can pass on to his sons. The notion that
the planting of trees is a sure sign that a person is putting down roots
in that place is not simply the analyst's own view, but is also that
informants are aware of. Thus, for example, one Grube man replied that
he had not planted any trees there 'because I am not interested in living
here'. On the other hand, one may point to the case of a Grube village
elder who had planted 2 mango, 10 palm, 3 silk cotton and 3 paw-paw trees
near his V.R.A. house, explaining to me that he was planting for the
future, for his sons and grandsons. In fact, of the 94 male household
heads surveyed at New Grube, 80.9% have planted trees there.

Another indicator of the people's intention to stay is provided
by their finally bringing certain religious objects from their old sites
and their rebuilding of shrines at the new site; thus, it was not until
mid-1969 that a *kabuno* in Grube and one in Banda Grube built their respective ancestor shrine in the V.R.A. site; at the time of my departure at
the end of 1969, neither Dentemanso nor Banda Grube people had yet 'moved'
their particular village-protecting deity.

The fact that many men intend to build, or have built, additional
housing at the site, that inheritors do use the V.R.A. houses, and that

224   *CHANGING SOCIAL STRUCTURE IN GHANA*

there is conflict between the village-groups over which *odikro* should
be the head of the site - all these signs may also be taken as indices
of the firm intention of those concerned to remain at the site[11].
Moreover, 75.5% of the 94 male household heads state that they are
satisfied with their present location in the site; perhaps more
importantly, 80.9% state that they are satisfied with their present
party- and side-neighbours, while only 11.7% would like to change
their neighbours; most, then, would not move away because of dislike
of their location or block neighbours. It must not be forgotten,
moreover, that these V.R.A. houses are the only form of compensation
that Nchumuru have received for their losses and removal; because of
this fact alone, most would stay. In addition, and as another key
index, there has not been a significant outflow of people from the
site since resettlement.

Conflict and social unease do exist between the village-groups
in New Grube. The passage of time, whose importance for changes in,
and the study of, social structure Fortes has emphasised (1949b),will
probably ease much of this. It is true that Western writers have
spoken of what I might call a new town's developmental cycle, of there
being an initial 'rather stormy period' or 'short phase of social dis-
location, followed by a fairly rapid recovery' and a phase exhibiting
'some degree of social and psychological stability' (Maule and Martin
1956;450,451). Moxon (1969:183) has recently indicated his opinion
that the V.R.A. towns will need an initial adjustment period of 10 years
before each site can 'adequately stand on its own feet'. At New Grube,
tension and conflict between the five village-groups will surely go on
for longer than 10 years, while some village-group differences (in custom
and sentiment) will surely persist for longer than a generation[12].
However, though problems of conflict and of social 'integration' remain,
it is clear from the foregoing that there are good grounds for saying
that New Grube, unlike the situation reported of certain southern V.R.A.,
sites, will not become a 'ghost town'.

CONCLUSION

In this paper, reporting on what was in some ways an exercise in
'experimental anthropology', I have examined some of the effects of a
major development project on the domestic life of members of one Ghanaian
ethnic group. In particular, I have tried to show how the new 'housing
environment' resulting from this project has affected, and conditions,
social relations, and thus how 'spatial relations directly shape structure' (Fortes 1949b:2). Contrary to Madge's assertion (1968:516), the
new type of housing has not simply 'sustained and reinforced existing
forms of family organisation'; the resettlement and rehousing project
has accentuated certain features of Nchumuru life, and has inhibited the
customary expression of others.

Furthermore, some years ago, J. Goody (1958:56) pointed out that
'co-residence is not an essential corollary of marriage'. On the basis
of the New Grube data presented above, I would suggest that the co-
residence of all its members is not essential to the definition, maintenance and persistence of the household or domestic group, though a
moderate to high degree of propinquity (e.g., the presence within the

RESETTLEMENT AND REHOUSING AMONG THE NCHUMURU 225

same village of nearly all effective members), a concomitant degree of direct, everyday interaction amongst most members, the reasonably regular and adequate performance of key domestic functions (to completely specify these is a problem, cf. Buchler and Selby 1968:47; one would expect such functions to receive differential weighting cross-culturally), and the existence of at least one anchoring, focal or nodal member (as opposed to peripheral, immature and/or temporarily absent members - e.g., a labour migrant) - all do seem to be necessary. Moreover, I would also suggest that the concept of 'domestic *network*' may prove to be of greater utility than that of 'household' for understanding and dealing with the New Grube situation, and with other such cases involving domestic fluidity and dispersion.

In any case, it should be emphasised how short a period of time it has been for Nchumuru domestic groups to be exposed to, and to respond to, the constraints and pressures (some transient) of New Grube's 'housing environment'; none have yet gone through a complete developmental cycle there.

In the course of his appraisal of Professor Fortes' work and thought, Worsley (1956:73) formulated the general hypothesis that 'enforced migration to new areas must inevitably weaken or at least alter the kinship system'; some such 'alterations' have been outlined here, though many of these have arisen not from the event of resettlement but rather from the additional constraints and readjustments experienced by the resettlers in the V.R.A.'s 'new town'. What the planners and the waters of change have wrought will affect Ghanaian life for generations yet to come; how gentle will the judgement of posterity be?

This brings me to my final point, the great significance of the Volta River Project for the future of Ghanaian social science and, indeed, for the development of a theory of social change in general. In concentrating on the Project's impact on domestic life in this paper, I have largely ignored certain other key research topics which should now be brought to the reader's attention. These topics include: the impact of population displacement on Local Council revenues and membership; the problems and opportunities created for the marketing of cash crops by the cutting of some ferry and road links and by the creation of others; changes in traditional farming practices necessitated by the new lake's having submerged land needed by a system of shifting cultivation (see Lumsden, 1973); changes in political allegiance in sites where persons formerly serving minor chiefs now find themselves dwelling in the same physical location with followers of more important chiefs or in the presence of such chiefs themselves; the occurrence of conflict and land disputes between resettlers and nearby non-resettled populations both before and after the 1966 coup; the extent to which resettlement and increased social scale have 'opened-up' tradition-oriented villagers to outside influences, to more effective control by the National government, and to religious 'conversions' as Christian missionaries find the V.R.A. sites more accessible than were the old villages; the impact on the resettlers' physical and mental health also needs urgent study. Each resettlement town is an example of a form of urbanisation; each polyethnic site contains and reflects in miniature the national problem of attaining some degree of social cohesion and the integration of somewhat competing groups into a viable whole. Each resettlement site, in itself and through controlled comparison with events in the other 51 towns, provides a laboratory situation in which

226 *CHANGING SOCIAL STRUCTURE IN GHANA*

all social scientists can analyse both general processes of change and the modes whereby people and groups manage psycho-social 'stress'[13]. Ecological and socio-economic changes, some being irreversible, have occurred and are occurring both above and below the Akosombo dam; the reverberations of the adjustments to such changes will continue on for decades to come; multidisciplinary longitudinal research is needed to examine and assess these topics and changes properly. In short, thanks to the Volta River Project, all Ghanaian social scientists now have in their own backyard many crucial, necessary and exciting research possibilities; the country as a whole now has a source of power for expanded industrial development; hopefully, some day soon, the resettlers themselves will benefit more fully and unambiguously from the Project. A co-ordinated research endeavour would surely help them attain more benefit, as the government and even the local Town Development Committees became aware of and acted on the research findings; these findings too will assist those involved in such major development schemes elsewhere and will contribute to sociological understanding of social change. By such research, moreover, future generations of Ghanaians will be enabled to make a more informed and more appreciative judgement of 'Akosombo' and its consequences.

ACKNOWLEDGEMENTS

I should like to express my gratitude to the Trustees of the Emslie Horniman Fund (Royal Anthropological Institute) and to the Canada Council for their financial support of this research. The co-operation of the Volta Resettlement Authority, Accra, and that of the Institute of Africa Studies, Legon, were much appreciated. The help of Mr. Eric Yaw Denteh and that of my five other research assistants were invaluable. Above all, I wish to express my gratitude to the Nchumuru people, to their Chiefs, Elders, Gods and Ancestors, for their friendship, libations, and assistance.

NOTES

1. See, for example, the classic work by Wilner *et al* (1962) which also includes a brief overview of forty other studies. The occurrence of 'social pathology' and ill-health as consequences of resettlement will be discussed elsewhere.

2. This would seem *not* to support the hypotheses of A. Inkeles and R. LeVine concerning parents mediating social change, and change leading to changes in child-rearing practices - unless one looks only at child-discipline (cf. R. LeVine *et al* 1967:216-17, and 219), but further work is needed here. A very few informants suggested that tinned milk was being used more now in the rearing of children.

3. For the somewhat similar 'fostering' mechanism amongst the Central Gonja, see E. Goody (1960 and 1970). Note the 'bilateral twist' to Nchumuru fostering, whereby a child may go to the mother's side as well as the father's, though Nchumuru procreation belief has it that the 'blood' of the father is always 'stronger' than the 'blood' of the

RESETTLEMENT AND REHOUSING AMONG THE NCHUMURU   227

mother. For this 'help', filiation rather than descent, is the
structural principle emphasised.

4. The paucity of cases recorded in Akaniem may indicate interviewer
    error in the census survey; other data show that several adults
    there were once fostered children, while the 16 year old new
    (and second) wife of the Akaniemhene was just leaving such a
    relationship.

5. That Nchumuru women are reportedly more 'touchy' under crowded
    conditions contradicts the recent findings of Ehrlich & Freedman
    (1971:13) that women under crowded conditions become more co-
    operative, while men become more competitive; or rather, it shows
    their findings to be culture-bound; their work is also inadequate,
    for our purposes, for their subjects were together in one room for
    only a 4-hour period. For a Scottish case in which increased
    space reduced intra-familial tension, see Hole (1959:165).

6. This question is taken from the Smith-Inkeles 'Minimal Scale of
    Individual Modernity', about which scale and its use amongst the
    Nchumuru more will be said in another place.

7. My data on the later career of such fostered children is not yet
    adequate for ascertaining the extent to which they may be said
    to undergo a markedly separate type of life-cycle, or have differ-
    ent life-chances, from that of non-fostered children; my impression
    is that it is not all that different.

8. Indeed,seemingly the only invariants to an Nchumuru 'marriage'
    today are (1) the necessity for the man to present drink, (2) for
    him to send someone to 'beg' for her, and (3) the necessity for
    him to attend and contribute in certain ways to his parents-in-
    law's funerals.

9. As noted, Nchumuru procreation beliefs would have it that the child
    is always the genitor's, even if he did not send food-stuffs to
    'feed the conception'; it happens, but very rarely (some 3 cases
    only), that in the latter situation the girl's father may refuse
    to let the genitor have the 'friendship child'; in only 1 recorded
    case did the girl refuse to name her lover.

10. Partly because the new lake has come closer to Akaniem's houses
     than the planners expected, the people are in the process of
     resettling themselves some 150-200 yards away from their present site.

11. The proposed major new agricultural scheme, WFP-356 (Lumsden 1973),
     if it is ever carried out at New Grube, may in future force some
     young people to leave the site and area.

12. For example, the slight linguistic differences between the village-
     groups in New Grube will probably merge and disappear, but the fact
     that one major village-group is of Sungwe *kasuro* and others are of
     Chachiae and Banda *nsuro* will continue to affect social relations
     and allegiances. Much depends (e.g., the degree of social integ-
     ration at New Grube) on what sort of stable, residential 'ward'
     system emerges (for the roadway within the site acts as but an

228 *CHANGING SOCIAL STRUCTURE IN GHANA*

imperfect social boundary between angry Sungwae and Chachiae *nsuro* representatives), and on what is done about the local land disputes, and about the headship of the whole site.

13. The concept of 'stress' is crucial for understanding such resettlement situations, where groups and individuals are attempting to cope (adaptively or maladaptively) with a number of exogenous and endogenous stressors. This chapter was written before one's own conceptualisation of 'stress', one set within a general systems theory approach, had reached the stage of elaboration later presented in my Cambridge Ph.D. thesis, chapters One and Six. The most advanced statement of my model of 'an open system under stress' is to be found in my 1974 paper entitled 'Towards a systems model of stress' (40pp.), prepared for the NATO Conference on 'Dimensions of Anxiety and Stress' (Oslo, 1975).

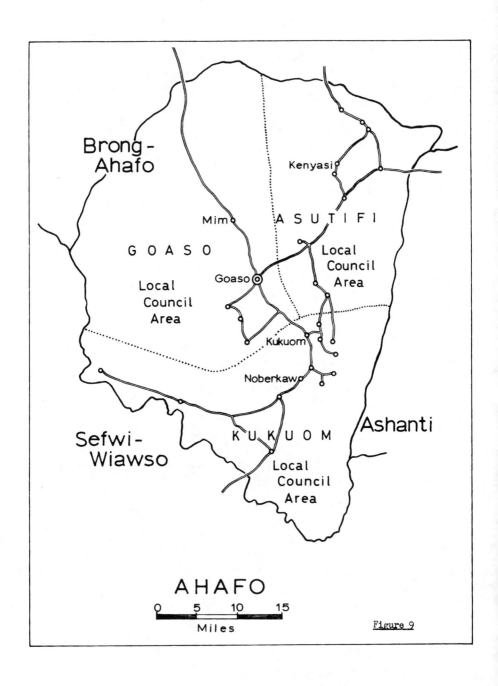

COMPOSITION AND PROCEDURE IN AHAFO COUNCILS

A. F.   R O B E R T S O N

Introduction

In recent years social anthropologists have become interested in the
relationship between the organisation of decision-making bodies and the
procedures they use (Bailey 1965, Richards and Kuper 1971). In this essay
I have argued that an examination of this relationship may explain certain
consequences of local government change in Ahafo more helpfully than simple
contrasts between 'tradition' and 'modernisation'. The essay focuses on the
procedural problems of the new Local Council Management Committees in Ahafo
(see fig. 9) and interprets these in terms of discontinuities between their
composition and the manner in which they are expected to operate.

Fig. 9 indicates the relationships among the three decision-making
bodies discussed here. The Local Councils which existed throughout Ghana
from 1952 until the overthrow of the Nkrumah government in 1966 have been
replaced by special committees appointed by the central authorities to
manage Local Council affairs. The predecessors in local government of
both the Management Committees and the Local Councils were the traditional
councils of chiefs and elders. Described as Stool Councils in fig. 9
these are still in operation, although the range of functions they perform
has been reduced. During a year's study of local government and public
decision-making in Ahafo I came to know the personnel, procedure and problems of the Management Committees quite well, and had opportunities to
compare them with other bodies operating at that time, notably the Stool
Councils. Between 1968 and 1969 I attended twenty full meetings of the
three Management Committees in Ahafo and was soon impressed by the nature
and intensity of the procedural traumas I witnessed. Central authorities
seem to have taken it for granted that these Committees would not only
perform the functions of the Local Councils but would also operate like
them in other respects, particularly in their adherence to procedural
rules. Although members were appointed by the Commissioner for Local
Government the composition of the Management Committees was intended to
give at least the illusion of popular representation; there even appeared
to be a tacit assumption that the Committees would operate more expedi-
tiously than the Local Councils for which they deputised, being released
from normal electoral responsibilities and enjoying the direct sanction
of superior authority.

I should make it clear at the outset that I found the integrity,
diligence and competence of the Management Committees in Ahafo admirable.
What was so conspicuous was the contrast between their calm and proficient
exterior image and the difficulties they so often experienced within the
council chamber. Efforts to follow 'proper Local Council rules' often
reduced decision-making to deadlock. Inevitably, solutions were sought
by deviating from the rules and on these occasions similarities between
the behavior of the Management Committees and the Stool Councils were

230 *CHANGING SOCIAL STRUCTURE IN GHANA*

striking. A plausible explanation might be that when the Management Committee members are frustrated in their efforts to adopt 'modern' procedures they lapse into 'traditional' styles of decision-making. Such an explanation would seem to underrate the sophistication and experience of most of the people involved, and in any case the behavioural similarities very often turn out, on closer examination, to be no more than superficial. The alternative explanation offered here is that there are similarities between the organisation of the Management Committees and the Stool Councils which may be related directly to similarities in their decision-making procedures, and that these features may be contrasted sharply with the organisation and procedural rules of the Local Councils.

Stool council organisation in Ahafo

Ahafo is in the forested cocoa and timber producing region of western Ghana. The pattern of settlement, which has profound effects on indigenous political organisation, is typical of the forest regions of southern Ghana. Communities have developed from small nuclei which were originally established as hunting camps. Out-migration from these nuclei has led to growth of subordinate village communities on land controlled by the central 'capital' town. The government now recognises twenty-eight of these units in Ahafo as distinct realms (*aman*), each administered by a chief (*ohene*) and a council of between 3 and 12 elders. Between 1958 and 1966 the 28 *aman* were united within the structure of an autonomous Ahafo State (fig. 9) under the paramountcy of the chief of Kukuom, but this constitution has been suspended and is the subject of vigorous political dispute (Dunn and Robertson 1973). It is essentially membership of the Ahafo State which entitles the chief of each *oman* to the rank *ohene* and to claim a particular Ahafo stool (*nkonnua*), the symbol of his office. It is primarily within this context that a chief and his elders may be described as constituting the Stool Council.

The *oman* in Ahafo is an economic and political association of co-resident units based on the mutual recognition of the authority of a chief or headman. The coherence of each unit is expressed today in the idiom of a common community of origin within or beyond Ahafo and also in terms of common matrilineal descent. Chiefship is supposedly vested in the matri-lineage of the original founder of the community, and other units which have become established over time are entitled to representation on the Stool Council. It is essentially in terms of the political and historical precedence among these units that the statuses of their respective elders on the Stool Council are differentiated (Robertson 1973). Elders are ranked according to the pre-colonial pattern of military alliance - for example *nifahene* (chief of the right wing) and *kyidomhene* (chief of the rear guard). The distribution of authority among these ranks is expressed today in the right to perform certain ceremonial functions and in terms of seating and speaking protocol during Stool Council sessions. A few elders are appointed without regard to their membership of a particular community unit, ostensibly on the strength of their personal qualities. These are non-hereditary offices, often allocated 'without portfolio' but more often given an executive designation, for example, the important *okyeame* (speaker) or the *sanaahene* (treasurer). In Ahafo it is even quite common to appoint an eminent 'stranger' to such offices.

COMPOSITION AND PROCEDURE IN AHAFO COUNCILS 231

Even today, when the government of the town or village is assisted by separate development committees consisting mainly of ordinary towns-folk, the Stool Council has important public functions (Robertson 1971). It deals with matters concerning the spiritual welfare of the community, land allocation and disputes of a minor and local nature. All issues are raised officially through the chief and all decisions are ultimately sanctioned by him. He is the moderator of competing interests within the Stool community and its agent in external affairs; reciprocally, he is sanctioned by the external authority of the state and is to some extent its agent within the community. As many writers have stressed, in his political actions the chief is bound to take the counsel of his elders - who also have an important 'say' in his appointment. As mode-rator of community affairs his role is mainly supervisory and his active engagement in Stool politics is effectively constrained by the insistence that on all formal occasions he should communicate through his official speaker, the *okyeame*. The rites of passage at 'enstoolment' emphasise his acquisition of the spiritual authority of his Stool predecessors and demand that his personal behaviour befit the office entrusted to him. He must not eat or drink in public, he must settle all outstanding dis-putes he may have within the community before he accedes, and today it is even asserted that he should not display sectional interest to the extent of selling all his cocoa to one particular dealer or worshipping at one particular church.

The growth of the local councils

Until 1951 the Stool Councils and the senior Divisional and State bodies (e.g. the Ashanti Confederacy Council) formed the basis of the Native Administration system in the Gold Coast. Busia (1951) has des-cribed the modification of the higher levels of chiefship, the processes of secularisation and centralisation resulting from half a century of involvement in colonial government, but it seems that the councils in the towns and villages were much less affected. The dissatisfaction of the younger and better educated people was directed primarily against the higher echelons of Native Authority and it was mainly with these levels that the constitutional changes of the 1950s were concerned. Growing nationalist pressures and a series of political disorders led to a Local Government Ordinance in 1951 which provided for a uniform system of Local and District Councils, two thirds of whose members were popularly elected. It was agreed however that the chiefs could not be displaced completely and the remaining seats were allocated to 'Tradi-tional Representatives'.

This mixed membership proved vexatious, although it was one of the more conspicuous shortcomings of the new Local Authority system. Control of revenue, corruption, inadequate staff and flagging public enthusiasm were all major problems. In 1961 a new Local Government Act of the Convention People's Party government sought full democratisation of the Councils; at the same time the enduring authority of the chiefs was grudgingly recognised in a Chieftaincy Act, by which they were accorded specific, if reduced functions. These changes did not resolve one major defect of the Local Councils - the system of public representation.

There are three Local Council areas in Ahafo: Asutifi, Goaso and Kukuom. Until the police-military coup d'état of 1966 the towns and villages of Ahafo were grouped into wards, units which had no pre-existing

232   *CHANGING SOCIAL STRUCTURE IN GHANA*

geographical significance and which often aggregated communities which were long term economic and political rivals. Complaints of bias were often levelled against councillors, one village saying its representative was favouring his home town. Under the traditional conciliar system each community had a chief or headman to pursue its interests for it, a concise political responsibility which the local councillor could rarely enjoy. The procedural traumas which these difficulties caused within the Council chamber often show through the tight-lipped minutes, and the lack of confidence with which these bodies were viewed by their public is part of an unfortunate heritage which today's Management Committee have been obliged to confront.

The Local Councils were disbanded shortly after the coup d'état of February 1966 which ousted the C.P.P. government of Kwame Nkrumah. Small management committees were appointed to transact business but these were reconstituted and enlarged in 1967 when it became clear that the re-establishment of elected Local Councils would be long delayed. In Ahafo three Management Committees each consisting of ten men and a woman transacted Council business under the close supervision of the District Administrative Officer resident in Goaso. His vigilance over all transactions was probably more intensive in Ahafo than in many other Districts, and it was mainly on his insistence that the Committees were obliged to conduct their affairs according to Local Council rules and standing orders. Each Council retained its executive staff, led by the clerk and treasurer, and other employees such as rate collectors continued to carry out their normal functions. The pattern of relationships with superior ministerial authority remained much the same. In matters of representation and composition, however the Management Committees were organised on new and radically different terms.

The management committees: representation and participation

In ideal at least, the Local Councillors were equal representatives of equal segments of the public. The democratic expectation was that the criteria of representation would create no role-differentiation among members, and that there would be no uneven distribution of authority. The office of chairman was filled on internal criteria, the members themselves electing one of their number on the strength of his personal qualities. Thereafter it was his duty to administer a set of very detailed and clearly defined procedural rules which were externally prescribed and externally sanctioned. Unlike the Stool Council, there was no authority structure built into Local Council composition and this, as I shall argue, severely restricted the procedural freedom it enjoyed. If we were to refer to the ideal types suggested by Bailey (1965), we might say that the Local Council was quite definitely an *arena* council, the Stool Council much more of an élite. The intention behind the organisation of the Management Committees set up after the 1966 coup d'état was to give them the appearance of popular representation and to make them look as much like an effective Local Council as possible. There was, however, no question of popular elections, and little opportunity to cast membership in terms of clearly demarcated segments of the public. The result has been something like an 'élite' council, in Bailey's terms, a body with a pronounced internal authority structure, concerned to isolate its transactions from public view in a way quite contrary to Local Council expectations. This feature of its organisation has nevertheless given it the capacity to set its own procedural

COMPOSITION AND PROCEDURE IN AHAFO COUNCILS   233

rules when attempts to follow Local Council drill end in deadlock. As a self-administering unit with one dominant participant - the District Officer - it bears quite close comparison with the Stool Council.

Six of the eleven Management Committee members were ordinary citizens appointed by the Ministry of Local Government on the recommendation of the District and Regional Officers. Criteria of selection were that they should be residents of the area, be literate in English, have a record of public service, be 'of good character', and have had no culpable association with the proscribed Convention People's Party. The Chairman was specified by the Ministry. One member was to be a 'Woman Representative' - the first time a lady had sat in a Local Council in Ahafo. These 'Ordinary Members' were mainly professional people, including a headmaster, a retired police officer and three timber merchants. Two described themselves unequivocally as farmers, but were very much the new, literate style of agricultural entrepreneur. Two of the 11 members were 'Traditional Representatives', chiefs or, where a literate candidate could not be found, local elders. The remaining three members were civil servants, representatives of the Education, Health and Community Development Departments. Shortage of personnel necessitated some doubling-up; one Community Development and one Education officer each served on two Management Committees and the acting Health Superintendent was obliged to serve on all three. This, and the fact that the staff of the three Councils were in quite close touch, helped to keep the three bodies in contact with each other, and at times even inspired some competitive zeal.

The Committees must be seen in the context of the sober and self-critical months following the overthrow of the Nkrumah government. There was a genuine concern about the scrupulous and orderly conduct of public affairs, and there were many references at meetings to the campaign for 'Civic Education' in which the future Prime Minister, Dr. Busia, was at that time engaged. Everyone concerned with the Committee was aware of the corruption of their Local Council predecessors, and was anxious to avoid a similar reputation. Members were nervous about revenue matters and as a result were reluctant to delegate financial business to sub-committees. Solicitude about matters of 'proper procedure' was conspicuous, and above all there was a heavy reliance on the direction of the District Officer and the advice of the Council staff. It could be said that the District Officer used the Committees to a substantial extent as a 'rubber stamp', and for this reason was concerned that their organisation and composition should appear orthodox. However, the greater part of Local Council business consists of simple political economising on a community basis: there is a budget of £n for new school classrooms - shall we build them in town A or in town B? On such issues the District Officer's prime concern was that an effective decision should be reached which would not cause disputes and jealousy.

For members themselves, ' proper procedure' was something of a moral imperative, lapses conjuring up uncomfortable memories of past corruption. As the cries of 'you can't do that!' or 'let's have a little order here' indicated, the procedural rules heavily inhibited them in their efforts to transact business. For technical guidance they often looked to the staff; apologising for his own part in a failure to arrive at a decision, one Traditional Member said 'the clerk must teach us the ways of government'. Concerned to keep such deference in check, the District Officer was often obliged to point out that 'Members are the bosses of the Staff, not the other way round'.

234 CHANGING SOCIAL STRUCTURE IN GHANA

Individuals were very much in two minds about their participation on these Committees. It was certainly an honour to be chosen by the government; on the other hand their relationships with the public were ambivalent and their relationships with each other in the Council chamber frustrating. 'Ordinary Members' in particular were confused about the interests they were supposed to represent. Sometimes they were encouraged to speak out for the particular communities in which they lived, while on other occasions they were reprimanded by the District Officer for being too partisan in this regard and told that they should have the diffuse, corporate interests of the Local Council area as a whole at heart. Again, efforts to appear 'unbiased' were liable to be construed as lack of enthusiasm. The District Officer once told me that in recommending members he had sought a 'trouble-free balance' in which none of the keenly-competitive local interests was over-represented. Members were sensitive to this - indeed three of them on the Goaso Committee who were all residents of the town of Mim themselves expressed concern about their possible bias.

The 'Official Members' played a different and very distinctive role. They took their places on the Committees by virtue of their bureaucratic offices. Moreover, as none of them was permanently resident in Ahafo, they had a certain professional detachment about local affairs. On the one hand their greater familiarity with official paperwork and 'committee procedure' helped to expedite matters. But they were apt to take a somewhat patronising attitude to other members, explaining details on the balance sheets to them or prompting 'call the chairman to call the clerk to read the Works Foreman's report'. They seemed in no doubt that they had the interests of the area as a whole at heart, nevertheless they were essentially the representatives of the government departments to which they were responsible. This gave them confidence which the others lacked but also made them more punctilious and liable to protract the discussion of an issue. They soberly reminded their committee colleagues that they were answerable to their departments for their part in Council transactions, and that they had to send copies of the minutes together with their own reports to their superiors. They also saw themselves as in competition with one another for available resources and on more than one occasion the District Officer was obliged to remind a zealous official that 'the Local Council is not for schools alone, you know'. They took great delight in voting each other into tedious and time-consuming Council duties and chased commas and spelling mistakes through each other's reports, questions and written motions.

More than any other category, the 'Traditional Members' were perplexed about the terms on which they were supposed to participate. They were not permitted, as the traditional system demanded they should, to speak out for their own communites, nor were the Committees supposed to discuss 'chieftaincy affairs'. Instead, chiefs were expected to contribute in terms of a vague, generalised notion of 'traditional interest', an idea which seems to have more meaning in central government circles than in Ahafo. Perhaps the qualification which might best enable them to perform according to official expectation is education rather than their inherent 'traditionalness'. Absenteeism was far higher among the Traditional Members than any other category, and I am sure this is closely related to the discomfort they often experienced in the Council chamber. At a meeting in Asutifi the District Officer remarked wryly that one chief on the Committee had obviously absented himself rather than become involved in the discussion of a rating complaint from his own townsmen. On another occasion an elder

COMPOSITION AND PROCEDURE IN AHAFO COUNCILS 235

was embarrassed by complaints about Council amenities in his town and when his chief was summoned to present the community's point of view, he clearly found his position untenable. When the chief had departed in high dudgeon, the Chairman demanded: 'you supported the chief just now - were you afraid that they would beat you if you hadn't, when you got home? Chief X thinks you are the representative of himself, not the whole area. He must not accost the members one-by-one'.

The Lady Members were victims of a good deal of male chauvinism occasioned by their apparent impassivity at meetings. 'She sits there as if she was watching a play' remarked one member to another. 'Next time we'll sell her a ticket' was the reply. The frequent request from the District Officer: 'what does our woman representative have to say about this?' usually elicited no more than an embarrassed smile, quite understandable in a society which does not in other contexts expect a lady to speak her mind in all-male company. One may refer here to the Stool Council on which one woman, the Queen Mother, has an important position. My own observation and those of other fieldworkers in the Akan area, make it clear that although she may have a great deal of influence behind the scenes the Queen Mother rarely contributes to debate. She is a leader among the townswomen, who prefer to settle their affairs among themselves, away from the menfolk.

Members were quick to make accusations of bias when discussion became heated, and on more than one occasion the placatory cry went up 'we are not sectional here'. Such a claim would hardly be appropriate in the Local Council, but Committee Members were touchy about the constructions others put on their motives. On one occasion an Education Officer complained that aspersions were being cast on his request for funds for a Catholic school on the grounds that he, as a Catholic, was showing undue interest. However, internal differentiation among members contrasted sharply with the united front they presented to the outside world. They were uncomfortably aware that there was little to lead the public to suppose that any of their interests were specifically represented. This was once discussed at a meeting when it was pointed out that everyone connected with the Management Committee was seen as belonging to a single category, and an unfavourable one at that. The term *councilfuo*, council people, was applied without discrimination to everyone from the rate collectors to the chairman. The District Officer complained on many occasions that members tended to speak of the Committee as 'you' rather than using the more responsible 'we'; significantly he regarded this as bad usage inherited from the Local Councils. Once he felt obliged to warn the Committees darkly that telling members of the public 'I have put your plea to the Council but they have rejected it' was tantamount to subversion and might even warrant criminal charges. Contrary to the democratic principles of the Local Council, the strength of the Committees was in their closed, élite status with regard to the people of Ahafo. An awareness of this status and of the marked internal distinctions among members, so evocative of Stool Council organisation in Ahafo, must go far towards explaining the procedural traumas experienced within the Council chamber.

236   *CHANGING SOCIAL STRUCTURE IN GHANA*

<u>Stool council and management committee: procedural similarities</u>

Returning briefly to the Stool Council, one may, I think, see the connection between its organisation and the way its proceedings are controlled. The regulation of transactions does not really depend on the application of a defined and standardised set of procedural rules so much as on protocol which reflects the structure of authority within the council. Taking a necessarily summary view I would describe the procedure of an Ahafo Stool Council as follows. Meetings are convened on the chief's direction in a special chamber of the 'palace' several times a month. They are occasioned by some routine business such as recurrent festivals but are usually called *ad hoc* when a particular issue is presented to the chief: a quarrel in the town, a breach of custom or a letter about sanitation from the District Office. Sessions are exclusive and privileged, although in reality open doors and windows make it difficult to prevent an audience gathering. Punctuality is not stressed, though at an early stage in the proceedings the chief pours an inaugural libation of gin which marks the commencement of business in earnest. When the issue has been explained, either by the spokesman (*okyeame*) or by a petitioner, the opinion of each elder, seated in rank order around the chief, is sought, usually but not necessarily starting with the most junior. Ideally the last opinion to be expressed is that of the chief; coming *ex cathedra*, it constitutes the final decision and marks the conclusion of discussion. After the first statements of opinions, a pattern of freer discussion, always addressed to the chief, establishes itself. The treatment of the issue is cyclic and repetitive, involving summaries for the benefit of frequent latecomers. Great importance is attached to good rhetoric, temperate behaviour, and respect to other elders - above all to the chief. Abusiveness in this context is a <u>sin</u> and as such must be expiated by the ritual sacrifice of a <u>sheep.</u> Nevertheless, everyone must have the fullest opportunity to speak and members are more piqued if they are denied this than if their point of view does not win through. Tangential issues and matters of personal character are explored at will and - very important - elders and others in attendance are allowed to excuse themselves to consolidate opinions or clarify particular points in small groups outside. Solutions are almost invariably sought in terms of elaborated verbal formulae, decisions to which no one objects being pursued by continual re-statement and re-phrasing. One Ahafo chief described decision-taking in his Council thus:

> 'If they (the elders)all agree I shall confirm their decision. If they say something I disagree with I shall ask them to explain again. They say 'I have taken this or that stand for this or that reason'. I have to tell them if I find their explanations unclear and we consider the whole issue again. Then, when I am satisfied, the matter is decided.'

This indicates both the constructive role of the counsellors and the subtle influence of the chief. The predominant tactic of 'talking it out' often makes meetings very lengthy and it is by no means clear whether the passing-around of gin expedites or protracts matters. The final phase of decision-making is the chief's pronouncement, which may be broadcast in the streets by the town crier or referred to another

COMPOSITION AND PROCEDURE IN AHAFO COUNCILS 237

appropriate body such as the town Development Committee.

As I have observed, the Local Council has explicitly no formal differentiation of authority among members. Composition is in terms of equal representation of equal segments of the public. The role of chairman is confined to the administration of a set of detailed, prescribed rules of procedure, externally sanctioned in terms of superior political authority. The Council itself does not have an internal authority structure in terms of which it can devise, adjust and autonomously apply its own procedural rules. *Faute de mieux,* the Management Committees are characterised by a marked pattern of internal authority differentiation, most noticeable in terms of the participation of the District Administrative Officer. They are obliged to masquerade as Local Councils with egalitarian, representative composition, a discontinuity which we may see expressed in decision-making traumas. Nevertheless it is important to stress that they do have the internal authority to override the procedural strictures of Local Council drill and find 'informal' solutions to decision-making problems. It is mainly because of this organisational facility that their procedural tactics bear comparison with the Stool Councils.

The District Officer - overshadowing all Management Committee transactions - insisted that meetings should be held at regular monthly intervals (I believe that in many other parts of Ghana they were convened less frequently). Members were much concerned about the spatial and temporal boundaries of meetings, and soon became suspicious if they thought that business was being transacted outside the Council chamber. Nevertheless, the staff, the Official Members and the District Officer prepared much of the business in advance, submitting it at meetings cut and dried for a decision. Meetings were often lengthy, $7\frac{1}{2}$ hours being the longest continuous session of the 20 I attended. As time dragged on, members would permit themselves a feeling of martyrdom to the public interest, recognising the need to 'thrash things out' fully. After a meticulous discussion of the annual estimates, the Goaso chairman closed a meeting with an altruistic sigh: 'let us thank ourselves for wasting our time about the Nation's business'. The need for punctuality and advance notice of absence was always being stressed, and in bad weather members from distant communities felt obliged to turn up an hour or two before meetings were scheduled to start. The quorum was meticulously observed and on two occasions business was brought to a halt for half an hour while an Official Member was called out to deal with some urgent matter. Meetings began promptly with a Christian prayer, which marked the commencement of formal business, the extinguishing of cigarettes, the donning of serious faces and the transition from the vernacular into English. A closing prayer marked the transition out of this formal context again and the adjournment of the meeting *en bloc* to the nearest bar. There it never failed to surprise me how quickly and completely the recriminations and acrimony were dispelled.

Ghanaian Local Council meetings, like their British counterparts, were statutorily open to the public; this would have been anathema to Management Committee Members, laying open all the problems of representation and composition. To ease matters the District Officer ruled that as they were, in a sense, committees of the former Local Councils, meetings could properly be held in camera. Members were sensitive about

238 *CHANGING SOCIAL STRUCTURE IN GHANA*

spatial seclusion, chasing away bystanders and concerned that no outsider should be aware of the individual views expressed. Thus protected, an Official Member felt able to assure his colleagues: 'here we talk openly, without fear.' The two occasions on which members complained of 'leaks' were bitter indeed, and the bland, impersonal style of the minutes reflected concern for privilege. The coming-and-going characteristic of many Stool Council meetings would have been viewed with great suspicion by the Management Committees. A member who was queried for periodically slipping out of the Council chamber explained that this was only to satisfy his craving for tobacco and that he always stood by a window where he could hear the proceedings.

The distinctions among categories of member were quite clearly apparent. Traditional Members wore the toga-style cloth and sandals which are the uniform of the Stool Council. The official all wore lightweight shirts and trousers and, bristling with pens, briefcases and files contrived to look more businesslike than the Ordinary Members. The Health Superintendent distinguished himself with an impressive field uniform of khaki and a solar topee, and the Woman Member, smartly wigged and colorfully dressed , was no less conspicuous in spite of her silence. Seating was habitual, but studiously avoided any grouping of membership category. The District Officer was somewhat uneasy about any distinctive placing of the chairman, particularly in Goaso, which boasted a high podium. He once remarked that such distinction was evocative of the 'the tyranny of the old regime' and advocated 'a more egalitarian and intimate' arrangement. By the next meeting, the old pattern had reasserted itself. The staff sat at a separate table, and so often it was between the two groups, the policy-makers and the executive, that the most heated arguments were conducted.

All Management Committee business was transacted in English - with a few relevant exceptions. This clearly inhibited some members, who were also struggling with the added burden of officialdom. One reason for the rigid insistence on the use of English was that the District Officer, a southerner, was not fluent in Twi, the vernacular. Inevitably the Official Members proved the most competent, while the Traditional Members made conspicuously heavy weather. As for the lady representative, her silence was once discussed - in her absence - at a meeting, and linguistic incompetence ruled out. The suggestion that the use of Twi might increase her active participation was hotly countered by one Official: 'such a suggestion is offensive to a supposedly educated group'. Nevertheless, the vernacular was always used in the Committee's dealings with Council employees and outsiders, an indication of the value of the alien medium in insulating transactions from public scrutiny. Again, it was necessary to have recourse to Twi to break a deadlock in discussion or to resolve a misunderstanding. It was also the medium for angry or impatient outbursts.

Council communication, with its abundance of minutes, reports, letters, balance sheets and so on, implies high standards of literacy and numeracy, and it was clear that Ordinary and Traditional Members were often at sea. This did not help them to 'keep a watchful eye on the staff', as the District Officer continually exhorted them. To many of them, the slow and obscure written transactions of the Council appeared inhibiting, and such issues as rates and exemption clearly required face-to-face consultation with petitioners. The District

COMPOSITION AND PROCEDURE IN AHAFO COUNCILS

Officer once interrupted proceedings to question the motives of a
Traditional Member who wanted to 'look at the face' of a candidate
for a Council typing post. On another occasion the droll Health
Superintendent lampooned the stiff bureaucratic proceedings involved
in the selection of District representatives for the electoral colleges
required in connection with the convening of a National Constituent
Assembly in 1968. Members of the Committees were obliged to vote for
people they did not know personally, so he enquired of one woman candidate: 'this Effua, is she plump or is she emaciated? This Constituent
Assembly will need a sound physique, you know.'

Most business was raised routinely, through the clerk and treasurer
in consultation with the Chairman. The latter was reminded from time to
time by the District Officer that his honorarium of £ 25 a month was paid
in recognition of these additional duties. 'You must come in two, three
days before meetings' he advised, 'you must tie everything up before and
after.' Ordinary Members were often scolded for not thinking up bright
questions and motions to table in advance, a failure in their 'representative' duties; yet it was clear that ideas came to mind in abundance
during the actual transaction of business, when they were liable to be
ruled out of order. Ordinary Members also complained that some of their
suggestions were filtered out in advance by the staff on the grounds
that they were superfluous or inappropriate; thus one complaint about
the flyblown calabashes in which palmwine was dispensed was dismissed
because it fell more within the competence of the town Development
Committees. This contrasts with the Stool Council where virtually
everything is relevant, if not actionable. Nevertheless the rubric
'any other business' at the end of the agenda was interpreted very
liberally, but although discussion ranged wide, it was rarely minuted.

Discussion is usually the most prominent feature of a decision-
making session in any council, and the different ways in which it is
controlled are of great interest. In the Stool Council, the chief is
quite passive with regard to the subject-matter of discussion, but very
active - usually through the medium of his official 'speaker' - in the
control of discussion. The Local Council chairman, elected by his
colleagues in terms of his personal qualities, applied very different
sanctions, prescribed standing orders and procedural rules. The role
of Management Committee chairman was disturbed by several ambiguities
he enjoyed. The Asutifi chairman was a headmaster, the Kukuom chairman a clinic attendant, and the Goaso chairman, Mr. A.W. Osei former
opposition (United Party) M.P. for the Ahafo area. Mr. Osei had not
only the advantage of parliamentary experience, he enjoyed considerable local respect, enhanced very greatly by the reversal of the
fortunes of the Convention People's Party in the 1966 coup. His right
to the chair would never have been questioned by other Goaso members,
whereas it would be fair to say that neither of the other two chairmen
would have been elected unanimously. In terms of the ambiguous composition of the Committees, Mr. Osei had clear advantages over the other
two in that he enjoyed both the external sanction of the Ministry and
the internal sanction of his colleagues. His participation was more
extensive than his Kukuom and Asutifi counterparts and the District
Officer, whose involvement was significantly reduced, once remarked
'Goaso is the only Committee which I can reasonably leave to its own
devices'. Certainly the procedural crises which dogged the other two
Committees affected Goaso less, and the fact that only in Goaso was any

240   *CHANGING SOCIAL STRUCTURE IN GHANA*

business entrusted to sub-committees may be taken as an indication of mutual confidence among members.

I measured and counted contributions at five meetings of each of the three Management Committees between August 1968 and April 1969 (fig. 10). The extent of the District Officer's participation is perhaps the most striking point, a measure not only of his active engagement in transactions but also of his continuous instruction, criticism and advice on procedural matters. He took the inexperience of members very much to heart and regarded Committee transactions at least in part as exercises in 'Civic Education.' He tended to delegate much of this role to the chairman and the clerk in Goaso, the latter being a very senior and well qualified officer, recently returned from a study-trip to West Germany. He spoke for a total of four hours and ten minutes over the five sessions, nearly half the total speaking time - extensive participation indeed when one considers our own generally mute clerks here in Britain. Other categories of Member speak very much in accordance with the differentiation of authority in Committee composition which I have described earlier. Kukuom had one very active and forceful Ordinary Member who has been responsible for the extent of his category's speaking time; the Lady Member in that body was either absent or completely silent. I hope that this figure will help to allay the suspicion that the Committees operate only as rubber stamps for the District Officer and Council staff. It would seem appropriate to re-emphasise at this point that much of the business transacted was the humdrum allocation of resources among local communities - contentious, but not always of great interest to the administrators.

The Local Council rule that a speaker may address himself no more than three times to a particular motion was not rigorously enforced, indeed it was usually held to be important that members should have the opportunity to 'talk things out to clear matters up' - a tactic very reminiscent of the Stool Council. At times, however, a chairman was censured by the District Officer for sitting back and allowing members to talk their way to a solution: 'you have to be dynamic, lead the discussion. I'm not supposed to be telling you this ....' Often it was difficult to encourage members to speak without equivocation on delicate issues - notably where the internal relationships of the Council were at stake. An almost meaningless, oblique allusion (how did the new Council messenger get his job?) turns out to imply something much more complex and delicate (did the clerk give the job arbitrarily to his brother-in-law?). Once the District Officer was moved to intervene: 'what is your ulterior motive? I find that when some of you ask questions like this, there is usually something more substantial afoot.' The Local Council demanded blunt,prepared statements and questions which are necessarily clear. In preferring to approach internal problems through their peripheral details, the Management Committee is behaving in a decorous and deferential way very reminiscent of the Stool Council.

In the ways it actually took decisions the Committee behaved quite contrary to Local Council expectations, where it is statutorily expected that a majority vote will be taken on a member's motion. It was particularly on this matter that Management Committee members found the application of formal, overt procedural rules inappropriate. Votes were taken on only eleven occasions, although 170 items of business were transacted during the 20 meetings I attended. Three of these votes,

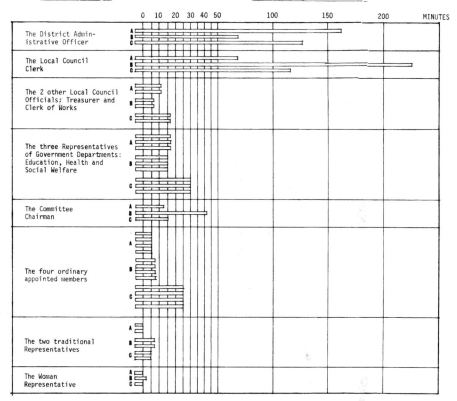

Figure 10 The Total duration of speaking time* of each category of Local Council Management Committee member in each of the 3 Committees in Ahafo over five meetings, 1968-9.

A = Asutifi Committee; B = Goaso Committee; C = Kukuom Committee

*Only contributions in excess of four seconds duration were measured

COMPOSITION AND PROCEDURE IN AHAFO COUNCILS 241

concerning the National Constituent Assembly, were compulsory. It seems significant that 5 of the remaining 8 concerned the internal relationships of the Council - staff matters and sub-committee appointments. The remaining three votes were taken within a short period by one of the Committees, when a bitter inter-personal dispute was obstructing business. The fastidiousness of the voting was striking. Two or three times a secret ballot was demanded in preference to a show of hands and once when papers were being counted by the clerk it was discovered that one had been spoiled accidentally. To demand a correction would have involved the explicit identification of the voter, however obvious the culprit may have been. The chairman ruled that all votes should be recast and more than that, a different colour of paper was to be used.

Nothing caused quite as much anguish as the chairman's casting vote. The Goaso chairman was required to do this once and felt obliged to remark that it was 'an unpleasant duty' but that he had to be 'strong minded'. The Kukuom chairman, who enjoyed less informal authority, was involved in the casting-vote predicament twice. On the first occasion he was taken to task by the leader of the opposing point-of-view for 'using his vote in a partisan fashion' and on the second, when he chose to withdraw his first vote and abstain, he was accused of 'bad chairmanship'. On two occasions Official Members pressed for a show of hands and proved quick to raise them; it was many seconds before the last Ordinary or Traditional Member raised his or hers, by which time it had become clear which way the wind was blowing.

Committee Members preferred more informal ways of taking decisions. It is tempting to follow Bailey and describe such tactics as 'consensual', a mode of decision-making which he correlates with his 'elite' type of council, and contrasts with the majority vote. If the assumption that these are polar opposites is faulty, the assumption that consensus is a single definable phenomenon is more so. It may be taken to include simple affirmation of a proposal or the elimination of dissent by a wide variety of tactics. Parts of the process could be described as 'mutual agreement', 'squaring','compromise', 'undeclared abstention', 'voting-with-the-feet' all of which I have observed in many different councils and many of which Bailey himself uses as synonyms for 'consensus'. However, the steamrollering of opposition by an adroit talker can hardly be bracketed with the positive idea of smiling unanimity. I value the kind of distinction Bailey is trying to make, but prefer to see it in terms of a gradation of <u>formal regulation</u> (of which the majority vote is an extreme example). This, of course, bears on my assumption that <u>informal</u> control of procedure is a feature of councils with a clearly defined internal structure of authority.

Masquerading as Local Councils, the Committees could find informal processes of decision-making every bit as taxing as the use of the majority vote. Decisions were described in the minutes as 'unanimous' but in Ghana this connotes 'with good will' rather than the literal meaning. I think that the most common feature of unregulated decision-making in public bodies is the elaboration of a verbal formula to which no-one ultimately objects. The formal demands of the Local Council reverse this procedure; the verbal formula is set down at the outset as a motion which is either accepted or rejected, the limits of flexibility being either an amendment from the mover or the admission of a counter motion. In practice Committee members reformulated nearly every motion jointly, chipping in words here and there without too much regard for total coherence. As official records demanded

242   *CHANGING SOCIAL STRUCTURE IN GHANA*

a clear pronouncement, it usually fell to the clerk to write out the final version after the meeting, but as this could bring indignant queries from members at subsequent meetings, clerks felt obliged to protract discussion to get the precise wording agreed. This involved calling for a proposer and a seconder,which again revealed members' discomfort about formal procedure. It was a standing joke that while people were reluctant to move even a vote of thanks, they would gladly move for one thing - the adjournment.

Other formal constraints inhibited the informal 'talking out' of solutions. The temporal and spatial confinement prevented 'squaring' - as Cornford called it - and such Stool Council tactics as walking out of the meeting to consult. Private conversations within the Council chamber were quickly stopped by the others with the complaint that it was rude or, significantly, <u>unfair</u>. However, when prodedural constraints were proving obstructive and aggravating, the District Officer now and then sanctioned a 'brief recess' which permitted free conversation and almost invariably solved the problem.

The bland, circumspect style of the minutes gave no clue to the vigour of debate or the procedural traumas experienced at meetings. Everyone was concerned to assert an image of concerted activity both to their public and to superior authority, and the written accounts of transactions were aseptic and depersonalised. A large proportion of each meeting was devoted to perusal of the previous minutes, and on one occasion this took nearly four hours, two thirds of a very long session. Amendments and revocations were viewed with great disfavour as they appeared to indicate the Committee's vacillation and indecision. 'This is not a club where we can say one thing and reverse it later', the Goaso chairman told his colleagues, 'our minutes are sent to the Regional Office'. Members were aware of the extent to which they were at the mercy of the staff in such matters; they could, one Official Member told me, 'publicly sabotage' the efforts of the Management Committee.

CONCLUSION

The development of a national system of local government has been one of the most intractable problems in the growth of Ghana as a modern state. Efforts to establish popularly elected Local Councils have met with frequent frustration, making it necessary on several occasions to entrust their functions to specially appointed committees of management. Although the Local Councils themselves may not have endured, the strong organisational and procedural ideals governing them have persisted; standing surrogate for the Local Councils the contemporary Management Committees have been saddled with formal procedural rules - diligently applied by the District Officer - which are clearly incompatible with the terms in which they have been organised. Lapses from strict Local Council procedure during Management Committee meetings are strongly evocative of decision-making patterns in the traditional Stool Council. It would, however, be inexact and misleading to account for these similarities simply in terms of the Management Committee's switching' in and out of traditional procedural styles. A more detailed comparison of the Stool Council and the Management Committee serves to highlight the discontinuities between the composition of the Committee and the procedures expected of it. Both bodies, unlike the former Local Council, have

COMPOSITION AND PROCEDURE IN AHAFO COUNCILS 243

clearly defined internal authority structures and patterns of role-differentiation among members. While this inhibits the appointed Management Committee's efforts to perform like an elected Local Council, it also enables it to waive strict adherence to the procedural rules of the Local Council when difficulties arise, and to seek solutions by less inhibited discussion and less formal decision-making tactics. It can do so because within the group there is authority, vested primarily in the role of the District Officer, to override formal rules and to control decision-making informally.

THE VILLAGE SCHOOLTEACHER IN GHANA

PENELOPE ROBERTS

Introduction

Ghana spends nearly one quarter of the National Budget on education. Following the introduction of fee-free compulsory primary education in 1961, enrolment rose precipitately reaching in certain areas something like 90% of children of schoolgoing age, although in other areas, notably the North, only one out of two children is yet attending school. The development of the educational system has been accompanied by studies in the appropriate curricula for mass education in a developing countries. Some of the unwelcome consequences such as increasing unemployment, the drift to urban areas and the rejection of full-time farming as a way of life among educated youth, have been the subject both of research and of some attempts at corrective measures. Little has been written, however, on the purveyor of education himself, the teacher. The subject of the present paper concerns the prestige and social status of elementary schoolteachers in village communities in Sehwi Wiawso state, Western Ghana[1].

The status of teachers

There are as yet few studies of the role and status of the teacher in his workplace in any part of the world. Most writers have measured his status vis à vis other comparable professions. Foster (1965), for instance, found in Ghana that the status of elementary school teachers ranked very low in the perceptions of secondary school students in comparison with that of doctors or lawyers. But the educational achievements of secondary school students already exceed those of many teachers, and their career expectations, therefore, are unlikely to be directed towards the level of such teachers with whom, in any case, they may no longer interact. The majority of adults with whom an elementary school teacher interacts during the course of his professional career in a rural, farming community are themselves illiterate. Such people are unlikely to have the same career expectations as secondary school students, and their perceptions of the status of teachers is at least likely to be based on different criteria of achievement and different perceptions of prestige.

Moreover, social ranking between professions makes the assumption that there are comparable criteria which can be measured: criteria such as level of income, security of tenure, promotion prospects and so on. Such criteria can hardly be used to compare the teacher and the farmer. The monthly pay cheque is a remuneration of a completely different nature from the income of the farmer which varies according to the time of year and from year to year, which must be estimated in kind as well as in cash which may depend on his position within the family and the number of

246 CHANGING SOCIAL STRUCTURE IN GHANA

children he has. While the actual income of a farmer may, with difficulty, be converted into cash and compared with that of the teacher, the social value of the income has also to be taken into account. The teacher may earn more each month than the farmer, but spend much of it on food: the farmer may have no cash in his pocket but can provide his visitors generously with food and drink at the end as well as the beginning of the month. The social status of the teacher in the community is likely to be based on such values.

The little that is known of the status of teachers does at least point to some variation. In some cases, although the institution of western education is a new one, teachers have inherited role statuses which already existed in traditional society. In Burma, for instance, teachers in Government schools receive the respect offered to monastic teachers of the old order (Nash 1970) while in Japan they have preserved to some extent the traditional attitudes towards 'men of knowledge' (Singleton 1967).

Traditional Sehwi society did not, however, possess roles into which modern teachers could conveniently fit. The educational process was diffuse, all adults being in a general way responsible for bringing up children, acquainting them with appropriate behaviour, customs and traditions. Training in special skills generally took place within the family, crafts being passed down from father to son and mother to daughter. While there were priests (*komie*), they did not teach except to their own apprentices and, moreover, their position could hardly be inherited by the Western-type teachers whose almost exclusive function in the early days of education was to impart Christianity. The role of the school teacher has to some extent had to be 'invented' and so has the social status attached to it.

It has been suggested that while the teacher in Africa may have a low professional status, he may be compensated by high status in his workplace (Jones 1962). This suggestion seems to derive from the fact that since education itself is highly valued in many parts of Africa, so too will be the teacher. But the values attached to education have clearly changed and continue to do so. When education first arrived in the area now known as Ghana, for instance, a negative value was placed upon it. It was seen as a positive threat to the integrity of society and to the authority of its ruler[2]. Such an attitude changed, however, when positive benefits could be obtained in the shape of careers in trade and in administration in the developing Colonial Governments. Foster (1965) has shown that the type of education in demand has consistently paralleled the opportunities for employment available. During this period, literacy was such a rare commodity that a minimal amount opened up considerable prospects, and the teacher who provided such a commodity may well have been highly valued. Such a period is clearly remembered in Sehwi since the first school was not opened until 1915. In those days, teachers did indeed occupy an exclusive social position, descriptions suggesting that they were regarded almost as highly as the District Commissioner and other Government agents. So great indeed was the demand for the services of teachers that when neither Government nor Missions could supply them, communities built their own schools and found and paid their own teachers.

But a third stage has now been reached. In consequence of the massive increase in the provision of elementary schooling and a corresponding failure

THE VILLAGE SCHOOL TEACHER IN GHANA 247

to provide employment opportunities in the modern sector, the education which the village schoolteacher can supply is almost completely devalued. Whereas once the Middle School Leaving Certificate opened up prospects in a variety of careers, it is now virtually a worthless commodity except as a basic qualification for further education. The teacher is no longer the only literate member of a community - even the smallest village has young men and women who have completed their elementary education. The only difference between them and the teacher is that they are unemployed while the teacher is not, for over 50% of teachers in Sehwi had no more than elementary schooling themselves.

This phase in the development of education has not been reached in many other parts of Africa or the developing world. It forms the background, however, to the following study.

Research methods

Since the subject of research is the position of the teacher in the community, the nature of the community - its political and social organisation, its values and attitudes - becomes the primary object of study. But this is in itself presents an immediate methodological problem. The number of teachers in any community is small: how is it to be determined that a community's attitudes towards teachers may not have been evolved from the limited experience of its own very few teachers? What would one community's attitudes have in common with another's and how could the teacher's role and status within the society as a whole be discovered?

Primary schools (covering the first 6 years of elementary education) are to be found in most villages with a population of over 300, which is in fact the average size of a village in the State. But such schools never had an enrolment to justify the employment of teachers for each class: on average such schools had 3 teachers for 6 classes, sometimes there was only one teacher for all the classes. Larger towns and villages with populations of over 800 also had middle schools (the last four years of elementary education), which served surrounding areas. While close observation of a community was desirable, the research period was divided between one small village with a primary school and three teachers, and two larger and adjacent villages with primary and middle schools in each and a total of 19 teachers. In addition several other communites were visited regularly and many others periodically. Finally, two sets of questionnaires were sent out to over 800 teachers in the Educational District requesting information on the background of the teachers, their problems and their attitudes. In these ways some of the problems of the small size of the teacher unit were ameliorated.

In an analysis of the social status of the teacher, two systems, which apparently have nothing in common, need description. The first is the structure of the community where the teacher works, together with the values and attitudes of its members. In Sehwi Wiawso the community is a unit of the traditional State, deriving its structure and function from its position within it. The second system is that of the teaching profession itself: its organisation and recruitment, the qualifications and characteristics of its members. With this information, the compatibilities and conflicts between the two systems begin to emerge.

Sehwi Wiawso State

Sehwi Wiawso State (*Wiawsoman*) is one of three Sehwi states, the traditions, political and social organisation of which are closely linked to those of other Akan states of the central forest region of Ghana. Its eastern frontier lies across the Tano River while in the west it borders the Ivory Coast. It is bounded to the north by Ahafo and to the south by Aowin and Denkyera. Until 30 years ago it was extremely sparsely populated and even in 1960, population density was less than 30 per square mile. Moreover, most of the population is centred round the capital, Wiawso, in the east and only in the last decade has the land in the west been opened up to Sehwi and stranger cocoa farmers following the exploitation of the forests by timber companies.

The factors behind the sparse population lie partly in the history of the State. Tradition records a long series of migrations to this area of refugees from war, fugitives from justice and people seeking new land. Very few Sehwi claim to be indigenous to the area and they are no doubt descendants of even earlier migrations. Despite the social and political links with the areas from which Sehwi originally migrated, however, notably with the Ashanti confederacy of which Sehwi subsequently became a tributary state, Sehwi language belongs to the Anyi-Baulé branch of Akan which is mainly spoken in the Ivory Coast and is not easily intelligible to Asante-Twi speakers of the south of Ghana. The language is an important symbol of Sehwi cultural identity and is used as a factor in political and legal relations with recent farming immigrants who do not speak Sehwi.

The political organisation of Sehwi Wiawso resembles that of other Akan states, political office being linked with the military organisation. The Omanhene is selected from the royal matrilineage (*abusua dihyie*) called *Asangera*, said to be the same as the Oyoko matrilineage which provides the Omanhene of several other Akan states. He is served by a Council of Chiefs who are the heads of seven military divisions (*fekuo*) each of which include branches of all the matrilineages in the state and one branch each of the royal matrilineage[3]. The State Council also includes a number of important sub-Chiefs with specific functions in the constitution. These chiefly titles and offices are vested in local lineages whose members elect their own head but a title can be removed from a lineage with the consent of the Council in cases of treachery or subversion.

Apart from these hereditary offices, there are also a number of appointive offices in the power of the Omanhene. Chief of these are that of *okyeame* who act as spokesmen, advisers, representatives of the Omanhene and his Ambassadors[4]. There are also the *Apamfoe* or councillors, men who have achieved distinction in their own careers and whose abilities have been harnessed by the State to its own ends.

The Omanhene is titular owner of the land which is administered by a hierarchy of lesser chiefs, rank being expressed by the right to greater privileges and powers such as that of direct access to the Omanhene's Council, ability to hear legal cases upon the swearing of the Omanhene's oath and so on.

The smallest political unit of the state is the village (*kro*) which has its own chief and councillors. Not all conglomerations of populations

THE VILLAGE SCHOOL TEACHER IN GHANA

are *kro* as such. Migrant farming communities, for instance, may not constitute a recognised political unit, and have access to legal and political representation only through the Chief of the land upon which they are settled or through the Chief of the land from which they migrated. The Chief of a *kro* may himself be of any rank within the State structure but administers the *kro* through hereditary and appointed elders whose titles and ranks are the same as those at the State Council itself. The royal lineage is generally that of the first settlers of the land, while other offices are held by lineages who subsequently migrated. From time to time lineages die out or leave to seek new land and more recently immigrated lineages can achieve office.

A *kro* is a politically autonomous unit in its internal affairs. It elects its own chief who only has to be ratified by the Omanhene or a senior Chief to whom he swears loyalty. It makes and administers its own body of bye-laws and distributes its land among its members and to strangers.

Most of the villages which have only a primary school are relatively undifferentiated farming communities. The major cash crop is cocoa; subsistence crops such as cassava and plantain are cultivated by slash and burn methods and are mainly the responsibility of women. Such a village possesses virtually no modern amenities. Only the capital town of Wiawso has electricity and a water supply, while there are no tarred roads within the state. There are a few stores with a tiny stock; storekeepers and artisans such as potters and carvers are also part-time farmers. Very little is grown for sale in markets owing to poor transport facilities. Apart from teachers, there are no wage-earners within such villages; agricultural officers, sanitary inspectors and so on live in the capital and visit rarely. Daily life is governed entirely by the agricultural cycle; non-farmers are an anomaly. Teachers are the only adults, apart from the aged and the sick, who stay in the villages on a farming day.

Larger villages with middle schools are generally market centres and they present greater occupational variation, many women being full time petty traders. Better transport facilities provide for greater movement in and out of the village. Even so they are basically farming communities.

Education in the village

Although the diffusion of education in Sehwi lagged considerably behind other parts of southern Ghana, present rates of enrolment into primary schools are high. It is the exception rather than the rule to find a boy not attending school in a village which has one, although this is less true of girls. Distance to schools is an important factor and children of outlying communities without schools are less likely to be enrolled.

Enrolment is, however, slowly deteriorating for two reasons. First, during the period 1961-66, elementary schooling was fee-free, parents having only to provide books and uniforms. In 1966 school book fees were instituted. While these are very small (£1.50 p.a. in primary schools, £3.00 p.a. in middle schools) parents contend that they are a burden. Moreover, while it probably cost parents just as much to buy books themselves these did become their own property, whereas now they are the property of the school. Secondly, parents are becoming increasingly aware

250 *CHANGING SOCIAL STRUCTURE IN GHANA*

that elementary education does not guarantee a job and few Sehwi can afford secondary school fees. Although they wish their children to be educated so that they can participate more freely in the bureaucratic stucture of the modern state, and so that they can read letters and newspapers and keep accounts, part of the motivation of sending and keeping a child in school has gone. While over 50% of the schools in Sehwi were opened in the period 1961-66, in 1970 quite a number of primary schools were closed down or amalgamated owing to low enrolment.

Nevertheless, even the smallest village is certain to have a number of young men who have fully or partially completed elementary school. These include young men who have worked for short periods in jobs requiring education - as messengers, clerks, perhaps even teachers - and those who are still seeking an opportunity to find employment. In the village they are now starting to farm.

One of the few jobs available to holders of a Middle School Leaving Certificate with no further education is that of Pupil Teacher; many school in small villages in Sehwi were staffed entirely by them.

The teaching profession

Elementary schools are run either by Local Councils or by Churches: in both cases all teachers are employees of the Ministry of Education which pays their salaries. Teacher training facilities are mainly provided by the Ministry of Education. The usual qualification for Teacher training is the Middle School Leaving Certificate. Teacher training is free, unlike secondary schooling. The course is four years and teaches up to a standard of fourth year secondary school, with the addition of education and teaching practice. Teachers then register either with a Regional Ministry of Education or with a Church Educational Unit and these allocate postings. Teachers are bound by contract to work for five years. School-leavers who apply but fail to gain entrance to a Training College may be employed as Pupil Teachers for a maximum of five years.

The District Education Office makes the decision as to where schools are to be built: in some cases this is upon application from a village which must show evidence that there are at least 12 children of school-going age ready to enrol. The Local Council is responsible for building schools but in fact many primary schools are built and maintained by the community. The community may provide its own school but it may not employ its own teachers. And there is no contract between the community and the District Education Office or the Local Council relating to the school or to the teachers. The community has no direct means of controlling its teachers; teachers are neither employed, paid, transferred nor dismissed by the community; they teach the children but have no contract with the parents to teach them according to their own standards.

The teachers in Sehwi

The teachers in Sehwi had certain marked characteristics. 90% of them were males; the few females received more favourable postings and were usually to be found in the larger town rather than the small villages. 85% of them were under the age of 30, the peak age being 24 to 25[5]. Over 50% of them were Pupil Teachers; of these the majority were Sehwi since

THE VILLAGE SCHOOL TEACHER IN GHANA　　　251

Pupil Teachers were usually employed locally. Over 50% of the total
were strangers to the District. Most teachers spent only two or three
years in one community before seeking a transfer and very few had more
than two or three years teaching experience. 90% of teachers were of
the first generation in their family to be educated.

Teacher Training is free and provides access to a higher level of
education than a child from a poor home could otherwise obtain. A
majority of trained teachers in Sehwi did not regard their job as a
terminal vocation. On the contrary, while the salaries for teachers
are commensurable with those for members of other professions with
equivalent educational qualifications, it was felt that the conditions
of service were not and this caused great dissatisfaction. One of the
greatest causes for complaint lay in the peculiar circumstances of a
teacher's job which require him, almost alone of educated men, to live
in small villages : just the kind of life which his education might be
expected to allow him to leave behind. Training Colleges with their
facilities such as electricity, medical treatment, libraries and the
company of fellow students, are not the best preparation for the conditions of a village. While many Pupil Teachers had no equivalent experience, their choice lay between going to Training College or going
back to farming. Most teachers were serving their bond and hoping,
perhaps in vain owing to the unemployment situation, to find an alternative occupation. This attitude certainly affected teacher relations
with the community; indeed nobody regarded teaching as a particularly
desirable employment. Illiterate parents, almost as much as their
educated children, hoped that if their children did seek salaried employment, it would at least have better prospects than those of teaching.

The fact that the majority of teachers had a number of characteristics in common made it relatively easier to generalise about their position in the community. In one sense the problem is reduced to the status
attached to 'young male stranger'. It was under this head that most
people discussed teachers. But the teacher is a 'young male stranger'
of a particular kind; he is not formally dependent upon the community's
resources for his subsistence; he has not achieved his authority over
children with the community's consent. These characteristics can now
be discussed in relation to the structure, attitudes and values of the
community.

The age factor

Age is in part an ascriptive factor in the acquisition of social
status and prestige in Sehwi society. It is not entirely so, for a
young man (or woman) may be elected to office and therefore become an
'elder' *(mpayine)*. Even so, he would be expected to take advice from
his 'elders'. The category of 'elders' is opposed in constitutional
terms to that of *mmerandie*. This term has often been translated into
English as 'young men'; strictly speaking it means 'commoners', that is,
people who do not hold office. The association between office and age,
however, is apparent.

A single man has lower status than a married man. A young man is
unlikely to build a house of his own until he has a wife; until that
time he lives with his father or lineage kin[6] and is under their domestic

252 *CHANGING SOCIAL STRUCTURE IN GHANA*

authority. Indeed, without a wife it is difficult for a man to start a farm and become economically self-sufficient.

Over half the teachers in the sample stated that they were married. Even so, teachers rarely lived with their wives especially if they had been posted to remote villages. There was a strong tendency among teachers to regard their postings as temporary and in any case they were usually away from their workplace during vacations. Many of their wives were petty traders and it was therefore better economically for them to live in larger villages or towns. Even if they were farmers themselves, the teacher as stranger has no right to land in his workplace (although the community may give him some) and therefore his wife's labour was of little value to him there . Also because they were strangers in the community, teachers did not build houses in their workplace, unless perhaps it was a large town where they could gain extra income from rent.

In effect, therefore, most teachers lived the life of young, unmarried males. In small villages they were generally provided with free accommodation tion in the house of an elder. Their relationship to their landlord was similar in many respects to that of an unmarried son to his father and they usually addressed him as 'father'. His wives prepared the teacher's meals, also without payment. The 'father' acted on his behalf in relations with the community if these were not of a professional nature. In return, the teacher owed the services of a son although he was not generally called upon to fulfil them.

The teacher as stranger

Only 48% of teachers in the sample were Sehwi. Of these, 10% were working in a Sehwi state other than that of their birthplace. Of the remaining 52%, 35% came from other Akan-speaking areas, mainly Ashanti, Denkyera and Fante. 17% came from non-Akan speaking areas, mainly Ewe. Very few stranger teachers learnt to speak Sehwi and while in most cases Asante-Twi provided a common language, many Ewe teachers spoke no Twi and had no common language with the community.

The language difficulties of stranger teachers created both social barriers and professional problems. In extreme cases their choice of friends was limited to other teachers, to the few English speakers in a community, generally young men rather than elders, and to migrant farmers in the locality who were similarly cut off in their social relations. Such teachers had to use English as their medium of instruction in schools, and found their professional contacts with parents severely hampered on such issues as the collection of school fees and the organisation of communal labour for the schools.

Nevertheless, language problems were usually no more than an indication of the more fundamental problems of being a stranger in a community in which citizenship rights are based upon the ascriptive criteria of lineage membership. Membership of a matrilineage incorporated into the state is the basic qualification for citizenship. Incorporation implies that the matrilineage owns a stool and title to office within the state, thus having direct political representation. The *kro* where the stool and title are vested is where the primary identity of the citizen lies, for it is in that place that a person holds rights to land and can succeed to

THE VILLAGE SCHOOL TEACHER IN GHANA

253

political office. While a man whose matrilineage holds stool and office in the village of X may settle in the village of Y for the purposes of farming, he has no access to hereditary office there and his primary rights as a citizen remain in the village of X. A woman who marries virilocally retains her citizenship in the village where her matrilineage holds office. When settlement for the purposes of farming or marriage takes place in other villages within the state in which a man's citizenship is primarily vested, he never at any time loses his direct representation through his matrilineage. When, however, a man settles in a State other than that where his rights of citizenship are vested, he has no direct representation and is therefore not a citizen of that state.

The term used to describe both men who are resident in a village other than that of their own matrilineage and men resident in a state where they have no citizenship rights is *wohoe*, which may be translated as 'stranger'. It is clear that there are, or at least have been in the past, means whereby a *wohoe* can 'convert' to the status of citizen. Oral history of the foundation of the State describes this expressly. Incoming groups in the successive waves of migration were offered titles and land in order to effect incorporation. During this period, the development of the state depended upon the increase of its manpower. Wealth accrued to the community from the labour and tribute of those who worked on its land and the ability to attract people to settle was of primary importance. Newcomers were offered the protection of representation in the state.

Nevertheless, the obligations of a citizen and those of a *wohoe* are clearly distinguished. The citizen has free access to land belonging to his matrilineage: he does not pay tribute on it nor share any part of its produce. His obligations as a citizen are to pay levies when they are demanded by the village through his matrilineal head, to observe the laws and rituals of the community and to contribute labour towards communal tasks. The stranger, on the other hand, has to pay tribute on the land and the crops he produces, but he may not pay levies and need not contribute his labour.

While differing rights in land are a fundamental aspect of the distinction between the status of citizen and stranger, a more relevant distinction for the purpose of this paper lies in the nature of the authority that a community can exert over its citizens as against strangers. The community holds authority over its members because vested in it are the rights upon which a citizen depends: his right to land, his right to office, his identity as a citizen. It is the place where the individual is most willing to expend labour and wealth in the accumulation of prestige, for by these means he increases his chances of gaining office and acquiring power. In order to do this, he must be seen to be obeying the laws and customs of the community. To take an example, a certain village totally prohibited the possession of dogs because of the presence of a god. While this caused considereble inconvenience since dogs are normally used for hunting, none of the citizens flouted the custom. One stranger, however, was able to do so by building his house outside the ritual boundary of the village, a thing which no citizen would consider doing. The home town is also the place where most people are actively concerned in the good behaviour of a member of the family, to protect it from disrepute. Nothing could be more explicit than the disgusted comment of an elder on the drunken behaviour of a visiting Census officer: 'He would not behave like that if he were at home'

254 *CHANGING SOCIAL STRUCTURE IN GHANA*

The community, therefore, exercises legitimate authority over its members because their own rights are dependent upon the proper exercise of their responsibilities. Only those members of lineages incorporated into the community may elect their Chief and only they may destool him.

However, the teacher's rights are not dependent upon the community, but upon the Ministry of Education which employs him, pays him, posts him and transfers him. The teacher is not responsible for the organisation and success of his school to the community where it is situated, but to the Local Education Office which has no established or contractual relationship with the community at all.

Of the total sample of teachers, only 6% were working in the villages where their citizenship rights were based. By far the vast majority were strangers in this sense to the system of authority within the community where they worked. The community might invent means to exercise control over its teachers, but they were otherwise not responsible to it.

The community did seek such means by which to control its teachers. Most teachers in villages (although not in towns) were given free accomodation and food; land was made available to them if they required it for their own farms; and since they generally had neither wife nor children to work their land, they were permitted to use the labour of their pupils. In this way the community sought to establish relations with the teacher of the kind which it had with its individual members: to act as the source of their livelihood. At the same time, the community did not normally demand of its teachers the corresponding obligations of a citizen. Perhaps the most relevant of these was the obligation to contribute labour to communal enterprises, an obligation which would normally fall upon its young male members (*mmerandie*).

The rationale of this exception seemed to derive from the allocation of a total social identity to certain status or occupational categories. The category 'elder' was exempt from communal labour whatever the actual age of the incumbent. So too was the category 'schoolboy'. In the latter case, a young man who was attending school (elementary or secondary) was exempt even during vacations. Teachers were exempted on a similar principles; it was evident that their total social identity was derived from their occupation since they were invariably addressed as 'Teacher' and many people knew them by no other name. This identity, however, only operated where their profession took them; teachers were not exempted in their home town, if it was not their place of work, where their identity derived from their ascriptive age and political status.

In such circumstances as these, teachers often lived better than they would in their home towns, for these 'privileges' were not clearly accompanied by equivalent responsibilities or, to put it more precisely, in their role as teachers they were not accountable to the community. It became clear that deteriorating relationships between teachers and the community generally developed from the failure of a teacher to acknowledge the privileges by fulfilling the required obligations. When they too blatantly ignored the obligations that the community demanded of them as teachers, the community was forced into alternative action.

The teacher's role

The community's interpretation of the teacher's role almost invariably related less to his professional abilities and more to the performance of the expectations associated with the social category 'teachers'. This was perhaps not surprising since it was difficult for illiterate parents to judge the progress of their children in school, a place which they rarely visited. The expectations concerning a teacher's behaviour were logically those which corresponded to his privileges, which were something like those of an elder. To some extent, the community had handed over to him the responsibility for bringing up children and therefore he had to be an exemplary adult, as well as a 'teacher of books'. The most important criteria were his behaviour towards women, his abstention from drinking and smoking, his presence in school during school hours (the nearest a community was able to judge of his professional competence), his treatment of the children and his participation in the affairs of the community.

His relations with women made him extremely vulnerable to accusations of failure to live up to expectations since as a wage-earning stranger a teacher has many advantages over other young men. Almost none of the restrictions existing between the sexes apply to the teacher. The Sehwi matrilineage is exogamous but sanctions are rarely applied to sexual intercourse between distant members of the same matrilineage provided marriage does not occur. Within the local lineage, sanctions would be strictly applied but a stranger teacher does not have any such links with members of the community. Moreover, even if a teacher is of Akan origin and therefore a member of a matrilineage known to Sehwi, many people will not know what lineage he belongs to. Sexual relations are also forbidden between close members of the same patriline (*wodaa*), again a set of relations which the stranger teacher does not possess. Theoretically, the stranger teacher has sexual access to a far greater number of women in the community than any other young man.

Moreover, fathers are responsible for the sexual misdemeanours of their sons and are liable for any debts arising from them. They are, therefore, expected to check any tendency towards illicit relationships. The teacher has no father or kinsman to perform such a function. In the crowded circumstances of village domestic life, few young men have a room of their own to indulge in even licit sexual relations; the teacher is an exception to this. Moreover, sexual relations are forbidden in the farms and the forest; one of the few places relatively far from the surveillance of adults and yet not outside the village proper is the school. It is frequently mentioned as a place where unmarried men and women consort and not surprisingly the teacher is suspect from his connection with it. Many parents forbid their daughters to attend night study in school for this very reason. In order to find a girl most young men have to go outside their home village where they are not under the supervision of their parents.

It is commonly acknowledged that young girls like boy friends who can buy them gifts. While a teacher many not be rich, he will certainly have more cash than an unemployed young man whose farm has not yet started to produce crops. Brokensha (1966) has commented on this factor in other parts of Ghana where teachers and lorry drivers (another category of wage-earning stranger) are the people most commonly charged with

256 *CHANGING SOCIAL STRUCTURE IN GHANA*

the seduction of girls. Traditionally, the penalties of seducing an unmarried girl, provided she had passed menstruation, were not very serious. If she became pregnant, the seducer was required to provide for her subsistence during her pregnancy and for that of the child during a period of six months after birth. He then paid a sum of money (*esi ase* - 'to put her behind') to her father and that ended his responsibility. Such a sum may have been as little as two or three pounds. A quite remarkable change in customary law has taken place on this point. Sums up to £300 are demanded, and sometimes awarded, in arbitration or in public courts, for a seduction of unmarried girls, particularly schoolgirls. Most of the men named in such cases are teachers. It is admitted that the teacher may not always be responsible. What is significant is that he is one of the few men who might be supposed to be able to afford such high sums and who would not be able to bring familial pressure upon the girl's family to reduce the penalty. The combination of a teacher's greater advantages in relation to girls, and his greater vulnerability as a wage-earning stranger, makes him suspect in more cases than those in which he is probably guilty. But his behaviour is required to be exemplary, and to most teachers the risks of involving themselves with women are one of the most serious problems in their relations with the community.

Restrictions concerning the teacher's freedom to smoke and drink are perhaps of a similar nature. A young man's tendencies in this respect are normally limited by his means and by parental supervision, both of which restrictions are less in the case of a stranger teacher. But in addition his job requires him to be in charge of children and young adults and therefore he is expected to behave as if he were a parent, although in many cases he is little older than the people he teaches.

When the teacher's behaviour in the performance of his role failed to live up to the expectations of the community, then explicit and sometimes severe sanctions were used, directed towards correcting his behaviour or seeking his expulsion from the community. It was his status as stranger which made him particularly vulnerable to such attacks. For instance, I have stated that the teacher in a village is perhaps fed and housed freely in order to create obligations on his part. It must be pointed out, however, that such privileges are also necessities from the point of view of the teacher. Almost alone in a village, he is not self-sufficient in foodstuffs nor can he demand accommodation as a member of a family. When cash is available to a farmer, he need rarely spend it on food but on things which can only be obtained with cash - clothes, transport, medical treatment and so on. The farmer provides his own subsistence to such an extent that small villages rarely contain a market and there is only casual selling of basic foodstuffs often at inflated prices. The sparse and scattered nature of settlement in Sehwi causes markets to be few and far apart and they are usually held in any case on a teacher's working day when he is not free to travel. It is perfectly understood that the non-farmer is in difficulties over food and that the community will have to feed him. While the frequent complaints of teachers about food shortages may sometimes derive from their lack of control over the source of food, when a teacher had incurred displeasure, the community reacted by denying him food. Such crises are documented in teacher's letters of complaint to the Education Office when requesting transfers; no more effective measure than the refusal of food could be taken by the community should it want to get rid of its teachers or to check their behaviour.

THE VILLAGE SCHOOL TEACHER IN GHANA 257

Other attacks were observed which were perhaps of a similar nature in that they were attacks against the life, if not the livelihood, of the teacher. For instance, 'juju' objects (*amoen*) were placed on the teachers' desks. While teachers claimed that they could not be harmed by them, they were certainly understood as signs of aggression. *Amoen* are a conventional means of mystical attack against strangers.

But direct sanctions against teachers may not be effective if the community intends to use them to cause their transfer to another village. For the Education Office does not withdraw teachers on the grounds that they have failed to establish good relations with the community: it will only do so when evidence is provided that the teacher has transgressed the Code of Discipline. This code provides penalties for offences similar to those which the community itself might try to sanction. There are penalties for absenteeism and drinking and smoking in school hours but the penalties are demotion rather than transfer. The only offence which is sanctioned by dismissal is the seduction of a schoolgirl.

For effective action against the teacher, therefore, the community has to approach the Education Office directly and provide charges which can be substantiated. Yet there are no established channels through which it can do so. The community may use the infrequent visits of an Education Officer to make its complaints. Or it may write to the Education Office. There are many examples of such letters in the files, signed by Chiefs and Elders, or by Village Development Committees. There are also a number of unsigned letters by accusation. Whether signed or unsigned, they all receive the appellation 'anonymous' by the Education Office and the general attitude towards them, of which perhaps the name is evidence, is that they are illegitimate approaches to authority, not sanctioned by the structure of the educational system. Even when such complaints are investigated, the community is not necessarily satisfied with a verdict against it, and may go on to appeal to an alternative authority. One village, for example, with a long history of difficulties with its untrained teachers, took them to Court. The difficulties were of the kinds referred to above. The teachers were frequently absent from school and one of them seduced a village girl. The elders summoned the teachers to reproach them for their behaviour but there was no improvement. Direct physical attacks then began; the houses of the teachers were stoned and their property stolen from the school. The elders asked the Education Office to take action but nothing was done. The community then made a decision that the teachers should become liable to perform communal labour from which as was customary they had previously been exempt. The teachers failed to comply and the community charged them in the Magistrate's Court with refusal to obey its bye-laws. The Magistrate ruled that the teachers could not be liable to communal labour since their professional tasks should occupy them sufficiently. Having failed in their appeal to two types of authority, the community took the final measure of withdrawing their children from school. This action ultimately succeeded in getting rid of the teachers, though perhaps not in the fashion which the community intended, since the school was temporarily closed down and finally amalgamated with another several miles away.

The obligation to do communal labour is an important reference of status and citizenship. In this case, and it was not   unique, the community's action developed from the principles already described. By offering teachers the privileges of citizens, without the concomitant

CHANGING SOCIAL STRUCTURE IN GHANA

obligations, the community expects the teachers to carry out the obligations associated both their professional and social roles. When the
teachers fail to do so, such privileges are withdrawn and in this case
it seemed as if the community had decided that since the teachers were
behaving no better than other young men in the community, then they
should be obliged to carry out the responsibilities of such other
young men.

The difficulties and hostility which a teacher encounters arise
in many respects from incompatible role expectations. His personal
status as a young man conflicts with his professional status as a
teacher, for a young man is not responsible for children, is not
required to be over-circumspect in his relations with women, nor to
be too restrained in his use of alcohol. While there are limitations
on this behaviour, a young man is expected to look for girls and to
drink in a moderate fashion[7]. But a young man will also be expected
to participate in the affairs of the community and by so doing build up
his prestige to the point where he can achieve positions of responsibility.

The stranger is not restricted from the performance of formal or
non-formal offices in the community provided they are not ascriptive.
Indeed, appointive offices are often filled by strangers, perhaps
because they are expected to work harder for the benefit of the community as a whole rather than for segments of it. Skills in oratory and
diplomacy and experience in affairs outside the State, have been employed
by the State whether they belonged to a stranger or a citizen. One of
the skills in great demand at present is literacy and experience in
bureaucratic procedures. Teachers in the past possessed these skills
almost to the exclusion of anybody else. They were the letter writers
and ambassadors of their communities. But they have now lost their
monopoly. A man will invariably prefer to ask his schoolboy son to
write his letters for him; it is better than a stranger knowing of his
private affairs. A Chief employs an educated citizen to look after his
affairs in negotiations with the Local Council or other Government body.
Nevertheless, if a stranger has skills superior to those to be found
locally, then his services will be exploited. In one village a stranger
farmer who had worked for many years in a bureaucratic position was in
constant demand in negotiations with the Local Council over roofing sheets
for the school. The community was well aware that its own pupil teachers
had no experience in such matters.

The position of a trained teacher was somewhat different; his experience was seen to be greater. But he had to show evidence that he was
willing to participate, and that he was capable of discharging the responsibilities. Few trained teachers reached this point, for one of their
major disadvantages lay in the very short time most of them spent in a
single community, generally not long enough to establish themselves as
eligible for office.

In the questionnaires, teachers were asked to state if they held any
office within the community where they worked. Such offices were chairman
or member of Village Development Committees; membership of church committees, civic societies, sports clubs, and so on, all of them elective.
About a quarter of the teachers in the sample held such an office and they
possessed marked characteristics: they were rather older than average and
they had worked in the village for a longer period. The differences between

THE VILLAGE SCHOOL TEACHER IN GHANA

the chances of a Sehwi and a non-Sehwi teacher were not significant. Only the very few teachers who happened not only to be Sehwi but also working in their home towns held a greater chance of holding office.

CONCLUSION

The role of the teacher in Sehwi demands that he behave as an exemplary adult, bearing the privileges and obligations of such a status. But the teachers which the Education Office supplies to the villages are young men. While a young man who is a member of the community has a vested interest in building up his reputation there, a stranger's right to ascriptive office is elsewhere and his interest in building up his prestige is low since he cannot transfer it to his home. While a stranger is not excluded from office and responsibility, he must demonstrate his capacity for carrying it, a process which takes time and familiarisation. While the teacher once had exclusive skills which would perhaps have overridden other factors, these have now become more diffuse and his position must rest upon what he can make of himself in the community. But the teacher does not want to live in a farming village any more than other educated young men who migrate to the towns; his interest lies not in building up a reputation for himself there but in finding a way of getting out of his present situation. A majority of trained teachers were doing no more than working out their bonds after which they hoped to be able to invest their education in some more attractive enterprise; the untrained teachers hoped to get their free education and would then follow suit. With a few notable exceptions, teachers in Sehwi were members of a dissatisfied profession who found few compensations in terms of the social status accorded to them in their place of work.

NOTES

1. This paper is based on fifteen months' fieldwork in Ghana between June 1969 and October 1970. The research was financed by grants from the Smuts Memorial Fund and a Henry Ling Roth Scholarship.

2. It is commonly stated of education in the early days in West Africa that the first children to be sent to school were slaves. The then Omanhene of Sehwi Wiawso is recorded as having had a strong dislike for the introduction of both Christianity and a school in 1915. One, he said, was good for strangers but not for his people; the other he had to be forced to build.

3. While the named matrilineages of Akan culture are also present in Sehwi, the 'indigenous' Sehwi do not belong to such matrilineages and many other people know themselves only by the name of a distant but traceable ancestress.

4. The Omanhene of Sehwi Wiawso was traditionally not allowed to cross the River Subrae, which forms the eastern boundary of the State and is the national god of Sehwi. Foreign relations had to be conducted by his junior chiefs or appointed officers.

260   *CHANGING SOCIAL STRUCTURE IN GHANA*

5.   The characteristics of teachers in Sehwi were not markedly different from those in other parts of Ghana. See Chacko and Subrahmanya (1969).

6.   A man usually continues to live in his father's house until his father dies or until he inherits from his mother's brother. Only if his father were neglecting him, or if his mother's brother requested permission from the father to have the son, would he otherwise leave.

7 .   Certain social occasions, such as funerals, permit a man to get drunk.

REFERENCES

ACQUAH, I. 1950 *Marriage and family life among educated Africans in urban areas of the Gold Coast*. Unpub. MSc thesis, University of London.

ALLAND, A. 1963 'Residence, domicile and descent groups among the Abron of the Ivory Coast' *Ethnology*, 2, 276-81.

ALUKO, S.A. 1965 'How many Nigerians? an analysis of Nigeria's census problems, 1901-1963', *J. mod. Afr. Stud.*, 3, 371-92.

AMSELLE, J.-L. 1971 'Parenté et commerce chez les Kooroko' in: *The development of indigenous trade and markets in West Africa*, ed. C. Meillassoux, London.

ANKRAH, E.M. 1973 'Women's liberation: has the African woman settled for tokens?' *New Blackfriars*, 54, 264-74.

ANON. 1971 'The challenge of rapid urbanization to Nigerian local government'. Paper presented at the Fourth National Conference on Local Government. mimeo.

ARIES, P. 1962 *Centuries of childhood, a social history of family life*, trans. R. Baldick, New York.

ARONSON, D.R. 1970 *Cultural stability and social change among the Ijebu Yoruba*. Unpub. PhD thesis, University of Chicago.

ASANTE, D. 1886 'Eine Reise nach Salaga und Obooso durch die Länder im Osten des mittleren Volta', *Mitt. geogr. Gesellschaft zu Jena*, trans. J. Christaller, 4, 15-40.

AZU, G. 1974 *The Ga family and social change*. Leiden.

BAILEY, F.G. 1965 'Decisions by consensus in councils and committees' in: *Political systems and the distribution of power*. ASA monograph no 2, London.

BANTON, M. 1957 *West African city: a study of tribal life in Freetown*. London.

BARAN, P. 1973 *The political economy of growth*. Harmondsworth.

BARNARD, G. 1968 *Ville africaine, famille urbaine: les enseignants de Kinshasa*. Paris.

BARTH, F. (ed.) 1963 *The role of the entrepreneur in social change in northern Norway*. Acta Universitatis Bergensis, no. 3, Bergen.

——— 1969 *Ethnic groups and boundaries: the social organization of culture differences*. London.

BASCOM, W.R. 1942 'The principle of seniority in the social structure of the Yoruba', *American anthropologist*, 44, 37-46.

——— 1969 *The Yoruba of southwestern Nigeria*. New York.

BECKETT, W.H. 1944 *Akokoaso: A survey of a Gold Coast village*. LSE monograph soc. Anthrop. no. 10, London.

BENDER, D. 1967 'A refinement of the concept of household: families, co-residence, and domestic functions', *American anthropologist*, 69, 493-504.

——— 1970 'Agnatic or cognatic? A re-evaluation of Ondo descent', *Man* (NS) 5, 71-87.

——— 1971 'De facto families and de jure households in Ondo', *American anthropologist* 73, 223-41.

BIEBUYCK, D. (ed.) 1963 *African agrarian systems*. London.

BOHANNAN, P. 1963 *Social anthropology*. New York.

BOHANNAN, P. & L. 1968 *Tiv economy*. London.

262   *CHANGING SOCIAL STRUCTURE IN GHANA*

BOSERUP, E.   1970 *Woman's role in economic development*. London.
BOSMAN, W.   1967 *A new and accurate description of the coast of Guinea*
   (4th ed). London.
BOTT, E.   1957 *Family and social network*. London.
BOWDICH, T.E.   1872 *Mission from Cape Coast to Ashantee*. London.
BRADBURY, R.E.   1957 *The Benin Kingdom*. Ethnographic Survey of Africa,
   London.
BRAY, J.M.   1968 'The organization of traditional weaving in Iseyin,
   Nigeria', *Africa*, 38, 270-9.
BROKENSHA, D.   1962 *Volta resettlement: ethnographic notes on some of*
   the southern areas. Legon.
—— 1966 *Social change at Larteh, Ghana*. Oxford.
BUCHLER, I. & H. SELBY 1968 *Kinship and social organization*. London.
BUSIA, K.A.   1950 *Report on a social survey of Sekondi Takoradi*. Accra.
—— 1951 *The position of the chief in the modern political system of*
   Ashanti. London.
—— 1954 'The Ashanti of the Gold Coast' in: *African worlds*, ed. D. Forde,
   London.
CALDWELL, J.C.   1968 *Population growth and family change in Accra: the new*
   urban élite in Ghana. Canberra.
—— 1969 *African rural-urban migration: the movement to Ghana's towns*.
   Canberra.
CARROLL, V. (ed.) 1970 *Adoption in eastern Oceania*. Hawaii.
CHACKO, V.J. & M.T. SUBRAHMANYA 1969 'Middle school teachers in Ghana',
   Institute of statistical, social and economic research technical
   publications, no. 7, Legon.
CHAMBERS, R. (ed.) 1970 *The Volta resettlement experience*. London.
CHAPIN, F.   1938 'The effects of slum clearance and rehousing on family
   and   unity relationships in Minneapolis', *American J. sociology*,
   43, 744-63.
CLAPPERTON, H. & R. LANDER 1829 *Journal of a second expedition into the*
   interior of Africa. London.
CLARKE, E.   1966 (2nd ed.) *My mother who fathered me*. London.
CLIGNET, R.   1970 *Many wives, many powers*. Evanston, Ill.
—— & J. SWEEN 1969 'Social change and type of marriage', *American J.*
   sociology, 75, 123-45.
COHEN, Abner 1965 'The social organization of credit in a West African
   cattle market', *Africa*, 35, 8-20.
—— 1966 'Politics of the kola trade', *Africa*, 36, 18-36.
—— 1969 *Custom and politics in urban Africa*. London.
COHEN, R.   1967 *The Kanuri of Bornu*. New York.
CORNFORD, F.M.   1908 *Microcosmographia academica*. London.
CRUIKSHANK, B.   1853 *Eighteen years on the Gold Coast*. London.
DANQUAH, J.B.   1922 *Akan laws and customs*. London.
—— 1928 *Cases in Akan law*. London.
DEBRUNNER, H.   1959 *Witchcraft in Ghana*. Kumasi.
DE GRAFT-JOHNSON, K.E.   1966 'The evolution of elites in Ghana' in: *The*
   new elites of tropical Africa, ed. P.C. Lloyd, London.
DERRETT, J.D.M. (ed.) 1965 *Studies in the laws of succession in Nigeria*.
   London.
DILLON, E.J.   1895 *The sceptics of the Old Testament*. London.
DIOP, A.B.   1965 *Société toucouleur et migration*. Dakar.
DOUGLAS, M.   1963 *The Lele of the Kasai*. London.
DUNN, J. & A.F. ROBERTSON (in press) *Dependence and opportunity: political*
   change in Ahafo, Ghana. Cambridge.

REFERENCES

DUPIRE, M. 1960 *Planteurs autochtones et étrangers en Basse-Côte d'Ivoire Orientale,* Etudes Eburnéennes VIII, Abidjan.

DURKHEIM, E. 1950 *Rules of sociological method.* (first pub 1895) Illinois.

—— 1964 *The division of labour in society.* Illinois.

EHRLICH, P. & J. FREEDMAN 1971 'Population, crowding and human behaviour', *New scientist and science J.,* 50,10-14.

ELIAS, T.O. 1963 *Nigerian land law and custom.* London.

ELLIS, A.B. 1887 *The Tshi-speaking peoples.* London.

EPSTEIN, A.L. 1961 'The network and urban social organization', *Rhodes-Livingstone institute J.,* 29 (reprinted in Mitchell, 1969).

EYRE-SMITH, St. J. 1933 *A brief review of the history and social organization of the peoples of the northern territories of the Gold Coast.* Accra.

FADIPE, N.A. 1970 *The sociology of the Yoruba.* ed. F.O. Okediji & O.O. Okediji. Ibadan.

FALADE, S. 1963 'Women of Dakar and the surrounding urban area' *Women in tropical Africa.* ed. D. Paulme, London.

FARBER, B. (ed.) 1966 *Kinship and family organization.* New York.

FFOULKES, A. 1908-9 'Borgya and Abirwa', *J. African Soc.,* 8, 387-97.

FIELD, M.J. 1940 *Social organisation of the Ga people.* London.

—— 1958 'Mental disorders in rural Ghana' *J. mental science.* 101, 1043-51.

—— 1960 *Search for security: an ethnopsychiatric study of rural Ghana.* London.

FOGARTY, M.P. et al. 1971 *Sex, career and family.* London.

FORDE, D. 1960 'The cultural map of West Africa: Successive adaptations to tropical forest and grasslands' *in: Cultures and societies of Africa* eds S. & P. Ottenberg, New York.

—— 1964 *Yakö studies.* London.

FORTES, M. 1936 'Culture contact as a dynamic process', *Africa,* 24-55.

—— 1945 *The dynamics of clanship among the Tallensi.* London.

—— 1948 'The Ashanti social survey: a preliminary report', *Rhodes-Livingstone institute J.,* 6.

—— 1949a 'The homestead and the joint family' in: *The web of kinship among the Tallensi* London, 44-77.

—— 1949b 'Time and social structure: an Ashanti case study' in: *Time and social structure and other essays,* London.

—— 1949c *The web of kinship among the Tallensi.* London.

—— 1950 'Kinship and marriage among the Ashanti' in: *African systems of kinship and marriage,* eds. A.R. Radcliffe-Brown & D. Forde, London.

—— 1958 'Introduction' in: *The developmental cycle in domestic groups,* ed. J. Goody, Cambridge.

—— 1963 'The "submerged descent line" in Ashanti' *Studies in kinship and marriage* ed I. Schapera, RAI occasional paper no. 16.

—— 1965 'Discussion' of a paper by Hes on 'Housing and mental health' *Ciba symposium on transcultural psychiatry,* eds. A. deReuck & R. Porter, London, 128, 132-3.

—— 1969 *Kinship and the social order.* Chicago.

—— 1970 *Kinship and the social order.* London.

—— 1973 'The Akan family system today' *Legon family research papers* no. 1, I.A.S. Legon.

—— & S.L. FORTES 1937 'Food in the domestic economy of the Tallensi', *Africa,* 9, 237-276.

—— & D. MAYER 1969 'Psychosis and social change among the Tallensi of northern Ghana', *Psychiatry in a changing society* eds S. Foulkes & G. Prince, London, 33-73.

FORTES & W. STEEL & P. ADY 1947 'Ashanti survey, 1945-6: An experiment in social research' *Geographical J.*, 60, 149-179.
FOSTER, P.J. 1965 *Education and social change in Ghana*. London.
FRAENKEL, M. 1964 *Tribe and class in Monrovia*. London.
FRANK, A.G. 1969 'The sociology of development and the underdevelopment of sociology' *Latin America: underdevelopment or revolution*. New York, 21-94.
FULLER, F. 1921 *A vanished dynasty*. London.
GAILEY, H.A. 1971 *The road to Aba*. London.
GALLETTI, R. et al. 1956 *Nigerian cocoa farmers*. London.
GARLICK, P.C. 1971 *African traders and economic development in Ghana*. London.
GEERTZ, C. 1963 *Peddlers and princes*. Chicago.
GIDDENS, A. 1971 *Capitalism and modern social theory*. Cambridge.
GIL, B., A.F. ARYEE & D.K. GHANSAH 1964 *Special report E. Tribes of Ghana*. Census office, Accra.
GONZALES, N.S. 1960 'Household and family in the Caribbean', *Social and economic studies*, 9, 106.
—— 1969 *Black Carib household structure*. Seattle.
GOODE, W.J. 1963 *World revolution and family patterns*. Illinois.
GOODY, E.N. 1961 *Kinship, marriage and the developmental cycle among the Gonja of northern Ghana*. Unpub. PhD thesis, University of Cambridge.
—— 1966 'Fostering of children in Ghana: a preliminary report' *Ghana J. Sociol.*, 2, 26-33.
—— 1969 'Kinship fostering in Gonja: deprivation or advantage?' *Socialization: the approach from social anthropology*, ed. P. Meyer, London.
—— 1970a 'Legitimate and illegitimate aggression in a West African state' in *Witchcraft, confessions and accusation*, ed. M. Douglas, London.
—— 1970b *The Kpembe study: a comparison of fostered and non-fostered children in eastern Gonja*. Manuscript report, SSRC, London.
—— 1971a 'Varieties of fostering', *New society*, 5th Aug, 237-9.
—— 1971b 'Forms of pro-parenthood: the sharing and substitution of parental roles' in: *Kinship*, ed. J. Goody, London.
—— 1973 *Contexts of kinship*. Cambridge.
—— & C.L. MUIR 1972 *Factors related to the delegation of parental roles among West Africans in London*. Manuscript report, SSRC, London.
GOODY, J.R. 1952 LoDagaa fieldnotes.
—— 1956 'A comparative approach to incest and adultery', *British J. sociology*, 7, 286-305.
—— 1957 'Anomie in Ashanti', *Africa*, 27, 356.
—— 1958a 'The fission of domestic groups among the LoDagaa' in: *The developmental cycle in domestic groups*, ed. J. Goody, Cambridge.
—— 1958b *The developmental cycle in domestic groups*. Cambridge.
—— 1959 'The mother's brother and the sister's son in West Africa', *JRAI* 89, 61-88.
—— 1961 'Religion and ritual: the definitional problem', *British J. sociology*, 12, 142-63.
—— 1962 *Death, property and the ancestors*. London.
—— 1969 *Comparative studies in kinship*. London.
—— 1970 'Marriage policy and incorporation in northern Ghana' in: *From tribe to nation in Africa*, eds R. Cohen & J. Middleton, Scranton, Pa.
—— 1972 *The myth of the Bagre*. Oxford.
—— 1973 'Polygyny, economy and the role of women' in: *The character of kinship*, ed. J. Goody, Cambridge.

REFERENCES

265

GOODY, J.R. (ed.) 1973 *The character of kinship*. Cambridge.
—— & J. BUCKLEY 1973 'Inheritance and women's labour in Africa' *Africa*, 43, 108-20.
—— & I. WATT 1963 'The consequences of literacy', *Comparative studies in society and history*, 5, 304-45.
GOUGH, K. 1952 'Changing kinship usages in the setting of political and economic change among the Nayars of Malabar' *JRAI* 82, 71-88.
—— 1961 'The modern disintegration of matrilineal descent groups' in: *Matrilineal kinship*, eds. D.M. Schneider & K. Gough, Berkeley.
GRANDMAISON, C. 1969 'Activités économiques des femmes dakaroises', *Africa* 39, 139-52.
—— 1973 'Roles traditionnels féminins et urbanisation: Lebou et Wolof de Dakar', *Annales de l'Université d'Abidjan*, Série F, Ethnosociologie Tome 4.
GRAY, R.F. & P.H. GULLIVER (eds.) 1964 *The family estate in Africa: studies in the role of property in family structure and lineage continuity*. London.
GREENSTREET, M. 1972 'Social change and Ghanaian women' *Canadian J. African Studies*, 6, 351-5.
GROVE, G.M. 1966 'Some aspects of the economy of the Volta delta (Ghana)', *Bulletin de l'Institut Fondamental d'Afrique Noire*, 28 (B), 381-432.
GUGLER, J. 1972 'The second sex in town' *Canadian J. African Studies*, 6, 289-301.
GUTKIND, P.C.W. 1965 'African urbanism, mobility and the social network' *International J. comparative sociology*, 6, 48-60.
GUYER, J.M. 1972 *The organizational plan of traditional farming*, Unpub. PhD thesis, University of Rochester, N.Y.
HALIBURTON, G.M. 1971 *The prophet Harris: a study of an African prophet and his mass movement in the Ivory Coast and the Gold Coast, 1913-1915*, London.
HARRINGTON, M. 1965 'Resettlement and self-image', *Human relations*, 18, 115-37.
HARRIS, R. 1965 'Interstate succession among the Mbembe of South-Eastern Nigeria' in: *Studies in the laws of succession in Nigeria*, ed. J. Derrett, Oxford, 91-138.
HART, J.K. 1969 *Entrepreneurs and migrants – a study of modernisation among the Frafras of Ghana*, Unpub PhD thesis, University of Cambridge.
—— 1970 'Small-scale entrepreneurs in Ghana and development planning', *J. development studies*, London, July, 104-20.
—— 1971 'Migration and tribal identity among the Frafras of Ghana', *J. Asian and African studies*, Leiden, 6, 21-36.
—— 1973 'Informal income opportunities and urban employment in Ghana', *J. mod. Afr. Stud.*, 11, 61-89.
—— 1974 'Migration and the opportunity structure: a Ghanaian case study' in: *Modern migrations in Western Africa*, ed. Samir Amin, London.
HENDERSON, R.N. 1973 *The King in every man*, New Haven, Conn.
HERBST, P.G. 1952 'The measurement of family relationships', *Human relations*, 5, 3-36.
—— 1954 'Conceptual framework for studying the family' in: *Social structure and personality in a city*, eds. O.A. Oeser & S.B. Hammond, London.
HERSKOVITZ, M.J. & W. HARWITZ (eds.) 1964 *Economic transition in Africa*, London.
HILL, P. 1956 *The Gold Coast cocoa farmer*. Oxford.
—— 1958 'Women cocoa farmers' in: *The Ghana Farmer*, Dept. of Agriculture, Accra.

HILL, P. 1963a 'Three types of Southern cocoa farmer' in: *African agrarian systems* ed. D. Biebuyck, London.
—— 1963b *The migrant cocoa farmers of Southern Ghana*. Cambridge.
—— 1963-4 'Pan-African fisherman', *West Africa* 28 Dec 1963 & 4 Jan 1964.
—— 1969 'Hidden trade in Hausaland' *Man* (NS), 4, 392-409.
—— 1970a *The occupations of migrants in Ghana*. Ann Arbor, Michigan.
—— 1970b *Studies in rural capitalism*. Cambridge.
—— 1972 *Rural Hausa: A village and a setting*. Cambridge.
—— 1974 'Big houses in Kano Emirate', *Africa*, 44, 117-35.
HOFFER, C.P. 1972 'Mende and Sherbro women in High Office', *Canadian J. African Studies* 6, 151-64.
HOLE, V. 1959 'Social effects of planned rehousing' *Town planning review* 30, 161-73.
HOROWITZ, M. 1967 *Morne-paysan: peasant village in Martinique*. New York.
HOSELITZ, B. 1952 'Entrepreneurship and economic growth' *American J. economic sociology* 12, 97-110.
HUTTON, W. 1821 *A voyage to Africa*. London.
IFEKA-MOLLER, C. 1973 '"Sitting on a man: colonialism and the lost political institutions of Igbo women": a reply to Judith Van Allen' *Canadian J. African Studies* 7, 317-18.
JONES, S.H.M. (ed.) 1962 *Handbook for African teacher organizations*. World conference of organizations of the teaching profession.
KABERRY, P.M. 1952 *Women of the grassfields: A study of the economic position of women in Bamenda, British Cameroons*. London.
KAMARCK, A. 1967 *The economics of African development*. London.
KATZIN, M. 1964 'The role of the small entrepreneur' in: *Economic transition in Africa*, eds. M. Herskovits & M. Harwitz, London, 179-98.
KEMP, D. 1898 *Nine years at the Gold Coast*. London.
KILSON, M.D. DeB. 1967 'Continuity and change in the Ga residential system' *Ghana J. sociology*, 3.
KLUCKHOHN, C. 1944 *Navaho witchcraft*. Cambridge, Mass.
LANDER, R. & J. 1832 *Journal of an expedition to explore the course and termination of the Niger*. London.
LEACH, E.R. 1968 'Marriage and divorce: the cereal packet norm', *Guardian*, London, Jan 29.
LEVINE, R.A. 1966 'Sex roles and economic change in Africa', *Ethnology* 5, 186-93.
—— et al. 1967 'Father-child relationships and changing life-styles in Ibadan, Nigeria', in: *The city in modern Africa* ed. H. Miner, London.
LEVTZION, N. 1968 *Muslims and chiefs in West Africa*. Oxford.
LEWIN, K. 1948 'The background of conflict in marriage', in: *Resolving social conflicts*, ed. G.W. Lewin, New York.
LEWIS, I.M. (ed.) 1966 *Islam in tropical Africa*. London.
LITTLE, K. 1957 'The role of voluntary associations in West African urbanization', *American anthropologist*, 59, 579-96.
—— 1965a *Social anthropology in modern life*. Inaugural lecture no.23, University of Edinburgh.
—— 1965b *West African urbanization*. Cambridge.
—— & A. PRICE 1967 'Some trends in modern marriage among West Africans', *Africa* 37, 407-24.
LLOYD, P.C. 1954 'The traditional political system of the Yoruba', *Southwestern journal of anthropology*, 10, 366-84.
—— 1955 'The Yoruba lineage', *Africa*, 25, 235-51.
—— 1962 *Yoruba land law*. London.

REFERENCES 267

LLOYD, P.C. 1965 'Yoruba inheritance and succession', in: *Studies in the laws of succession in Nigeria*, ed. J. Derrett, Oxford.
—— (ed.) 1966a *The new elites of tropical Africa*. London.
—— 1966b 'Agnatic & cognatic descent among the Yoruba', *Man* (NS), 1, 484-500.
—— 1967a 'The elite' in: *The city of Ibadan*, eds. P.C. Lloyd, A.L. Mabogunje & B. Awe, Cambridge.
—— 1967b *Africa in social change*. London.
—— 1968 'Divorce among the Yoruba', *American Anthropologist*, 70, 67-81.
LONG, N. 1968 *Social change and the individual*. Manchester.
LORING, W. 1956 'Housing characteristics and social disorganization', *Soc. problems*, 3, 160-8.
LUCAS, D. 1973 'Nigerian women and family resources', paper presented at Family Research Seminar, Institute of African Studies, University of Ghana. Mimeographed.
LUCKHAM, L.R. 1971 *The Nigerian military*. Cambridge.
LUMSDEN, D.P. 1971 'Schooling, employment, and Lake Volta: the Nchumuru case in Ghana', *Manpower and unemployment research in Africa*, 4, 26-45.
—— 1973 'The Volta River project: village resettlement and rural animation', *Canadian J. African studies*, 7, 115-32.
MADGE, J. 1968 'Housing: social aspects', *International encyclopaedia of the social sciences* 6, 516-21.
MAHLY, E. 1885 'Zur Geographie und Ethnographie der Goldküste', *Verhandlungen der naturforschenden Gesellschaft in Basel*, 7, 809-52 and map 13.
MANDEL, E. 1968 *Marxist economic theory*. London
MANOUKIAN, M. 1951 *Tribes of the northern territories of the Gold Coast*. London.
MARRIOTT, M. 1955 'Little communities in an indigenous civilization'. in: *Village India: studies in the little community*, ed. M. Marriott, Chicago.
MARRIS, P. 1961 *Family and social change in an African city*. London.
MARX, K. 1970 *Capital vol. I*. London.
MATHEWSON, R.D. 1967a 'Note on Bagyamso excavation', *Archaeology in the Volta basin, 1963-66*, University of Ghana, 16-18.
—— 1967b 'The painted pottery sequence in the Volta basin', *The West African archaeological newsletter*, University of Ibadan, 8, 24-31.
MAULE, H. & F. MARTIN 1956 'Social and psychological aspects of rehousing', *The advancement of science*, 12, 443-53.
MAYER, P. 1961 *Tribesmen or townsmen: conservatism and the process of urbanization in a South African city*. Cape Town.
MCCALL, D. 1961 'Trade and the role of wife in a modern West African town', in: *Social change in modern Africa* ed. A. Southall, London.
MEAD, M. (ed.) 1955 *Cultural patterns and technical change*. Mentor books.
MEILLASSOUX, C. 1964 *Anthropologie économique des Gouro de Cote d'Ivoire: de l'économie de subsistance à l'agriculture commerciale*. Paris.
—— 1968 *Urbanization of an African community*. Seattle.
MERTON, R.K. 1957 *Social theory and social structure*. Illinois.
MEYEROWITZ, E. 1962 *At the court of an African king*. London.
MILONE, V.M. & G.O. OLAORE 1971 'Tentative population projections for western Nigeria from air photographs and house occupancy measurements', *Nigerian opinion*, 7, 71-4.

CHANGING SOCIAL STRUCTURE IN GHANA

MINTZ, S.W. 1971 'Men, women and trade', *Comparative studies in society and history*, 12, 247-69.
—— 1973 'A note on the definition of peasantries', *J. peasant studies*, 1, 91-106.
MITCHELL, J.C. 1969 *Social networks in urban situations: analyses of personal relationships in central African towns*. Manchester.
MOGEY, J. 1955 'Changes in family life experienced by English workers moving from slums to housing estates', *Marriage and family living*, 17, 123-8.
MORGAN, Edmund S. 1944 *The Puritan family, religion and domestic relations in 17th century New England*. Boston.
MORTON-WILLIAMS, P. 1956 'The Attinga cult among the S.W. Yoruba', *Bull. IFAN*. 18.
MOXON, J. 1969 *Volta, man's greatest lake: the story of Ghana's Akosombo dam*. London.
MUIR, C.L. & E.N. GOODY 1972 'Student parents: West African families in London', *Race*, 13, 329-36.
NADEL, S.F. 1935 'Witchcraft and anti-witchcraft in Nupe society', *Africa*, 8, 423-47.
—— 1942 *A Black Byzantium: The Kingdom of Nupe in Nigeria*. London.
NASH, M. 1970 'Education in a new nation. The village school in upper Burmah', in: *From child to adult*, ed. J. Middleton, New York.
NICOLAS, G. 1964 *La vallee du Gulbi de Maradi: enquête socio-économique*, IFAN-CNRS, Bordeaux.
NUKUNYA, G.K. 1957 'Onion farming by the Keta lagoon', *Bull. Ghana geogr. Soc.*, 2, 12-15.
—— 1969 *Kinship and marriage among the Anlo Ewe*. London.
OBI, S.N.C. 1963 *The Ibo law of property*. London.
OESER, O.A. & S.B. HAMMOND 1954 *Social structure and personality in a city*. London.
OLLENNU, N.A. 1958 *Principles of customary land law in Ghana*. London.
—— 1966 *The law of testate and intestate succession in Ghana*. London.
OPOKU, K.A. 1970 'A directory of spiritual churches in Ghana', *Research review* 7, 98.
OPPONG, C. 1965 *Some sociological aspects of education in Dagbon*. M.A. thesis, Institute of African studies, Legon.
—— 1969a *Matriliny and marriage*. Paper presented at a conference on networks, Leiden, Afrika-Studiecentrum, September.
—— 1969b 'Education of relatives' children by senior civil servants in Accra' *Ghana J. child development,* 2.
—— 1969c 'A preliminary account of the role and recruitment of drummers in Dagbon', *Research review*, 6, 38-51.
—— 1970a 'Conjugal power and resources: an urban African example' *J. marriage and family*, 32, 676-80.
—— 1970b *Aspects of conjugal relationships among Akan senior civil servants in Accra*. PhD thesis, University of Cambridge, published as *Marriage among a matrilineal elite* Cambridge (1974,q.v.).
—— 1971a 'Urban household budgets', Paper presented at an interdisciplinary seminar on the family among the Akan and Ewe, published in *Legon family research papers, 1,* 1974.
—— 1971b 'Family change in Africa: a review', *Research review*, 7, 1-17.
—— 1971c '"Joint" conjugal roles and "extended families"', *J. comparative family studies*, 11, 178-87.
—— 1972A 'Norms and variations: a study of Ghanaian students' attitudes to marriage and family living' Paper presented at the 2nd interdisciplinary seminar on the family, Legon, forthcoming in *Legon family research papers, 3*.

REFERENCES

—— 1972b 'Education and change: the domestic system of an educated urban elite',*Research review,* 8.
—— 1972c 'The conjugal family "open" or "closed": prescribed norms for family relationships among Ghanaian university students', *Research review,* 8.
—— 1973 'Decision making and the exchange of resources among some urban Akan couples', forthcoming in *J. Asian and African studies,* special issue, ed. M. Fortes.
—— 1974 *Marriage among a matrilineal elite.* Cambridge.
OTTENBERG, S. 1968 *Double descent in an African society: The Afikpo village groups.* Seattle.
—— & P. (eds.) 1960 *Cultures and societies of Africa.* New York.
PAINE, R. 1963 'Entrepreneurial activity without its profits' in: *The role of the entrepreneur in social change in northern Norway,* ed. F. Barth, 33-55.
PAINTER, C. 1967 'The distribution of Guang in Ghana, and a statistical pre-testing of 25 (31) idiolects' *J. West African languages,* 4, 25-78.
PARKIN, D. 1972 *Palms, wine and witnesses.* San Francisco.
PEIL, M. 1971 'The expulsion of West African aliens', *J. mod. African Stud.,* 9, 205.
PFEFFERMAN, G. 1968 *Industrial labour in the republic of Senegal.* New York.
PLANT, J. 1937 'Family living space and personality development' in: *A modern introduction to the family,* eds. N. Bell & E. Vogel, London, 510-20 (in 1st ed. only).
PLATT, J. 1969 'Some problems in measuring jointness of conjugal role relationships', *Sociology* , 3, 287-98.
PLOTNICOV, L. 1970 'Rural-urban communications in contemporary Nigeria', in: *The passing of tribal man,* ed. P. Gutkind.
PRIESTLEY,M. 1969 *West African trade and coast society: a family study.* London.
QUANSAH, S.T. 1956-7 'The shallot industry, incorporating a recent survey of the Anloga growing area' *New Gold Coast farmer* 1, 45-9.
RADCLIFFE-BROWN, A.R. 1950 'Introduction', *African systems of kinship and marriage,* eds. A. Radcliffe-Brown & D. Forde, London, 1-85.
RAINWATER, L. 1965 *Family design.* Chicago.
RAMSEYER, F.A. & KUHNE, J. 1875 *Four years in Ashantee.* London.
RATTRAY, R.S. 1915 *Ashanti proverbs.* Oxford.
—— 1923 *Ashanti.* London.
—— 1927 *Religion and art in Ashanti.* Oxford.
—— 1957 (2nd ed) *Ashanti law and constitution.* Oxford.
REDFIELD, R. 1947 'The folk society', *American J. Sociology,* 52, 293-308.
RICHARDS, A.I. & KUPER, A. (eds.) 1971 *Councils in action.* Cambridge.
ROBERTSON, A.F. 1971 'The development of town committees in Ahafo, western Ghana', in: *Councils in action,* eds. A.I. Richards & A. Kuper, Cambridge.
—— 1973 'Histories and political opposition in Ahafo, Ghana', *Africa,* 43, 41-58.
ROSSER, C. & C. HARRIS 1965 *The family and social change.* London.
ROSTOW, W. 1960 *The stages of economic growth.* Cambridge.
ROUCH, J. 1956 'Migration au Ghana, 1953-55' *J. Soc. africanistes,* 26, 33-196.
SANDAY, P.R. 1973 'Female status in the public domain', in: *Woman, culture and society,* eds. M.Z. Rosaldo and L. Lamphere, Stanford.
SANFORD, M.S. 1971 *Disruption of the mother-child relationship in conjunction with matrifocality: A study of child-keeping among the Carib and Creole of British Honduras.* PhD dissertation, Catholic University of America.

SARBAH, J.M. 1897 *Fanti customary laws*. London.
SCHILDKROUT, E. 1970a 'Government and chiefs in Kumasi Zongo', in: *West African Chiefs*, eds. M. Crowder & O. Ikemi, Ile-Ife.
—— 1970b 'Strangers and local government in Kumasi', *J. mod. Afr. Stud.*, 8, 251-69.
—— 1973a 'Ethnicity and generational change in Ghana' in: *Urban ethnicity*, ed. A. Cohen, ASA monograph 12, London.
—— 1973b 'The fostering of children in urban Ghana: problems of ethnographic analysis in a multi-cultural context', *Urban anthropology*, 2.
SCHNEIDER, D.M. & K. GOUGH 1961 *Matrilineal kinship*. Berkeley.
SCHUMPETER, J. 1961 *The theory of economic development*, trans R. Opie, New York.
SCHWARZ, A. 1972 'Illusion d'une émancipation et aliénation réelle de l'ouvrière zaïroise', *Canadian J. Afr.*,6, 183-212.
SINGLETON, J. 1967 *Nichu: a Japanese school*. New York.
SKINNER, E.P. 1960 'Labour migration and its relationship.to socio-cultural change in Mossi society', *Africa*, 30, 375-99.
—— 1963 'Strangers in West African societies', *Africa*, 33, 307-20.
—— 1964a 'West Africa economic systems', *Economic transition in Africa*, eds. M. Herskovitz & W. Harwitz, London.
—— 1964b 'Intergenerational conflict among the Mossi: father and son', *J. conflict resolution*, 5, 55-60.
SMITH, M.G. 1955 *The economy of Hausa communities of Zaria*. London.
—— 1962a *Kinship and community in Carriacou*. New Haven.
—— 1962b *West Indian family structure*. Seattle.
SMITH, R.T. 1956 *The negro family in British Guiana*. London.
—— 1968 'Family: comparative structure', *International encyclopaedia of the social sciences* 5, 301-13.
SMYTHE, H.H. & M.M. 1960 *The new Nigerian elite*. Stanford.
SOUTHALL, A. (ed.) 1961 *Social change in modern Africa*. London.
SPENS, T. 1969 *Family structure in a Dominican village*. PhD thesis, University of Cambridge.
STACEY, M. 1969 'Family and household', *Comparability in social research* ed. M. Stacey, SSRC review, 6, London, 32-55.
STAPLETON, G.C. 1959 'Nigerian in Ghana', *West Africa*, 2814,175.
STEIN, J.T.H. 1929 'Agriculture in the Keta-Ada district' *Gold Coast Department of Agriculture Bull.*22, 152-60.
TALMON- GARBER, Y. 1962 'Social change and family structure', *International social sciences journal*, 14, 468-87.
TETTEY, D.K. 1960 'Shallot industry in South Anlo' unpub. dissertation for B.A. hons. degree, University of Ghana, Legon.
TIGER, L. 1967 'Bureaucracy and urban symbol systems' in: *The city in modern Africa*, ed. H. Miner, London.
TOOTH, G. 1950 *Studies in mental illness in the Gold Coast*. London.
WARD, B.E. 1956 'Some observations on religious cults in Ashanti', *Africa*, 26, 47-60.
WATSON, W. 1970 'Migrant labour and detribalization' in: *Black Africa*, ed. J. Middleton, London.
WEBER, M. 1958 *The Protestant ethic and the spirit of capitalism*. New York.
—— 1962 *Basic concepts in sociology*, trans. H.P. Secher, London.
WHITEFORD, J. 1877 *Trading life in western and central Africa*. Liverpool.
WILKS, I. 1961 *The northern factor in Ashanti history*. Legon.
WILNER, D. et al. 1962 *The housing environment and family life*. Baltimore.
WILSON, G. & M. 1945 *The analysis of social change*. Cambridge.

REFERENCES

WINIET, Governor *Journal* ADM 1/451 Ghana national archives.
WOODMAN, G.R. 1969 'Some realism about customary law: the West
    African experience', *Wisconsin law review*, 1.
WORSLEY, P. 1955 'The kinship system of the Tallensi: a revaluation',
    JRAI 86, 37-75.
YALMAN, N. 1967 *Under the bo tree*. Berkeley.
YOUNG, M. & P. WILLMOTT 1957 *Family and kinship in East London*. London.
ZOLBERG, A.R. 1968 'The structure of political conflict in the new
    states of tropical Africa', *American political science review*,
    62, 70-87.

BIBLIOGRAPHY

GENERAL

BIRMINGHAM, W., NEUSTADT, I. & OMABOE, B.N. (eds) *A study of contemporary Ghana. Vol II: some aspects of social structure.* London, 1967.
LLOYD, P.C. *Classes, crises and coups: themes in the sociology of developing countries.* London, 1971.

HISTORY

AGBODEKA, F. *African politics and British policy in the Gold Coast, 1868-1900: a study in the forms and force of protest.* London, 1971.
AJAYI, J.F.A., & CROWDER, M. (eds) *History of West Africa. Vol. I.* London, 1971.
CROWDER, M. (ed) *West African resistance: the military response to colonial occupation.* London, 1971.
DAAKU, K.Y. *Trade and politics on the Gold Coast, 1640-1720.* London, 1971.
DICKSON, K.B. *A historical geography of Ghana.* Cambridge, 1969.
FAGE, J.D. *Ghana: a historical interpretation.* Madison, 1966.
FORDE, D., & KABERRY, P.M. (eds) *West African kingdoms in the nineteenth century.* London, 1967.
FYNN, J.K. *Asante and its neighbours.* London, 1971.
KIMBLE, D. *A political history of Ghana: the rise of Gold Coast nationalism, 1850-1928.* Oxford, 1963.
PRIESTLEY, M. *West African trade and coast society: a family study.* London, 1969.
TORDOFF, W. *Ashanti under the Prempehs, 1883-1935.* London, 1965.

POLITICS

ANKRAH, K.E. A search from within: an examination of nepotism, tribalism and other cultural situations in Ghana. In: *Windows on Africa* ed: Parsons, R.T. Leiden 1971.
APTER, D.E. *Ghana in transition*. Revision of 'Gold Coast in transition'. New York, 1968.
—— Ghana. In: *Political parties and national integration in tropical Africa,* eds: Coleman, J.S. & Rosberg, C.G., California, 1964.
—— & LYSTAD, R.A. Bureaucracy, party and constitutional democracy: an examination of political role systems in Ghana. In: *Transition in Africa: studies in political adaptation,* eds: Carter, G.H. & Brown, W.O. Boston, 1958.
AUSTIN, D. *Politics in Ghana, 1946-1960.* London, 1964.
—— *Ghana observed.* London, 1973.
—— Elections in an African rural area. *Africa* 31, 1, 1961.
—— & TORDOFF, W. Voting in an African town (Kumasi). *Polit. Stud.,* 8, 2, 1960, 130.

BIBLIOGRAPHY

AWOONOR, K. Kwame Nkrumah: symbol of emergent Africa, *Afr. Rep.*, 17 6, 1972, 22.
BERG, E.J. The economic basis of political choice in French West Africa, *Amer. Polit. Sci. Rev.*, June 1960, 391.
BING, G.H.C. *Reap the whirlwind: an account of Kwame Nkrumah's Ghana 1950-1966.* London, 1968.
BRETTON, H.L. *The rise and fall of Kwame Nkrumah - a study of personal rule in Africa.* London, 1967.
BUSIA, K.A. The prospects for parliamentary democracy in the Gold Coast, *Parliamentary Affairs*, 5, 4, 1952, 438.
CALLAWAY, B.J. Transitional local politics: tradition in local government elections in Aba, Nigeria, Kete, Ghana, *Afr. Stud. Rev.* 15, 3, 1961, 403.
—— & CARD, E. Political constraints on economic development in Ghana, in: *The state of the nations*, ed. Lofchie, M.F., California, 1971.
COHEN, D.L. The Convention People's Party of Ghana: representational or solidarity party, *Canad. J. Afr. Stud.*, 4, 2, 1970, 173.
CROOK, R. Colonial rule and political culture in modern Ashanti, *J. Commonwealth polit. stud.*, 9, 1, 1973, 3.
DOWSE, R.E. *Modernisation in Ghana and the USSR: a comparative study.* London, 1969.
DRAH, F.K. Political tradition and the search for constitutional democracy in Ghana: a prolegomenon, *Ghana J. Sociol.*, 6, 1, 1970, 1.
DUNN, J. & ROBERTSON, A.F. *Dependence and opportunity: political change in Ahafo.* Cambridge, 1974.
ESSEKS, J.D. Political independence and economic development: the case of Ghana under Nkrumah, *Western Polit. Quart.*, 24, 1, 1971, 59.
FOLSON, B.D.G. The development of socialist ideology in Ghana, 1949-1959, *Ghana Soc. Sci. J.*, 1,1, 1971, 1.
FOSTER, P. & ZOLBERG, A.R. *Ghana and the Ivory Coast: perspectives on modernisation.* Chicago & London 1971.
GOODY, J. Consensus and dissent in Ghana, *Political Sci. Quart.* 83, 3, 1968, 337..
GREENSTREET, D.K. Trends in decentralisation in Ghana, *Q.J. Adm.* 5, 2, 1971, 167.
HAYWARD, F.M. Rural attitudes and expectations about national governments: experiences in selected Ghanaian communities, *Rural Africana* 18, 1972, 40.
IKOKU, S.G. *Le Ghana de Nkrumah.* Paris, 1971.
JAHODA, G. Nationality preferences and national stereotypes in Ghana before independence, *J. Soc. Psych.* 50, 1959, 165.
LEFEVER, E.W. *Spear and sceptre: army, police and politics in tropical Africa.* Washington, 1970.
LEWIS, W.A. *Politics in West Africa.* London, 1965.
MAHONEY, W. Nkrumah in retrospect, *Rev. Polit.* 30, 2, 1968, 246.
MOHAN, J. Ghana parliament and foreign policy, 1957-1960, *Econ. Bull. Ghana.* 10, 4, 1966, 29.
OMARI, T.P. *Kwame Nkrumah, the anatomy of an African dictatorship.* London, 1970.
OWUSU, M. *Uses and abuses of political power: a case study of continuity and change in the politics of Ghana.* Chicago, 1970.
PINKNEY, R. *Ghana under military rule, 1966-1969.* London, 1972.
PRICE, R. A theoretical approach to military rule in new states: reference-group theory and the Ghanaian case, *World Polit.* 23, 3, 1971, 399.
—— Military officers and political leadership: the Ghanaian case, *Comp. Polit.* 3, 3, 1971, 361.

274   *CHANGING SOCIAL STRUCTURE IN GHANA*

RUNCIMAN, W.G. Charismatic legitimacy and one-party rule in Ghana,
      Archiv. Europ. Sociol., 4, 1963, 148.
RYAN, S. The theory and practice of African one-partyism: the Conven-
      tion People's Party (Ghana) re-examined, *Canad. J. Afr. Stud.*,
      4, 2, 1970, 145.
SAFFU, E.O. Nkrumah and the Togoland question, *Econ. Bull. Ghana*, 12,
      2/3, 1966, 37.
THOMPSON, W.S. *Ghana's foreign policy, 1957-1966: diplomacy, ideology
      and the new state.* Princeton, 1969.
TIGER, L. Bureaucracy and charisma in Ghana, *J. Asian Afr. Stud.*, 1,
      1, 1966, 13.
TRIULZI, A. The Asanthene-in-Council: Ashanti politics under colonial
      rule, 1935-1950.*Africa*, 42, 2, 1972, 98.
WALLERSTEIN, I. *Africa: the politics of independence.* New York, 1961.
—— *The road to independence: Ghana and the Ivory Coast.* Paris and
      the Hague, 1964.
—— (ed) *Social change: the colonial situation.* New York, 1966.
WELCH, C.E. Praetorianism in Commonwealth West Africa, *J. Mod. Afr.
      Stud.*, 10, 2, 1972, 203.
WERLIN, H.H. The roots of corruption: the Ghanaian enquiry, *J. Mod.
      Afr. Stud.*, 10, 2, 1972, 247.

TRADITIONAL AUTHORITIES

BUSIA, K.A. *The position of the chief in the modern political system of
      Ashanti.* London, 1951.
CROWDER, M & IKIME, O. (eds.) *West African chiefs: their changing status
      under colonial rule and independence.* New York, 1970.
FORTES, M. & EVANS-PRITCHARD, E.L. (eds.) *African political systems.*
      London, 1940.
LLOYD, P.C. Traditional rulers,In: *Political parties and national
      integration in tropical Africa,* eds. Coleman, J.S. & Rosberg, C.G.,
      California, 1964.
SKINNER, E.P. Traditional and modern patterns of succession to political
      office among the Mossi of the Voltaic Republic, *J. Human Rel.*, 8,
      1960, 394.
—— *The Mossi of the Upper Volta: the political development of the
      Sudanese people.* Stanford, 1964.
ZAJACZKOWSKI, A. La structure du pouvoir chez les Ashanti de la période
      de transition. *Cah. Et. Afr.*, 3, 12, 1963, 458.

LOCAL GOVERNMENT AND ADMINISTRATION

ACQUAH, I. The development and functioning of municipal government in
      Accra, *Proc. Conf. West Afr. Inst. Soc. Econ. Res. 1956.*
ADU, A.L. *The civil service in new African states.* London, 1965.
FOLSON, D.D.C. Coussey and local government structure in Ghana, *Econ.
      Bull. Ghana*, 8, 1, 1964, 3.
GREENWOOD, A.F. Ten years' local government in Ghana, *J. Local Admn.,
      Overseas*, 1, 1, 1962, 23.
LADOUCEUR, P. The Yendi chieftaincy dispute and Ghanaian politics,
      Canad. J. Afr. Stud., 6, 1, 1972, 97.
NSARKOH, J.K. *Local government in Ghana.* Accra, 1964.
ROBERTSON, A.F. The development of town committees in Ahafo, Western Ghana,
      In: *Councils in Action,* eds. Richards, A. & Kuper, A.,London, 1971.

BIBLIOGRAPHY 275

SCHILDKROUT, E. Strangers and local government in Kumasi, *J. Mod. Afr. Stud.*, 8, 2, 1970, 25.
WRAITH, R. *Local government in West Africa.* London,1964.
WRAITH, R. & SIMPKINS, E. *Corruption in developing countries.* London, 1963.

COMMUNITY STUDIES

BROKENSHA, D. *Social change at Larteh, Ghana.* Oxford, 1966.

LAW

ALLOTT, A.N. *Essays in African law, with special reference to the law of Ghana.* London , 1960.
BENTSI-ENCHILL, K. *Ghana Land Law: an exposition, analysis and critique.* London, 1964.
ELIAS, T.O. *Ghana and Sierra Leone: the development of their laws and constitutions.* London, 1962.
HARVEY, W.B. A value analysis of Ghanaian legal development since independence, *Univ. Ghana Law J.*, 1, 1, 1964, 4.
—— *Law and social change in Ghana.* Princeton, 1966.
JUERGENSMEYER, J.C. African presidentialism: a comparison of the 'executive' under the constitutions of the Federation of Nigeria, the Federal Republics of the Congo and Cameroon, and the Republics of Ghana, Chad, Congo and the Entente, *J. Afr. Law*, 8, 3, 1968, 157.
KYEREMATEN, A.A.Y. *Inter-state boundary litigation in Ashanti.* Leiden, 1971.
MENSAH- BROWN, A.K. The nature of Akan native law: a critical analysis, *Sociologus*, 20, 2, 1970, 123.
MURRAY, P. & RUBIN, L. *The constitution and government of Ghana.* London, 1964.
OLLENNU, N.A. *Principles of customary land law in Ghana.* London, 1962.
—— The changing law and law reform in Ghana, *J. Afr. Law*,15, 2, 1971, 132.
RATTRAY, R.S. *Ashanti law and constitution.* 2nd ed., Oxford, 1957.
SEIDMAN, R.B. The Ghana prison system: an historical perspective, In: *African Penal Systems*, ed. Milner, A., London, 1969.

ELITES

CLIGNET, R.P. & FOSTER, P. Potential elites in Ghana and the Ivory Coast: a preliminary comparison, *Amer. J. Sociol.*, 70, 1964, 349.
——,—— *The fortunate few: a study of secondary schools and students in the Ivory Coast.* Evanston, 1966.
DE GRAFT-JOHNSON, J.C. The evolution of elites in Ghana, In: *The new elites of tropical Africa*, eds: Lloyd, P.C. & Forde, D. London, 1970.
FRIEDMANN, J. Intellectuals in developing societies, *Kyklos*, 13, 1960, 518.
GOODY, J. Class and marriage in Africa and Eurasia, *Amer. J. Sociol.*, 76, 4, 1971, 585.
GRUNDY, R.W. The 'class struggle' in Africa: an examination of conflicting theories, *J. Mod. Afr. Stud.*, 2, 3, 1964, 379.
LLOYD, P.C. *The new elites of tropical Africa.* London, 1970.
MERCIER, P. Aspects des problèmes de stratification sociale dans l'ouest africain, *Cah. Int. Soc.*, 16, 1954, 47.
NADEL, S.F. The concept of social elites, *Int. Soc. Sci. Bull.*, 8, 1956, 413.

276 *CHANGING SOCIAL STRUCTURE IN GHANA*

PAUVERT, J.C. Le problème des classes sociales en Afrique équatoriale, *Cah. Int. Soc.*, 19, 1955, 76.
SAUNDERS, J.T. & DOWUONA, M. (eds.) *The West African intellectual community*, Papers from Int. Seminar at Freetown, Dec. 1961. Ibadan, 1962.
SHILS, E. Intellectuals and democratic development, In: *Africa the dynamics of change*, eds. Passin, H. & Jones-Quartey, K.A.B. Ibadan, 1963.
TARDITS, C. The notion of the elite and the urban social survey in Africa, *Int. Soc. Sci. Bull.*, 8, 1956, 492.

EDUCATION

CALDWELL, J.C. Extended family obligations and education: a study of an aspect of demographic transition among Ghanaian University students, *Population Stud.*, Nov. 1965, 183.
CURLE, A. Nationalism and higher education in Ghana, *Univ. Quart.*, 16, 3, 1962, 229.
—— *Educational problems of developing societies, with case studies in Ghana, Pakistan and Nigeria.* New York, 1973.
DOGBE, S. Which way Ghana education? *Insight and Opinion*, 6, 3, 1971, 46.
FINLAY, D.J. et al. Ghana, In: *Students and politics in developing nations*, ed. Emmerson, D.K. London, 1968.
FOSTER, P.J. Ethnicity and the schools in Ghana, *Comp. Educ. Rev.*, 1962, 127.
—— Secondary schooling and social mobility in a West African nation, *Sociol. Educ.*, 37, 1963, 150.
—— Secondary school-leavers in Ghana: expectations and reality, *Harvard Educ. Rev.*, 34, 1964, 537.
—— *Education and social change in Ghana.* London, 1965.
GOODY, J. Restricted literacy in N. Ghana, In: *Literacy in traditional societies*, ed. Goody, J. Cambridge, 1968.
GRINDAL, B.T. *Growing up in two worlds: education and transition among the Sisala of Northern Ghana.* New York, 1972.
HAIZEL, E. Literacy and adult education in Ghana, In: *Continuing literacy*, ed. Clarke, R.F. Kampala, 1968.
HAYWARD, F.M. Ghana experiments with civic education, *Afr. Rep.*, 16, 5, 1971, 24.
HINCHCLIFFE, J.K. A comparative analysis of educational development in Ghana and the Western region of Nigeria, *Nigerian J. Econ. Soc. Stud.*, 12, 1, 1970, 103.
—— The rate of return to education in Ghana, *Econ. Bull. Ghana*, 1, 2, 1971, 45.
HURD, G.E. & JOHNSON, T.J. Education and social mobility in Ghana, *Sociol. Educ.*, 40, 1, 1967, 55.
JAHODA, G. The social background of a West African student population, *Brit. J. Sociol.*, 5, 1954, 355.
JONES-QUARTEY, K.A.B. The Ghana press, In: *Report on the press in West Africa.* Ibadan, 1960.
LEWIS, L.J. *Education and social growth.* Edinburgh, 1956.
MCWILLIAM, H.O.A. *The development of education in Ghana: an outline.* London, 1959.
OMARI, T.P. Changing attitudes of students in West African society towards marriage and family relationships, *Brit. J. Sociol.*, Sept. 1960, 197.
PEIL, M. Ghanaian university students: the broadening base, *Brit. J. Sociol.*, 16, 1, 1965, 19.

BIBLIOGRAPHY 277

PEIL, M. The influence of formal education on occupational choice.
    Canad. J. Afr. Stud., 7, 2, 1973, 199.
RATHBONE, R.J.A.R. Education and politics in Ghana In: *Africana
    collecta*, ed. Oberndorfer, D. Freiburg, 1968.
WILLIAMS, T.D. Some economic implications of the education explosion
    in Ghana In: *World Year Book of Education 1965*.

ECONOMICS

ADDO, W.O. Immigration into Ghana: some social and economic implications
    of the Aliens Compliance Order of 18-11-69. *Ghana J. Sociol.*, 6,
    1, 1970, 20.
AGAMA, G.K. Population and manpower development in Ghana. *Nigerian J.
    Econ. Soc. Stud.*, 11, 3, 1969, 285.
ARHIN, K. The Ashanti rubber trade with the Gold Coast in the eighteen-
    nineties. *Africa*, 42, 1, 1972, 32.
BECKETT, W.H. *Akokoaso.* London, 1947.
BECKMAN, B. Economic policy and the distribution system in Ghana, 1960-
    1966. *Res. Rev.*, 4, 3, 1968, 83.
BIRMINGHAM, W., NEUSTADT, I., OMABOE, E.N. (eds.) *A study of contemporary
    Ghana, Vol.1: the economy of Ghana*. London, 1966.
BISSUE, I. Ghana's seven-year development plan in retrospect. *Econ. Bull.
    Ghana*, 11, 1, 1967, 21.
CHRISTIANSEN, J.B. Marketing and exchange in a West African tribe.
    Southwestern J. Anthrop., 17, 1961, 124.
DE GRAFT-JOHNSON, J.C. Some population and related problems in the
    Ghanaian economy. *Econ. Bull. Ghana*, 1, 1, 1971, 18.
EWUSI, K. *West African economies: some basic economic problems*. Legon,
    1971.
FAGERLUND, V.G. & SMITH, R.H.T. A preliminary map of market periodicities
    in Ghana. *J. Dev. Areas*, 4, 3, 1970, 333.
GARLICK, P.C. *African traders in Kumasi*. Legon, 1959.
—— African and Levantine trading firms in Ghana. *Proc. Conf. Nigerian
    Inst. Soc. Econ. Res.*, 1960.
—— *African traders and economic development in Ghana*. London, 1971.
GENOUD, R. *Nationalism and economic development in Ghana*. New York, 1969.
GREENHALGH, C. Income differentials in the Eastern Region of Ghana.
    Econ. Bull. Ghana, 2, 2, 1972, 3.
HART, K. Small scale entrepreneurs in Ghana and development planning.
    J. Dev. Stud., 6, 4, 1970.
HILL, P. *Studies in rural capitalism in West Africa*. Cambridge, 1970.
HOPKINS, A.C. *An economic history of West Africa*. London, 1973.
JAHODA, G. 'Money-doubling' in the Gold Coast: with some cross-cultural
    comparisons. *Brit. J. Delinquency*, 8, 1958, 266.
KAY, G.B. (ed.) *The political economy of colonialism in Ghana: a collec-
    tion of documents and statistics, 1900-1960*. New York, 1972.
KILLICK, A. Price controls in Africa - the Ghanaian experience. *J. modern
    African stud.*, 11, 3, 1973, 405.
—— & SZERESZEWSKI, R. The economy of Ghana In: *The economies of Africa,*
    eds. Robson, P. & Lury, D.A. London, 1969.
LIMBERG, L. The economy of the Fanti Confederation. *Trans. Hist. Soc.
    Ghana*, 11, 1970, 83.
LOKEN, R.D. *Manpower development in Africa*. New York, 1969.
MABOGUNJE, A. *Regional mobility and resource development in West Africa*.
    Montreal, 1972.

278 *CHANGING SOCIAL STRUCTURE IN GHANA*

MCCALL, D.T. The Koferidna market In: *Markets in Africa*, eds. Robson,
    P. & Dalton, G. Evanston, 1962.
MCKIM, W. The periodic market system in northeastern Ghana. *Econ. Geog.*,
    48, 3, 1972, 14.
MEILLASSOUX, C. (ed.) *The development of indigenous trade and markets in
    West Africa*. London, 1971.
NYPAN, A. *Market trade: a sample survey of market traders in Accra*.
    Legon, 1960.
OKALI, C. & KOTEY, R.A. *Akokoaso: a resurvey*. Legon, 1971.
POLEMAN, T.T. The food economies of urban middle Africa: the case of
    Ghana. *Food Res. Inst. Stud.*, 11, 2, 1961, 121.
QUANSAH, S.T. The Gonja settlement and development scheme - Ghana. *Econ.
    Bull. Ghana*, 2, 1, 1972, 14.
RADO, E.R. The African contractor and the Gold Coast building industry.
    Proc. Conf. West Afr. Inst. Soc. Econ. Res., 1956.
SKINNER, E.P. Trade and markets among the Mossi people In: *Markets in
    Africa*, eds. Bohannan, P. & Dalton, G. Evanston, 1962.
VAN APELDOORN, G.J. *Markets in Ghana: a census and some comments*.
    Legon, 1972.

AGRICULTURE

BECKETT, W.A. *Koransang: a Gold Coast cocoa farm*. Accra, 1945.
BENNEH, G. Small scale farming systems in Ghana. *Africa*, 43, 2, 1973,134.
DJEAGBO, G. & MATE, A. Settlement and farming in the Manya Krobo district.
    Bull. Ghana Geog. Ass., 7, 1/2, 1962, 54.
DUMETT, R. The rubber trade of the Gold Coast and Asante in the nineteenth
    century. *J. Afr. Hist.*, 12, 1, 1971, 79.
HILL, P. The pledging of Gold Coast cocoa farms. *Proc. Conf. West Afr.
    Inst. Soc. Econ. Res. 1956.*
—— Women cocoa farmers. *The Ghana farmer* , Dept. of Agriculture,
    Accra, 1958.
—— *Migrant cocoa-farmers of Southern Ghana*. Cambridge, 1963.
—— Three types of Southern Ghanaian cocoa farmers In: *African agrarian
    systems*, ed. Biebuyck, D. London, 1963.
LA-ANYANE, S. *Ghana agriculture: its economic development from early times
    to the middle of the twentieth century*. London , 1963.
MIRACLE, M.P. The smallholder in agricultural policy and planning: Ghana
    and the Ivory Coast 1960-1966. *J. Dev. Areas*, 4, 3, 1970, 321.
NICHOLAS, M.S.O. Resettlement agriculture In: *Volta resettlement symposium
    papers, 1965*. Kumasi.
QURAISHY, B.B. Land tenure and economic development in Ghana. *Présence
    Afr.*, 77, 1971, 24.
STOCES, F. Agricultural production in Ghana 1955-1965. *Econ. Bull. Ghana*,
    10, 3, 1966, 3.
UCHENDU, V.C. *Field study of agricultural change: the cocoa farmers of
    Akim Abuakwa, Eastern region, Ghana*. Stanford, 1969.
—— & ANTHONY, D.R.M. *Economic, technical and cultural determinants of
    agricultural change in tropical Africa: preliminary report No. 3*.
    Stanford, 1969.
WILLS, J.B. (ed.) *Agriculture and land use in Ghana*. London, 1962.

BIBLIOGRAPHY   279

URBANISATION AND MIGRATION

ACQUAH, I. *Accra survey: a social survey of the capital of Ghana, formerly called the Gold Coast, undertaken for the West African Institute of Social and Economic Research, 1953-1956.* London, 1958.
ADDO, W.O. Some demographic aspects of urbanization in Ghana, 1931-1960. *Ghana Soc. Sci. J.*, 1, 1, 1971, 50.
BUSIA, K. *Social survey of Sekondi-Takoradi.* London, 1950.
CALDWELL, J.C. *African rural-urban migration: the movement to Ghana's towns.* Canberra, 1969.
DATE-BAH, E. Informal relations among employees of a Ghanaian factory. *Ghana Soc. Sci. J.*, 2, 1, 1972, 86.
DICKSON, K.B. Nucleation and dispersion of rural settlements in Ghana. *Ghana Soc. Sci. J.*, 1, 1, 1971, 116.
FORTES, M. The Ashanti social survey: a preliminary report. *Rhodes-Livingstone Inst. J.*, 6, 1948, 1.
—— Some aspects of migration and mobility in Ghana. *J. African Asian Studies*, 6, 1971, 1.
GRINDAL, B.T. Islamic affiliations and urban adaptation: the Sisala migrant in Accra, Ghana. *Africa*, 43, 4, 1973, 333.
KUPER, H. (ed.) *Urbanization and migration in West Africa.* California, 1965.
PEIL, M. Unemployment in Tema: the plight of the skilled worker. *Canad. J. Afr. Stud.*, 3, 2, 1969, 409.
—— The expulsion of West African aliens. *J. Mod. Afr. Stud.*, 9, 2, 1971, 205.
—— *The Ghanaian factory worker.* Cambridge, 1972.
ROUCH, J. Migration au Ghana, 1953-1955. *J. Soc. Afr.*, 26, 1956, 33.
SKINNER, E.P. Labour migration and its relationship to socio-cultural change in Mossi society. *Africa*, 30, 4, 1960, 375.

RESETTLEMENT

AMARTEIFIO, G.W. Social welfare In: *Volta resettlement symposium papers 1965.* Kumasi.
BROKENSHA, D. *Volta resettlement: ethnographic notes on some of the southern areas.* Legon, 1962.
CHAMBERS, R. (ed.) *The Volta resettlement experience.* London, 1970.
DODOO, M.A. Case study of a resettlement town, New Mpamu In: *Volta resettlement symposium papers 1965.* Kumasi.
HUSZAR, L. Resettlement planning In: *Volta resettlement symposium papers 1965.* Kumasi.
KALITSI, E.A.K. Present and future problems of administering resettlement towns In: *Volta resettlement symposium papers 1965.* Kumasi.
MOXON, J. *Volta, man's greatest lake: the story of Ghana's Akosombo dam.* London, 1969.

VOLUNTARY ASSOCIATIONS

BERG, E.J. & BUTLER, J. Trade unions In: *Political parties and national integration in tropical Africa.* eds. Coleman, J.S. & Rosberg, C.G., California, 1964.
DATTA, A.K. & PORTER, R. The Asafo system in historical perspective. *J. Afr. Hist.*, 12, 2, 1971, 279.

280 *CHANGING SOCIAL STRUCTURE IN GHANA*

HODGE, P. The Ghana workers' brigade; a project for unemployed youth. *Brit. J. Sociol.*, 15, 1964, 113.
JOHNSTONE, T.J. Protest, tradition and change: an analysis of southern Gold Coast riots 1890-1920. *Economy and Society*, 1, 1972, 164.
LITTLE, K. *West African urbanisation: a study of voluntary associations in social change.* Cambridge, 1966.
ROBERTSON, A.F. African and European social clubs in rural Ghana. *Race*, 12, 2, 1970, 107.
WALLERSTEIN, I. Voluntary associations In: *Political parties and national integration in tropical Africa.* eds. Coleman, J.S. & Rosberg, C.G., California, 1964.

RELIGION

BAETA, C.G. *Prophetism in Ghana: a study of some 'spiritual' churches.* London, 1962.
—— (ed.) *Christianity in tropical Africa.* London, 1968.
BARTELS, F.L. *The roots of Ghana Methodism.* London, 1965.
BUSIA, K.A. The Ashanti In: *African Worlds.* . . ed. Forde, C.D. London, 1954.
FERNANDEZ, J.W. Rededication and prophetism in Ghana. *Cah. Et. Afr.* 10, 2, 38, 1970, 228.
FIELD, M.J. *Search for security: an ethno-psychiatric study of rural Ghana.* London, 1960.
GOODY, J. Anomie in Ashanti. *Africa*, 27, 4, 1957, 356.
—— Reform, renewal and resistance: a Mahdi in Northern Ghana In: *African perspectives*, eds. Allen, C. & Johnston, R.W. Cambridge, 1970.
HALIBURTON, G.M. *The Prophet Harris: a study of an African prophet and his mass movement in the Ivory Coast and the Gold Coast, 1913-1915.* London, 1971.
JAHODA, G. Magic, witchcraft and literacy. *Lumen Vitae*, 16, 2, 1961, 137.
—— Persistence of supernatural beliefs among Ghanaian university students In: *Witchcraft and healing.* Edinburgh, 1969. (Proc. seminar).
—— Supernatural beliefs and changing cognitive structures among Ghanaian university students. *J. Cross-Cult. Psychol.*, 1, 2, 1970, 115.
KILSON, M. Ambivalence and power: mediums in Ga traditional religion. *J. Relig. in Africa*, 4, 3, 1972, 171.
LEVTZION, N. *Muslims and chiefs in West Africa.* Oxford, 1968.
OPOKU, K.A. A directory of spiritual churches in Ghana. *Res. Rev.*, 7, 1, 1970, 98.
SARPONG, P.K. The sacred stools of Ashanti. *Anthropos*, 62, 1/2, 1967, 1.
SAWYERR, H. *God: ancestor or creator? Aspects of traditional belief in Ghana, Nigeria and Sierra Leone.* London, 1970.
TRIMINGHAM, J.S. *A history of Islam in West Africa.* London, 1970.
WARD, B.E. Some observations on religious cults in Ashanti. *Africa*, 26, 1, 1956, 47.
WILLIAMSON, S.G. & DICKSON, K.A. (eds.) *Akan religion and the Christian faith: a comparative study of the impact of two religions.* Accra, 1965.

POPULATION

CALDWELL, J.C. Fertility attitudes in three economically contrasting regions of Ghana. *Econ. Dev. Cult. Change*, 15, 2, 1967, 217.

BIBLIOGRAPHY

281

CALDWELL, J.C. *Population growth and family change in Africa: the new urban elite in Ghana.* Canberra, 1968.
—— & OKONJO, C. (eds.) *The population of tropical Africa.* London, 1968.
POOL, D.I. Social change and interest in family planning in Ghana: an exploratory analysis. *Canad. J. Afr. Stud.*, **4**, 2, 1970, 207.

FAMILY

CRAWFORD, T. Ghana: marriage and divorce. *Afr. Law Stud.*, 4, 1971, 27.
FIELD, M.J. *Search for security: an ethno-psychiatric study of rural Ghana.* London, 1960.
FORTES, M. Time and social structure In: *Social structure*, ed. Fortes, M. Oxford, 1949.
—— *The web of kinship among the Tallensi.* London, 1949.
—— Kinship and marriage among the Ashanti In: *African systems of kinship and marriage.* eds. Radcliffe-Brown, A.R. & Forde, D. London, 1950.
—— & MAYER, D.Y. Psychosis and social change among the Tallensi of Northern Ghana. *Cah. Et. Afr.*, **6**, 21, 1966, 5.
GOODY, E. Fostering of children in Ghana: a preliminary report. *Ghana J. Sociol.*, **2**, 1, 1966, 26.
—— Kinship fostering in Gonja: deprivation or advantage? In: *Socialization: the approach from social anthropology.* ed. Mayer, P. London, 1970.
—— *Contexts of kinship.* Cambridge, 1973.
—— Marriage policy and incorporation in Northern Ghana In: *From tribe to nation in Africa.* eds. Cohen, R. & Middleton, J., Scranton, Pa., 1970.
—— Polygyny, economy and the role of women In: *The character of kinship.* ed. Goody, J. Cambridge, 1973.
GREENSTREET, M. Social change and Ghanaian women. *Canad. J. Afr. Stud.*, **6**, 2, 1972, 351.
JAHODA, G. Boy's images of marriage partners and girl's self images in Ghana. *Sociologus*, 8, 1958, 155.
—— *White man: a study of the attitudes of Africans to Europeans in Ghana before independence.* London, 1961.
—— Aspects of westernization: a study of adult-class students in Ghana. *Brit. J. Sociol.*, Part I - **12**, 4, 1961, 375: Part II - **13**, 1, 1962,43.
KAYE, B. *Bringing up children in Ghana.* London, 1962.
LITTLE, K. *African women in towns: an aspect of Africa's social revolution.* Cambridge, 1974.
MILLS-ODOI, G. *The La family and social change.* Leiden, 1973.
NUKUNYA, G.K. The Gluckman hypothesis and marital instability in Anlo. *Ghana J. Sociol.*, **6**, 1, 1970, 79.
OMARI, T.P. Changing attitudes of students in West African society towards marriage and family relationship. *Brit. J. Sociol.*, Sept. 1960, 197.
OPLER, M.K. Cultural definitions of illness: social psychiatry views inter-cultural and inter-class communication in Ghana In: *Man's image in medicine and anthropology.* ed. Galdston, I. New York, 1963.
OPPONG, C. *Marriage among a matrilineal elite.* Cambridge, 1974.
POOL, J. A cross-comparative study of aspects of conjugal behaviour among women of three West African countries. *Canad. J. Afr. Stud.*, **6**, 2, 1972, 233.
VERSTRAELEN, F.J. *Catholic missionaries, marriage and family life in Ghana.* Legon, 1969.

INDEX

Abron, 221
Ahafo, 229-43
Akan, 53, 74, 81, 83, 85, 93, 121,
  175, 181-200, 248, 255
Akaniem village, 203, 206-22
  passim
aliens, expulsion of, 37, 41-2
Alland, A., 221
Amselle, J.-L., 46
Anloga, 59-69
Arab, Arabic, 46, 47, 170, 172
Asante, Ashanti, 92-3, 103, 107-17,
  120, 169, 178, 248

Barnard, G., 82
Bailey, F. G., 232
Bender, D., 222
Bolgatanga, 15, 18, 19, 21, 23,
  24, 26
bridewealth, 19-20, 212, 213, 214
Brokensha, D., 255
Busia, K., 37, 231, 233

Carib people, 137, 152, 154
Chapin, F. S., 207
chiefs, 20, 97-8, 110, 203, 230-1,
  248
children, 48, 52, 68, 77, 78, 112,
  173, 187-93; fostering of, 137-
  65; and Volta River resettlement
  project, 207-13 *passim*
Christians, 30, 31, 52, 67, 75,
  85, 101, 103, 105
civil servants, 187, 233
Clarke, E., 137
clientage, 176
Clignet, R., 76, 84, 86
cloth, 41, 45, 46, 51, 53
cocoa, 80, 128, 131, 249
Cohen, A., 38, 42, 54, 75
committees, 229-43; Yoruba Parapo,
  52
community, definition of, 7-8; Ewe,
  59-71; multi-ethnic, 167-9; Yoruba migrant, 37-55
conversion, religious, 91-106
councils, Ahafo, 229-43

Creole, 152, 154
crops, 121, 123, 249; cash crops,
  59-71
cults, 96-100, 102-3; anti-witchcraft cults, 101-17
currency, 42

Dagomba, 53
dances, 91
Dillon, E. J., 92
divorce, 83-6, 102, 216-17
dogs, 253
Douglas, Mary, 99, 100
dress, 238

education, 67, 68, 245-60
elites, 15-16, 82, 89, 181-200
entrepreneurs, 1-34
Ewe, 59-71, 85, 142, 144, 146, 181,
  183-7 *passim,* 198

Fanti, 142, 144, 146, 182
farming, 59-71, 119-36, 221
fishing, 61
food, 68, 123, 215-16
Forde, Daryll, 122
Fortes, M., 14, 19, 20, 107, 120,
  201, 209, 221
Foster, P. J., 246
fostering, 138-65
Frafra, 3, 4, 5, 14-34

Ga, 74, 81, 85, 144, 181, 183,
  184-7, 198
Galletti, R., 80
gandu system, 126-7, 130
gods, 94, 96, 103, 107
Gonja, 92, 96, 139, 140, 143, 145,
  147
Goody, J. R., 107, 108, 119, 224
Gonzalez, N. S., 151
Grandmaison, C., 86
Gurensi, 14, 18

Hausa, 37, 38, 45, 52, 54, 74, 75,
  119, 123-9
Hill, Polly, 75

284

Horowitz, M., 137
houses, housing, 68, 169-75, 170-5, 201-28
household, farming, 119-32

Ibo, 80, 82, 85
inheritance, 19-20, 62-3, 81, 127-31, 173-4
Islam, 26, 31, 52, 75, 87, 101, 103, 105, 108, 123, 169, 170

kin, kinship: Akan, 182-7; foster-ing of children, 137-63; Frafra, 4, 8, 16, 17, 20-9; and migration 47-55; in multi-ethnic dwellings, 167-79; Nehumuru, 103; Yoruba, 43, 49, 50
Kooroko, 46
Krobo, 142, 144, 146

land, 19, 20, 59, 62-3, 69, 127, 128, 253
Lele, 91, 99-100
Lewis, I. M., 102
Lloyd, P. C., 86, 131 n., 187
Lodagaa, 92-105 *passim*
Loring, W., 107
LoWiili, 95
Lucas, D., 82

Madge, J., 221
Mandel, E., 10
markets, 21, 40-1, 45, 75
marriage, 51, 73, 75, 76, 78, 81-7, 119-20, 125-7, 187, 211-15, 252
Marris, P., 76, 83
Marxism, 2, 6, 7, 10, 13
masks, 91
Mbembe, 125-6
Meillassoux, C., 74
Meyerowitz, Eva, 93, 103
migration, migrants, 3, 14-15, 21, 22, 23, 29, 37-57, 67, 154, 168-89, 253
missionaries, missions, 67, 101-2, 109, 225
Mossi, 37, 45, 172, 175
myths, 103-5

Nadel, S. F., 91
Namdam, 14
Nchumuru, 201-28
New Grube town, 204-26
Nupe, 85, 91

Oppong, Christine, 82

Papatia village, 203, 210-19
Parapo committee, 52-3
Plant, J., 207
polygyny, 76, 86, 88, 89, 119-20, 124, 200-11, 215, 216, 222-3.
prostitutes, 77-8

religion, traditional, 91-106, 208, 209, 223, 225
resettlement, 201-26

Sanford, M., 151, 152, 153-4, 155
savings, 10, 11
school teachers, 245-60
Schumpeter, J., 6
Schwarz, A., 74
seduction, 255-6
Sehwi village, 245-60 *passim*
sexual relations, 209, 255, 256
shallots, 61-9
Smith, M. G., 137
smuggling, 42
songs, 206
sons, in farming household, 125-7, 129, 130
Southall, A., 80
Spens, T., 154, 155
Stacey, M., 222
Stein, J. T. H., 61-2
surpluses, 10, 11, 13, 19

Tallensi, 14, 17, 19, 32, 91, 123
Tamale, 38-52
Tiv, 122-3
traders : women, 39-41, 73-7, 81, 83, 90, 206, 217, 252; Yoruba, 39-48
Twi, 238, 248

villages, 19-21, 24-5, 205-22; school teachers in, 245-60
Volta River Resettlement Project, 201-26

Ward, Barbara, 107, 116
Watt, I., 91
wealth, 1, 2, 17, 21
Weberian tradition, 2, 30, 31
West Indians, 148-63
Whiteford, J., 61
witchcraft, 85, 96-9, 107-17
women: cocoa farmers, 131; council-

lors, 233, 235, 238; factory workers, 77; farmers, 121-5; housing, 174; inheritance, 173; migrants, 75; prostitutes, 77-8, roles, 73-91; social life, 87-88; taboos, 208; traders, 39-41, 73-7, 81, 85, 90, 206, 217, 252; witches, 98, 99, 111, 112, 114; work, 184-7

Yakö, 122
Yoruba, 37-57, 74, 76, 80, 83, 85, 88, 121, 128

zongo, 168-73